A READER'S GUIDE TO
J.D. SALINGER

Time magazine, September 15, 1961: J.D. Salinger at the peak of his popularity. Reprinted courtesy of TimePix.

A READER'S GUIDE TO J.D. SALINGER

Eberhard Alsen

Emmanuel S. Nelson, Advisory Editor

GREENWOOD PRESS
Westport, Connecticut • London

Library of Congress Cataloging-in-Publication Data

Alsen, Eberhard.
    A reader's guide to J.D. Salinger / Eberhard Alsen.
      p. cm.
    Includes bibliographical references and index.
    ISBN 0–313–31078–5 (alk. paper)
    1. Salinger, J.D. (Jerome David), 1919—Criticism and interpretation—Handbooks,
manuals, etc. I. Title.
PS3537.A426Z538   2002
813'.54—dc21   2002067919

British Library Cataloguing in Publication Data is available.

Library of Congress Catalog Card Number: 2002067919
ISBN: 0–313–31078–5

First published in 2002

Greenwood Press, 88 Post Road West, Westport, CT 06881
An imprint of Greenwood Publishing Group, Inc.
www.greenwood.com

Printed in the United States of America

The paper used in this book complies with the
Permanent Paper Standard issued by the National
Information Standards Organization (Z39.48–1984).

10 9 8 7 6 5 4 3

Once more for Doreen, Emilia, and Louisa

Contents

Prologue

"Yet there is method in't"

In *The Catcher in the Rye,* the sixteen-year-old Holden Caulfield observes that most people are crazy about cars. As for himself, he would rather have a horse because a horse is at least human. And in "Seymour—An Introduction," the ten-year-old Seymour Glass watches his younger brother Buddy play marbles and lose steadily. Then Seymour tries to snap Buddy's losing streak by asking him if he could try not aiming so much.

There are many non-sequiturs such as these in Salinger's fiction. These statements are apparently illogical; yet there is method in them because they begin to make sense once we study the vision of life that they embody. My aim in this book is to guide the reader in such a study.

I believe that we can only achieve an adequate understanding of the vision of life in an individual work of literature if we read additional works that the same author wrote around the same time. That is the only way to get a good sense of the basic outlook of the author at that time. After all, it is an author's ideology or complex of attitudes that forms the spiritual core of his or her work, and out of that spiritual core grow the work's content and form.

This book is organized in such a way that it will help the new reader decide on his or her own approach to Salinger's work, that is, which works to read first and which works to read next, and it will help the reader who is already familiar with one or the other of Salinger's works to deepen his or her appreciation and understanding. For one thing, the overall organization of this book allows the reader to place in chronological context the particular works he or she is interested in. For another, the organization of each individual chapter allows the reader to compare what fiction by Salinger he or she has already read to Salinger's other works in terms of such specific aspects as narrative structure, point of view, characterization, symbolism, and themes.

This book also contains resources for the reader who wants to go beyond close readings of the texts. The introduction provides such biographical information as is reflected in Salinger's fiction, and subsequent chapters analyze the content and form of specific works, summarize major interpretations, and provide suggestions for further readings. Finally, in the appendix section, the reader will find an index of Salinger's fictional characters—from his apprentice stories to his last published work—a chronology of major events in the Glass Family Series, and a brief essay outlining Salinger's philosophy of composition, based on statements that Salinger and his fictional characters have made about the craft of writing.

One of Seymour Glass's statements about writing concerns the choice of what to write about. In a letter, he tells his younger brother to ask himself "what piece of writing in all the world Buddy Glass would most want to read if he had his heart's choice." Then Seymour advises his brother: "You just sit down and shamelessly write the thing yourself."

In writing this book, I shamelessly followed Seymour's advice, because when I first discovered Salinger's fiction, I wished there had been a reader's guide such as this one. There wasn't then, but now there is.

A READER'S GUIDE TO
J.D. SALINGER

Introduction

Salinger's Life as Reflected in His Fiction

> It is my rather subversive opinion that a writer's feelings of
> anonymity-obscurity are the second-most valuable property
> on loan to him during his working years.
>
> J.D. Salinger

There is to date no authorized biography of J.D. Salinger because Salinger has steadfastly opposed any books about his life. In 1986, when Ian Hamilton tried to publish a biography entitled "J.D. Salinger: A Writing Life," Salinger sued Hamilton's publisher, Random House, because he felt the book contained too much material from his unpublished letters. In a notorious case that went all the way to the United States Supreme Court, Salinger forced Random House to withdraw the book. Ian Hamilton later published a much-altered version entitled *In Search of J.D. Salinger* (1988).

Hamilton's book contains very few facts that shed light on Salinger's fiction beyond what had been mentioned in various biographical magazine pieces and in Warren French's book, *J.D. Salinger* (1963, rev. ed. 1976). The same is true for Paul Alexander's book, *Salinger: A Biography* (1999). However, the memoir of Salinger's daughter Margaret, *Dream Catcher* (2000)—unkind though it is to her father—presents quite a bit of new information, and some of it corrects mistakes of previous biographers.

When we examine the available biographical information and compare it to the content of Salinger's work, we find that throughout his career Salinger has worked details from his life into his fiction. However, except for a few instances, the crucial events in his stories are pure invention. On the other hand, several of Salinger's fictional characters seem to be alter egos at various stages of his life, from the adolescent prep school student Holden Caulfield in *The Catcher in the Rye* to the middle-aged writer and literary shut-in Buddy Glass in the Glass Family Series.

CHILDHOOD

Jerome David Salinger was born in 1919 in New York City. Two of his alter egos, Holden Caulfield and Buddy Glass, were also born in New York, and Buddy Glass was born the same year as J.D. Salinger. Moreover, just like Holden Caulfield and Buddy Glass, Jerry Salinger also had parents who were of different religions. His mother was Christian and his father was Jewish. However, while Salinger had only one sibling—an older sister by the name of Doris—Holden and Buddy each have several siblings.

When Salinger was born, his family lived on upper Broadway. A year later, they moved to 113th Street, three blocks from 110th Street and Riverside Drive, where Seymour and Buddy Glass lived during their elementary school days. The Salingers later moved several times to more fashionable addresses. They eventually wound up at 1133 Park Avenue, in the same general neighborhood, where Holden Caulfield's affluent parents lived.

Young Jerry Salinger first attended public schools in Manhattan. When he did poorly in mathematics, his father transferred him to the McBurney private school, but Jerry but flunked out after a year. This private school shows up in *The Catcher in the Rye* when Holden Caulfield and his fencing team travel to New York for a fencing meet with the McBurney team.

Another detail from Salinger's childhood reflected in *The Catcher in the Rye* has to do with the Museum of Natural History, located just across Central Park from where both Jerry Salinger and Holden Caulfield lived. In a 1944 contributor's note for *Story* magazine, Salinger says that he fondly remembers the American Indian Room "where I used to drop my marbles all over the floor" ("Contributors" [1944] 1). In *The Catcher in the Rye*, Holden explains that the floor of the Indian Room was all stone, and if a person dropped some marbles, they would bounce all over the place like madmen and make a terrible racket.

When Jerry Salinger was eleven years old, his parents sent him to Camp Wigwam, a summer camp in Waterford, Maine. In "Hapworth 16, 1924," Salinger transformed that camp into Camp Hapworth, the setting of one of the Glass Family stories. That camp is also in Maine, but the two campers, Seymour and Buddy Glass, are much younger than Jerry Salinger was (seven and five, respectively). Furthermore, while young Jerry Salinger was a good mixer and participated fully in the camp's activities—he even helped put on a play—Seymour and Buddy are "ostracized" because they are both child prodigies.

ADOLESCENCE

Salinger's hit-and-miss schooling is reflected chiefly in *The Catcher in the Rye*. After Jerry Salinger flunked out of the McBurney School in Manhattan, his father enrolled him in a boarding school, Valley Forge Military Academy in Pennsylvania. That boarding school is the model for Pencey Preparatory School for Boys in *The Catcher in the Rye*. That school is also located in Pennsylvania.

Two incidents from Jerry Salinger's time at Valley Forge Military Academy found their way into *The Catcher in the Rye.* One is the suicide of a fellow student. Salinger fictionalized that incident in the story of James Castle who jumps out of a second story window to escape from some bullies at the prep school that Holden attended before Pencey. Another incident is mentioned by Salinger's daughter Margaret. She remembers her father confessing that while he was at Valley Forge, "he, like Holden lost the fencing team's gear on the subway" (*Dream Catcher* 33).

However, what is known about Salinger's stay at Valley Forge Military Academy also reveals significant differences between his and Holden's personalities and life experiences. For instance, unlike Holden Caulfield, who hated school and was an outsider, Jerry Salinger seems to have thrived at Valley Forge Military Academy. He got above average grades, and he was a joiner rather than a rebel. Warren French reports that Salinger belonged to "the Glee Club, the Aviation Club, the French Club, the Non-commissioned Officers' Club, the Mask and Spur (a dramatic organization), and he also served during his senior year as literary editor of *Crossed Sabres*, the academy yearbook" (22). Most importantly, unlike Holden Caulfield, Jerry Salinger did not flunk out of prep school, and he did not have to be committed to a sanatorium for physical and mental rehabilitation.

AN ABORTIVE COLLEGE CAREER

Echoes of Salinger's decision not to finish college sound through several of his stories. After he graduated from Valley Forge in 1936, he enrolled at New York University but dropped out after less than a year. At this point, his father, Solomon Salinger, an importer of cheeses and Polish hams, decided to apprentice him to the cheese and ham importing business and sent him to Austria and Poland. A biographical note that accompanies "The Heart of a Broken Story" in *Esquire* states that Salinger "visited pre-Anschluss Vienna when he was eighteen, winning high honors in beer hoisting. In Poland he worked in a ham factory and slaughter house" ("Backstage" [1941] 24).

The story "A Girl I Knew" reflects some of Salinger's experiences in Vienna. It is the most autobiographical of his early stories. Like Salinger, the young narrator of the story quits college during his freshman year and is sent to Vienna for language study. The narrator's unrequited love for a pretty Jewish girl named Leah may also be autobiographical, for in a letter that Salinger wrote to Ernest Hemingway from Germany in 1945, he says that now that the war is over, he hopes to have a chance to get to Vienna "to put ice skates on the feet of a Viennese girl again." Also, when Salinger was in Vienna before the war, he lived with a Jewish family. His daughter Margaret reports that "he loved this family" but that "they were all killed in concentration camps" (*Dream Catcher* 39). So was Leah in "A Girl I Knew."

Like the narrator of "A Girl I Knew," Salinger also went back to college after he returned from Europe. In the fall of 1938, he enrolled at Ursinus College in Pennsylvania. At Ursinus he wrote a column for the *Ursinus Weekly*. In a piece entitled "The Skipped Diploma: Musings of a Social Soph," he explains his motivation for returning to college: "Once there was a young man who ... did not want to go to work for his Daddykins—or any other unreasonable man. So the young man went back to college" (2). Apparently Ursinus did not have anything to offer that interested Salinger because he dropped out and returned to New York. Salinger evokes the atmosphere of insipid college parties in his first published story, "The Young Folks" (1940).

The following fall, in 1939, Salinger enrolled in Whit Burnett's short story writing course at Columbia University. That course launched Salinger's career as a writer. He wrote "The Young Folks" for that course, and it was published in *Story* magazine which was edited by Whit Burnett. This experience shows up in Salinger's fiction when Buddy Glass also takes a short story course at Columbia University from a "professor B" ("Introduction" 154). And, like J.D. Salinger, Buddy Glass also became a professional writer without ever having received a college degree.

FREE-LANCE WRITING

During the years 1940 to 1942 only two of Salinger's experiences show up in his fiction. One is his stint as an entertainment director for the younger set on the cruise ship *Kungsholm*; the other is his work as a free-lance short story writer.

Salinger's experience of working on a cruise ship is reflected in the story "A Young Girl in 1941 with No Waist at All." That story takes place on the *Kungsholm* as she cruises the Caribbean. The girl in the story is unsuccessfully wooed by a college freshman named Ray Kinsella who has taken a temporary job as "a member of the ship's Junior Entertainment Committee."

Another one of Salinger's experiences during that time was his struggle to get stories accepted by the so-called "slick" magazines. His efforts paid off in 1941 when he had one story published by *Collier's* and another by *Esquire*. In the *Esquire* story, the narrator shares his unsuccessful attempt "to write a lovely tender boy-meets-girl story" for *Collier's* magazine. Because he is unable to write such a story for *Collier's*, he instead writes a "boy-doesn't-meet-girl" story for *Esquire* and calls it "The Heart of a Broken Story."

During this stage in his career, Salinger also wrote his first two stories about men in the military. After World War II had started in Europe and the United States had not yet entered the war, the American public demanded upbeat stories about young men in the Army. Even though Salinger was, at this point, not in the military, he cranked out two such formula stories for *Collier's*. Each of them was advertised as "A Complete Short Story on this Page," and their titles are "The Hang of It" (1941) and "Personal Notes of an Infantryman" (1942).

MILITARY LIFE IN THE UNITED STATES

Salinger was drafted in April of 1942, and most of the stories he wrote during the next two years deal with people who are living on Army bases in the United States. Salinger's basic training at Fort Dix and Fort Monmouth, New Jersey, his stint as an instructor at a U.S. Army Air Force base in Bainbridge,

Georgia, and his attendance at the Signal Corps School in Nashville, Tennessee, provided him with the milieu for the stories: "Soft-Boiled Sergeant" and "This Sandwich Has No Mayonnaise." These two stories are not as light-hearted as "The Hang of It" and "Personal Notes of an Infantryman" because the two protagonists lose a good friend and a brother, respectively: One is killed at Pearl Harbor and the other is missing in action in the Pacific.

More importantly, though, Salinger had, up to this point, led a very privileged upper-middle-class life, and his experiences in the military exposed him for the first time to members of the American working class. He seems to have been fascinated with the way the "other half" lived and talked, and he made three fictional forays into that social territory. In the stories "Soft-Boiled Sergeant," "Both Parties Concerned," and "Elaine," the central characters all belong to the lowest stratum of American society and speak very slangy, ungrammatical English.

When Salinger was assigned to the Counter Intelligence Corps and was waiting to be shipped off to Europe, his anticipation is reflected in two stories, "Once a Week Won't Kill You" and "Last Day of the Last Furlough." Both deal with characters who are about to leave for the European Theater of Operations. "Once a Week" contrasts the somberness of the soldier who is about to go to war with the frivolity of his wife who can think only of the wonderful shopping opportunities he will have when he gets to London. In "Last Furlough," Salinger creates his first war-time alter ego: The protagonist, Sergeant John F. "Babe" Gladwaller has the same Army identification tag number as Staff Sergeant Jerome David Salinger, ASN 32325200. But above all, Gladwaller expresses Salinger's own ambivalence toward the war. On the one hand he is opposed to all war, on the other hand he knows that Hitler and Hirohito's armies must be stopped.

THE WAR EXPERIENCE

Salinger's experiences in World War II show up in fewer stories than one would expect considering that he kept writing and publishing stories straight through from D-Day on June 6, 1944, to V-E Day on May 7, 1945—that is, from the day of the invasion of Europe to the day that Nazi Germany surrendered.

In 1944, the Army sent Salinger to Tiverton in Devonshire, England, where he was trained by the Counter Intelligence Corps. His CIC section was attached to the 12th Infantry regiment of the 7th Army, and that regiment fought in the five major European campaigns of World War II. These five campaigns were officially called Normandy, Northern France, Rhineland, Ardennes, and Central Europe. Toward the end of the war, Salinger's regiment participated in the occupation of Southern Germany, and during the last days of the war, Salinger saw with his own eyes what the concentration camps were all about.

Although Salinger kept writing and sending stories to magazines all through 1944 and 1945, his war experiences show up in only three stories and then only indirectly. The stories are, "A Boy in France," "The Stranger," and "For Esmé—with Love and Squalor."

When we consider the stories Salinger wrote during the war, we need to realize that he was not a combat infantryman. As a member of the Counter Intelligence Corps, his job was to interview prisoners of war and civilians in order to collect information on enemy troop strength, number of tanks, location of heavy artillery, supply depots, and so forth. He was attached to the headquarters of the regiment which was located quite a distance behind the front lines, and he had a jeep at his disposal so he could quickly get to wherever there were prisoners of war or civilian refugees to be interviewed.

Although Sergeant Salinger did not participate in the day-to-day combat with the Germans, he must have occasionally come under enemy fire. This is suggested in two stories. In the story "The Stranger," Sergeant Babe Gladwaller reports that his friend Vincent Caulfield was fatally wounded by a mortar shell while he was far behind the front lines where he and some other GIs were warming themselves at a fire near a medics' tent. Gladwaller reports that Caulfield "died in the medics' CP tent about thirty yards away" ("Stranger" 77). And in "For Esmé—with Love and Squalor," a Counter Intelligence Sergeant and his jeep driver accidentally wind up in an area that has just come under German artillery fire. The driver, Corporal Clay, remembers that as they drove into the town of Valognes, "we got shelled for about two goddam hours." He also remembers a "goddam cat I shot that jumped up on the hood of the jeep when we were layin' in that hole" ("Esmé" 110).

The episode of Corporal Clay shooting the cat was probably inspired by an incident involving Ernest Hemingway. Several biographers report that Hemingway visited Salinger's regiment and got into an argument with someone about the comparative accuracy of the German Luger pistol and the U.S. Army issue .45. Hemingway supposedly demonstrated the accuracy of the Luger by shooting the head off a chicken (Skow 13, French 25). Sergeant X was appalled at Corporal Clay's killing of the cat and used the words "cruel," "brutal," and "dirty" to describe Clay's behavior. We can imagine that Salinger felt the same way about Hemingway killing the chicken. And Hemingway didn't even have Corporal Clay's excuse that he was "temporarily insane" because he was under enemy fire ("Esmé" 110).

It is probably because Salinger was not a combat infantryman that his war stories don't ever show soldiers in battle situations. However, in one story, he illustrates the psychological after-effects of combat. "A Boy in France" begins in the evening after a battle. The protagonist, Babe Gladwaller, wants to bed down for the night in an abandoned German foxhole, but he first has to scoop out the blood-soaked blanket of its former inhabitant. Then, in an inner monologue, his mind begins to unravel as he imagines being back home in the United States and bolting the door to his room behind him. In the rest of the inner monologue, Gladwaller says four more times "and I'll bolt the door." This is his mind's attempt to shut the bloody fighting of the day out of his memory. Like some of the infantrymen in Salinger's regiment, Gladwaller was close to what was then called "combat fatigue," that is, post-traumatic stress disorder.

NERVOUS BREAKDOWN

Sergeant Salinger's nervous breakdown at the end of World War II is reflected in the nervous breakdowns of Sergeant X in "For Esmé—with Love and Squalor" and of ex-sergeant Seymour Glass in "A Perfect Day for Bananafish."

We know about Salinger's nervous breakdown from a letter he wrote to Ernest Hemingway. The two met twice during the war. Several biographers have assumed that Salinger's nervous collapse was due to "combat fatigue," but that is not likely since Salinger was not a combat soldier. It is more likely that his nervous breakdown was due to the horrifying sights and smells of his visit to one of Germany's most gruesome concentration camps.

Salinger's daughter Margaret was the first person to mention Salinger's concentration camp experience. In her memoir, *Dream Catcher,* she writes: "As a counter intelligence officer my father was one of the first soldiers to walk into a certain, just liberated, concentration camp. He told me the name, but I no longer remember." She also quotes her father as saying, "You never really get the smell of burning flesh out of your nose, no matter how long you live" (*Dream Catcher* 55). The reason Margaret Salinger doesn't remember the name of the camp is that it is not as well known as the infamous names of Dachau and Auschwitz.

The concentration camp that Salinger walked into must have been the camp near the village of Hurlach, Bavaria, seven miles north of the city of Landsberg. That camp was not occupied by Salinger's regiment but by elements of the 12th Armored Division. However, Salinger could easily have gotten to that camp, because on April 27, 1944, the day that the camp was first discovered by GIs, the command post of Salinger's regiment was located in the village of Aga-wang, 15 miles northwest of the camp, and two days later, the command post was in the village of Winkl, only nine miles east of the camp (Johnson 391).

The camp near Hurlach was officially called Kaufering Lager IV. It was one of 11 slave labor camps that housed a total of 22,000 Jewish prisoners. This slave labor force was used in the construction of a gigantic underground aircraft factory on the outskirts of the city of Landsberg. In that factory, the jet fighter plane Messerschmitt Me 262 was scheduled to be mass-produced at 900 planes a month. Kaufering IV was a catchall camp for the sick prisoners of the other small camps in the area. It was therefore named the "Krankenlager" (camp for the sick). But it was actually an extermination camp because the sick prisoners were simply allowed to die from their illnesses or from starvation.

On the day before Americans troops occupied the area, the SS guards evacuated some 3,000 prisoners via railroad boxcars and killed all those that were too sick or too weak to travel. They shot, clubbed, and hacked to death 92 prisoners, and they burned alive 268 others by locking them in wooden barracks and setting the barracks on fire (Posset 41). When the Americans arrived, all the SS guards were gone and only a handful of prisoners were still alive. They had escaped extermination by hiding from the SS. In addition to the 360 prisoners whom the SS had killed before pulling out, the GIs found two mass graves containing the bodies of another 4,500 prisoners who had died from sickness or malnutrition.

The first American soldiers who arrived at the camp found that the barracks and the corpses of the prisoners in them were still burning. Sergeant Robert T. Hartwig remembers that when he and his jeep driver approached Hurlach, "we knew we were near a camp because of the sickening odor of burning bodies" (Saks 118), and Corporal Pete Bramble reports that "the stench was terrible, especially the burning corpses" (Bramble 1). Photos taken by Sergeant Hartwig, Corporal Bramble, and other American soldiers show dozens of smoldering corpses in the ruins of the burned-out barracks. These pictures support the assumption that it was at the Kaufering camp that Salinger encountered the smell of burning flesh which he said he would never be able to get out of his nose (the pictures can bee seen in Ken Bradstreet's combat history of the 12th Armored Division entitled *Hellcats,* on the web site of the Simon Wiesenthal Multi Media Learning Center, and on the web site *The Twelfth Armored Division and the Liberation of Death Camps*).

Salinger never described in writing what he witnessed at the Kaufering concentration camp, but the effect that this experience had on him does show up in his fiction. That effect is the nervous breakdown which he suffered some time in May of 1945. From the undated letter that Salinger wrote to Ernest Hemingway, we know that he checked himself into "a General Hospital in Nürnberg" because he had been in "an almost constant state of despondency." Internal evidence suggests that the letter was written in May of 1945, shortly after the liberation of the concentration camps in Bavaria. In this letter—which can be examined in the Princeton University Library—Salinger worries that he may receive a psychiatric discharge from the Army. This suggests that his case must have been severe.

Salinger's nervous breakdown is best reflected in his most autobiographical story, "For Esmé—with Love and Squalor." The central character in the story is Staff Sergeant X, a member of the Counter Intelligence Corps. At the beginning of the story, he is being trained at an Army base in a small town in the South of England. This town is modeled after Tiverton in Devonshire where Staff Sergeant Salinger himself was trained by the CIC. After D-day, Staff Sergeant X participated in the five major European campaigns, and so did Staff Sergeant Salinger. At the end of the war, Sergeant X winds up in the fictitious town of Gaufurt, Bavaria, where interrogates Nazi civilians. Similarly, Sergeant Salinger wound up in the town of Weißenburg, Bavaria, where he also interrogated suspected Nazis.

Even though Sergeant X's nervous breakdown is the subject of "For Esmé—with Love and Squalor," the story describes only the symptoms and not the causes. This is because the story skips from a few days before the D-Day invasion to a time "several weeks after V-E Day" [Victory in Europe] ("Esmé" 104). Sergeant X has just returned from a two-weeks' stay at an Army hospital in Frankfurt, Germany, where he has been treated for a nervous breakdown. It is significant that he calls it a "nervous breakdown" and not "combat fatigue." Whatever treatment Sergeant X received did not help much because upon his return, he still feels "his mind dislodge itself and teeter, like insecure luggage on an overhead rack" ("Esmé" 109). Also, his driver, Corporal Clay, tells him that "the goddam side of your face is jumping all over the place" (109). Moreover, the sergeant's hands shake so much that when he tries to write, his writing is "almost entirely illegible" (105). The same happened to Sergeant Salinger's handwriting. When Salinger's daughter Margaret read through her father's wartime letters, she found that during the spring and summer of 1945, his handwriting became "something totally unrecognizable" (*Dream Catcher* 68).

POST-WAR CIVILIAN LIFE

The events that occurred in Salinger's life between the end of World War II in 1945 and his sudden success with *The Catcher in the Rye* in 1951 did not leave much of an imprint on his fiction. The only story of that time period that contains biographical material is "For Esmé—with Love and Squalor" (1950).

"For Esmé" not only reflects Salinger's nervous breakdown but also a romantic end-of-the-war experience. In the story we are told that several weeks after V-E Day, Sergeant X arrested and interrogated an unmarried woman who "had been a low-level official in the Nazi Party, but high enough by Army Regulations standards, to fall into an automatic-arrest category" ("Esmé" 105). The woman had in her possession a book by the Nazi propaganda minister, Joseph Goebbels, entitled *Die Zeit ohne Beispiel* (The Time without Equal). On the title page, the woman had inscribed the sentence, "Dear God, life is hell." Underneath that inscription, Sergeant X—his hands shaking uncontrollably—tries to write a quotation from Dostoevsky, "Fathers and teachers, I ponder, 'What is hell?' I maintain that it is the suffering of being unable to love" ("Esmé" 105).

We learn from Margaret Salinger that Sergeant X's arrest of this fictitious German woman has a striking parallel in actual life. Like Sergeant X, Sergeant Salinger also arrested a woman who was a minor official in the Nazi Party. Her name was Sylvia, and Sergeant Jerry Salinger fell in love with her. The upshot was, so Margaret Salinger reports, that "she and Jerry were married by summer's end" (*Dream Catcher* 71). Margaret Salinger here corrects a mistake that Salinger scholars have perpetuated for many years, namely the bogus information that Salinger's first wife Sylvia was from France and that she was a doctor (see Hamilton 97, Alexander 109).

We may wonder how far the similarities between Sylvia Salinger and the Nazi woman in "For Esmé" went. Since Sylvia was a member of the Nazi Party, it is possible that she, too, owned the Goebbels book and that she is the original author of the inscription, "Dear God, life is hell." This inscription may well have been what endeared her to Salinger. After the horrendous experience of his visit to the Kaufering concentration camp, Jerry Salinger may also have come to believe that "life is hell," and he may have felt that the only way to get out of this hell was to reassert his ability to love.

Unfortunately, Salinger's first marriage disintegrated after he brought Sylvia home to New York. Apparently Sylvia could not get along with Salinger's family. Margaret Salinger reports that her aunt Doris said about Sylvia, "She was *very* German," and that her father said "Sylvia hated Jews as much as he hated Nazis" (*Dream Catcher* 71). At any rate, Sylvia returned to Germany, and the marriage was dissolved.

While Salinger's personal life wilted, his writing career went into full bloom. He signed a contract with the *New Yorker*—then the most prestigious venue for short fiction in America—and in December of 1946, that magazine finally published a story about Holden Caulfield which Salinger had originally submitted in 1941. The title of that story is "Slight Rebellion off Madison." Subsequently, Salinger expanded that story into the novel, *The Catcher in the Rye.* The novel came out in 1951 and made Salinger into a celebrity and a wealthy man.

None of the events that occurred in Salinger's life after his return from Germany show up his fiction, except that one of Salinger's alter egos, the writer Buddy Glass, suggests that he is the author of *The Catcher in the Rye* ("Introduction" 111).

CONVERSION TO VEDANTA HINDUISM

Approximately a year after the publication of *The Catcher in the Rye,* there occurred an event that had a profound effect on Salinger's life and his fiction. That event was his discovery of and conversion to Vedanta Hinduism which he studied at the Ramakrishna-Vivekananda Center in New York. That center is on East 94th Street, only a few blocks from where Salinger's parents lived on Park Avenue.

Salinger apparently discovered Vedanta via the biography of the Hindu saint Sri Ramakrishna, for in March of 1952, he sent a copy of *The Life of Sri Ramakrishna* to a British publisher urging him to bring out an English edition (Hamilton 127). Vedanta is the most philosophical and the most ecumenical branch of Hinduism. Its ecumenical nature is evident in the chapel of the Ramakrishna-Vivekananda Center in New York. On the altar, there is a statue of Ramakrishna, but in niches on the right and left walls there are icons of Gautama Buddha and the Virgin Mary with the Christ Child.

When Salinger took his course of studies at the center in 1952, it was directed by Swami Nikhilananda. Salinger later gave Nikhilananda a copy of *Franny and Zooey* (1961) with an inscription in which he says that he wrote the book "to circulate the ideas of Vedanta" (Paniker 2). Salinger kept up his association with the Center at least until the late seventies. When I took my course of studies at the Center in 1977, Nikhilananda's successor, Swami Adiswaranda, told me that Salinger corresponded with him occasionally and that the previous year, Salinger had attended the Center's annual retreat on an island in the St. Lawrence River. I attended the same retreat the following year, but Salinger didn't show up.

Salinger's conversion to Vedanta Hinduism is reflected in the story "Teddy" (1953). The story is a Socratic dialogue between the ten-year-old child prodigy Teddy McArdle and a skeptical education professor by the name of Bob Nicholson. In that conversation, Teddy provides an exposition of the basic ideas of Vedanta Hinduism: the belief in reincarnation, which Teddy says "isn't a theory"; the belief that "everything [is] God"; and the goal of all Hindus which is "to stop getting born and dying all the time [and] staying with God, where it's really nice" ("Teddy" 188-191).

Salinger's fiction reveals that his interest in Vedanta Hinduism lasted from "Teddy" (1953) all the way to his last published novella "Hapworth 16, 1924"

(1965). In his long letter from Camp Hapworth, the seven-year-old Seymour asks to be sent *Raja-Yoga* and *Bhakti-Yoga*, two Vedanta texts by Swami Vivekananda. Seymour says about Vivekananda that he is one of the "giants of this century," and he also says that his, Seymour's, "personal sympathy for him will never be outgrown or exhausted as long as I live" ("Hapworth" 92).

Whether or not Salinger himself outgrew or exhausted his own sympathy for Vivekananda and his interest in Vedanta Hinduism will remain a mystery for some time since he does not plan to publish again during his lifetime. In a National Public Radio interview in September of 2000, Margaret Salinger said that her father "has been writing every day" and that "he is planning to publish after his death." She also revealed that Salinger has a filing system with "red dots on stories that are ready to go, should he die" and that "a green dot meant that these require some editing" ("Margaret Salinger on J.D. Salinger"). Salinger's posthumous work will show if he remained a Vedantist for the rest of his life or if he experienced another major ideological change such as the one back in 1952.

Salinger's preoccupation with religious themes had a devastating effect on the critical reception of his work. Ever since the publication of the novella "Zooey" (1957), there have been more negative than positive reviews of his work, and the criticism has focused—more often than not—on his religious ideas. But Salinger was aware of the risk he was taking in writing fiction that is essentially religious. In the novella "Zooey," the narrator Buddy Glass says that his brother Zooey has warned him that his, Buddy's, fiction contains "a too vividly apparent transcendent element of sorts" and that this "can only expedite, move up, the day and hour of [his] professional undoing" (48). This warning, so Buddy says, is something to give a writer pause. But that's all it does. It gives him pause; it doesn't stop him from writing what he feels he must write. Salinger leaves no doubt that he shares Buddy's attitude because in the dust cover notes for *Franny and Zooey* (1961), he explicitly refers to Buddy Glass as "my alter-ego and collaborator."

THE LIFE OF A LITERARY SHUT-IN

In 1953, Salinger decided he needed to get away from the publicity circus that inevitably swirls around a successful author. He therefore bought an old, unwinterized farmhouse on a hill outside Cornish, New Hampshire, and he has been fanatical in guarding his privacy there.

Salinger's reclusive life is reflected in "Seymour—An Introduction" when Buddy Glass calls himself "a literary shut-in" because he lives in a little house on a mountainside, deep in the woods Upstate New York, not far from the Canadian border,

In "Seymour—An Introduction," Salinger makes fun of the misinformation that began to circulate about him soon after he withdrew to the woods of New Hampshire. Buddy Glass mentions that he occasionally receives get-well-cards from readers who believe the rumors that he spends one-half of each year in a Buddhist monastery and the other half in a mental institution.

However, while Buddy Glass welcomes it when people drop by at his hermitage in the woods, J.D. Salinger has been known to threaten uninvited visitors with a shotgun. Unlike Salinger, Buddy loves to discuss his work with visitors, especially what he has written about his brother Seymour. He says he absolutely yearns to be questioned about his late brother and will happily talk about him for hours. But then he imagines what his hospitality might ultimately lead to. Academics and curious lay people might arrive by the busload, and some of them might even parachute into his yard wearing cameras. Humorous though this passage in "Seymour—An Introduction" is, it spells out what must be one of J.D. Salinger's worst nightmares.

J.D. SALINGER AND BUDDY GLASS

The relationship between Salinger's life and his fiction is epitomized in the relationship between himself and Buddy Glass. Although Salinger calls Buddy Glass his alter ego, the similarities between the lives of the two are balanced by differences. They were both born in 1919, grew up in the same neighborhoods of Manhattan, took a short story course from Whit Burnett at Columbia University, served in Europe during World War II, and retreated to the woods after they became famous writers. But in addition to these similarities, there are major differences. Unlike Buddy, who was a child prodigy, Salinger was an average student; and unlike Buddy, who is a bachelor and a teacher at a college, Salinger has married three times, has two children, and despises people who teach at colleges. Moreover, the most traumatic event in the life of Buddy Glass, the suicide of his beloved brother Seymour, has no direct parallel in the life of J.D. Salinger.

What is more important than the external similarities and differences between J.D. Salinger and Buddy Glass is their identical visions of life and views of art. From what we know about Salinger's religious studies and from what we can deduce from the form of his fiction, Buddy Glass is indeed his alter ego and spokesman when it comes to religion and art.

Buddy Glass speaks not only about his own religious beliefs but also about Salinger's when he says in "Seymour—An Introduction" that his roots in Eastern Philosophy are planted in the New and Old Testaments, Advaita Vedanta Hinduism, and classical Chinese Taoism. He then uses Vedanta terms to describe himself as a fourth-class Karma Yogin who is also attracted to the path of Jnana Yoga (See "Introduction" 208).

This declaration contains five ideas that need to be explained. First of all, Advaita Vedanta—or non-dualistic Vedanta—is the most philosophical branch of Hinduism and teaches that man and God are not two but one because *Brahman*, or God, dwells in man's soul as *Atman*. Second, Advaita Vedanta sees other religions such as the Judaism of the Old Testament, the Christianity of the New Testament, and classical Taoism as expressions of the same religious truth. Third, a *karma yogin* is a person who pursues his spiritual advancement via the path of scrupulous fulfillment of everyday duties. Fourth, *jnana yoga* is the path of spiritual advancement via knowledge and learning. And finally, a fourth-class *karma yogin* is a person in the fourth stage of life, or *sannyasa*, the monk or teacher stage (see Vivekananda, *Karma Yoga* 20).

The views on art and writing that Buddy Glass expresses in "Seymour—An Introduction" also seem to be identical with Salinger's views. The four most important ideas that inform this view of art are (1) that all true art originates in divine inspiration; (2) that the true artist is a seer who sees more than ordinary mortals; (3) that the form of true art is organic because it is created spontaneously; and (4) that true art has both a secular and a divine purpose, it should "please or enlighten or enlarge" its audience to within an inch of its life. These ideas are epitomized in the advice that Seymour gives Buddy about his writing when he tells him: "Follow your heart, win or lose" ("Introduction" 160).

But Salinger did not write *The Catcher in the Rye* and *Nine Stories* according to these ideas. At that stage of his career he still followed accepted methods of composition and pursued themes that had universal appeal. However, the loose structure and the religious themes in "Zooey," "Seymour—An Introduction," and "Hapworth 16, 1924" suggest that Salinger accepted the fatal advice of his brainchild Seymour Glass and decided to follow his heart rather than proven recipes for success.

The connections that I have pointed out between Salinger's life and his fiction show that although his fiction contains many autobiographical details, he is not an autobiographical writer in the same way that Ernest Hemingway was. Unlike Hemingway, Salinger does not build his stories and novels around major events in his life. Hemingway, for instance, used one of the most traumatic events of his life, his being wounded in World War I, as a crucial part of the plots in two novels (*A Farewell to Arms* and *Across the River and Into the Trees*) and in several short stories (Vignette VI in *In Our Time*, "Now I Lay Me," "In Another Country," and "A Way You'll Never Be"). By contrast, what was probably the most traumatic event of Salinger's life, his nervous breakdown at the end of World War II, is treated not directly but only vaguely and in terms of its after effects in only two stories, "For Esmé—with Love and Squalor" and "A Perfect Day for Bananafish."

The difference between the way that Salinger and Hemingway used their own war experiences in their fiction is chiefly due to their different attitudes toward war. While Hemingway saw war as a test of manhood, Salinger could see nothing positive in war and did not think people should write fiction about it. He expressed this attitude through Babe Gladwaller in the early story "Last Day of the Last Furlough." Referring to World War II, Gladwaller says that "it's the moral duty of all the men who have fought and will fight in this war to keep our mouths shut, once it's over, never again to mention it in any way. It's time we let the dead die in vain." Gladwaller continues to argue that if all those who have fought in the war come back, "all of us talking, writing, painting, making movies of heroism and cockroaches and foxholes and blood, then future generations will always be doomed to future Hitlers. It's never occurred to boys to have contempt for wars, to point to soldiers' pictures in history books laughing at them" ("Last Day" 62). But Salinger's contempt for war and for soldiers is only part of the reason why his fiction isn't more directly autobiographical.

The main reason why real life experiences do not play as important a role in Salinger's fiction as in Hemingway's is that their views of art are very different. While Hemingway started out as a journalist who had a great respect for real-life events as the basis of art, Salinger started out as a writer of fiction who had an even greater respect for imagination as the basis of art. I will analyze Salinger's view of art in detail in Appendix III: "Salinger's Philosophy of Composition."

WORKS CITED

"A.G. 'Pete' Bramble. 12th Armored Division." The Twelfth Armored Division and the Liberation of Death Camps. <http://www.acu.edu/academics/history/12ad/campsx/bramble.htm>

Alexander, Paul. *Salinger: A Biography*. Los Angeles: Renaissance, 1999.

Bramble, A.G. "Kaufering IV, After Being Burned by the Retreating German Soldiers" [Photo]. The Twelfth Armored Division and the Liberation of Death Camps. http://www.acu.edu/academics/history/12ad/campsx/burning.gif>

"Charred bodies discovered upon liberation by US troops" [Photo]. Simon Wiesenthal Multi Media Learning Center. <http://motlc.wiesenthal.com/gallery/pg01/pg7/pg01738.html>

French, Warren. *J.D. Salinger*. New York: Twayne, 1963.

Hamilton, Ian. *In Search of J.D. Salinger*. New York: Random House, 1988.

Hartwig, Robert T. "Inmates Were Rounded Up and Placed in this Barracks" [Photo]. The Twelfth Armored Division and the Liberation of Death Camps. <http://www.acu.edu/academics/history/12ad/campsx/c-01.gif>

Hemingway, Ernest. *Across the River and Into the Trees* [1950]. New York: Scribner's, 1998.

___ . *A Farewell to Arms* [1929]. New York: Scribner's, 1969.

___ . "In Another Country." In *The Short Stories*, 267-272.

___ . *In Our Time* [1925]. New York: Scribner's, 1958.

___ . "Now I Lay Me." In *The Short Stories*, 363-371.

___ . *The Short Stories of Ernest Hemingway*. New York: Scribner's, 1966.

___ . "A Way You'll Never Be." In *The Short Stories*, 402-414.

Johnson, Gerden F. *History of the Twelfth Infantry Regiment in World War II*. Boston: Twelfth Infantry Regiment, 1947.

"Margaret Salinger on J.D. Salinger." *The Connection*. Natl. Public Radio. WBUR Boston. 14 September 2000. <http://www.theconnection.org/ archive/2000/09/0914b.shtml>

Paniker, Sumitra. "The Influence of Eastern Thought on 'Teddy' and the Seymour Glass Stories of J.D. Salinger." Diss. U of Texas at Austin, 1971.

Posset, Anton. "Die amerikanische Armee entdeckt den Holocaust." *Themenhefte Landsberger Zeitgeschichte* 2 (1993): 35-41.

Saks, Julien, Colonel. "GIs Discover Holocaust." In *Hellcats* [WW II Combat History of the 12th Armored Division]. Ed. Ken Bradstreet. Paducah, KY: Turner, 1987, 117-120.

Salinger, J.D. "Backstage with *Esquire*." *Esquire* 16 (September 1941): 24.

___ . "Both Parties Concerned." *Saturday Evening Post* (26 February 1944): 14, 47-48.

___ . "A Boy in France." *Saturday Evening Post* (31 March 1945): 21, 92.

___ . *The Catcher in the Rye* [1951]. New York: Bantam, 1964.

___ . "Contributors." *Story* 25 (November-December 1944): 1.

___ . "Elaine." *Story* 26 (March-April 1945): 38-47

___ . "For Esmé—with Love and Squalor." In *Nine Stories* [1953]. New York: Bantam, 1964, 87-114.

___ . *Franny and Zooey* [1961]. New York: Bantam, 1964.

___ . "A Girl I Knew." *Good Housekeeping* 126 (February 1948): 37, 186, 18-196.

___ . "The Hang of It." *Collier's* (12 July 1941): 22.

___ . "Hapworth 16, 1924." *New Yorker* (19 June 1965): 32-113.

___ . "The Heart of a Broken Story." *Esquire* 16 (September 1941): 32, 131-133.

___ . "Last Day of the Last Furlough." *Saturday Evening Post* (15 July 1944): 26-27, 61-62, 64.

___ . Letter to Ernest Hemingway. [nd.] Ernest Hemingway Collection. Princeton, NJ: Princeton University Library.

___ . Letter to Whit Burnett. 28 June 1944. Archives of Story Magazine and Story Press. Princeton, NJ: Princeton University Library.

___ . "Once a Week Won't Kill You." *Story* 25 (November-December 1944): 23-27.

___ . "Personal Notes of an Infantryman." *Collier's* (12 Dec. 1942): 96.

___ . *Raise High the Roof Beam, Carpenters and Seymour—An Introduction* [1963]. New York: Bantam, 1965.

___ . "The Skipped Diploma: Musings of a Social Soph." *Ursinus Weekly* (10 October 1938): 2.

___ . "Soft-Boiled Sergeant." *Saturday Evening Post* (15 April 1944): 18, 82, 84-85.

___ . "Teddy." In *Nine Stories* [1953]. New York: Bantam, 1964, 166-198.

___ . "This Sandwich Has No Mayonnaise." *Esquire* 24 (October 1945): 54-56, 147-149.

___ . "A Young Girl in 1941 with No Waist at All." *Mademoiselle* 25 (May 1947): 222-223, 292-302.

___ . "The Young Folks." *Story* 16 (March-April 1940): 26-30.

Salinger, Margaret. *Dream Catcher*. New York: Washington Square, 2000.

Skow, John. "Sonny: An Introduction." *Time* (15 September 1961): 84-90. Rpt. in *Salinger: A Critical and Personal Portrait*. Ed. Henry A. Grunwald. New York: Harper, 1962, 3-18.

SUGGESTIONS FOR FURTHER READING

Haveman, Ernest. "The Search for the Mysterious J.D. Salinger: Recluse in the Rye." *Life* (3 November 1961): 129-144.

Hoban, Phoebe. "The Salinger File." *New York* (15 June 1987): 36-42.

Maxwell, William. "J.D. Salinger." *Book-of-the-Month Club News* (July 1951): 5-6.

Rosenbaum, Ron. "The Man in the Glass House." *Esquire* (June 1997): 41-53, 116-121.

Chapter 1

The Early Stories

It's always the best way to rectify a mistake *before* it's made.

Mrs. Odenhearn in
"A Young Girl in 1941 with No Waist at All."

In 1939, the twenty-year-old J.D. Salinger took a short story writing course from Whit Burnett at Columbia University. Burnett was the editor of the literary magazine *Story*. He liked one of Salinger's stories so much that he published it in his magazine the following year. "The Young Folks" appeared in the March-April 1940 issue, and it was accompanied by the following biographical information: "J.D. Salinger, who is twenty-one years old, was born in New York. He attended public grammar schools, one military academy, and three colleges, and has spent a year in Europe. He is particularly interested in playwriting" ("Contributors" [1940] 2). Salinger's interest in playwriting waned during the forties, and Herschel Brickell, the editor of *Prize Stories of 1949*, reported that Salinger told him "he may start a novel sooner or later, but says that since he is essentially a short-story writer he will drop the project if he feels he is abusing what talent he has, or spreading it too thin" (Brickell 249).

By the time Salinger made that statement in 1949, he had published over 20 stories, among them two that focus on a character named Holden Caulfield who later became the protagonist of *The Catcher in the Rye*. These stories appeared in "slick" magazines such as *The Saturday Evening Post* (five), *Collier's* (four), *Esquire* (two), *Cosmopolitan* (two), but also in the intellectually more ambitious *New Yorker* (five) and *Story* (four). Salinger wrote most of these stories while he was in the Army during World War II. When *Story* magazine published "Once a Week Won't Kill You" in the November-December issue of 1944, Salinger said in a "Contributors" note that he was currently a soldier in Germany and that he was "still writing whenever [he] can find the time and an unoccupied foxhole" ("Contributors" [1944] 1). Ten of Salinger's 20 uncollected stories involve characters who are in the Army, the rest of them are mostly about male-female relationships, and two deal with the pressures faced by artists.

Salinger did not want to see his early work reprinted. When an individual who called himself John Greenberg published Salinger's early stories in an unauthorized two-volume edition, entitled *The Complete Uncollected Short Stories of J.D. Salinger* (Berkeley, 1974), Salinger sued the person for violation of the copyright law and told a *New York Times* reporter: "I'm not trying to hide the gaucheries of my youth. I just don't think they're worthy of publishing" (Fosburgh 69).

While Salinger's early stories aren't exactly "gaucheries," they lack the structural coherence and the clarity of purpose that distinguish his mature work. Some of these stories are formula magazine fiction—for example, "The Hang of It" and "Personal Notes of an Infantryman"—but others contain ambitious experiments with plot, point of view, and style—for example, "The Heart of a Broken Story," "The Varioni Brothers," and "Blue Melody." The uncollected early stories are worth studying because they help us understand the development of Salinger's narrative techniques, his thematic interests, his view of human nature, and his vision of life.

CRITICAL RECEPTION

At the time of their publication, Salinger's early stories did not attract any critical attention. Some of the reviewers of *The Catcher in the Rye* (1951) commented in passing on Salinger stories that had recently appeared in the *New Yorker*, but it wasn't until the late fifties that critics began to analyze Salinger's apprentice work.

An early positive response to Salinger's apprentice fiction came from Ernest Hemingway. Shortly after the liberation of Paris, Salinger sought out Hemingway who was holding court at the Ritz Hotel. Salinger showed him the story "Last Day of the Last Furlough," which had just been published in the *Saturday Evening Post,* and Hemingway is reported to have said about Salinger: "Jesus, he has a helluva talent" (Skow 13).

The first critic to evaluate the early stories was Ihab Hassan in his 1957 essay "Rare Quixotic Gesture: The Fiction of J.D. Salinger." Hassan said about them: "The majority of these pieces make an uneasy lot, and some of them are downright embarrassing—it is gratifying to find that Salinger has excluded them all from his collection [*Nine Stories*]" (143). The following year, in *The Fiction of J.D. Salinger* (1958), Frederick Gwynn and Joseph Blotner offered a slightly more positive view of the 20 uncollected stories. Although they judged most of them to be either "commercial stories" or "arty sketches," they singled out six pieces as worthwhile because they "develop attitudes and relationships and names that end in the fruitful Caulfield and Glass families with whom Salinger is later to feel so much at home" (9). A year later, in a negative assessment entitled "The Love Song of J.D. Salinger" (1959), Arthur Mizener said about Salinger's apprentice work that it will disappoint the reader who might expect to find in it the same powers of observation and sense of experience as in Salinger's later work. Mizener concluded: "The first published stories deal, in a mechanical and overingenious way, with the superficial interests of magazine readers of the time" (25).

Warren French and John Wenke are two critics who see greater value in Salinger's uncollected stories than the earlier critics. French's book *J.D. Salinger* (1963) provides so far the most extensive analysis of Salinger's early fiction. French discusses 15 stories and spends an entire chapter on the novella "The Inverted Forest" which he believes to be the most important example of Salinger's early work. Other pieces that French considers to have merit are the story "Elaine" which he calls "genuinely moving" (51) and the Babe Gladwaller story "Last Day of the Last Furlough" which he calls "one of the best of Salinger's uncollected stories" (60). However, French refers to another Babe Gladwaller story, "The Stranger," as "one of Salinger's most complete failures" (63) because he finds its plot and its hero's motivation totally unconvincing. According to French, the major problem with Salinger's early stories is that "Salinger continued to grind out for the slicks the fodder that sentimentalists thrive upon" (58). French singles out "Soft-Boiled Sergeant" as the most sentimental of the early stories and he also objects to the sentimentality in "Once a Week Won't Kill You," "Both Parties Concerned," and "A Boy in France."

The most recent appraisal of Salinger's early stories is that of John Wenke in his book *J.D. Salinger: A Study of the Short Fiction* (1991). Wenke says about Salinger's uncollected stories that they are "neither all failures nor a trove of unacknowledged masterpieces." They range, in Wenke's opinion, from "brief sentimental failures" such as "The Hang of It" to "highly sophisticated, carefully refined pieces" such as "The Varioni Brothers" and "The Heart of a Broken Story" (5).

THEMES

Four recurring themes in Salinger's early fiction are that of unhappy male-female relationships, that of premature death, that of the devastating effect of war on the minds and emotions of soldiers and their families, and that of the frustrating relationship between artists and their society. Some stories develop more than one of these themes.

The theme of unhappy male-female relationships occurs in various forms in 12 of the 20 uncollected stories. Two sub-types of this theme are those of unrequited love and bad marriages. In four stories, the unrequited love theme is the primary and in four it is a secondary theme.

Salinger's very first story, "The Young Folks," deals with the unsuccessful attempts of Edna Phillips, an unattractive college girl, to arouse the romantic interest of a geeky young man by the name of William Jameson. They are attending a party at a friend's house, and Edna lures William onto a dimly lit terrace, hoping he will make an amorous advance. But he doesn't because he is fascinated with the prettiest girl at the party, a small blonde by the name Doris Leggett, who totally ignores him.

Another tale about an individual who is unsuccessful in winning another person's affection is "The Heart of a Broken Story." This is the story of a young printer's assistant by the name of Justin Horgenschlag who develops a crush on a girl he sees on the Third Avenue Bus in New York. The narrator imagines how Horgenschlag might go about declaring his love to the girl, and he develops a number of different scenarios, none of which seem realistic. Thus the story ends without Horgenschlag ever having talked to the girl.

In "A Young Girl in 1941 with No Waist at All," we get a double dose of unrequited love. In that story, an eighteen-year-old girl by the name of Barbara takes a Caribbean cruise with the mother of her wealthy fiancé. During that cruise, she meets the Yale freshman Ray Kinsella who is working on the Junior Entertainment Committee of the cruise ship. After an evening of frenzied kissing, Ray proposes marriage to Barbara, but she rejects the proposal. The next day Barbara tells her fiancé's mother that she is not going to marry her son because she doesn't feel ready to get married to anybody yet. The story has a more upbeat ending than the others that deal with the theme of unrequited love because, as the mother of Barbara's fiancé says, "it's always the best way to rectify a mistake *before* it's made" (361).

By contrast, the saddest unrequited-love story is "A Girl I Knew." The story is told by a young American by the name of John who has come Vienna in 1936 to improve his German. A pretty Jewish girl by the name of Leah helps him with his language study by conversing in German with him for an hour each day. John falls in love with Leah but then finds out that she is engaged to be married to a young Polish businessman. After John leaves Vienna, he and Leah lose touch, and when he returns at the end of World War II, he finds out that Leah has died in a concentration camp.

A story that involves the unrequited love theme as well as the theme of a bad marriage is "The Long Debut of Lois Taggett." In that story, the heiress Lois Taggett marries the handsome man of her dreams but then divorces him when it becomes clear that he was only after her money and doesn't love her at all. She finds out that her love is unrequited when her husband deliberately hurts her by burning the back of her hand with a cigarette and by smashing her foot with a golf club. She eventually remarries, and her new husband is an unattractive and uncultivated person whose love she does not reciprocate.

The bad marriage theme is the major one in two stories about very young couples. In "Both Parties Concerned," a teenage marriage is on the rocks because the nineteen-year-old husband is more interested in going out every night than in staying home with his seventeen-year-old wife and their baby. And in the story "Elaine," another young marriage collapses right after the wedding ceremony when the mother of the sixteen-year-old bride and the mother of the groom get into a fistfight.

The second most important theme in Salinger's early fiction is that of premature death. It occurs in nine of the twenty stories. In "The Long Debut of Lois Taggett," the baby of Lois and Carl suffocates in its crib. In "The Varioni Brothers," the writer Joe Varioni is accidentally shot to death by a gangster who is trying to kill his brother. In "Soft-Boiled Sergeant," a soldier gives his wife the details of the combat death of his best friend. In "Last Day of the Last Furlough" and "This Sandwich Has no Mayonnaise," Vincent Caulfield grieves over the loss of his younger brother Holden who is missing in action and is presumed dead. In "Once a Week Won't Kill You," the protagonist's aunt Rena went insane when her fiancé died in World War I. In "The Stranger," Babe Gladwaller seeks out Vincent Caulfield's former girlfriend to give her an eyewitness account of Vincent's war time death.. In "A Girl I Knew," a young American falls in love with a Jewish girl who eventually dies in a concentration camp. And in "Blue Melody," the black blues singer Lida Louise dies from a burst appendix because two for-whites-only hospitals refuse to treat her.

A third recurring theme in the early stories is that of the psychological effects of war on soldiers and their families. This theme is developed in six stories. The four most notable ones deal with two friends, John F. "Babe" Gladwaller and Vincent Caulfield. Three of the Gladwaller/Caulfield stories illustrate the way people react to the death of loved ones, and one illustrates the way soldiers react to the carnage of war. In "This Sandwich Has No Mayonnaise," Vincent Caulfield has just learned that his younger brother Holden is missing in action somewhere in the Pacific. Vincent simply cannot concentrate on the job he is supposed to be doing because his mind runs berserk. He keeps thinking: "Missing, missing, missing. Lies! I'm being lied to. He's never been missing before. He's one of the least missing boys in the world.... Why lie about something as important as that? How can the Government do a thing like that? What can they get out of it, telling lies like that?" (55).

In "Last Day of the Last Furlough," we see how the war makes two peaceful men accept the necessity of killing enemy soldiers. Vincent Caulfield is visiting Babe Gladwaller and his family on the day before the two are to be shipped off to join the fighting in Europe. During a dinner conversation, Babe takes exception to his father's nostalgic stories of World War I and gives a long anti-war speech to the effect that it is the glorification of one war that causes the next: "If German boys had learned to be contemptuous of violence, then Hitler would have had to take up knitting to keep his ego warm" (62). But near the end of the story, there is a shift in Babe's attitude toward war. This shift begins when Vincent tells Babe that he feels murderous because his younger brother Holden is missing in action. Vincent says: "I want to kill so badly, I can't sit still." After some reflection, Babe Gladwaller says: "I believe in this war. If I didn't I would have gone to a conscientious objectors' camp and swung an ax for the duration. I believe in killing Nazis, and Fascists, and Japs" (61-62).

Another Babe Gladwaller story, "A Boy in France," illustrates the way the bloody business of being a soldier affects a person's mind. The story begins in the evening after a battle when Babe Gladwaller is too tired to dig his own fox-hole and luckily finds one abandoned by the Germans. However, there is a bloody blanket at the bottom of it on which a German soldier has apparently died. Babe fishes out the blanket and scoops out some of the bloody soil underneath before he spreads out his own blanket. Once settled, he tries to shut the gruesome events of the day out of his mind. He does that by thinking of locking himself in his room at home in the United States. In his inner monologue, the metaphoric phrase "and I'll bolt the door" occurs so often (seven times in one paragraph) that we get the impression Babe's mind is off its hinges.

In "The Stranger," we find that Babe Gladwaller, like Sergeant X in the later story "For Esmé—with Love and Squalor," has not come through the war with all his faculties intact. Babe returns to the United States before the end of the war and goes to see a former girlfriend of Vincent Caulfield's to tell her about Vincent's death. Babe wants to make sure that Vincent's girl doesn't have any romantic notions of how Vincent died. He tells himself: "Don't let Vincent's girl think that Vincent asked for a cigarette before he died. Don't let her think that he grinned gamely, or said a few choice last words." Babe tells the girl that Vincent didn't hear the mortar shell that hit him and that "he had too much pain in too large an area of his body to have realized anything but blackness." After telling about Vincent's death, Babe starts crying and apologizes to the girl, "I'm acting very peculiarly. I don't know what's the matter" (77). At this point, we speculate that Babe Gladwaller might have come home before the end of the war because the Army discharged him early for psychiatric reasons.

"Soft-Boiled Sergeant" is another story in which a soldier objects to romantic notions of combat death and grieves about the loss of a friend. The protagonist, a corporal by the name of Philly Burns, has a wife who likes to see the kind of war movies in which handsome men always get shot in such a way that it doesn't spoil their good looks, and they always have time to make impressive speeches before they die, and they always get fancy funerals with a bugler playing taps. To convince his wife that this is not what combat death is like, Philly describes for her the death of his friend, Sergeant Burke. Burke died at Pearl Harbor while saving the lives of three young recruits. He was machine-gunned by a Japanese airplane and wound up with four holes between his shoulders and half of his jaw shot off. Philly concludes his story by saying: "He died all by himself, and he didn't have no message to give to no girl or nobody, and there wasn't nobody throwing a big classy funeral here in the States, and no hot-shot bugler blowed taps for him" (85). When Philly's wife breaks down crying, she helps Philly cope with the loss of his friend.

A fourth theme that is developed in Salinger's early stories is that of the defeat of the artist by society. This is the central theme in two stories, "The Varioni Brothers" and "Blue Melody." "The Varioni Brothers" deals with two artists—Sonny the composer and Joe the writer—whose popular songs make them rich and famous. When Joe wants to quit the partnership to finish a novel he has been working on for many years, his greedy brother won't let him go because no one can write better song lyrics than Joe. Then one day, Sonny loses 40,000 dollars in a poker game with a gangster boss and refuses to pay up because he claims the man cheated. The gangster sends a hit man to kill Sonny, but the man accidentally kills Joe instead. Wracked by guilt, Sonny gives up fortune and fame, collects all of Joe's papers, and begins to piece together the novel he would not let his brother finish. Talking about his work on his brother's novel, Sonny says, "I hear the music for the first time in my life" (77). What he means is that he was never truly inspired while he was composing his successful popular tunes, but he is inspired now that he is struggling to put together a true work of art.

While the artist in "The Varioni Brothers" is thwarted by materialism, in "Blue Melody" the artist is destroyed by racism. At the beginning of the story, the narrator makes the claim that the story is not intended as "a slam against one section of this country" (51-112). Yet the main story line tells of the black blues singer Lida Louise whose appendix bursts and who dies because she is turned away by two Tennessee hospitals that refuse to treat blacks.

NARRATIVE STRUCTURE AND POINT OF VIEW

The narrative structures of Salinger's early stories vary from straightforward to highly complicated. On the straightforward end we get three types of structures: Simple, chronological narratives that cover very short time spans such as "Both Parties Concerned" or "Once a Week Won't Kill You," stories with surprise endings such as "The Hang of It" and "Personal Notes of an Infantryman," and stories such as "The Young Folks" and "Slight Rebellion Off Madison" that seem like small stage plays because they consist almost entirely of dialogue. On the more complicated end, we also get three types of narrative structures: Stories such as "Soft-Boiled Sergeant" and "Blue Melody" which cover large periods of time in the lives of their characters, stories such as "This Sandwich Has No Mayonnaise" and "The Stranger" in which the inner monologues are more important that the exterior action, and stories such as "The Varioni Brothers" and "The Inverted Forest" whose narratives are divided into segments told by different narrators.

Four of Salinger's early stories have a structural peculiarity which recurs Salinger's later novellas, and that peculiarity is the use of two central characters rather than one. For instance, in the story "The Hang of It," we can't tell if the central character is Colonel Harry Pettit or his son, the recruit Bobby Pettit. Similarly, in "Personal Notes of an Infantryman," the protagonist could be either the narrator, Captain Lawlor, or his father who is a recruit in Lawlor's regiment. In "Soft-Boiled Sergeant," we also have a double focus on the narrator Philly Burns and on his mentor and friend, Sergeant Burke. And in "The Varioni Brothers," the title already suggests that the story has a dual focus on Sonny, the musician, and Joe, the writer. We find the same structural peculiarity in Salinger's early novella, "The Inverted Forest," and in his later "Raise High the Roof Beam, Carpenters," "Zooey," and "Seymour—An Introduction."

Salinger's most ambitious experiment in narrative structure is "The Heart of a Broken Story." It is subtitled a "satire," and the narrator explains that he was going to write it for *Collier's* magazine as "a lovely tender boy-meets-girl story." But as he explains: "I couldn't do it with this one. Not and have it make sense" (32). So he decides to write a story for *Esquire* magazine instead in which the boy does not meet the girl. The story is not only "broken" because the boy does not meet the girl but also because it actually consists of five different versions of the boy-does-not-meet-girl scenario.

At the beginning of the story, the protagonist, a printer's assistant named Justin Horgenschlag, develops a crush on a girl by the name of Shirley Lester while riding on a Third Avenue Bus in New York. In the first scenario, Horgenschlag is as suave and debonair as a movie star and sweeps Shirley off her feet. But the narrator rejects that possibility as unrealistic because Horgenschlag is really a geek. In the second scenario, Shirley rejects Horgenschlag because he acts exactly the way that a slightly dim-witted printer's assistant would really act. In the third, the narrator has Horgenschlag collapse, grab Shirley's legs, and tear her stockings, hoping that she will give him her address so he can buy her new stockings. But the narrator surmises that this ploy would fail and that Shirley would not give Horgenschlag her address. Besides, Horgenschlag would not do anything so rash in the first place.

Next, the narrator embarks on a convoluted fourth scenario in which Horgenschlag gets desperate, grabs Shirley's handbag, and runs off with it. Horgenschlag is arrested, hauled into court, and sentenced to one year in prison. While in prison, Horgenschlag writes two letters to Shirley in which he apologizes and declares his love. Shirley answers the first letter out of pity but doesn't reply to the second one in which Horgenschlag begs her to visit him. In despair, Horgenschlag participates in a seventeen-man jailbreak and is shot and killed. The narrator comments: "And, thus, my plan to write a boy-meets-girl story for *Collier's*, a tender, memorable love story, is thwarted by the death of my hero." But the story isn't over yet because the narrator erases the fourth scenario by telling us that "Horgenschlag never would have been among those seventeen desperate men" (132).

The narrator then goes on to develop a fifth version of the boy-doesn't-meet-girl story. He goes back to the scenario in which Horgenschlag steals Shirley's purse and winds up in jail, but he now imagines what might happen if Horgenschlag were to write a more effective letter. The narrator composes such a letter and also a positive reply from Shirley in which she says: "I don't care if you're not a success, or that you're not handsome, or rich, or famous, or suave" (132). She ends the letter by asking: "Please let me know when I may come to see you" (133). But then the narrator tells us that Horgenschlag and Shirley don't have it in them to write such letters. Consequently, "Justin Horgenschlag never got to know Shirley Lester," and both of them eventually found other partners. The narrator concludes the story with these words: "And that's why I never wrote a boy-meets-girl story for *Collier's*. In a boy-meets-girl story the boy should always meet the girl" (133).

As this plot analysis shows, "The Heart of a Broken Story" is a tour de force in narrative structure and narrative technique. The story is not really about unrequited love but about writing formula magazine fiction. As a story about writing a story, "The Heart of a Broken Story" anticipates by over 20 years the metafiction of experimental postmodernists such as John Barth, Robert Coover, and Raymond Federman.

At the beginning of his storytelling career, J.D. Salinger favored the third person objective point of view, probably because it gave his stories the feel of theater plays and he was interested in playwriting. But he soon began to experiment with various subjective narrative perspectives, and he even tried his hand at stories with more than one narrator and multiple points of view.

In his first two stories, "The Young Folks" and "Go See Eddie" (both 1940), Salinger used the third person objective point of view which Ernest Hemingway loved because it is extremely realistic and because it forces the reader to collaborate in creating the story. Narratives that use this point of view give the impression that the narrator is as objective and uninvolved as a movie camera. By not revealing anything at all about what his characters are thinking or feeling (or almost nothing as in the case of Salinger's first two stories), the author makes his reader deduce his characters' mental and emotional states from their body language and from their speech mannerisms. Salinger used this narrative perspective in four uncollected stories, and it reappears later in five pieces of his 1953 collection *Nine Stories*.

In most of Salinger's early fiction, the point of view is subjective. Eight of the 20 stories are first person narratives, and four of the stories that are told from the third person point of view and use a center-of-consciousness perspective. This is a limited-omniscient, third person point of view that is almost as subjective as first person. Moreover, in some of these center-of-consciousness narratives, we get a switch to the first person during the central characters' inner monologues. This is the case in "The Last Day of the Last Furlough," "This Sandwich Has No Mayonnaise," "A Boy in France," and "The Stranger."

In three early stories, Salinger uses more than one narrator and therefore more than one narrative perspective. These stories are "Soft-Boiled Sergeant," "Blue Melody," and "The Varioni Brothers."

In terms of narrative perspective, "The Varioni Brothers" is the most experimental of Salinger's early stories because it is told by three different narrators. "The Varioni Brothers" starts out with an editor telling us that "while Mr. Penney is on his vacation, his column will be written by a number of distinguished personalities from all walks of life. Today's guest columnist is Mr. Vincent Westmoreland, the well-known producer, raconteur and wit" (12). The second narrator, Westmoreland, then tells us the story of the Varioni brothers' financial success as writers of popular songs, of Joe Varioni being mistakenly killed by a gangster who was gunning for his brother Sonny, and of Sonny's mysterious disappearance at the height of his career. The major part of the story is told by a third narrator, the college English instructor Sarah Daley Smith, who says that she has "the inside dope on Sonny Varioni" (13). She begins by telling of her futile efforts, back in 1926, to talk Sonny Varioni into releasing his brother Joe from his song writing duties so he could finish a novel he was working on. After Joe was killed, Sarah did not hear from Sonny for 15 years. But recently, in 1941, Sonny Varioni turned up at her college with a trunk full of manuscript material and asked her for a place to stay so he could finish his brother Joe's novel. And that's the straight dope about him.

If we count as shifts in point of view the first person inner monologues in the third person narratives "Last Day of the Last Furlough," "This Sandwich Has No Mayonnaise," "A Boy in France," and "The Stranger," then it turns out that more than half of Salinger's early third person narratives have a shifting rather than a fixed point of view. Thus the experiments that Salinger made with narrative structure and point of view show that during his apprentice years he was not just trying to write stories that the magazines would buy but that he was discontent with conventional narrative techniques and kept looking for new ways of telling stories.

CHARACTERIZATION AND STYLE

When we browse through Salinger's early stories, we will be struck by how different the characters are from those in *The Catcher in the Rye* and the later short fiction. While Holden Caulfield and the Glass children have been rightfully dubbed misfits and outsiders, most of the characters in the early stories are

conformists. Another striking thing about Salinger's early characters is that the
majority of the women are depicted unsympathetically, with the manipulative
female being a recurring type. As far as techniques of characterization is concerned, the early stories are already quite sophisticated, especially the first person narratives where the burden of characterization is carried by the style. In the
later forties, Salinger not only found the voice of Holden Caulfield but was also
moving toward the whimsical style of Buddy Glass, the narrator of the Glass
Family Series.

The most prevalent character type in the early stories is the conformist. This
is not surprising because Salinger wrote most of his early stories for mass-
market magazines and therefore created characters whose values were in line with
those of society at large. The conformity is especially obvious in the soldiers
who are the central characters in nine of the twenty early stories. But there are
also a number of civilian protagonists who conform to society's ideals and values or at least try to.

A good specimen of a military conformist is the protagonist in "The Hang Of
It." He is a recruit whom his drill sergeant calls "the clumsiest gink" he has
ever seen. But the young man tells the sergeant he'll get "the hang of it yet"
because, as he says, "I like the Army. Some day I'll be a colonel or something"
(22). In another one of the war time stories, "Last Day of the Last Furlough,"
the praise of military conformity gets a bit cloying when the central character
says: "GIs—especially GIs who are friends—belong together these days. It's
no good being with civilians any more. They don't know what we know and
we're no longer used to what they know" (62).

But it is not only the soldiers in Salinger's early fiction who are conformists;
most of the civilians also want to fit in. This is especially apparent among the
female characters. For instance, the wallflower Edna in "The Young Folks" is
desperate to follow the example of other couples at a party who are kissing and
necking on a dark terrace. But she is unsuccessful in arousing amorous feelings
in the young man that the hostess has steered her way. Another female conformist is the debutante in "The Long Debut of Lois Taggett." Although she
comes from a very wealthy family, she takes an office job in her uncle's firm
because "it was the first big year for debutantes to Do Something" (28). And at
the bottom of the social scale there is yet another female conformist, the title
character in the story "Elaine." She and her mother are described as "living in a
Hollywood-and-radio-promoted world peopled with star newspaper reporters,
crackerjack young city editors, young brain surgeons, intrepid young detectives,
all of whom crusaded or operated or detected brilliantly when they were not
sidetracked by their own incorrigible charm" (41).

Even though most of the characters in Salinger's early fiction are conformists,
there are a few who are misfits or outsiders. For instance, two female characters
rebel against social conventions, and two early versions of Holden Caulfield
rebel against the kind of future their fathers have planned for them.

Helen Mason in "Go See Eddie" flaunts social morality by having affairs
with married men, and Barbara, the title character in "A Young Girl in 1941
with No Waist at All," rebels against the notion of marriage as a career goal for
women.

The rebellion of the two Holden Caulfields in "I'm Crazy" and "Slight Rebellion Off Madison" is much milder than that of the Holden Caulfield in *The Catcher in the Rye*. One of the two early Holdens says: "I knew that I wasn't going to be one of those successful guys [and] that I wouldn't like working in an office" ("Crazy" 51), and the other one also dislikes what the future holds for him: "I'd have to work at my father's office and ride in Madison Avenue buses and read newspapers" ("Slight Rebellion" 84). Although the two early Holdens are non-conformists because they don't want to join the rat race for money and power, they do not rail against the conformists for being "phonies" as does the Holden in *The Catcher in the Rye*. In fact, the word "phony" does not appear in either one of the early Holden Caulfield stories. Moreover, as one of the two titles indicates, the rebellion of the two Holden prototypes is only a "slight rebellion."

Of the few non-conformists in Salinger's early stories, the most admirable are Sonny Varioni in "The Varioni Brothers" and young Rudford in "Blue Melody." In "The Varioni Brothers," the composer of popular tunes, Sonny Varioni, becomes a non-conformist when he gives up fortune and fame in order to put together his dead brother's unfinished novel. He forsakes the American Dream for two reasons. One is that he feels guilty because the bullet that killed his brother was intended for him. The other reason is that while working with his brother's manuscripts, Sonny comes to realize that it is more worthwhile to strive for artistic than for financial success.

The second admirable non-conformist in Salinger's early fiction is Rudford in "Blue Melody." His non-conformity has to do with the issue of race because Rudford swims against the stream of racism in Southern society when he befriends the piano player Black Charles and his niece, the blues singer Lida Louise.

In addition to the conformist and the rebel, another recurring character type in Salinger's uncollected stories is the manipulative woman. Not all of the female characters in the early stories are of this type. In fact, four women are portrayed positively. They are Ruthie in "Both Parties Concerned," Juanita in "Soft-Boiled Sergeant," Barbara in "A Young Girl in 1941 with No Waist at All," and Leah in "A Girl I Knew." However, the negative female characters outnumber the positive ones.

Salinger's very first story, "The Young Folks," presents us with a negative female character who is memorable because she is not only manipulative; she also lies and steals. She is the college girl Edna Phillips, and she has a hard time making friends because she is tall and unattractive. At a party, she lures a young man by the name of William Jameson to the dimly-lit terrace by claiming that there is some liquor out there. Instead, there are only other couples are making out. When Jameson wants to go back inside she says: "It's so grand out here. Amorous voices and all" ("Folks" 28). Then she tries to arouse Jameson's romantic interest by telling him that the previous summer, a college graduate took her out a number of times and in return expected her to have sex with him. She says that she refused because "It's gotta be the real thing with me" (29). But Jameson doesn't want to be Edna's "real thing" and abandons her. Later Edna lies to the hostess and says that Jameson is a trifle too "warm-blooded" for her but that luckily she is "still all in one piece" (30). As the story ends, Edna finds that her cigarette case is empty; so she sneaks into an upstairs room and steals a dozen cigarettes from the parents of her host.

The title character in "The Long Debut of Lois Taggett" is also manipulative and doesn't get what she wants. Lois Taggett divorces her first husband when she finds out that he has a vicious streak. Later she accepts a marriage proposal from a chunky young man by the name of Carl Curfman. Because Carl is not as debonair as her first husband was, Lois resolves to break him of all the habits she dislikes about him. She makes him stop wearing white socks with dark suits, and she makes him stop slicking down his hair with hair cream. She makes him inhale his cigarettes—which he had never done before—and she tries to make him take longer steps when they dance—which he finds hard to do because he's so short. But these attempts to turn Carl into someone as suave as her first husband do not succeed. Lois eventually gives up and accepts that she is doomed to spend her life with "the man she didn't love" (34).

An even more negative female character in Salinger's early fiction is Helen Mason in "Go See Eddie." She is a young actress who can't keep her hands off married men. Because of her amorous adventures, Helen has lost interest in her career. Talking to her brother Bobby, Helen defends her most recent affair with a man named Phil Stone by saying that he is "a really grand person" and that their love for each other is "the real thing" (123). Her brother Bobby thinks that it is a shame she has put her affair with Phil ahead of her career, and he therefore tells Helen to see a friend of his, Eddie Jackson, who might cast her in a show he is going to direct. By re-starting Helen's stalled career, Bobby hopes to get her so preoccupied that her affair with Phil Stone will fizzle. But at the end of the story, we realize that Helen is not going to see Eddie because she makes two phone calls, one to end her affair with Phil Stone and the other to set up a tryst with yet another married man.

But the most manipulative of all the female characters in Salinger's early fiction is Bunny Croft in the novella "The Inverted Forest." She steals the poet Raymond Ford away from his wife and then ruins his career. I will analyze her characterization in the chapter devoted to "The Inverted Forest."

As far as techniques of characterization are concerned, Salinger's interest in playwriting stood him in good stead, for in early stories such as "The Young Folks," "Go See Eddie," and "Once a Week Won't Kill You," he relies almost entirely on dialogue to develop the personalities of his characters. And in the best of the first person narratives, he creates voices that reveal his good ear for the way people from different walks of life speak. This is a quality of his fiction that was later praised by many critics. In Philly Burns in "Soft-Boiled Sergeant" and Billy Vullmer in "Both Parties Concerned," Salinger seems to have re-created working class people whom he met in the Army, and in the language of the Holden Caulfield prototype of "I'm Crazy," he seems to have re-created the way he himself talked when he was a prep school student.

While Salinger's first person narrators Philly Burns, Billy Vullmer, and Holden Caulfield sound very authentic, even more memorable characters in Salinger's early fiction are Babe Gladwaller and Vincent Caulfield. The characterizations of Babe Gladwaller and Vincent Caulfield are so successful because Salinger gives us the feeling that we know these two people better than their own friends and kin do, and he does that by giving them contradictory personality traits and by using inner monologues to let us in on their most secret thoughts.

Both Babe and Vincent are educated people with a literary bent, but despite their education and literary interests, both feel at home with the less well-educated people in the lower ranks of the Army (both Babe and Vincent are sergeants). Moreover, Salinger gives Babe and Vincent additional depth through inner monologues whose subjects have nothing to do with the external action. In "This Sandwich Has No Mayonnaise," Vincent tries to cope with the news that his younger brother Holden is missing in action. Interspersed among bits of GI conversation is Vincent's continuous inner monologue in which he repeats that he can't believe Holden is missing. As Vincent's mind gets used to the idea of Holden's probable death, he realizes that Holden is still here in his mind: "Here," Vincent says to himself, "not missing, not dead, not anything but Here" (149).

An even more moving inner monologue occurs in the story "A Boy in France" when Babe Gladwaller tries to go to sleep in a foxhole, but he first has to block out of his mind the battle in which he fought that day. He tries to do that when he imagines locking himself in his room at home in America:

I'll be home and I'll bolt the door. I'll put some coffee on the stove, some records on the phonograph, and I'll bolt the door. I'll read my books and I'll drink the hot coffee and I'll listen to the music, and I'll bolt the door. I'll open the window, I'll let in a nice quiet girl—not Frances, not anyone I've ever known—and I'll bolt the door. I'll ask her to walk a little bit in the room by herself, and I'll look at her American ankles, and I'll bolt the door. I'll ask her to read some Emily Dickinson to me—that one about being chartless—and I'll ask her to read some William Blake to me—that one about the little lamb who made thee—and I'll bolt the door. She'll have an American voice, and she won't ask me if I have any chewing gum or bonbons, and I'll bolt the door. (21)

The pathological repetition of the phrase "and I'll bolt the door" suggests that all is not well with Babe Gallagher's mind. But his army buddies will never know. Before he goes to sleep, Babe calls to the man in the next foxhole: "You on tonight, Eeves?... Wake me if anything gets hot or anything" (92)

Finally—on a much lighter note—I want to point out that in the early stories we already find a peculiarity of the characterization in Salinger's later fiction, and that is his tendency to give his characters names that have double letters in them. Examples are Edna Phillips and William Jameson in "The Young Folks," Harry and Bobby Pettit in "The Hang of It," Lois Taggett and her first husband Bill Tedderton in "The Long Debut of Lois Taggett." And so on and so forth through Billy Vullmer in "Both Parties Concerned," Mattie Gladwaller in "A Boy in France," Corinne von Nordhoffen in "The Inverted Forest," and Peggy Moore in "Blue Melody," all the way to "Slight Rebellion Off Madison" where we learn that Holden Caulfield's middle name is "Morrisey."

What does this doubling of letters in the names mean? In Salinger's later fiction—as I will show in subsequent chapters—the doubling of letters in the names of Buddy, Boo Boo, Zooey, and Franny Glass, points to motifs of doubling in both the form and the content of the stories. In the early fiction, we find double protagonists in four stories and one novella, but doubling motifs are in evidence in only three pieces. In "The Hang Of It," Private Harry Pettit comes across as the double of his father, Colonel Billy Pettit, because he is being trained by the same drill sergeant as his father once was, and he is just as inept a recruit. In "The Varioni Brothers," Joe is killed by a bullet intended for his brother Sonny, and Sonny later tries to assemble the novel that he had prevented his brother Joe from finishing. And in "The Inverted Forest," Raymond Ford elopes with Bunny Croft because she reminds him of his mother.

Salinger's style in his early stories reveals his fondness for the fiction of Stephen Crane, Ring Lardner, Ernest Hemingway, and Scott Fitzgerald. However, as early as the mid-forties, Salinger began to develop the whimsical style that eventually found full expression in the convoluted language of Buddy Glass, the narrator of the Glass Family Series.

Salinger seems to have studied Ring Lardner's first person narratives very carefully in order to learn how to create a narrator's personality through the way he speaks. This does not yet work very well in "The Hang of It" (1941), "The Heart of a Broken Story" (1941), and "Personal Notes of an Infantryman" (1942) because the narrators' personalities remain nondescript. But in "Soft-Boiled Sergeant" (1944) and "Both Parties Concerned" (1944), Salinger successfully uses ungrammatical and slangy diction to create two colorful, uneducated narrator-protagonists, one of them likable and the other a louse. Salinger does an even more convincing job in using language to characterize the narrator-protagonist in "I'm Crazy" (1945). This is the story in which a prototype of Holden Caulfield is expelled from prep school and comes home to New York to tell his parents. When Salinger expanded this story into the novel *The Catcher in the Rye*, he got rave notices for the expert way in which he delineates Holden's character through his speech mannerisms.

Salinger also seems to have studied Ernest Hemingway's short stories to learn how to write effective dialogue. The Hemingway influence is very apparent in Salinger's first story "The Young Folks" where the narrative passages sound unnatural while the dialogue is very realistic. Compare the style in the following two passages. Here is a narrative passage:

About eleven o'clock, Lucille Henderson, observing that her party was soaring at the proper height, and just having been smiled at by Jack Delroy, forced herself to glance in the direction of Edna Phillips, who since eight o'clock had been sitting in the big red chair, smoking cigarettes and yodeling hellos and wearing a very bright eye which young men were not bothering to catch. (26)

Aside from the ill-advised Faulknerian length of the sentence, what is off-putting about the style is the tortured phrases "yodeling hellos" and "wearing a bright eye." By contrast, the dialogue between Edna Phillips and Bill Jameson sparkles with Hemingwayesque authenticity:

> "What's the matter?" he asked.
> "Just look at that sky," Edna said.
> "Yeah. I can hear somebody talkin' over there. Can't you?"
> "Yes, you ninny."

"Wuddaya mean, ninny?"
"Some people," Edna said, "wanna be alone."
"Oh. Yeah. I get it."
"Not so loud. How would you like it if somebody spoiled it for you?"
"Yeah. Sure," Jameson said. (28)

This bit of dialogue reveals the story's central conflict in a nutshell. Edna wants Bill to feel romantic, but Bill isn't interested.

Salinger's style not only gives away that he studied Hemingway but also that he studied Fitzgerald. Several of the uncollected stories contain passages that seem parodies of Fitzgerald's style. The most obvious example is the last sentence of the story "A Young Girl in 1941 with No Waist at All." That sentence reads as follows:

The fragile hour was a carrier of many things, but Barbara was now exclusively susceptible to the difficult counterpoint sounding just past the last minutes of her girlhood. (302)

Yet another classic American author who seems to have influenced the style of Salinger's early stories is Stephen Crane. In *Maggie: A Girl of the Streets* (1896), Crane uses the device of repetition to reveal a character's limited intelligence. For instance, Maggie's seducer Pete keeps repeating himself constantly as for instance when he brags about a fight he had with another man: "'Aw, go ahn!' I says, like dat. 'Aw. go ahn,' I says. See? 'Don' make no trouble,' I says, like dat. 'Don' make no trouble.' See?" (Crane 22). In several early stories, Salinger similarly suggests a character's slowness of mind by making him repeat himself. For instance, in the story "Elaine," the bridegroom wants to keep his bride from walking out on him on his wedding day and says to her mother, "Listen ... she's my wife, see. I mean she's my wife. If she don't come with me, I can get it annulled, the marriage" (47). Similarly, the teenage narrator in "Both Parties Concerned" is getting into a fight with his wife and tells us: "'Something's the matter,' I said. I know her like a book. I mean I know her like a book" (14). And even the Yale freshman in "A Young Girl in 1941 with No Waist at All" reveals himself to be a simpleton by repeating himself when he tells his flame Barbara: "In other words, if two people love each other they oughta stick together. I mean they really oughta stick together" (297).

By 1945, Salinger had begun to develop the whimsical style that later became the trademark of his alter ego Buddy Glass, the narrator of most of the Glass family stories. Salinger did not use this style in his stories quite yet, but he used it in a biographical note that accompanied the publication of his story "This Sandwich Has No Mayonnaise" in *Esquire*:

I've been writing short stories since I was fifteen. I have trouble writing simply and naturally. My mind is stocked with some black neckties, and though I'm throwing them out as fast as I find them, there will always be a few left over. ("Backstage" 34).

The "black neckties" that Salinger wanted to throw out as soon as he found them were probably the conventional elements of style, borrowed from classic writers, elements that he had used to dress up his early fiction and make it look respectable.

It wasn't until 1948 that the style of Salinger's later fiction began to show up in his stories. Two passages that illustrate this style occur in "A Girl I Knew" and "Blue Melody." In "A Girl I Knew," the narrator has this to say about the inane German conversations he had with a Viennese girl named Leah:

If I should go to Hell, I'll be given a little inside room—one that is neither hot nor cold, but extremely drafty—in which all my conversations with Leah will be played back to me over an amplification system confiscated from the Yankee Stadium. (189)

In a similarly quirky passage, the protagonist of "Blue Melody," a young man named Rudford, is introduced to the husband of his childhood sweetheart, and the narrator describes the encounter in this way: "The husband's name was Richard something, and he was a Navy flier. He was eight feet tall, and he had some theater tickets or flying goggles or a lance in one of his hands. Had Rudford brought a gun along, he would have shot Richard dead on the spot" (119). No more black neckties here.

SETTINGS AND SYMBOLS

Salinger's uncollected stories feature a wider range of settings than his later work, both in terms of time, geography, and social milieu. Except for "Hapworth 16, 1924," the events in Salinger's later fiction all take place in the now time, that is, right around the time the stories were published. However, "The Hang of It" juxtaposes events in 1917 to recent ones in 1941, "The Inverted Forest" also starts in 1917 and ends in the late 1940s, "The Varioni Brothers" begins in 1926 and ends in 1941, and "Blue Melody" begins in 1944, but the major events of the plot occur in 1936.

While Salinger's later fiction—with three exceptions—all takes place in and around New York City, we get more geographical variety in the early stories. "This Sandwich Has No Mayonnaise" takes place on an Army base in Georgia; "A Young Girl in 1941 with No Waist at All" takes place on a cruise ship in the Caribbean; "A Boy in France" takes place on a battlefield in Normandy; "The Varioni Brothers" takes place in Chicago and in Waycross, Illinois; "A Girl I Knew" takes place in Vienna, Austria; and "Blue Melody" has two settings, war-time Luxembourg and Agersburg, Tennessee, before the war.

Finally, Salinger's early stories also offer a greater variety than the later ones in terms of the social environment in which the events occur. The characters in Salinger's later fiction all belong to the upper middle class and are all college educated. In the uncollected stories, however, the characters range from millionaires to people from the bottom rung of the social ladder. To mention only the extremes, the narrator of "Soft Boiled Sergeant" meets the title character when they are both hobos riding freight trains, and the couple in the story "Elaine" are a middle-school drop-out and a movie usher. On the other hand, in "The Long Debut of Lois Taggett," the title character's "coming out" party is described as "a five-figure, la-de-da, Hotel Pierre affair," and in "The Inverted Forest," the poet Raymond Ford is the son of an alcoholic waitress, but he later marries the daughter of a millionaire.

The uncollected stories do not contain much symbolism, but what there is works quite well; moreover, some of it recurs in Salinger's later work. One typical Salinger symbol in the early stories is the younger sibling whose welfare preoccupies an older brother, as is the case with Babe Gladwaller's younger sister Mattie in "Last Day of the Last Furlough" and "A Boy in France" and with Vincent Caulfield's younger brother Holden in "This Sandwich Has No Mayonnaise." This younger sibling is a symbol of innocence that needs to be protected. This symbol re-occurs later in "For Esmé—with Love and Squalor," *The Catcher in the Rye*, "Raise High the Roof Beam, Carpenters," and "Hapworth 16, 1924."

Another early symbol that shows up in Salinger's later fiction is the frequently re-read letter of a loved person which helps the protagonist cope with his problems. This symbol first shows up in "A Boy in France" (1945) where Babe Gladwaller beds down in a foxhole and re-reads for the thirtieth time a letter from his young sister Mattie. It shows up again in "A Girl I Knew" (1948) where the narrator carries a letter from a Viennese girl with him for months "opening and reading it in bars, between halves of basketball games, in Government classes, and in [his] room" until it gets almost too stained to be legible (194). Such letters reappear in Salinger's later fiction, in "Franny," "Raise High the Roof Beam Carpenters," "Zooey," and "Seymour—An Introduction."

Two symbolic kinds of behavior from the early stories that show up again in Salinger's later fiction are the compulsive nail-biting and the chain-smoking of some characters. Both types of behavior suggest troubled states of mind. They appear for the first time in Salinger's first story "The Young Folks" (1940) where Edna chain-smokes and the boy she is with, William Jameson, bites his fingernails. Nail-biting and/or chain-smoking also appear in "The Inverted Forest" and again in Salinger's mature work, in "Pretty Mouth and Green My Eyes," "Just Before the War With the Eskimos," *The Catcher in the Rye*, and "Franny."

Two fairly subtle symbols in the early stories that don't recur later on are the white socks of Lois' husband in "The Long Debut of Lois Taggett" and the white pocket comb of the effeminate Teddy in the story "Elaine." The white socks that her husband wears with dark suits represent everything uncouth that Lois Taggett dislikes about him, and Teddy Schmidt's white pocket comb represents his effeminate traits which make Elaine's mother decide that she doesn't want Elaine to stay married to "that sissy."

Even more subtle is Salinger's handling of the symbolism in the two early Holden Caulfield stories. In "I'm Crazy," he invents the symbol of the ducks in Central Park when the sensitive Holden wonders more than once what happens to the ducks in winter when the lagoon freezes over. And in "Slight Rebellion Off Madison," Salinger comes up with the Thoreauvian image of a cabin by a brook as a counter-symbol to the kind of urban conformity that Holden wants to escape from. I will discuss both symbols at length in the chapter on *The Catcher in the Rye*.

INTERPRETATIONS

There are very few interpretations of individual early stories. However, a number of critics have commented on the major themes of Salinger's uncollected fiction as a whole. Most of these essays or book chapters spend no more than a paragraph or two on the few stories they choose to discuss. However, Warren French, James Lundquist, John Wenke, and William Purcell each discuss over half a dozen stories and single out some of them for a more detailed analysis than the rest.

In his essay, "J.D. Salinger: The Development of the Misfit Hero," Paul Levine comments on eight of the early stories. His purpose in dealing with them is to show that the "misfit heroes" in Salinger's later fiction have precursors in his apprentice work. Says Levine: "The hero in every Salinger story becomes a reflection of a moral code arising out of a cult of innocence, love, alienation, and finally redemption." According to Levine, the basic predicament in all of Salinger's fiction, including the early stories, is that "a moral hero [is] forced to compromise his integrity within a pragmatic society" and that "the hero's misfitness in the modern world resolves as a moral problem rather than as the bitter fruit of a social injustice" (107). Levine supports this thesis chiefly with references to the defeat of the protagonists in "The Varioni Brothers" and "The Inverted Forest." However, he also comments on the Babe Gladwaller/Vincent Caulfield stories. Levine concludes: "All of Salinger's wartime stories accentuate the hero's isolation from the good past and the corrupt world.... What is so horrifying is neither war's physical brutality nor society's overt prejudices but rather the subtle dehumanization, the insidious loneliness, and the paralyzing lovelessness" (108).

Just as Paul Levine projects back into the early stories the misfit heroes of Salinger's later fiction, so William Wiegand, in his essay "Seventy-eight Bananas," projects backward his interpretation of "A Perfect Day for Bananafish." In that story, Seymour Glass tells a little girl a story about the bananafish who swim into a hole and eat so many bananas that they can't swim out again. As a result they die of banana fever. After telling that story, Seymour commits suicide. Wiegand interprets this suicide as the result of Seymour having contracted the deadly disease of banana fever: "Seymour, a bananafish himself, has become so glutted with sensation that he cannot swim out into society again." Wiegand asserts: "In general, the bananafish diagnosis applies to all the Salinger invalids" and that "in going back, we find the bananafish in embryo even in Salinger's earliest stories." Wiegand claims that what is distinctive about the early stories is "a particular undertone of very imminent tragedy: the moment imperiled by what is to come. Even the glimpses of life we get away from the front are fraught with a fragile sense of impermanence" (125-126). Wiegand then focuses on the war time stories "Last Day of the Last Furlough," "A Boy in France," and "The Stranger," and says:

The Babe Gladwaller stories ... foreshadow what is to become the chief concern in Salinger's fiction, but they remain unfocused. The war is still an irrelevant part of them—irrelevant because it was too easy to blame the war for the hero's state of mind when probably Babe Gladwaller had an incipient case of banana fever. It took Salinger some years to define Babe Gladwaller's feelings as a disease, to recognize, in other words, that so-called normal people were not affected with these strange symptoms of chronic hypersensitivity and sense of loss. (127)

To date, only four uncollected stories—aside from the novella "The Inverted Forest"—have been analyzed in more than a paragraph and by more than one critic. They are "The Heart of a Broken Story" (1941), "The Varioni Brothers" (1943), "Last Day of the Last Furlough" (1944), and "Elaine" (1945).

The most detailed analysis of "The Heart of a Broken Story" is that of John Wenke in his book *J.D. Salinger: A Study of the Short Fiction* (1991). In "The Heart of a Broken Story," the narrator develops and rejects several improbable variations of a boy-meets-girl scenario. Wenke says about this story:

Well before meta-fiction became fashionable, Salinger unmakes—that is, he deconstructs—the form of the sentimental love story, presenting, as it were, a series of subjunctive counterlives that emerge and dissolve in a skein of comic improbabilities. Salinger anticipates the self-reflexivity associated with such recent postmodern practitioners as John Barth, Kurt Vonnegut, Thomas Pynchon, and Philip Roth. He also anticipates the self-reflexivity of the Glass stories, especially "Seymour." (12)

As far as the story's theme goes, Wenke concludes that "The Heart of a Broken Story" is important because it "constitutes [Salinger's] earliest attack on phony art" (14).

The story "The Varioni Brothers" has received its most thorough analysis from Warren French in his 1963 book *J.D. Salinger.* French says that the central theme of the story concerns the role of the artist in modern American society and that this is the first time Salinger has dealt with this theme. "The Varioni Bothers" is about the songwriter Sonny Varioni who wants to put together a novel that his dead brother Joe could not finish because he, Sonny, pressured him into writing song lyrics instead. French calls the story a "morality play" and says that it deals with a question that has always troubled artists working in a materialistic society: "Should one settle for commercial success or labor over a great work of art that may go unnoticed?" (56-57). French also points out two parallels between "The Varioni Brothers" and Salinger's later novella "Seymour—An Introduction." He says that both stories deal with talented college English instructors who are also writers, who die prematurely, and who each have a brother who has made it the primary concern of his life to prepare for public presentation "the remarkable remains of his dead brother's unacknowledged genius" (57-58).

"Last Day of the Last Furlough" is the story that William Purcell analyzes in more detail than any other in his article "World War II and the Early Fiction of J.D. Salinger" (1991). The story is about Babe Gladwaller and Vincent Caulfield, two friends whose army units are about to be shipped overseas. Purcell points out that "Last Furlough" is one of four early stories in which Salinger creates "two sensitive but opposing archetypes—the 'romantic idealist' (Babe) and the 'disillusioned realist' (Vincent)" (85). Ultimately, so Purcell argues, Salinger has more sympathy for the romantic than the realistic outlook:

It is true that Babe's romantic outlook on life makes him appear naive almost to the point of foolishness. Yet, it seems to me that what Salinger is principally doing is not so much cataloging a desperate attempt to cling blindly to a sentimental, carefree and contented lifestyle, as he is contrasting two possible responses to the circumstances of the times: One, Babe Gladwaller's, is an affirming, if somewhat desperate, faith in the basic decency of mankind. The other, Vincent's more mature 'realistic' outlook, is a capitulation to cynical pessimism which leads ultimately to lonely isolation and alienation. (86-87)

Purcell implies that it is Babe Gladwaller's romantic outlook that underlies most of Salinger's later fiction.

The most interesting interpretation of "Elaine" is the one in James Lundquist's book *J.D. Salinger* (1979). Lundquist suggests that the story "gives us another side of Salinger and a significant clue to an attitude toward sexuality that becomes increasingly apparent in his fiction" (21). Lundquist reminds us that "Elaine" is the story of a beautiful but mentally retarded girl who has sex with a movie usher under the Coney Island boardwalk and then marries him only to have her mother force her to walk out on her new husband. To console Elaine, her mother takes her to a Henry Fonda movie. Lundquist believes that Salinger treats Elaine's plight with sympathy and he says that at a first glance the story's message seems to be that "Elaine, as well as most people, is better off going to the movies than in trying to deal with complexities of life that are indeed beyond her" (21). However, Lundquist suggests that on a deeper level, the story may be saying something else, and this something else is that "Salinger is suspicious of marriage as a solution to anything" (22).

CONCLUSION

Although Salinger's early stories make interesting reading because they reflect the preoccupations of Americans during World War II, most of them do not have much merit as works of art, and Salinger showed good judgment in not reprinting them. However, readers who want to study Salinger's development as a writer will find much in the early stories that sheds light on his later work.

For one thing, they will find that most of Salinger's early stories are very different from *The Catcher in the Rye*, *Nine Stories*, and the Glass Family Series. This difference is due primarily to a more pessimistic vision of life which is expressed in the recurring themes of unhappy male-female relationships and premature death.

An even more noticeable difference between Salinger's early and later fiction is that most of the protagonists in the early stories are conformists rather than misfits or rebels as in Salinger's later work. Also, while Salinger's later fiction—with very few exceptions—is set in the New York area and in the present time, the settings of the early stories range from Illinois, Georgia, and Tennessee, all the way to France, Germany, and Austria, and several stories take us back to the nineteen-twenties and earlier. Moreover, while the social environment of Salinger's later fiction is predominantly upper middle class, some of his early stories create working class milieu.

However, there are a few early stories that do foreshadow Salinger's later fiction. For instance, the central characters in "I'm Crazy" and "Slight Rebellion Off Madison" are early versions of Holden Caulfield in *The Catcher in the Rye*. Moreover, Babe Gladwaller in "Last Day of the Last Furlough," "A Boy In France," and "The Stranger" is a prototype for Sergeant X in "For Esmé—with Love and Squalor," and Robert Waner in "The Inverted Forest" is a prototype for Buddy Glass in the Glass Family Series. In addition, a number of the early stories share two peculiarities with Salinger's later fiction, and those are the employment of double protagonists and the use of names with double letters in them, as in Harry and Bobby Pettit in the early story "The Hang of It" and Franny and Zooey Glass in the later novella "Zooey." Another trait of some early stories that recurs in the Glass Family Series is flexible or multiple points of view achieved by the use of more than one narrator, by inner monologues, or by the inclusion of letters and diary entries. Two stories that contain such experiments with point of view are "The Varioni Brothers" and "Blue Melody."

The differences and similarities between Salinger's early stories and his later work, both in terms of artistic merit and content, are best exemplified in what I would consider the worst and the best of the early stories, "The Hang of It" and "A Girl I Knew." Those are the two stories that I would recommend to fans of Salinger's fiction who want no more than a quick taste of his early work.

To fully appreciate Salinger's early stories, a reader would have to be well acquainted with his later work. Digging up the early stories in old magazines would therefore not make sense for someone who has just started to read Salinger. Or, to put it differently, the early stories should only be read by aficionados of Salinger's fiction who have already read everything else by him and still yearn to read more. And the over-the-top fanatics who have read all the uncollected stories and still are not satisfied can travel to the Princeton University Library and read the five unpublished stories listed below.

Students who are looking for Salinger stories to analyze that have not already been over-interpreted will be very happy with what they can find in old issues of such magazines as *Story*, *Collier's*, and *The Saturday Evening Post*. The pieces that have already received quite a bit of attention are the two Holden Caulfield stories "I'm Crazy" and "Slight Rebellion Off Madison" and the four stories whose interpretations I summarized above. However, three early stories are especially deserving of attention because they are so different from Salinger's later work and because so little has been written about them. They are "Both Parties Concerned," "Soft-Boiled Sergeant," and "Blue Melody."

WORKS CITED

Brickell, Herschel. "J.D. Salinger." In *Prize Stories of 1949: The O. Henry Awards*.
        New York: Doubleday, 1950, 249.
"Contributors." *Story* 16 (March-April 1940): 2.
Crane, Stephen. *Maggie: A Girl of the Streets* [1896]. New York: Signet, 1991.

Fosburgh, Lacey. "J.D. Salinger Speaks About His Silence." *New York Times* (3 November 1974): 1, 69.

French, Warren. *J.D.* Salinger. New York: Twayne, 1963.

Grunwald, Henry A., ed. *Salinger: A Critical and Personal Portrait.* New York: Harper, 1962.

Gwynn, Frederick L., and Joseph L. Blotner. *The Fiction of J.D. Salinger.* Pittsburgh: U of Pittsburgh P, 1958.

Hassan, Ihab. "Rare Quixotic Gesture: The Fiction of J.D. Salinger." *Western Review* 21 (Summer 1957): 261-280. Rpt. in Grunwald 138-163.

Levine, Paul. "J.D. Salinger: The Development of the Misfit Hero." *Twentieth Century Literature* 5 (October 1958): 92-99. Rpt. in *J.D. Salinger and the Critics.* Ed. William F. Belcher and James W. Lee. Belmont, CA: Wadsworth, 1962, 107-115.

Lundquist, James. *J.D. Salinger.* New York: Ungar, 1979.

Mizener, Arthur. "The Love Song of J.D. Salinger." *Harper's Magazine* 218 (February 1959): 83-90. Rpt. in Grunwald 23-36.

Purcell, William F. "World War II and the Early Fiction of J.D. Salinger." *Studies in American Literature* (Kyoto) 28 (1991): 77-93.

Salinger, J.D. "Backstage with *Esquire*." *Esquire* 24 (October 1945): 34.

____ . "Blue Melody." *Cosmopolitan* 125 (September 1948): 51, 112-119.

____ . "Both Parties Concerned." *Saturday Evening Post* (26 February 1944): 14, 47-48.

____ . "A Boy in France." *Saturday Evening Post* (31 March 1945): 21, 92.

____ . *The Catcher in the Rye* [1951]. New York: Bantam, 1964.

____ . "Contributors." Story 26 (November-December 1944): 1.

____ . "Elaine." *Story* 26 (March-April 1945): 38-47.

____ . "For Esmé—with Love and Squalor." In *Nine Stories* [1953]. New York: Bantam, 1964.

____ . "A Girl I Knew." *Good Housekeeping* 126 (February 1948): 37, 186, 188-196.

____ . "Go See Eddie." *University of Kansas City Review* 7 (December 1940): 121-124.

____ . "The Heart of a Broken Story." *Esquire* 16 (September 1941): 32, 131-133.

____ . "I'm Crazy." *Collier's* (22 December 1945): 36, 48, 51.

____ . "Last Day of the Last Furlough." *Saturday Evening Post* (15 July 1944): 26-27, 61-62, 64.

____ . "The Long Debut of Lois Taggett." *Story* 21 (September-October 1942): 28-34.

____ . "Once a Week Won't Kill You." *Story* 25 (November-December 1944): 23-27.

____ . "Slight Rebellion Off Madison." *New Yorker* (21 December 1946): 82-86.

____ . "Soft-Boiled Sergeant." *Saturday Evening Post* (15 April 1944): 18, 82, 84-85.

____ . "The Stranger." *Collier's* (1 December 1945): 18, 77.

____ . "This Sandwich Has No Mayonnaise." *Esquire* 24 (October 1945): 54-56, 147-149.

____ . "The Varioni Brothers." *Saturday Evening Post* (17 July 1943): 12-13, 76-77.

____ . "A Young Girl in 1941 with No Waist at All." *Mademoiselle* 25 (May 1947): 222-223, 292-302.

____ . "The Young Folks." *Story* 16 (March-April 1940): 26-30.

Skow, John. "Sonny: An Introduction." *Time* (15 September 1961): 86-90. Rpt. In Grunwald 3-18.

Wenke, John. *J.D. Salinger: A Study of the Short Fiction.* Boston: Twayne, 1991.

Wiegand, William. "Seventy-eight Bananas." *Chicago Review* 11 (1958): 3-19. Rpt. in Grunwald 123-136.

SUGGESTIONS FOR FURTHER READING

Salinger, J.D. "The Children's Echelon." [nd.] Archives of Story Magazine and Story Press. Princeton, NJ: Princeton University Library.
___ . "The Last and Best of the Peter Pans." [nd.] Archives of Story Magazine and Story Press. Princeton, NJ: Princeton University Library.
___ . "The Magic Foxhole." [nd.] Archives of Story Magazine and Story Press. Princeton, NJ: Princeton University Library.
___ . "The Ocean Full of Bowling Balls." [nd.] Archives of Story Magazine and Story Press. Princeton, NJ: Princeton University Library.
___ . "Two Lonely Men." [nd.] Archives of Story Magazine and Story Press. Princeton, NJ: Princeton University Library.

Chapter 2

"The Inverted Forest"

A poet does not invent his poetry—he finds it.

Raymond Ford

When *Cosmopolitan* magazine published "The Inverted Forest" in December of 1947, the editors introduced it with this build-up:

To say that this short novel is unusual magazine fare is, we think, a wild understatement. We're not going to tell you what it's about. We merely predict you will find it the most original story you've read in a long time—and the most fascinating. (73)

Salinger never reprinted "The Inverted Forest" between its own covers, probably because he realized that it is much inferior to his later work. He must therefore have been chagrined when *Cosmopolitan* magazine reprinted "The Inverted Forest" in its "diamond jubilee" issue in March of 1961, 10 years after the publication of Salinger's masterwork, *The Catcher in the Rye.*

Like several of Salinger's earlier stories, "The Inverted Forest" prefigures his later tendency to give equal emphasis to two major characters so that we can't tell who the central character is supposed to be. "The Inverted Forest" starts out as the story of an eleven-year-old girl, Corinne von Nordhoffen. She is the daughter of a Long Island millionaire, and she has a crush on one of her public school classmates, Raymond Ford, the son of an alcoholic waitress. Corinne has invited Raymond to her birthday party, but Raymond doesn't show up because his mother has just been fired from her job, and the two of them are in the process of moving away.

The plot then follows Corinne's life for the next 20 years. She inherits the family fortune, goes to college, spends a few years in Europe, and then begins to work for a magazine in New York City. Raymond Ford re-enters Corinne's life when they are both thirty years old, and he has become a celebrated poet and

is teaching at Columbia University. When they meet, she finds that he has
turned out to be very good looking and that she now has an even bigger crush
on him than she did when they were children. The two get married, but their
marital bliss is short-lived. After only four months of marriage, Raymond runs
away with Bunny Croft, one of his admirers.

A year and a half later, Corinne finds out that Raymond and Bunny are living
in an industrial city in the Midwest. Corinne travels to that city, hoping to take
Raymond back home with her. But she finds that Raymond has become an
alcoholic and that Bunny is preventing him from writing poetry. Instead,
Bunny wants him to write commercial fiction. Nevertheless, Raymond refuses
to come home with Corinne. He is totally browbeaten by Bunny because she
reminds him of his mother. The novella ends with Corinne walking back to the
train station through the snow.

CRITICAL RECEPTION

"The Inverted Forest" did not receive critical attention until Salinger had become a well-established figure in American literature. The first critic to evaluate
"The Inverted Forest" was Ihab Hassan in his 1957 essay "Rare Quixotic Gesture: The Fiction of J.D. Salinger." This is Hassan's judgment:

The piece is at best terrifying, at worst awkward, and its style vacillates between
glamour and doom. The story unfolds ponderously; the introduction, midway, of a
narrator who sees the action both in the first and the third person seems like the intrusion of a Nick Carraway gone slightly schizophrenic. (144)

A year after Hassan, Frederick Gwynn and Joseph Blotner offered the next
evaluation of "The Inverted Forest." In their book, *The Fiction of J.D. Salinger,* they call the plot "irredeemably fantastic" (12), and they wonder "what *is*
significant about what *has* happened?" (14). Guessing that it is Raymond
Ford's forest that is inverted, the two critics say: "We have never been able to
see this submerged forest for the mass of roots crawling about on the surface"
(14).

The same year as Gwynn and Blotner, Paul Levine also discussed "The Inverted Forest." Levine's essay, "J.D. Salinger: The Development of the Misfit
Hero," is chiefly interpretive rather than evaluative. But Levine finds the novella to be a valuable part of Salinger's canon because he believes that the vision
of life in Salinger's early fiction culminates in "The Inverted Forest" and that
Raymond Ford is a character type "later to be developed into Seymour Glass"
(108).

Even more positive about "The Inverted Forest" is Warren French in his 1963
book, *J.D. Salinger.* French asserts that "this novelette provides important evidence about some of the persistent assumptions underlying its author's creations" (68). He says about "The Inverted Forest" that "it is cerebral enough to
require the reader's cooperation" but that "in terms of artistic satisfaction, this
cooperation is not repaid" (68). French argues that "if we follow the theory expounded in the story, the reader's needs do not matter anyway" because "The
Inverted Forest" is really "an allegorical statement of the idea that the artist

doesn't have any social obligations" (68). French dismisses previous negative assessments of "The Inverted Forest" by arguing that Salinger should not be treated as a realist: "As psychologically realistic fiction, 'The Inverted Forest' is surely one of the least satisfactory tales ever written, but it can be justified as an allegory" (71).

However, 25 years later, in his book *J.D. Salinger, Revisited* (1988), French admitted that his earlier judgment of "The Inverted Forest" was too generous and that the novella has "few redeeming features." Above all the protagonist's "fatal attraction to a scheming woman (Bunny) who reminds him of his mother fails to move the reader." Moreover, French now says that in the entire novella "none of the characters is plausible" (29).

NARRATIVE STRUCTURE AND POINT OF VIEW

In "The Inverted Forest," Salinger takes his experiments with plot and point of view a step further than he did earlier in "The Varioni Brothers." He again gives equal emphasis to two major characters, he tells part of the story in the form of diary entries and letters, and he again employs multiple points of view. "The Inverted Forest" is even more experimental than "The Varioni Brothers" because its narrative technique is self-reflexive; that is, one of the two narrators intrudes into the story to comment on his storytelling.

Shifts in point of view divide the novella into three major parts. The first part covers a time span of almost 20 years, from Corinne's eleventh birthday to the time when she is thirty years old. This part begins with an excerpt from Corinne's childhood diary in which she prays to God that Raymond Ford will attend her birthday party because she loves him and plans to marry him. This is followed by an account of Corinne's eleventh birthday party and of her trip to town where she finds Raymond Ford and his mother on the way to the train station. Then we get a summary of Corinne's life from ages ten to thirty. The next dramatic scenes are between Corinne and her college friend, Robert Waner, who is now her boss at a New York magazine. She refuses Waner's engagement ring but accepts the gift of a book of poems from him. The poems happen to be by Raymond Ford whom Waner compares to Blake, Coleridge, Yeats, and Rilke. The rest of the novella's first part consists of a number of scenes developing Corinne and Raymond's relationship, their marriage, and the intrusion into their lives of Raymond's admirer Bunny Croft. This intrusion begins with a letter to Corinne in which Bunny asks that Raymond read some of her poems because she wants his advice. By the end of part one of the novella, Bunny has become a protégée of Raymond's.

Part two begins with a memo from Corinne to Robert Waner. In that memo she announces that she will tell him of the events shortly before and after Raymond's disappearance. She explains that she has written about these events as if she were a private detective keeping a diary. This private detective's log consists of two sections. The first has five entries (dated 10 May through 14 May 1937) and tells of the days preceding Raymond's elopement with Bunny. The second section consists of a single entry, dated 23 May 1937, and tells of the visit of Bunny's husband Howie Croft.

The third part of the novella begins when the diary format is abandoned without explanation and there is a shift back to an omniscient point of view. This last part covers the rest of Howie Croft's visit to Corinne and a single day in November of 1938 when Corinne tracks down Raymond and Bunny but is unable to talk Raymond into coming home with her.

Multiple love interests—in the form of two love triangles—tie the three major parts together. The first love interest is Corinne's childhood crush on Raymond Ford. With Raymond Ford out of the picture, the next love interest is Robert Waner's unrequited love for Corinne. This becomes a love triangle when Corinne hooks up with Raymond Ford again and decides to marry him despite Robert Waner's warning that Raymond won't be able to love her because he is cold as ice. A second love triangle is added when Bunny Croft appears on the scene and begins to make a play for Raymond. When Bunny gets Raymond away from Corinne for good, she dissolves both love triangles. In the end, it seems that a wiser Corinne is on her way back to New York where a person who truly loves her—Robert Waner—is faithfully waiting for her.

Like "The Varioni Brothers," "The Inverted Forest" employs multiple points of view. We not only have two major narrators, Robert Waner and Corinne von Nordhoffen, we also have additional shifts in narrative perspective because of the inclusion of a letter from Bunny Croft and the preposterous stories Bunny tells of her life in the mansion of her rich aunt.

The unusual thing about the narrative perspective in "The Inverted Forest" is that the main narrator, Robert Waner, intrudes several times to comment on the story he is telling. These intrusions involve a shift from a third person omniscient to a first person point of view. For instance, halfway through the first part of the novella, Waner identifies himself and says: "I think I'll say here, and then let it go, that I am Robert Waner. I don't really have a good reason for taking myself out of the third person" (79). But a few pages later, Waner switches from the third to the first person to comment on the lapse of time in his narrative. He says that he feels tempted to use two old Hollywood clichés, the calendar whose days get blown off and the tree that is transformed from being covered by snow to sporting lush spring foliage. In a third such intrusion, Waner justifies skipping over Corinne and Raymond's honeymoon by saying that he knows nothing about that honeymoon but that he would have been able to get the facts if he had wanted to pass them along to us. Waner intrudes one last time in the middle part of the novella when he says that he will reprint for us a note that Corinne sent him. What follows is Corinne's memo and her private detective log of the days immediately before and after Raymond and Bunny ran off together.

As we can see, "The Inverted Forest" (1947) anticipates the post-modernist fashion of self-reflexive fiction, that is, of a story told by a narrator who comments on the progress of his own narrative. Salinger used this self-reflexive narrative technique for the first time in 1941, in "The Heart of a Broken Story," and he did not return to it until 1955, in "Raise High the Roof Beam, Carpenters."

CHARACTERIZATION AND STYLE

In some places in "The Inverted Forest," the style is indistinguishable from that in Salinger's later fiction, but the description and motivation of the characters is not as convincing as it might be. However, as character types, Robert Waner and Raymond Ford anticipate the characters of Buddy and Seymour Glass. Moreover, Bunny Croft stands out as the most despicable female character in all of Salinger's fiction.

Robert Waner is one of several early prototypes for Buddy Glass, the very subjective narrator of the Glass Family Series. Both are literary men, Waner an editor on the staff of a literary magazine, and Buddy a teacher of creative writing and a fiction writer. Moreover, their literary tastes are very similar. Both lean toward the romantics, old and new, Blake, Keats, and Coleridge on the one hand, and Yeats and Rilke on the other. Moreover, both subscribe to the same romantic view of art as Raymond Ford, that is, to the belief that all great art grows out of divine inspiration and not out of mechanical composition. To quote Raymond Ford: "A poet doesn't invent his poetry—he finds it" (95). And finally, both Robert Waner and Buddy Glass are admirers of doomed geniuses, of Raymond Ford and Seymour Glass, respectively.

Raymond Ford is not the first doomed genius in Salinger's fiction. He is a further development of the brilliant lyricist and would-be novelist Joe Varioni in "The Varioni Brothers." Joe Varioni is shot to death before he can realize his full potential as an artist. However, Raymond Ford achieves the recognition that eluded Joe Varioni. Robert Waner describes Ford as Blake, Coleridge, and Rilke all in rolled into one, and then some. In addition, we learn that Raymond Ford twice won the Rice Fellowship for poetry and three times the Annual Strauss Award, and that he now spends half of his time writing poetry and the other half teaching at Columbia University.

Raymond Ford's accomplishments foreshadow those of Seymour Glass, the central character in the Glass Family Series. Not only was Seymour a child genius who entered Columbia University at fifteen, got his Ph.D. at eighteen, and was an associate professor at twenty-three, he was also—according to his brother Buddy—a great poet. In "Seymour—An Introduction," Buddy says about him that the world has had only three or four non-expendable poets and he thinks that posterity will eventually rank Seymour with those few. Also like Seymour Glass, Raymond Ford is fatally attracted to a woman who does not share his love of poetry.

Even though Bunny Croft's effect on Raymond Ford is less devastating than Muriel's effect on Seymour Glass, Bunny is still the most negative female character in all of Salinger's fiction. She pretends to be a twenty-year-old college girl who aspires to be a poet like Raymond Ford, but she is actually a thirty-one-year-old housewife, who is married to a salesman. The interesting thing about her characterization is that she is developed as a double for Raymond's mother. First of all, like Raymond's mother, Bunny is an alcoholic. Secondly, like Raymond's mother, she is a compulsive liar who loves to make up stories about her background. She not only claims to be a college student, but she also tells long stories about growing up in a huge mansion with her rich aunt. Thirdly, like Raymond's mother, Bunny has a violent streak, and her husband tells Corinne that Bunny often releases her anger by beating their eleven-year-old son. And finally, Bunny is just as verbally abusive as Raymond's mother. For instance, she tells Corinne that she and Raymond would be better off financially if "this big lug" would consider writing for money. And when Corinne is leaving their apartment, Bunny says to Raymond: "Turn on the hall light for Corinne, stupid" (109).

A major weakness in the characterization of Raymond Ford is that his reasons for taking up with Bunny Croft and staying with her are hard to believe. While Bunny's motivation is understandable—she finds Raymond attractive and she hopes that he can help her get published—Raymond's motivation for choosing Buddy over Corinne is unconvincing. Also, Salinger makes a better case for Raymond having been a non-drinker for many years because of his mother's alcoholism than he does for Raymond starting to drink after he hooks up with Bunny. And when Corinne asks him to come home with her, Raymond's refusal is not plausible. He says to Corinne that he "can't get away" because he is "with the Brain again." Because Corinne doesn't understand what he means, Raymond says: "You saw the original. Think back. Think of somebody pounding on the window of a restaurant on a dark street" (107). Raymond here reminds Corinne of her eleventh birthday when she came looking for him and found Raymond and his mother leaving the restaurant where his mother had worked. But it doesn't make sense for Raymond to call his mother "the Brain" because she was a very coarse person with a very limited intelligence and no education. Moreover, it is hard to believe that an internationally famous poet would choose to live in poverty and obscurity with an abusive, violent-tempered woman because that woman reminds him of his mother.

If we compare the style of "The Inverted Forest" to the style of Salinger's earlier stories, then we will find that by 1947 he had overcome his tendency to come up with stylistic innovations at all cost. His characters are no longer "mousing" into rooms, "little-girling" at each other, or "yodeling hellos." However, he still uses the Stephen Crane repetition to suggest dim-wittedness, as for instance, when Howie Croft says to Corinne: "I and Bunny haven't been gettin' along so good. We haven't been gettin' along so good the last coupla years.... She just changed a lot. I mean she just changed a lot" (102). And Salinger also hasn't quite shaken his fondness for the style of F. Scott Fitzgerald. We can see that when he makes the following comments about Corinne's travels in Europe:

She had a feeling that on arriving there she would respond more poignantly to the memory of things long over and ungracefully done with.... She studied and played, more or less after a fashion, in Paris, Vienna, Rome, Berlin, St. Anton, Cannes, Lausanne. She prescribed for herself some of the usual American-in-Europe neurotic fun, plus some accessible exclusively to girls who happen to be millionairesses.... Nobody, of course can make the American rich feel quite as filthy as can a poor-but-clean European (79).

Of course it isn't only the style that is reminiscent of Fitzgerald here, it is also the character type. Reading this passage, one can't help thinking of Fitzgerald's narrator saying in "The Rich Boy": "Let me tell you about the very rich. They are different from you and me" (177).

But in "The Inverted Forest," there are also passages that sound like Salinger's later fiction. In one such passage, Robert Waner reminds Corinne of kissing her in a taxicab. He says that there was something in the way she raised her arms to straighten her hat that he will never forget because she is "the greatest hat-straightener that ever lived." The style in this passage resembles that in the later story "Franny" (1955) when the narrator describes Franny's meeting with her boyfriend, Lane Coutell, in a train station. Franny throws her arms around Lane and gives him "a station-platform kiss" which was at once spontaneous and inhibited and had "somewhat of a forehead-bumping aspect."

In another passage from "The Inverted Forest," Robert Waner sounds very much like Buddy Glass in the later novella "Zooey" (1957). This happens when Robert Waner switches from third person to first person narration to identify himself as Robert Waner and when he says that he doesn't really have a good reason for taking himself out of the third person. This passage sounds very much like Buddy Glass identifying himself as the narrator of "Zooey" and saying: "We will, however, leave this Buddy Glass in the third person from here on in. At least I see no good reason to take him out of it" (50).

In summary, as far as characterization and style are concerned, "The Inverted Forest" shows that in 1947, Salinger was already growing into his mature style but that he still had difficulties in making his characters believable.

SETTINGS AND SYMBOLS

The temporal setting in "The Inverted Forest" is spelled out precisely. The novella begins with a diary entry dated December 31, 1917. This is the day before the 11th birthday of one of the two central characters, Corinne von Nordhoffen. She tells her diary that she loves her classmate Raymond Ford and that she must absolutely marry him or she'll die. Corinne and Raymond get married on April 27, 1937. On May 14, 1937, Raymond leaves Corinne and runs away with Bunny Croft. And it is in November of 1939, when Corinne tracks down her husband and Bunny Croft in a smog-bound industrial city in the Midwest.

As in most of Salinger's early fiction, the physical settings in "The Inverted Forest" are not described in detail and do not play an important role. Moreover, the descriptions that we do get are sparse. Similarly, there is practically no symbolism in the novella, and when Salinger makes a stab at it with a portentous metaphor, he misses the mark.

There are only two places in the novella where the physical environment is described, and in both cases the description is impressionistic. In one scene, the eleven-year-old Corinne and her father's secretary are looking for her classmate Raymond Ford whom she has invited to her birthday party. They encounter Raymond and his mother on a cold New Year's Day as they are leaving their apartment which is above the restaurant where Mrs. Ford had been working as a waitress. Before Mrs. Ford leaves, she expresses her anger at being fired by yelling obscenities at her former employer and pounding on the restaurant's dark display window. The narrator describes this window as "the place where normally lobsters could be seen winking on cracked ice" (77). The unusual thing here is that only part of what is being described—the dark window—is physical reality. The lobsters winking on cracked ice aren't actually there; they have been moved out of the show window for the night. The unusual nature of this descriptive passage suggests that Salinger prefers imagination to physical reality.

Another passage near the end of the novella shows just how sparse the descriptions of settings in Salinger's early fiction usually are. However, while this sparseness sometimes seems like a defect, in this case it makes an eloquent point. In the passage in question Corinne has finally tracked down Raymond and Bunny to a tenement building somewhere in the Midwest. When Corinne first sees Raymond, the narrator tells us: "Ford was sitting at a small bridge table with his back to the door. He was in his shirt sleeves. An undressed watty little bulb burned over his head.... Ford turned around in the wooden restaurant chair he was sitting on and looked at his visitor" (107). The description of the setting contains only three physical facts: a small bridge table, a naked light bulb, and a wooden chair. The sparseness of the furnishings of the room can suggest two things, either abject poverty or a monkish disdain for material possessions. As it turns out, both impressions make sense, for Raymond doesn't seem to be materialistic at all while Bunny chafes under their poverty. Moreover, the description of Raymond Ford in his Spartan room suggests that Salinger was groping for a way of using his settings to symbolize aspects of his characters' personalities, as he later does in *The Catcher in the Rye* and in *Nine Stories*.

Oddly enough, Salinger's use of symbolism is less effective in "The Inverted Forest" than in other early stories. For instance, the novella's title refers to a passage from a poem in Raymond Ford's book *The Cowardly Morning*:

> Not wasteland, but a great inverted forest
> with all foliage underground. (80)

Since Salinger took the novella's title from this passage, we would expect him to do something with the ideas of the "wasteland" and the "inverted forest." But he doesn't, unless the "foliage underground" is supposed to refer to Raymond Ford's subconscious Oedipal fixation on Bunny Croft.

Most of the symbolism in "The Inverted Forest" seems to be unintentional and has to do with the major characters. First of all, in sociological terms, Corinne von Nordhoffen can be seen to represent America's money aristocracy, Robert Waner the upper middle class, Bunny and Howie Croft the lower middle class, and Raymond Ford's mother the working class. And Raymond Ford himself can be seen to represent the person from a working class background who moves up to the top of the social ladder and then slides back down again. Although the characters can be interpreted as social symbols in this manner, it is doubtful that Salinger had that in mind. As far as Raymond Ford is concerned, it is less likely that Salinger wanted us to see him as an unsuccessful social climber than as a representative of all those artists who self-destruct because of psychological or hereditary problems—in Ford's case an Oedipus complex and an inherited tendency toward alcoholism.

The most obvious and least effective attempt to generate symbolic meaning in "The Inverted Forest" is Raymond Ford's use of the metaphor "the Brain" to characterize both Bunny Croft and his mother. Raymond tells Corinne that he must stay with Bunny because she is "the Brain," and when Corinne doesn't understand, he tells her that she, Corinne, has seen "the original," namely his mother. Normally the word "brain" has a positive connotation suggesting intelligence. However, neither Raymond's mother nor Bunny Croft comes across as an especially brainy person. The kind of twisted intelligence they share, however, is reflected in their propensity to invent stories about themselves that make them look more interesting and important than they really are. Here is Raymond's mother, an alcoholic waitress and single parent who has been fired from her job, and she says that she could go home this minute and say to her supposedly wealthy father, "'Dad, I'm tired of bein' an adventuress. I wanna settle down and take it easy for a while.' He'd be tickled a death. I'd make him the happiest Dad in the world" (78). Similarly, Bunny Croft misrepresents herself when she tells Raymond and Corinne Ford that she is a twenty-year-old college student who grew up in the mansion of her rich aunt, when she is really a thirty-one-year-old housewife who beats her eleven-year-old son and cheats on her salesman husband.

Another similarity between Raymond's mother and Bunny has to do with their similar violent streaks. Raymond used to come to school with his back full of bruises. That is how his classmates knew his mother beat him. While there is no evidence in the novella that Bunny beats Raymond, she is verbally abusive because she calls him, in front of Corinne, "stupid" and a "big lug." When Raymond does not protest this verbal abuse, we realize that he feels as intimidated by Bunny as he had been by his mother. It seems therefore that Salinger wanted us to read "the Brain" as a negative metaphor that refers to the oppressive deceitfulness of both Bunny Croft and Raymond's mother. But such an interpretation is a stretch which most readers probably won't make.

Moreover, the metaphor of "the Brain" works against a more common-sense interpretation of Raymond's mother as a symbolic figure. Given her social background, alcoholism, and coarse behavior, she can be seen as representing the overpowering negative hereditary and social influences that eventually destroy Raymond Ford's life. If it were not for his mother's coarseness, her alcoholism, and her violent temper, Raymond Ford would not have been attracted to Bunny Croft in the first place, nor would he have stayed with her after she became abusive and drove him to drink.

An analysis of Raymond's mother's influence on him and of the way the plot is constructed suggests a determinist view of life. Despite all the romantic ideas about art that are expressed by Robert Waner and Raymond Ford, the novella implies the belief that we are not the masters of our own lives but the slaves of our heredity and upbringing.

THEMES AND INTERPRETATIONS

Not much has been written about "The Inverted Forest." The few critics that do discuss "The Inverted Forest" focus either on psychological, sociological, or aesthetic themes or on a combination of those.

In the essay "Rare Quixotic Gesture: The Fiction of J.D. Salinger" (1957), Ihab Hassan says that it is "the outsider theme" that is crucial in "The Inverted Forest." Hassan feels that

the piece strikes with the impact of an old theme given a new Freudian wrench. Raymond Ford, the poet genius, once under the domination of his unspeakably coarse mother, grows up only to throw over marital love and self respect for a woman every bit as offensive as his parent. The Oedipal surrender is complete, the regression almost savage; [it is] a pathological submission of the outsider to the vulgarian. (144)

In short, Hassan sees "The Inverted Forest" as the pessimistic culmination of the first phase of Salinger's career. Comparing Raymond Ford to Seymour Glass, Hassan says that Raymond prefigures the Seymour of "A Perfect Day for Bananafish" because—like Seymour—Raymond "concedes the victory to the world much too easily" (145).

Paul Levine analyzes a similar theme as Hassan and also offers a pessimistic interpretation of "The Inverted Forest." In the 1958 essay "J.D. Salinger: The Development of the Misfit Hero," Levine says that the novella expresses "Salinger's early vision—the vision of something so terrible that it cannot be communicated" (108). Levine refers to the ending of "The Inverted Forest" and says about the protagonist Raymond Ford:

He returns to the miserable state of his childhood when he saw neither poetry nor the real world. Salinger's insight into his hero's dilemma is now clear. The point for Raymond Ford—as for Holden and Seymour—is that he is a misfit and can never be accepted by, or accept, society. His vision—like his unimpaired sense of taste—renders his problem insoluble. With it he cannot live in society; without it he cannot live with himself. (109)

The most detailed and ingenious interpretation of "The Inverted Forest" is a chapter of Warren French's 1963 book *J.D. Salinger*. The title of the chapter is "You, T.S. Eliot." According to French, the central theme of "The Inverted Forest" is an esthetic one because the novella is a clever allegory intended as an attack on T.S. Eliot's view of art, especially on his notions of artistic creation and of the responsibility of the artist to society.

French begins his interpretation by warning us not to accept Corinne's judgment that "everything was wrong" with Raymond Ford when she finally tracks Raymond down to the Midwestern tenement building where he lives with Bunny Croft. French argues that what Corinne considers "wrong" from her success-oriented point of view may be "right" from the point of view of "the artist who doesn't want to get anywhere anyway, but wants only to dwell in the 'inverted forest' of his imagination." It is in this inverted forest of the artist's imagination that his or her poetry grows. This is how French explains that Raymond Ford says he does not "'invent' poetry, employing the formulas that society provides, but 'finds' it in the mysterious depths of his imagination" (74).

And how is all this related to T.S. Eliot? French sees two connections. For one thing, unlike Raymond Ford's poetry which is "found" and not "invented," Eliot's poetry "is largely based on traditional learning—is 'invented' rather than 'found'." For another thing, "Eliot—like Corinne—wishes to reform the waste-land rather than to withdraw into 'the inverted forest'" (75). Thus, according to the view of art that the novella advocates, T.S. Eliot is not really a poet but only a versifier, because "the true artist cannot but chose to be completely irre-sponsible socially." According to such a view of art and of the artist, so French argues, "pursuit of one's artistic vision justifies ignoring all one's obligations to society." This view not only implies an attack on T.S. Eliot's aesthetics; it is also "identical with the Beatnik notion of 'disaffiliation'" (75).

In 1979, James Lundquist offered a two-pronged interpretation of "The In-verted Forest" that examines not only what the novella has to say about the theme of art and artists but also what it implies about the role of sex in people's lives. Taking a hint from the novella's title, Lundquist says that a key idea is that of inversion. The artist Raymond Ford is the character in the novella who is associated with the inverted forest, and Lundquist says about Ford that "the beauty he sees, the beauty which leads to his art, is all underground." Others can only see Raymond Ford's exposed roots, that is, his educational and family background, "but the real world of the artist is something only he can see.... The foliage wilts, and all that Ray has left is the wasteland—the cruel world that has made him what he is" (24).

Lundquist finds the novella "confused in its allegorical implications," but he says that in addition to the theme of the artist's conflict with the world, the novella also develops a sexual theme because throughout the novella, "the sheer threat of sexuality and marriage is an inescapable presence" (24). Lundquist believes that "sex generally has a destructive effect in Salinger's stories" and that "The Inverted Forest" confirms the notion that "for many of [Salinger's] charac-ters, love is simply impossible, or is represented in impossible terms, and this is what makes sex so negative a factor in his work" (25).

CONCLUSION

Salinger showed good judgment in never reprinting "The Inverted Forest." It is such a flawed performance in terms of plot construction and characterization that readers who have never read any Salinger before would probably not be in-spired to read any more of him afterwards. However, Salinger aficionados who have read everything he has published in hard covers would probably find "The Inverted Forest" very interesting because in its style, character types, and han-dling of point of view, the novella anticipates Salinger's later Glass Family Series.

In terms of Salinger's development as a writer, "The Inverted Forest" (1947) stands out as one of the three most experimental works of his early period, that is, the period before *The Catcher in the Rye* (1951). The other two stories are "The Heart of a Broken Story" (1941) and "The Varioni Brothers" (1943). In "The Inverted Forest," Salinger combined the self-reflexiveness of "Broken Story" with the multiple points of view of "Varioni Brothers." Moreover, Raymond Ford's belief that "a poet doesn't invent his poetry—he finds it" an-ticipates Buddy Glass's and J.D. Salinger's romantic belief in inspiration as the source of all art (see Appendix III: "Salinger's Philosophy of Composition").

"The Inverted Forest" is relatively untilled soil, and there are several thematic areas that may be fruitfully explored.   One is the theme of unrequited love (Corinne's for Raymond and Robert's for Corinne) that figures prominently in much of Salinger's apprentice fiction. Another theme is that of the difficulty of overcoming class differences (as between Raymond and Corinne) which also plays a role in some of Salinger's early stories. A third theme that has not yet been explored in "The Inverted Forest" is Raymond Ford's fondness for the romantic poets and for the romantic view of art. This theme links "The Inverted Forest" to the earlier "The Varioni Brothers" and to the later "Seymour—An Introduction."

WORKS CITED

Fitzgerald, F. Scott. "The Rich Boy." In *The Stories of F. Scott Fitzgerald.* Ed. Malcolm Cowley. New York: Scribner's, 1988, 177-208.

French, Warren. *J.D. Salinger.* New York: Twayne, 1963.

___ . *J.D. Salinger, Revisited.* Boston: G.K. Hall, 1988.

Gwynn, Frederick L., and Joseph L. Blotner. *The Fiction of J.D. Salinger.* Pittsburgh: U of Pittsburgh P, 1958.

Hassan, Ihab. "Rare Quixotic Gesture: The Fiction of J.D. Salinger." *Western Review* 21 (Summer 1957): 261-280. Rpt. in *Salinger: A Critical and Personal Portrait.* Ed. Henry A. Grunwald. New York: Harper, 1962, 138-163.

Levine, Paul. "J.D. Salinger: The Development of the Misfit Hero." *Twentieth Century Literature* 5 (October 1958): 92-99. Rpt. in *J.D. Salinger and the Critics.* Ed. William F. Belcher and James W. Lee. Belmont, CA: Wadsworth, 1962, 107-115.

Lundquist, James. *J.D. Salinger.* New York: Ungar, 1979.

Salinger, J.D. *Franny and Zooey* [1961]. New York: Bantam, 1964.

___ . "The Inverted Forest." *Cosmopolitan* 113 (December 1947): 73-80, 85-86, 88, 90, 92, 95-96, 98, 100, 102, 107, 109. Rpt. in *Cosmopolitan* 150 (March 1961): 111-132.

___ . *Raise High the Roof Beam, Carpenters and Seymour—An Introduction* [1963]. New York: Bantam, 1965.

___ . "The Varioni Brothers." *Saturday Evening Post* (17 July 1943): 12-13, 76-77.

SUGGESTIONS FOR FURTHER READING

Fosburgh, Lacey. "J.D. Salinger Speaks About His Silence." *New York Times* (3 November 1974): 1, 69.

Hamilton, Ian. *In Search of J.D. Salinger.* New York: Random House, 1988.

Hamilton, Kenneth. "The Interplay of Life and Art." In *J.D. Salinger: A Critical Essay.* Grand Rapids, MI: Eerdmans, 1967, 11-21.

Salinger, Margaret. *Dream Catcher.* New York: Washington Square, 2000.

Wenke, John. "The Uncollected Stories." In *J.D. Salinger: A Study of the Short Fiction.* Boston: Twayne, 1991, 4-7.

Chapter 3

The Catcher in the Rye

I'm quite illiterate, but I read a lot.

Holden Caulfield

J.D. Salinger invented the central character of *The Catcher in the Rye* 10 years before the publication of that novel. The sixteen-year-old Holden Caulfield first appears in the story "Slight Rebellion Off Madison" which Salinger sold to *New Yorker* magazine in 1941 and which he later transformed into Chapter 17 of *The Catcher in the Rye*. "Slight Rebellion" is the story of Holden's relationship with his girl friend Sally Hayes. Holden eventually alienates Sally by calling her "a royal pain" because she doesn't want to run away to the woods of Massachusetts or Vermont with him. *The New Yorker* shelved the story in 1941 but finally published it in 1946. Meanwhile, *Collier's* magazine printed another story about Holden Caulfield, "I'm Crazy" (1945). This story contains what amounts to a plot outline of *The Catcher in the Rye*. It begins with Holden saying good-bye to his history teacher Spencer at Pentey [sic] Preparatory School, and it ends with Holden sneaking into his parents' apartment in New York to talk to his sister Phoebe before telling his parents that he's been expelled from yet another school.

Another preliminary study for *The Catcher in the Rye* was "a novelette ninety pages long," so Salinger told William Maxwell, when Maxwell was writing a biographical piece about him for the *Book-of-the-Month Club News* in 1951. Maxwell reports that Salinger had the novelette accepted for publication in 1946 but that he withdrew it at the last minute and "decided to do it over again" (5). That ninety-page draft probably was an expanded version of "I'm Crazy" with "Slight Rebellion Off Madison" spliced into the middle of it.

CRITICAL RECEPTION

The Catcher in the Rye was received enthusiastically by the reading public. Even before its publication, it was adopted by the Book-of-the-Month Club, and it sold fabulously well. Ten years after its first publication, over a million and a half copies had been sold in the United States. It was translated into dozens of languages and put on the reading lists of high schools in America and in several European countries. To this day, the worldwide sales of *The Catcher in the Rye* still total close to a quarter million a year.

Surprisingly, the first reviews of *The Catcher in the Rye* were mixed. Some reviewers praised the novel as a significant success while others panned it as a disappointing failure. Still others were offended by what they called the book's vulgar and obscene language.

On the one hand, the *New York Times*, the *New Yorker*, and the *Saturday Review of Literature* reviewed the book positively. Nash Burger, in the *New York Times*, called *Catcher* "an unusually brilliant first novel" (19); N.S. Behrman, in the *New Yorker*, called it "a brilliant, funny, meaningful novel" (65); and Harrison Smith, in the *Saturday Review*, judged it to be "a remarkable and absorbing novel" (28) and "a book to be read thoughtfully and more than once" (30).

On the other hand, the *New Republic*, the *Atlantic Monthly*, and the *Nation* gave the novel thumbs-down reviews. Anne Goodman, in the *New Republic,* said that "the book as a whole is disappointing" (23). It is "a brilliant tour-de-force, but in a writer of Salinger's undeniable talent one expects something more" (24). Harvey Breit, in the *Atlantic Monthly*, made the point that Holden Caulfield is "an urban, transplanted Huck Finn" (6) but that unlike Twain's *The Adventures of Huckleberry Finn*, *The Catcher in the Rye* ultimately fails because "whatever is serious and implicit in the novel is overwhelmed by the more powerful comic element" (7). And in the *Nation*, Ernest Jones (not the Ernest Jones who was a disciple of Freud's) admitted that *The Catcher in the Rye* is "a case history of all of us," but he said that "though always lively in its parts, the book as a whole is predictable and boring" (25).

The aspect of *The Catcher in the Rye* that caused the greatest disagreement among reviewers is its style. For instance, Riley Hughes, the reviewer in the *Catholic World* complained about an "excessive use of amateur swearing and coarse language" (31), and Morris Longstreth, writing for the *Christian Science Monitor*, found the novel to be "wholly repellent in its mingled vulgarity, naïveté, and sly perversion." Longstreth concluded that *The Catcher in the Rye* "is not fit for children to read" (30). This judgment was shared, a decade later, by parents of high school students in places such as Louisville, Kentucky; Tulsa, Oklahoma; and San Jose, California where the school boards banned the novel because of its language.

More open-minded reviewers analyzed the novel's style objectively and noted the influence of Ring Lardner and Ernest Hemingway. Writing for the *New York Herald Tribune*, Virgilia Peterson said that "had Ring Lardner and Ernest Hemingway never existed, Mr. Salinger might have had to invent the manner of his tale." She described this "manner" by saying, "*The Catcher in the Rye* repeats and repeats, like an incantation, the pseudo-natural cadences of a flat, colloquial prose which at best, banked down and understated, has a truly moving impact and at worst is casually obscene." According to Peterson, the value of the book depends on Holden's "authenticity," that is, on "what Holden's contemporaries, male and female, think of him" (4).

The academic critics didn't have a go at the novel until the mid-fifties. The fact that the novel had become a best seller among adolescents rubbed some critics the wrong way but confirmed the opinion of others that with *The Catcher in the Rye* they had a new classic on their hands. The most positive of the early academic analyses is entitled "J.D. Salinger: Some Crazy Cliff" (1956). It was written by Arthur Heiserman and James E. Miller who bestowed epic grandeur on *The Catcher in the Rye* when they asserted that the novel belongs to the "ancient and honorable narrative tradition ... of the Quest" (196). The two critics saw similarities between *The Catcher in the Rye* and such masterworks of world literature as Homer's *Odyssey* and James Joyce's *Ulysses* and such American classics Mark Twain's *The Adventures of Huckleberry Finn* and F. Scott Fitzgerald's *The Great Gatsby*. They said about Holden Caulfield that "unlike other American knights errant, Holden seeks Virtue second to Love," and they explained Holden's quest by saying that he is "driven toward love of his fellow man" (197-198).

At the opposite end of the critical spectrum, George Steiner took issue with the exaggerated praise that other critics had heaped upon *The Catcher in the Rye*. In his article, "The Salinger Industry" (1959), Steiner granted Salinger that "he has a marvelous ear for the semi-literate meanderings of the adolescent mind" (82), and he admitted that Salinger is "a most skillful and original writer" (85). However, Salinger should not be praised "in terms appropriate to the master poets of the world." Salinger falls short of being a writer of the first rank, so Steiner argued, because he "flatters the very ignorance and moral shallowness of his young readers. He suggests to them that formal ignorance, political apathy and a vague *tristesse* are positive virtues" (83).

Subsequently, the critical pendulum swung in Salinger's favor, and since the early sixties, most critics have written appreciative analyses of *The Catcher in the Rye*.

NARRATIVE STRUCTURE AND POINT OF VIEW

In its narrative structure and point of view *The Catcher in the Rye* resembles Mark Twain's *The Adventures of Huckleberry Finn*. Like Twain's novel, Salinger's is told in the first person by an adolescent, the plot is episodic, the central conflict is between an adolescent and adult society, and the reader's interest is generated less by the events of the plot than by the unique personality of the narrator-protagonist.

However, the differences between *Catcher* and *Huck Finn* are more crucial than the similarities. First of all, the events in *The Catcher in the Rye* all occur on one weekend between Saturday afternoon and Monday morning while the events in *Huck Finn* span over two months. Secondly, the episodes in the plot are tied together more closely in *Catcher* than they are in *Huck Finn*. And thirdly, the conflict between Holden and adult society is resolved, whereas the conflict between Huck Finn and adult society remains unresolved. At the end of *Catcher,* Holden is getting ready to go back to school, but at the end *of Huck Finn*, Huck is getting ready to run away again, to "light out for the territory."

The events in *The Catcher in the Rye* follow one another in an almost random order, and the sequence of some of the events at Pencey Prep and the sequence of some of those in New York could be rearranged without damaging the plot. However, the episodes of the plot are strung like pearls on four narrative strands of different lengths. The two longer ones stretch through the length of the entire novel. They are Holden's conflict with the world of adults and his descent into an almost suicidal depression. The two shorter narrative strands are developed only in the second half of the novel. They are the decline of Holden's health and his inner change.

The novel's central conflict is between Holden and the adult world. It is due to Holden's unwillingness to become part of this world because most adults he knows are phonies, that is, people who claim to be something they are not. This central conflict is muted because Holden has more dramatic, face-to-face confrontations with people his own age than with adults. However, those with whom he does have such confrontation are adolescents who have already achieved the phoniness of adults. One such individual is Holden's roommate Ward Stradlater. Stradlater looks like a well-groomed individual but is a secret slob; moreover, in his relationships with girls, he has only one thing on his mind, and that is sexual conquest. Another adolescent who acts like an adult is Holden's girlfriend Sally Hayes, whom he calls "the queen of the phonies" because she is extremely concerned about appearances and, above all, because she acts as though she were already an adult.

During his conflict with Sally Hayes, Holden reveals that the kind of adult future Sally looks forward to is abhorrent to him. This conflict arises when Holden asks Sally to run away with him to the woods of Massachusetts or Vermont. He would get a job, and they would live in a cabin by a brook and maybe even get married. Sally tells Holden that his plan is an unrealistic fantasy because if he didn't get a job they'd both starve to death; besides they're still practically children, and they still have time to do all those things after he goes to college. She says: "There'll be oodles of marvelous places to go to." But Holden says it won't be the same after they are adults. If they wanted to go away they would have to telephone all their family and friends to say goodbye, and when they got to where they're going they would have to send back postcards. But what's worst, he would have to work in an office somewhere in Manhattan, ride to work in buses or cabs, read newspapers, and have other people over to play bridge.

Holden expresses a similar distaste for adult life when his sister Phoebe tells him that he has a very negative outlook and that there's nothing he wants to be when he grows up, not even a lawyer like his father. Holden says that lawyers are all right if they are committed to saving innocent people's lives. But that's not what lawyers do. All they do is make tons of money, play golf, buy expensive cars, and drink Martinis. In short, in Holden's view, even his own father is a phony because he is more interested in making money than in helping others.

Because he can't accept the kind of adult future that he describes to Sally and Phoebe, Holden decides to run away. He plans to hitchhike out West, get a job at a gas station, build himself a little cabin on the edge of the woods, and live there for the rest of his life. He'll pretend to be a deaf-mute so that he does not have to talk to adults.

Holden's conflict with the adult world is resolved because his little sister Phoebe makes him give up his rebellion. When Holden tells Phoebe about his plans to run away, Phoebe decides to skip school and come along with him. She is so persistent that Holden eventually tells her that he has changed his mind and that he is not going away anywhere. At this moment Holden's conflict with the adult world is resolved because he has decided to go home and confront his parents, even though he knows they will probably send him to a very strict military school.

Another pervasive narrative pattern that helps string together the episodes of the plot is Holden's emotional decline. We see the first symptom when he is on his way to say good bye to his history teacher at Pencey Prep. As he is about to cross a highway, he feels that he may disappear when he steps into the road. After he finishes packing his suitcase and gets ready to leave his dorm, he expresses his first death wish. He says that he felt so lonely that he almost wished he were dead. And when he actually walks out of the dorm, he breaks into tears.

Holden's death wish becomes more specific in New York after he gets beaten up by the pimp Maurice. He says he was thinking of committing suicide by jumping out of the hotel window. The next day, when he argues with his girlfriend Sally Hayes, he explains his crankiness by saying that he feels absolutely lousy. Later, that night, in the bathroom of a hotel bar, Holden once again breaks down and cries. And still later that same night, Holden's favorite teacher, Mr. Antolini, makes what Holden considers a homosexual pass at him and Holden says at this point that he was more depressed than he ever was in his entire life. The next morning, as Holden walks up Fifth Avenue toward Phoebe's school, he again has the strange sensation that he will disappear every time he crosses a street.

Holden finally overcomes his depression when he watches Phoebe go around and around on a carrousel in Central Park. He says that he didn't care that the rain was soaking him to the skin because he felt tremendously happy, and this happiness made him cry. Holden tries to explain this sudden emotional change by saying that Phoebe looked so nice riding the carrousel. But that is not much of an explanation. Apparently Holden doesn't understand himself why he is no longer depressed.

The explanation for Holden's sudden emotional uplift lies in his inner change which makes up another narrative strand in the novel. This change begins in the middle of the novel, on Sunday morning, when Holden starts to find out that not all people turn into phonies when they grow up. He finds that out when he gets to know two nuns while having breakfast in an inexpensive restaurant. He is especially taken with the nun who is an English teacher and who shares his fondness for Shakespeare's *Romeo and Juliet*. Holden later thinks of those two nuns when Phoebe accuses him of not liking anything or anybody. Even though he talked to the nuns for only a short while, they are now among his favorite people, along with his dead brother Allie and his favorite teacher Mr. Antolini. Holden's visit with Mr. Antolini also has a lot to do with his inner change because Antolini takes Holden's rebellion seriously and recognizes it as a moral and spiritual crisis. And even though Holden recoils when Antolini expresses his fondness for him by stroking his head, he recognizes that Antolini is a caring individual and not a phony.

Holden completes his inner change when he accepts responsibility for Phoebe. Phoebe threatens to quit school if Holden runs away, and Holden ends his rebellion so that Phoebe will go back to school.

The fourth narrative strand, that of Holden's deteriorating health, not only helps to tie the plot's episodes together, it also lends credibility to Holden's surrender to the adult world. It could even be argued that at the end of the novel he is simply too sick to rebel any longer. Holden alerts us to the deterioration of his health at the beginning of the novel when he explains why he is in a sanatorium in California: "I practically got t.b. and came out here for all these goddam checkups and stuff" (5). Holden's health seems fine until Sunday night when he gets drunk at a hotel bar and then tries to sober up in the men's room by soaking his head in a sink. Then he walks to Central Park to look for the ducks in the partially frozen lagoon. As ice is forming in his hair, he wonders if he is going to contract pneumonia and die. Then on Monday morning, as he is walking down Fifth Avenue, he begins to perspire heavily, and he feels that he is on the verge of vomiting. When he is at Phoebe's school where he gives the secretary a note for Phoebe, he suddenly needs to sit down because he again feels nauseous. A short time later, while he is waiting for Phoebe in the Metropolitan Museum of Art, he has to go to the bathroom because he feels a bout of diarrhea coming on. But before he can relieve himself, he passes out. Although he feels much better when he comes to, he later makes his condition worse by sitting on a park bench in the December rain while watching Phoebe ride the carrousel.

In addition to the four narrative strands of different lengths, what also ties together the novel's episodes is Holden Caulfield's distinctive voice. Salinger's choice of the first person point of view not only gives the novel its special flavor of authenticity, it also allows Holden to express thoughts and feelings that we would not be aware of if the novel were told by from an objective third person point of view. The choice of the first person point of view strengthens the reader's identification with the narrator-protagonist and ultimately makes the reader care more about the Holden's personality than the events of the plot.

The rightness of Salinger's decision in favor of the first person point of view becomes apparent when we compare a passage from "Slight Rebellion Off Madison" to the reworked version in *The Catcher in the Rye*. In the early story, Salinger uses an objective third person point of view. Therefore, we see Holden only from the outside and hear what he says, but we don't find out what he thinks and feels. In the early story, Holden tells Sally Hayes:

> "You don't see what I mean at all."
> "Maybe I don't. Maybe you don't either," Sally said.
> Holden stood up with his skates slung over one shoulder. "You give me a royal pain," he announced quite dispassionately. ("Rebellion" 84)

And that's how the scene ends in the short story. We don't find out what Holden thinks. We don't even find out how Sally reacts. Here now is the re-worked passage as it appears in the novel:

> "You don't see what I mean at all."
> "Maybe I don't. Maybe you don't either," old Sally said. We both hated each other's guts by that time. You could see there wasn't any sense in trying to have an intelligent conversation. I was sorry as hell I'd started it.
> "C'mon, lets get outa here," I said. "You give me a royal pain in the ass if you want to know the truth."
> Boy did she hit the ceiling when I said that. I know I shouldn't've said it and I probably wouldn't've ordinarily, but she was depressing the hell out of me. (*Catcher* 133)

The major difference between the scene in the story and the novel is that we learn much more about Holden's thoughts and feelings in the novel than we do in the story, and we can therefore identify more with him.

Another aspect of the narrative perspective in the novel is that Holden is occasionally able to step out of his own shoes and look at himself from the perspective of an outsider. Yet in other places, we find that he also has some blind spots in his view of himself.

The occasional objectivity of Holden's point of view is illustrated at the end of the passage in which he describes his fight with Sally Hayes. Holden says that he apologized like mad but that Sally wouldn't accept his apologies. In frustration, Holden did something he knows he shouldn't have done, he began to laugh. He admits that he has a very loud, stupid-sounding laugh, and in a typical Salingeresque non-sequitur, he says that if he ever sat behind himself in a movie theater and heard himself laugh like that, he'd lean over and tell himself to shut up.

On the other hand, there are a number of passages in the novel in which Holden demonstrates a blatant lack of self-perception. For instance, he doesn't even realize in retrospect, when he tells the story, how unrealistic he was when he asked Sally Hayes to run off to the woods with him and live in a cabin. When his money runs out so Holden said, he'll get a job to support the two of them. Here most readers will shake their heads about Holden's inability to see himself for what he is. Holden has never had to work for his money and probably would not like it at all. He can only entertain such notions because deep down he knows that he can always return to his affluent parents when things don't work out.

Thus the contrast between the blind spots in Holden's self-perception and his occasional ability to see himself exactly the way he is perceived by others is a unique element of the novel's narrative perspective. It helps to develop Holden into a fictional character who is unusually complex.

CHARACTERIZATION AND STYLE

One of the astonishing things about *The Catcher in the Rye* is that adolescents all over the world—boys as well as girls—continue to identify with Holden Caulfield even now, 51 years after the novel was first published. Two reasons for the universal appeal of Holden's personality offer themselves. One is that Salinger subordinated all other aspects of the novel to the development of Holden's character. For instance, it seems that he created the minor characters not to advance the plot but to shed light on Holden's personality, and that he even designed the symbolism to clarify what kind of person Holden is. But the main reason Holden is so believable is that—like most adolescents—he is full of contradictions and ambivalent feelings.

The contradictions in Holden's character are reflected in his appearance. Although he is only sixteen when the events of the novel take place, he six-foot-two-and-a-half and has a patch of gray hair on the right side of his head. Also, he wears a red hunting hat with the visor turned backwards which contrasts sharply with his sports coat and tie.

Holden is aware of some of the contradictions in his personality. One of these contradictions concerns his age. He sometimes acts as though he were much older than sixteen and sometimes as though he were much younger. On several occasions, Holden tries to pass himself off as older than he is. For instance, he invites two different cab drivers to stop at a bar for drinks and he tells the prostitute, Sunny, and the three girls from Seattle that he is twenty-two years old. But on other occasions, Holden also acts younger than his age, especially when he pretends to be a character in a movie. In one instance, he annoys his roommate Stradlater by tap-dancing all over the bathroom while Stradlater is shaving. Holden says that he is the Governor's son and that his father doesn't want him to be a tap dancer, he wants him to study at Oxford. But he can't help himself because dancing is in his blood. Holden even engages in make-believe when he doesn't have an audience. After he has been beaten up by the pimp Maurice, he pretends that he has been shot in the stomach. As he staggers around in his hotel room, he imagines that he is getting his automatic and that he is walking downstairs to find Maurice. He is clutching his stomach, and he is bleeding all over the stairs, but he finds Maurice and fires six bullets into his hairy belly.

Three other contradictions in Holden's character concern his attitudes toward the movies, literature, and religion. On the one hand, he goes to the movies often, imitates them, and at one point even gives us a long plot summary of a movie he went to see at Radio City, James Hilton's *Random Harvest*. But he makes the contradictory comment about the film that it was so "putrid" that he could not stop watching it. Elsewhere he says that he hates the movies like poison but that he gets a bang out of imitating them.

About his relation to literature Holden makes this contradictory statement: "I'm quite illiterate, but I read a lot" (18). But when Holden talks about Shakespeare's *Romeo and Juliet*, Thomas Hardy's *The Return of the Native* Scott Fitzgerald's *The Great Gatsby*, and Ernest Hemingway's *A Farewell to Arms*, we see that he is far from illiterate but has a good understanding of these works.

Holden's comments on religion are also contradictory. He claims that he is an atheist, but then he explains that he likes Jesus but he doesn't like the Disciples because they always let Jesus down. And Holden also shows a better understanding of the personality of Jesus than a Quaker classmate when they disagree about the fate of Judas. Holden says that he believes Jesus never sent Judas to hell. In short, Holden's sensitive comments about Jesus contradict his statement that he is an atheist.

Another major contradiction in Holden's character has to do with his attitude toward money. While he is disdainful of money and generous with it, he also has more respect for wealthy people than for people who are not so well off. Holden's generosity is illustrated when pays for the drinks of the three young women from Seattle with whom he dances on Saturday night and when he gives ten dollars to the nuns for their next collection and later frets that he didn't give them enough. But money itself doesn't mean much to him because he often forgets to pick up his change at restaurants and nightclubs. His disdain for money is also illustrated when he is down to his last four dollars and he uses the coins to skip them across the unfrozen part of the lagoon in Central Park.

Holden's disdain for money and his generosity stand in sharp contrast to statements that show him judging people by how much money they have. For instance, he mentions a roommate at a previous prep school who had very inexpensive suitcases while Holden had genuine cowhide bags from Mark Cross. Holden admits that he tends to dislike people just because they have cheap luggage. A moment later he tells us that one of the reasons he roomed with Stradlater at Pencey Prep is that Stradlater's suitcases were as good as his own. Holden again shows that he looks down on people who don't have much money when he walks behind a father, a mother, and a little boy who just came out of church on Sunday morning. Holden says he could tell they were poor. And then he explains that the father wore the kind of pearl-gray hat that poor fellows tend to wear when they want to look sharp.

And finally, like most adolescents, Holden has conflicting attitudes toward sex. He admits that he thinks about sex all the time and that sometimes he can imagine doing "very crumby stuff" if he had the opportunity. But when the opportunity does come up in New York, and he has a young prostitute in his hotel room, Holden suddenly isn't interested in sex. He says that he knows he is supposed to feel aroused when the girl pulls her dress up over her head, but he doesn't feel that way. Instead of feeling aroused by the girl, Holden feels sorry for her because she looks as if she is only sixteen, Holden's own age. That is why Holden says he felt more depressed than aroused.

Holden even has conflicting attitudes about necking. The previous year he made a rule that he was not going to neck with girls he did not respect. He broke that rule immediately because he spent that night necking with Anne Louise Sherman whom he considered a terrible phony. In short, Holden has the normal sexual urges of an adolescent, but he also has a conscience which tells him not to treat girls as mere sex objects.

Salinger gives Holden's personality additional depth through the secondary characters. Holden's attitudes toward and reactions to these people shed light on his likes and dislikes, especially since a number of the secondary characters seem to be pairs of opposites. Here we see another instance of Salinger's propensity to work in patterns of twos as in the doubling of letters in the names of characters and in his use of double protagonists in some of his early stories and his later novellas.

A pair of characters who reveal much about Holden's values are his older brother D.B., who is a successful writer, and his younger brother Allie, who died of leukemia. Holden's attitude toward D.B. is at best ambivalent and at worst negative. On the one hand, Holden says that D.B. is his favorite author, on the other hand he agrees with Antolini who said that a person who could write like D.B. should not write for Hollywood movies. And although Holden admires D.B. for making so much money, driving a Jaguar, and having a British movie actress for a girlfriend, he does call him a prostitute for selling out to Hollywood. If D.B. were not his brother, Holden would probably even call him a phony.

By contrast, Holden's attitude toward Allie is not only 100% positive but even worshipful. Holden says that Allie was the most intelligent person in the family. But what's even more important, Allie was also the kindest because Holden cannot remember that Allie ever got mad at anybody. Another thing that stands out about Allie is that he loved poetry so much that he copied his favorite poems on his baseball glove so he would have something good to read during the lulls in the games. Allie has remained Holden's favorite person even after his death, and Holden carries Allie's baseball glove around in his luggage as if it were a holy relic. In fact, Holden actually prays to Allie when he is about to cross a street and is afraid that he will disappear: "Allie, don't let me disappear, Allie. Please, Allie" (198). When we compare Holden's attitudes toward his brothers D.B. and Allie, we can see clearly that he respects Allie's kindness more than D.B.'s success.

That Holden ultimately judges people by how kind they are also becomes apparent when we examine his reasons for liking his former English teacher Antolini more than Spencer, his history teacher at Pencey. Holden tries to like Mr. Spencer and he even writes him a note so that Spencer won't feel so bad about flunking him. But when Holden goes to see him, Spencer is sarcastic and nasty while reading Holden's failing history exam back to him. Holden says that he won't ever forgive Spencer for his unkindness because if their roles were reversed, he would never have read that terrible exam out loud to Spencer.

While Mr. Spencer is too unkind to Holden, Mr. Antolini, Holden's English teacher from his previous prep school, is perhaps a bit too kind. One reason Holden likes Antolini is that he cared enough about James Castle, who committed suicide by jumping out of a window, to pick up his body and carry it to the infirmary. Moreover, Antolini is the only adult to take Holden seriously and reassure him that "many men have been just as troubled morally and spiritually as you are right now" (189). But when Holden wakes up on Antolini's couch at night to find Antolini patting his head and stroking his hair, he panics and thinks that Antolini is making a pass at him. Later Holden is no longer sure what Antolini's intentions were and starts thinking that even if Antolini is a homosexual, what counts is that he has been very kind to him.

That Holden tries to be more like Mr. Antolini than Mr. Spencer becomes apparent when we examine his relationship with another contrasting pair of minor characters, his roommate, Ward Stradlater, and his dorm neighbor, Robert

Ackley. Ackley has a misanthropic personality, a face full of pimples, and "mossy" teeth. Although Ackley is being ostracized by most of the students at Pencey Prep, and although Holden dislikes his personality, he feels sorry for Ackley and invites him to go out on the town with him on his last night at Pencey Prep. Holden is probably the first person at Pencey to voluntarily spend time with Ackley, and Holden probably does so because unlike many others at Pencey, Ackley is at least a genuine person and not a phony.

By contrast with Ackley, Stradlater is one of the wealthiest, best looking, and most popular students at Pencey Prep, and while Holden can't help admiring him, he ultimately dislikes him even more than Ackley because he is a phony. There are several reasons why Holden thinks Stradlater is a phony. Stradlater always looks well groomed, but he never cleans his rusty razor; he can convince people, especially girls, that he is sincere when he is really lying to them; and he acts as though he likes people even though he is only in love with himself. Holden should therefore despise Stradlater, but instead he lends him his new hounds-tooth jacket and writes an English Composition essay for him. But Holden later gets in a fight with Stradlater because he worries that Stradlater might have seduced Jane Gallagher who is an old friend of Holden's. Holden is concerned, because most of the other boys at Pencey only claim to have had sexual intercourse; but from talking to a couple of girls, Holden knows that Stradlater really did have sex with some of his dates. Thus when Holden says that he hates Stradlater's guts, this may be in part because he envies him.

Yet another pair of minor characters that shed light on Holden's personality are Jane Gallagher and Sally Hayes. The characterization of the two tells us much about Holden's attitude toward the opposite sex. Holden met Jane Gallagher in the summer of 1948 when her family and Holden's were neighbors at a summer resort in Maine. All summer, Holden and Jane played tennis and golf together, and in the evenings they went to the movies or played checkers. Holden's mother didn't think Jane was pretty, and Holden admits that she is "muckle-mouthed," by which he means she distorts her mouth a lot when she talks. But she has a terrific figure and above all a terrific personality. The two things that impress Holden most about Jane are that she always reads good books and that she never uses her kings when playing checkers but always keeps them in the back row because she likes the way the stacked-up pieces look when they are all lined up. Holden and Jane went around holding hands all the time, but they never actually necked. The two times they got close to getting physical were when Jane was crying and Holden kissed her tears away and when Jane suddenly put her hand on Holden's neck while they were watching a movie. Holden thinks that this is a typical thing for adult women to do to their children or their husbands, but if a young girl does it, it is unbearably pretty. In short, Jane Gallagher brings out a deep fondness in Holden, similar to what he feels for his dead brother Allie and for his little sister Phoebe.

We wonder therefore what Holden sees in his girlfriend Sally Hayes who is in many ways the opposite of Jane. For one thing, Sally is extremely good-looking and is very concerned about everybody's appearance. For instance, she tells Holden to grow out his crew cut because crew cuts are getting to be corny. Also, on their date, she wants to go skating at Radio City because she can rent one of those tiny skating skirts that look very good on her. Holden therefore calls Sally "the queen of the phonies" (116). However, when he meets her at the Biltmore hotel for their Sunday date, Holden is overwhelmed by how gorgeous she looks. He even says that as soon as he saw her, he felt he wanted to marry her. But in retrospect, he admits that this was a crazy idea because he didn't even like her very much. Aside from her phoniness, another one of the reasons Holden doesn't like Sally much is that she has a loud, embarrassing voice. But then Holden adds that Sally can get away with that kind of voice because she is so good-looking. Even though Holden finds Sally irritating, he starts necking with her as soon as they get in the back of a taxicab. Holden even tells Sally that he loves her, but then he explains to us that he was lying when he said that but that he meant it at the time. The reason Holden briefly feels he loves Sally is, of course, that she is willing to play kissing and groping games with him.

Holden can no longer overlook the differences in his and Sally's personalities when he finds out that she is actually looking forward to becoming an adult and living the kind of conformist upper-middle-class life that Holden rebels against. This is why he finally tells her that she gives him "a royal pain in the ass" and why he lets her go home by herself. He says that he should not have done that but that has he was totally fed up with Sally. Without being aware of it, Holden here affirms a mature preference for substance over appearance, for the terrific personality of Jane Gallagher over the terrific looks of Sally Hayes.

The most important minor character in the novel is Holden's ten-year-old sister Phoebe. She is so important because she brings out a belated sense of responsibility in Holden and makes him end his rebellion. Holden mentions Phoebe early on in the novel and says about her that she is extremely smart and pretty. She is "roller-skate-skinny" and has red hair similar to that of Holden's dead brother Allie. She gets straight A's in school, and she likes to write novels that she never finishes about a girl detective named Hazle Weatherfield. Holden considers Phoebe one of the very few people who really understand him. Phoebe's only fault, so Holden says, is that she is sometimes a bit too affectionate.

When we finally see Phoebe for the first time, we find that she is unusually perceptive and mature for a ten-year-old. Because Holden is home early for Christmas vacation and sneaks into the apartment, Phoebe figures out at once that Holden must have flunked out of yet another private school. When Holden tells her that he plans to hitchhike out West to work on a ranch in Colorado, Phoebe doesn't approve but gives him her Christmas money for travel expenses. Moreover, she also senses that Holden feels very depressed and lonesome. She therefore leaves school, packs her suitcase, and insists on coming along with Holden. Although Holden is moved by Phoebe's unconditional love, he won't allow her to run away with him. At this point Holden exhibits a sense of responsibility that we have not seen in him before. He accepts that he is his sister's keeper and that he must make sure Phoebe goes back to school. He therefore gives up his plan to run away and promises to go home and face his parents.

The way Holden Caulfield talks reveals just as much about the contradictions in his character as what he does. The silliness of Holden's speech mannerisms contrasts with his astute insights and his strongly held values. Taken out of context, almost any long quotation of what Holden is saying must seem insipid. For instance, Holden keeps attaching meaningless phrases such as "and all," "or something," and "or anything" to the end of many statements, as in "it's a pretty good book and all," "we could get married or something," and "there was no sun out or anything."

Moreover, like many adolescents who want to seem tough by sneering at the world, Holden attaches emphatic negative adjectives to nouns, adjectives such as "lousy," "goddam," "stupid," "crazy," "crumby," "corny," or "phony." For instance, on the first page of the novel, Holden says that he won't talk about his "lousy childhood" because he doesn't want to tell us his "whole goddam autobiography." And a few pages later, he talks about the "crazy cannon" on top of a "stupid hill" at Pencey Preparatory School.

Another speech mannerism is Holden's habit of attaching the adjective "old" to the names of people. This makes sense when he speaks of "old Spencer," his history teacher who is close to retirement. It does not make sense when he speaks of "old Phoebe," his ten-year-old sister. However the adjective "old" is not a term of endearment, as in Jay Gatsby's beloved phrase "old sport." Holden applies the adjective equally to people he likes and people he hates. For instance he talks about "old Maurice," the pimp who beats him up, and about "old Sally" who gives him "a royal pain in the ass."

And finally, Holden keeps repeating two statements that he is very fond of. One of them is "if you want to know the truth" and the other one is that something or someone "really kills me."

Since the style of *The Catcher in the Rye* is so distinctive, it begs to be parodied. And indeed, one of the reviews of the novel was written as a parody of its style. Here is part of the opening paragraph:

This girl Helga, she kills me. She reads just about everything I bring into the house, and a lot of crumby stuff besides. She's crazy about kids. I mean stories about kids. But Hel, she says there's hardly a writer alive can write about children.... It depresses her. That's another thing. She can sniff out a corny guy or a phony book as quick as a dog smells a rat. This phoniness, it gives old Hel a pain if you want to know the truth. That's why she came hollering to me one day, her hair falling over her face and all, and said I had to read some damn story in The New Yorker. Who's the author? I said. Salinger, she told me. J.D. Salinger. Who's he? I asked. (Stern 2)

SETTINGS AND SYMBOLS

The time and locations of the settings in *The Catcher in the Rye* can be established from information that Holden mentions in passing. The narrative begins on Saturday afternoon, the 17th of December 1949 at the Pencey Preparatory School for Boys in Pennsylvania, and it ends on Monday morning, the 19th of December, in New York City. Even though it is winter, there are almost as many scenes that take place outdoors as indoors. Most of the outdoor scenes occur in New York, and the most memorable one is the scene of Holden watching Phoebe ride the carrousel in Central Park in the pouring rain.

Like Salinger's earlier fiction, *The Catcher in the Rye* provides only sketchy, impressionistic descriptions of its physical settings. A typical example is the description of the home of Mr. Spencer, Holden's history teacher at Pencey Prep. After Holden rings the bell and Mrs. Spencer opens the door, Holden says: "They didn't have a maid or anything, and they always opened the door themselves. They didn't have too much dough" (5). And all that Holden mentions about the inside the Spencers' house is that Mr. Spencer, who had the grippe, was sitting in a big leather chair, wrapped in a blanket, and that "there were pills and medicine all over the place, and everything smelled like Vicks Nose Drops" (7). As this example shows, the social milieu seems to be more important in the settings of *The Catcher in the Rye* than the physical details.

What almost all the indoor settings—except for the Spencers' home— have in common is that the social environment is upper middle class. First of all, Holden says about the social milieu of Pencey Prep that quite a few of his fellow students come from very wealthy families. When he goes home to talk to his sister Phoebe, we find that his parents' apartment house is located in one of the most expensive areas of Manhattan, on 71st Street just off Fifth Avenue, and that the family has a live-in maid. Later, Holden visits his former English teacher, Mr. Antolini, and says that he lived in a "very swanky apartment" and that his wife "was lousy with dough." The only indoor settings in New York that are not upper middle class are the hotel where Holden meets the young prostitute Sunny and the restaurant where he meets the two nuns.

There are three settings in the novel that are important because they cannot be associated with social class and because they have symbolic significance. One of these settings is the room with the dioramas in the Museum of Natural History. That room is symbolic because Holden's fondness for it reveals his desire to have things always stay the same. Another of these symbolic settings is Phoebe's elementary school, the same school where Holden went he was younger. That school also symbolizes the kind of stability that Holden likes, and he is very much upset when that stability is threatened by obscene graffiti.

A third symbolic setting is an imaginary one. It is the cabin by a brook to which Holden wants to escape with Sally Hayes. Later in the novel, we get another version of that cabin to which he wants to escape by himself.

The Catcher in the Rye develops its meaning chiefly through its major symbols and through the change in the connotation of the central metaphor of the catcher in the rye. Like the symbolic settings in the novel, most of the symbolic objects contribute to the characterization of Holden Caulfield. Six major symbols in the novel are the ducks in Central Park, Holden's red hunting cap, the glass cases in the Museum of Natural History, the cabin by the woods to which Holden wants to escape, the obscene graffiti, and the carrousel in Central Park. An analysis of these symbols clarifies the inner change that Holden experiences.

Before discussing the novel's symbols, it is necessary to analyze the novel's central metaphor, Holden wanting to be the catcher in the rye. Holden comes up with the idea when his little sister Phoebe tells him that he doesn't like anything or anybody and that he doesn't even know what he would like to be when he grows up. Holden replies that he does know what he wants to be when he grows up. He says when he heard the song, "If a body catch a body coming through then rye," he decided that that's what he wants to be, the catcher in the rye. Phoebe corrects him and says that the line goes, "If a body meet a body coming through the rye," and that it is not from a song but from a poem by Robert Burns. This information doesn't make a difference to Holden, and he explains that he keeps picturing thousands of little children playing in an enormous field of rye which has a steep cliff at one end, and there are no adults around except for him. He says that if the little kids are running and not looking where they are going, "I have to catch everybody if they start to go over the cliff" (173). That's all he wants to do all day; that's the only thing he would really like to be, the catcher in the rye.

The way Holden explains why he wants to be the catcher in the rye shows the kindness and unselfishness of his character. However, the surreal nature of the metaphor also reveals Holden's unwillingness to face the real life choices he needs to make now that he is approaching adulthood. By the end of the novel, Holden realizes that children won't grow up if there's always someone there to protect them from all potential harm. He therefore gives up his dream of being the catcher in the rye and is ready to make a realistic choice of what he wants to do with his life.

As far the symbols in the novel go, the most obvious one is Holden's hat. Holden describes it as a red hunting hat with a very long visor. When Holden's dorm neighbor Ackley tells him that where he comes from, people wear that kind of hat to shoot deer in, Holden replies that his is not a deer shooting hat but a people shooting hat.

Holden's hat is a complex symbol because it suggests several interpretations of its meaning. For one thing, it can be seen as a badge of Holden's deliberate non-conformity. He bought it because it clashes with the rest of his getup, his sports coat and tie. Also, he likes to draw attention to the incongruous hat by wearing it with the visor turned backward. By turning the visor backward Holden suggests that his values are the reverse of what everybody else's are. It is also the way that baseball catchers wear their caps. Therefore Holden's turning the visor of the hat to the back can be seen as foreshadowing his desire to be the catcher in the rye. And finally, because Holden calls it a people shooting hat, it symbolizes his dislike of most of the people around him. This dislike is very obvious to those who know Holden well. For instance, both his sister Phoebe and his favorite teacher Antolini tell him that he hates more people than he likes.

Near the end of the novel the hat disappears temporarily because Holden gives it to Phoebe. It is significant that Holden does not have the hat when his inner change occurs, when he decides not to run away. The hat reappears on Holden's head—this time with the visor facing front—in the carrousel scene where it gives Holden protection while he is sitting on a park bench in the pouring rain.

Symbols that illustrate a more positive aspect of Holden's character than the hunting hat are the ducks in Central Park. Holden thinks of them for the first time while his history teacher is talking to him. He says he was not paying attention to Mr. Spencer because he suddenly started to wonder where the Central Park ducks go when the lagoon freezes over. Holden mentions the ducks in

Central Park several more times and even asks two New York cab drivers if they know what happens to the ducks when the lagoon freezes. Holden's obsession with the ducks has been interpreted in a number of different ways. It has been suggested that the ducks represent Holden who also feels he has no place to go and is being "frozen out." Another view is that the mystery of the disappearance of the ducks can be likened to the mystery of people's disappearance into death. Still another interpretation of the meaning of the ducks picks up on Holden's idea that maybe some park employee came with a truck and took them to a zoo for the winter. Thus, when Holden wonders about the fate of the ducks, he is really wondering if there is some benevolent authority, some God, that takes care of humans just as the zoo employee takes care of the ducks. But the most common sense interpretation is simply that Holden's concern for the well-being of the ducks illustrates an important character trait, his compassion for all living things.

Another important symbol in *The Catcher in the Rye* is the glass cases in the Museum of Natural History. These dioramas display life-size figures of Indians weaving blankets and Eskimos catching fish. They are what Holden likes best in the museum because even if he went there a thousand times, the Eskimo would still be catching the same two fish and the Indian squaw would still be weaving the same blanket. They would not be different even though he, Holden, would have changed. Holden concludes that certain things should always stay the same: "You ought to be able to stick them in one of those big glass cases and just leave them alone" (122). Here we realize that Holden is troubled by change in general. He knows that he himself can't help changing as he grows up, but he wants the things he likes to be exempt from change. But eventually, at the end of the novel, during the carrousel scene, he overcomes this desire for immutability.

A symbol that illustrates a more adult side of Holden's character than the glass cases with the Indians and Eskimos is the cabin in or on the edge of the woods. At a first glance, this symbol seems to represent only his wish to escape from the world of the phonies and from the kind of upper-middle-class future his parents have mapped out for him. But a close analysis shows that there is more to the symbol than that.

The cabin appears in two versions. Holden comes up with the idea of escaping to a cabin in the woods for the first time when he tries to get Sally Hayes to run away with him to Massachusetts or Vermont. He tells he that they will stay in a cabin camp until their money runs out. Then he will get a job somewhere, and they will live by a brook, and eventually they might get married. At this point, Holden's escape plan is still very sketchy. Later, he comes up with a more elaborate plan which includes the second version of the cabin. This time he plans to hitchhike to somewhere way out West where it is very pretty and sunny and where nobody knows him. He will get a job at a filling station, and he will pretend to be a deaf-mute. That way, he won't have to have "any goddam stupid useless conversations with anybody" (198). If someone wants to talk to him, the person has to write him a note on a piece of paper. With the money he earns at the gas station Holden plans to build himself a little cabin on the edge of the woods but not right in the woods because he wants the cabin to be in a place that is sunny all the time. He will do all his own cooking, and later on, he will meet a beautiful girl who is also a deaf-mute, and they will get married. If they have any children, they will hide them and home-school them. Holden imagines that he will not want to come home to New York until he is about thirty-five or until someone in the family gets very sick and wants to see him before the person dies. That will be the only reason for him to leave his cabin. He plans to invite his family to come and visit him in his cabin, but if any of them do anything phony, he won't let them stay.

In retrospect, Holden realizes that the part of his plan about pretending to be a deaf-mute was crazy, but he stresses that he really did decide to go out West. We therefore need to take his plan seriously. When we do, we realize that both versions of his dream of living in a cabin away from society involve his plan to eventually get married. In other words, Holden is realistic enough to know that once he is an adult, he will not want to live alone. This aspect of the cabin symbolism reveals that despite his dream of escape, Holden is on the verge of accepting adulthood.

When Holden crosses the threshold between adolescence and adulthood, two symbols help us understand his inner change. Both symbols show up near the end of the novel. One is the obscene graffiti and the other is the carrousel in Central Park. In both cases, we see a change in Holden's attitude toward those symbols.

Holden's initial response to the obscene graffiti is to erase them, to pretend that they were never there. The first "Fuck you" that Holden sees on a wall in Phoebe's school is written in crayon, and so he has no trouble rubbing it out. But the second "Fuck you" is scratched into a wall with a knife, and Holden can't erase it. At this point Holden comes to the realization that even if he had a million years, he could not erase half the "Fuck you" signs in the world. And then he sees another "Fuck you" in one of his favorite places of refuge in New York, the Metropolitan Museum of Art. This is very depressing to him, and he realizes that he will never find "a place that's nice and peaceful" because there aren't any such places. He says that even if you think you have found such a place, "somebody'll sneak up and write 'Fuck you' right under your nose" (204).

The graffiti can be seen as symbols of all the negative things that Holden wants children to be protected from. But he comes to realize that they cannot be protected from all of them. When Holden still thought he wanted to be the catcher in the rye, he believed he could rub out all the "Fuck you" signs in the world. By the end of the novel he knows he can't. Moreover, he also knows that he cannot escape to a place that is free from "Fuck you" signs. In short, the ubiquitousness of the "Fuck you" signs is one of the reasons Holden gives up his dream of escaping to a cabin by the woods.

The carrousel in Central Park is a symbol that also suggests a change in Holden, but it is a more complex symbol than the obscene graffiti. There's an obvious aspect to the meaning of the carrousel, an aspect that Holden seems to be aware of, and a less obvious aspect that he seems unaware of.

The less obvious aspect of the carrousel's meaning has to do with Holden's telling Phoebe that he changed his mind and that he is not going away anywhere. They are walking out of the zoo at Central Park and toward the carrousel, and it is starting to rain. Holden hears the carrousel music long before the carrousel comes into sight. The song is "Oh, Marie!" which Holden says he heard "about fifty years ago" when he was a little kid (210). This is one thing he likes about carrousels, he says, they keep on playing the same songs. Here Holden is still associating the carrousel with his childish desire to have things always stay the same, like the dioramas in the Museum of Natural History.

But when Holden and Phoebe come to the carrousel, Holden's attitude changes. Phoebe wants the two of them to take a ride together, but Holden tells her that he'll just watch her. Then he buys Phoebe a ticket and sits down on one of the benches surrounding the carrousel where the parents of the other children on the carrousel are sitting. When the rain starts coming down hard, the other adults seek shelter, but Holden continues sitting on his bench. He gets very wet, but he says he didn't bother to get out of the rain because he suddenly felt very happy about watching Phoebe ride the carrousel. He explains: "It was just that she looked so damn *nice*, the way she kept going around and around in her blue coat and all" (213).

The carrousel is therefore a symbol that has more than one level of meaning. Although it awakes childhood memories in Holden, it helps him define himself as being no longer a child. Watching Phoebe ride the carrousel brings Holden a vicarious enjoyment similar to that of the parents of the other children on the carrousel. It seems that he is enjoying his first taste of what it is like to be an adult and that he is enjoying it so much that he doesn't mind getting soaked to the skin in the heavy December rain.

All this is confirmed by what Holden actually realizes about the symbolism of the carrousel. On this particular carrousel the children are supposed to lunge upward and try to pull down a golden ring. Holden says that he is afraid Phoebe might fall off the carrousel horse, but he stops himself from doing or saying anything. He has come to understand that when children want to go for the golden ring, we should not stop them. He says: ""f they fall off, they fall off, but it's bad if you say anything to them" (211). Holden here realizes that the carrousel represents life and grabbing for the gold ring represents the chances that children must take in order to grow up. When we see Holden allow Phoebe take her chances, we realize that he no longer wants to be the catcher in the rye and that he has come to accept adulthood.

THEMES AND INTERPRETATIONS

There aren't many twentieth-century novels that have been more frequently analyzed in print than *The Catcher in the Rye*. Among the hundreds of interpretations, four trends stand out. One is an historical approach which relates *The Catcher in the Rye* to Mark Twain's *The Adventures of Huckleberry Finn*. Another is a sociological approach which treats the novel as social criticism. A third approach is psychological and focuses on Holden's transition from adolescence to adulthood. And a fourth approach examines the moral and religious implications of the novel.

The first systematic comparison of *The Catcher in the Rye* and *The Adventures of Huckleberry Finn* is Edgar Branch's essay "Mark Twain and J.D. Salinger: A Study in Literary Continuity." Branch says that "the two novels are clearly related in narrative pattern and style, characterization of the hero and critical import" (217). Moreover, Branch argues that *"Huckleberry Finn* and *The Catcher in the Rye* share certain ethical and social attitudes. Yet Salinger's critical view assumes a cultural determinism that in *Huckleberry Finn*, although always present, permits freedom through self-guidance" (216). Like many early critics, Branch sees the ending of *The Catcher in the Rye* as pessimistic and that of *Huckleberry Finn* as optimistic. He writes: *"Huckleberry Finn*, in short, recognizes both necessity and freedom, the restrictions limiting moral accomplishment and its possibility. *The Catcher in the Rye* leaves us doubtful that the individual, even assisted by the analyst's best efforts, can ever truly escape the double trap of society and self" (214-215). What further contributes to the "underlying despair of Salinger's book," so Branch says, is that Holden has not matured or learned anything by the end of the novel and that "Holden wants to remain forever the catcher in the rye" (215).

Unlike Edgar Branch and most early critics, Carl F. Strauch sees the ending of *The Catcher in the Rye* as optimistic. In his essay, "Kings in the Back Row: Meaning Through Structure—A Reading of Salinger's *The Catcher in the Rye*," Strauch says that "the conclusion is neither pessimistic nor, for that matter, ironical in any sense perceived thus far" (47). Strauch argues that by the end of the novel, Holden has "miraculously wrought his own cure" (48) because he has accepted a sense of responsibility. Strauch says: "The conclusion is, therefore, optimistic and affirmative" (48).

As Strauch describes it, the meaning of the novel is both psychological and philosophical because *Catcher* is a story of an irresponsible young neurotic who dies a figurative death and is reborn as a new, healthy, and responsible individual. The support for this reading of the novel comes from a detailed analysis of what Strauch calls its "interlocking metaphorical structure" (48). This structure consists of four stages in the novel, Holden's "neurotic deterioration," his "symbolical death," his "spiritual awakening," and his "psychological self-cure" (48).

Several later interpretations have analyzed *The Catcher in the Rye* in more rigid psychoanalytical terms. James Bryan's essay, "The Psychological Structure *of The Catcher in the Rye*" is a Freudian analysis which defines Holden's neurosis as "a frantic need to save his sister from himself" (107). Bryan bases this notion on the psychoanalytical axiom that "a sister is often the first replacement for the mother as love object, and that normal maturation guides the boy from the sister to other women." However Holden has a serious problem because "Holden's sexuality is swaying precariously between reversion and maturation" (107). Fortunately, so Bryan contends, "Phoebe's responses to Holden's secret needs become the catalyst for both his breakdown and his recovery" (111).

More recently there have been Adlerian and Lacanian readings of *The Catcher in the Rye*. In the essay, "Adlerian Theory and Its Application to *The Catcher in the Rye*—Holden Caulfield," R.J. Huber explains that Adlerian psychoanalysts are always interested in knowing whether an individual "feels competent or inferior, and whether [s/he] strives with or without social interest in mind" (47). Huber's conclusion is that Holden "reveals deep-seated inferiority feelings and a compensatory striving for grandiosity" (48).

The most fashionable psychological study of the novel is James Mellard's essay "The Disappearing Subject: A Lacanian Reading of *The Catcher in the Rye*." Mellard shares Carl Strauch's view that Holden eventually cures himself. According to Mellard, Holden passes through the Lacanian stages of "alienation" and "separation" from the "Other" but eventually achieves symbolic wholeness with that "Other" (203-204). Here is how Mellard describes the moment when Holden becomes whole again: "Restored to the only sort of fullness that shall ever be available to one who has acceded to the Symbolic, Holden is gripped by joy at this moment. Sitting on a bench in the sudden rain, watching Phoebe go around on the carrousel, at this final moment of the main narrative, Holden feels unbounded pleasure, perhaps a Lacanian *jouissance*" (211). Reacting to the argument of earlier critics that when Holden tells his story, he is a patient in a mental institution, Mellard says that "on the evidence of the story he tells, he no longer has any real need for therapy. He would appear to be as healthy, as 'whole,' as sane as anyone ever might be" (211).

Many critics have assumed that when Holden tells his story, he is a patient in a mental institution. But as early as 1963, Warren French pointed out that there's no textual proof for that assumption. In his book *J.D. Salinger*, French says: "Even though Holden acknowledges being attended by a psychoanalyst at the end of the book, his breakdown is clearly not just–or even principally—mental" (108). French points out that Holden is physically ill and that "his run-down physical condition magnifies the pain" of his "emotional and intellectual problems" (109). French describes the plot as being partially Holden's quest for sympathy for his physical condition and for a place of peaceful refuge. Being denied this sympathy and refuge, Holden physically collapses. But as French notes, there is another story intertwined with that of Holden's physical breakdown and that is "the story of the breaking down of Holden's self-centeredness and his gradual acceptance of the world that has rejected him" (115). What Holden learns from his experiences is "the injunction that we must all love each other" (116). But French does not believe that Salinger develops "the idea of universal compassion" convincingly in the novel: "The trouble with compassion is that, although without it one cannot be a decent human being, it cannot by itself provide a person with the means of making himself useful.... Being simply a saint requires no education" (118).

The notion that Holden is some kind of a saint or even a Christ figure is advanced in several interpretations of *The Catcher in the Rye*. For instance, in his essay "The Saint as a Young Man: A Reappraisal of *The Catcher in the Rye*," Jonathan Baumbach argues that what Holden wants is "to be a saint—the protector and savior of innocence. But what he also wants ... is that someone prevent *his* fall" (56). For this reason, so Baumbach says, "Holden's real quest throughout the novel is for a spiritual father" (56). However, Holden does not find such a spiritual father: "The world, devoid of good fathers (authorities), becomes a soul-destroying chaos in which his survival is possible only through withdrawal into childhood, into fantasy, into psychosis" (57). Holden's savior turns out not to be a father figure but his ten-year-old sister Phoebe. Baumbach concludes: "The last scene, in which Holden, suffused with happiness, sits in the rain and watches Phoebe ride on the merry-go-round, is indicative not of his crack-up, as has been assumed, but of his redemption" (471).

Although some critics have noted that Holden is not an average adolescent because he comes from a very wealthy family, it wasn't until the mid-seventies that we got a socio-economic interpretation of *The Catcher in the Rye*. In the essay "Reviewers, Critics, and *The Catcher in the Rye*," Carol and Richard Ohmann offer a Marxist interpretation of the novel. They call *The Catcher in the Rye* "a case study in capitalist criticism" (119) and note that "Salinger wrote about power and wealth and reviewers and critics about good and evil and the problems of growing up" (122). The Ohmanns agree with previous critics that "Holden's sensitivity is the heart of the book," but they disagree with everyone else when it come to the question "What does he reject?" (129) Yes, it is phoniness that Holden rejects, but the Ohmanns contend that "this phoniness is rooted in the economic and social arrangements of capitalism, and in their concealment" (130). The two critics cite a number of passages to prove that "the novel's critique of class distinction may be found, not just between the lines of Holden's account, but in some of his most explicit comments on what's awry in his world" (131).

The Ohmanns conclude with a speculation as to what response Salinger expected from his readers: "Given Salinger's perception of what's wrong, there are three possible responses: do the best you can with this society; work for a better one; flee society altogether" (134). The Ohmanns fault Salinger for Holden's response to this choice: "When Holden imagines an adult self he can think only of the Madison Avenue executive or the deaf-mute, this society or no society" (134). And yet, the two critics give Salinger credit for creating an accurate picture of social reality in mid-century America: "*The Catcher in the Rye* is among other things a serious critical mimesis of bourgeois life in the Eastern United States, ca. 1950—of snobbery, privilege, class injury, culture as a badge of superiority, sexual exploitation, education subordinated to status, warped social feeling, competitiveness, stunted human possibility, the list could go on" (135).

The Ohmanns here map out a list of socio-economic themes that could be profitably pursued in further interpretations of *The Catcher in the Rye*, but very little such criticism has been published in the meantime. In fact, since the mid-seventies, very little has been written about the novel that has not been said before. In addition to the Lacanian interpretation of James Mellard that I mentioned before, the only notable studies have been essays on the reception of *The Catcher in the Rye* by readers in foreign countries and by female readers in the United States.

A little known fact in Salinger lore is that *The Catcher in the Rye*—in the translation of Nobel Laureate Heinrich Böll (*Der Fänger im Roggen*)—was required reading in the West German secondary schools for over 20 years. In an article entitled "Jerome D. Salinger's Novel *The Catcher in the Rye* as Required Reading in Upper Level German Classes" (1968), Fritz Kraul defends that choice. Kraul notes that "Salinger's novel continues a narrative tradition which was based on novels of social criticism by writers such as Upton Sinclair and Sinclair Lewis." As Kraul describes it, *The Catcher in the Rye* "depicts the conflict between the individual and society, and in particular the difficulties which face today's American adolescents" (79). The novel is valuable because "it affords a picture of contemporary American society" and because Holden Caulfield's story is that of a "protest against society" (81). The chief targets of the protest are society's "conformity and the pressure to succeed" (83). As positive values the novel holds up "the selflessness of the two nuns, the courage of James Castle, and the patience of Holden's late brother Allie" (86).

More recently, *The Catcher in the Rye* has become the subject of gender criticism. In her essay, "Holden Caulfield: C'est Moi," Mary Suzanne Schriber points out that almost all previous criticism on *The Catcher in the Rye* was written by males. She cites a number of critics who admit that they identify with Holden and therefore assume that Holden's experiences and view of life are universal. Therefore, "the popularity and the ascription of broad significance and exceptional literary importance to *The Catcher in the Rye* can be traced to … assumptions that the male is the normative" (235). These assumptions, so Schriber argues, have led male critics to accord *The Catcher in the Rye* the status of a classic of America literature. Schriber disagrees because she claims that female readers do not identify with Holden the way male readers do because "an adolescent male WASP is not automatically nature's designated spokesperson for us all" (236). In short, Schriber argues that once the responses of female readers are considered, *The Catcher in the Rye* will no longer be rated as highly as it has been in the past.

CONCLUSION

Despite some feminist protests, there is almost universal agreement that *The Catcher in the Rye* is a classic of twentieth-century American literature. The novel deserves that distinction because it is an extremely well constructed piece of verbal art. But like all human creations, it is by no means perfect. What grates on some readers is that in two separate scenes taking place the same evening Holden's roommate Stradlater and his dorm neighbor Ackley both happen to trim their finger and toe nails in Holden's presence, that Holden pointlessly summarizes a "putrid" movie he has seen, that Mr. Antolini pontificates too much and says too little, and, above all, that Holden incessantly repeats phrases such as "it really kills me" and "if you want to know the truth." But these are quibbles over what not everyone thinks of as weaknesses. What makes up for these weaknesses (if they are such) are the novel's strengths in narrative structure, characterization, and symbolism.

While early critics of the novel stressed the episodic nature of the plot and were unable to see any development in Holden's character, it has by now been firmly established that the episodes of the plot are held together by several strands of narrative development and that one of them is a pattern of character change. In short, Holden is not a static character but experiences an inner change, and this change is a movement from adolescence to adulthood, from his immature desire to be the catcher in the rye to his mature understanding that if children want to grab for the gold ring, we should not stop them but let them take the risk of falling.

Another strength of the novel is the characterization of Holden as a very complex human being who is at once generous and materialistic, illiterate and well-read, an atheist and a fan of Jesus. Despite these contradictions, one thing stands out about him and that is his unusual kindness. This kindness extends to pimply fellow students, to ugly girls, to underage prostitutes, to nuns who will never eat at swanky restaurants, and to the freezing ducks in Central Park. And even though the minor characters are designed chiefly to bring out specific personality traits in Holden, most of them assume a life of their own in the reader's imagination, from the "muckle-mouthed" Jane Gallagher who keeps her kings in the back row during checkers to the hairy-bellied pimp Maurice who snaps his fingers very hard at the crotch of Holden's pajamas before beating him up.

Perhaps the most important and the most impressive aspect of the novel is its symbolism. None of the symbols are artificial, all of them occur naturally in the scenes in which they appear, and most of them allow several different interpretations. The most notable examples are Holden's hunting hat and the ducks in Central Park. Moreover, some of the symbols are constructed in such a way that the change in their meaning parallels the change in Holden's outlook. This is the case with the obscene graffiti in Phoebe's school and with the carrousel in Central Park. Parallel to the change in the meaning of those symbols, the central metaphor of the catcher in the rye also changes its connotation from positive to negative.

Because of the multi-layered narrative structure, the complex characterization of Holden Caulfield, the many memorable minor characters, and the rich symbolism, *The Catcher in the Rye* allows more interpretations than the average novel. This thematic richness is the ultimate proof that this novel is a work of art of the first rank.

Twenty-five years after the publication of *The Catcher in the Rye*, a critic noted that so much criticism had been written about it that it was hard to imagine that anyone could say anything new. And yet that same year, in 1976, Carol and Richard Ohmann published a Marxist analysis and pointed out a number of socio-economic themes that had not yet been pursued.

At this writing—51 years after the publication of *The Catcher in the Rye*—some of the themes pointed out by the Ohmanns still have not been explored, for instance the theme of social class and privilege and the theme of education subordinated to status. Also, we do not yet have any good psychological analyses of the novel. What we have so far are efforts to use the novel to illustrate psychological concepts rather than efforts to use psychological concepts to interpret the novel. Another approach to *The Catcher in the Rye* that has been neglected so far is the reader response approach. This is an approach that the novel definitely calls for because Holden Caulfield not only addresses a specific kind of reader, but his narrative is full of gaps for the reader to fill.

WORKS CITED

Baumbach, Jonathan. "The Saint as a Young Man: A Reappraisal of *The Catcher in the Rye*." *Modern Language Quarterly* 25 (December 1964): 461-472. Rpt. in Salzberg 55-64.

Behrman, N.S. "The Vision of the Innocent" [Review]. *New Yorker* (11 August 1951): 64-68.

Branch, Edgar. "Mark Twain and J.D. Salinger: A Study in Literary Continuity." *American Quarterly* 9 (Summer 1957): 144-58. Rpt. in Grunwald 205-217.

Breit, Harvey. "Reader's Choice" [Review]. *Atlantic Monthly* 188 (August 1951): 82. Rpt. in Marsden 6-7.

Bryan, James. "The Psychological Structure of *The Catcher in the Rye*." *Publications of the Modern Language Association* 89 (1974): 1065-1074. Rpt. in Salzberg 101-117.

Burger, Nash K. "The Catcher in the Rye" [Review]. *New York Times* (16 July 1951): 19.

French, Warren. "The Artist as a Very Nervous Young Man." In *J.D. Salinger.* New York: Twayne, 1963, 102-129.

Goodman, Anne. "Mad About Children" [Review]. *New Republic* 125 (16 July 1951): 20-21. Rpt. in Salzberg 23-24.

Grunwald, Henry A., ed. *Salinger: A Critical and Personal Portrait.* New York: Harper, 1962.

Hassan, Ihab. "Rare Quixotic Gesture: The Fiction of J.D. Salinger." *Western Review* 21 (Summer 1957): 261-280. Rpt. in Grunwald 138-163.

Heiserman, Arthur, and James E. Miller. "J.D. Salinger: Some Crazy Cliff." *Western Humanities Review* 10 (Spring 1956): 129-137. Rpt. in Grunwald 196-205.

Huber, R.J. "Adlerian Theory and Its Application to *The Catcher in the Rye*—Holden Caulfield." In *Psychological Perspectives on Literature: Freudian Dissidents and Non-Freudians.* Ed. Joseph Natoli. New York: Archon, 1984, 43-52.

Hughes, Riley. "The Catcher in the Rye" [Review]. *Catholic World* 174 (November 1951): 154. Rpt. in Salzberg 31.

Jones, Ernest. "Case History of All of Us" [Review]. *Nation* 173 (1 September 1951): 176. Rpt. in Salzberg 24-25.

Kraul, Fritz. "Jerome D. Salingers Roman 'Der Fänger im Roggen' als Pflichtlektüre im Deutschunterricht der Oberstufe." *Der Roman im Unterricht* 20 (1968): 79-86.

Longstreth, Morris. "Review of *The Catcher in the Rye*." *Christian Science Monitor* (19 July 1951): 7. Rpt. in Salzberg 30-31.

Marsden, Malcolm, ed. *If You Really Want To Know: A Catcher Casebook.* Chicago: Scott Foresman, 1963.

Maxwell, William. "J.D. Salinger." *Book of the Month Club News* (July 1951): 5-6.

Mellard, James. "The Disappearing Subject: A Lacanian Reading of *The Catcher in the Rye*." Rpt. in Salzberg 197-214.

Ohmann, Carol, and Richard Ohmann. "Reviewers, Critics, and *The Catcher in the Rye*." *Critical Inquiry* 3 (Autumn 1976): 15-37. Rpt. in Salzberg 119-140.

Peterson, Virgilia. "Three Days in the Bewildering World of an Adolescent" [Review]. *New York Herald Tribune Book Review* (15 July 1951): 3. Rpt. in Marsden 3-4.

Salzberg, Joel, ed. *Critical Essays on Salinger's The Catcher in the Rye.* Boston: G.K. Hall, 1990.

Schriber, Mary Suzanne. "Holden Caulfield: C'est Moi." In *Critical Essays on Salinger's The Catcher in the Rye.* Ed. Joel Salzberg. Boston: G.K. Hall, 1990, 226-238.

Smith, Harrison. "Manhattan Ulysses, Junior" [Review]. *Saturday Review of Literature* 34 (14 July 1951): 12-13. Rpt. in Salzberg 28-30.

Steiner, George. "The Salinger Industry." *Nation* 189 (14 November 1959): 360-363. Rpt. in Grunwald 82-85.

Stern, James. "Aw, the World's a Crummy Place" [Parody/Review]. *New York Times Book Review* (15 July 1951): 5. Rpt. in Marsden 2-3.

Strauch, Carl F. "Kings in the Back Row: Meaning Through Structure—A Reading of Salinger's *The Catcher in the Rye*." *Wisconsin Studies in Contemporary*

Literature 2 (Winter 1961): 5-30. Rpt. in *Salinger's "Catcher in the Rye":
Clamor vs. Criticism.* Ed Harold P. Simonson and Philip E. Hager. Boston:
D.C. Heath, 1963, 46-62.

SUGGESTIONS FOR FURTHER READING

Costello, Donald P. "The Language of *The Catcher in the Rye.*" *American Speech* 34
 (October 1959): 172-181. Rpt. in Salzberg 44-53.
Lundquist, James. "Against Obscenity: *The Catcher in the Rye.*" In *J.D. Salinger.*
 New York: Ungar 1979, 37-68.
Oldsey, Bernard. "The Movies in the Rye." *College English* 23 (December 1961):
 209-215. Rpt. in Salzberg 92-99.
Seng, Peter J. "The Fallen Idol: The Immature World of Holden Caulfield." *College
 English* 32 (December 1962): 203-209. Rpt. in Marsden 73-81.
Shulevitz, Judith. "Holden Reconsidered and All." *New York Times Book Review* (29
 July 2001): 23.
Vanderbilt, Kermit. "Symbolic Resolution in *The Catcher in the Rye:* The Cap, the
 Carrousel, and the American West." *Western Humanities Review* 17 (Sum-
 mer 1963): 271-277.
Weinberg, Helen. "J.D. Salinger's Holden and Seymour and the Spiritual Activist
 Hero." In *The New Novel in America: The Kafkan Mode in Contemporary
 Fiction.* Ithaca, NY: Cornell UP, 1970, 141-164.

Chapter 4

Nine Stories

My sister ... was drinking her milk, and all of a sudden I saw that *she* was God and the *milk* was God. I mean, all she was doing was pouring God into God.

Teddy McArdle in "Teddy"

After *The Catcher in the Rye* appeared in 1951, Salinger continued to publish short stories in the *New Yorker* and other magazines. In 1953, he collected what he considered his best short work and titled the collection *Nine Stories*. Seven of these pieces had appeared in the *New Yorker* between 1948 and 1953, and two of them had been published elsewhere: "Down at the Dinghy" in *Harper's* in 1949, and "De Daumier-Smith's Blue Period" in *World Review* in 1952. Some critics hailed the collection *Nine Stories* as an even greater achievement than *The Catcher in the Rye*. The two stories that received more critical attention than the rest are "A Perfect Day for Bananafish" and "For Esmé—with Love and Squalor."

Readers who come to *Nine Stories* after reading *The Catcher in the Rye* will be surprised at how different these stories are from the novel. First of all, the central characters in all but two of the nine stories are adults rather than adolescents or children, and the stories deal with such grown-up themes as unhappy marriages, child rearing, the psychological damage caused by war, marital infidelity, and Eastern philosophy. Secondly, the vision of life in the earlier of the nine stories is a pessimistic one while that in the later stories foreshadow the more optimistic and religious outlook of Salinger's Glass Family Series. And finally—unlike *The Catcher in the Rye*—most of the nine stories are told by third person narrators, and the two stories that are in the first person have adult narrators who sound more like Buddy Glass in the Glass Family Series than Holden Caulfield in *The Catcher in the Rye*.

CRITICAL RECEPTION

Predictably, most of the reviews of *Nine Stories* compared the book to *The Catcher in the Rye* and found it very different from the novel. In talking about the central characters in the nine stories, the anonymous reviewer for *Newsweek* noted that "even the mildest of Salinger's nine seems to verge on being an ogre" and that in some stories Salinger "reaches a new level of nightmarish reality" (98). To illustrate this point, the reviewer mentions the suicide of the protagonist in "A Perfect Day for Bananafish," the death of the title character in "Teddy," and the adulterous affair in "Pretty Mouth and Green My Eyes." Other reviewers called the stories "somber" and even "frightening," but most of them had positive things to say about Salinger's craftsmanship as a storyteller.

The most extravagant praise of *Nine Stories* came from novelist Eudora Welty who reviewed the collection for the *New York Times Book Review.* Welty begins with these words: "J.D. Salinger's writing is original, first-rate, serious and beautiful." She also says that the stories reveal a "sensitive eye," an "incredibly good ear," and an ephemeral quality of "grace." And although the stories are about "heartbreak" which is chiefly due to "the absence of love," there is "not a trace of sentimentality" in them (109). In fact, Welty liked *Nine Stories* better than *The Catcher in the Rye* because "all of [that novel's] virtues can be had in a short story by the same author where they are somehow more at home" (110).

Reviews of *Nine Stories* in other papers and magazines were not quite as enthusiastic as that of Eudora Welty. For instance, in his review for *Commonweal,* Seymour Krim said that two flaws in the stories are that "Salinger is sometimes over-sophisticated in his surface technique" and that "Salinger has an unsure grasp of the meaning of his material" (66). And in the *New York Herald Tribune Book Review,* Gene Baro credited Salinger with "considerable skill in telling his stories" but he found that "a few of these pieces seem uncommonly thin" (6).

Academic critics, however, saw more depth and a clearer vision of life in *Nine Stories* than did newspaper and magazine reviewers. Arthur Mizener, for example, said that while "*The Catcher in the Rye* does not quite come off as a whole; the best of these stories do." He explains: "They have, as the novel did not, a controlling intention which is at once complex enough for Mr. Salinger's awareness and firm enough to give it a purpose" (20). Mizener singled out "A Perfect Day for Bananafish" and "De Daumier-Smith's Blue Period" as the best stories in the collection and said that they "and large units of several other stories are better than anything in *The Catcher in the Rye*" (20). Ihab Hassan had similar high praise for *Nine Stories*. He placed the collection in the context of Salinger's development as a writer and suggested that the phase of his career in which he wrote *Nine Stories* "marks the level of his most sustained achievement" (144). This achievement reveals itself in "a constant energy of perception and irritation of the moral sense." What irritates Salinger, Hassan said, is "the primary fact of mendacity" because the stories all depict "a world which has lost its access to the simple truth" (144).

NARRATIVE STRUCTURE AND POINT OF VIEW

What the narrative structure of *Nine Stories* has in common with that of *The Catcher in the Rye* is that Salinger seems more interested in creating reader interest through fascinating characters than through gripping incidents. Moreover, when we examine the structure of the stories, we get the impression that Salinger was determined to get away from conventional patterns of storytelling. This is suggested by the fact that the majority of the stories do not have an obvious conflict and a clearly defined resolution. Instead, they develop their meaning in terms of subtle inner changes in the central characters. These inner changes are not explained to us by narrators but developed in terms of dialogue. In fact, most of the stories consist largely of dialogue with very few narrative passages. The two exceptions are the first person narratives of "The Laughing Man" and "De Daumier-Smith's Blue Period."

Because the narrators in *Nine Stories* rarely explain what is going on inside the minds of the characters, we need to pay very close attention to what the characters say and what their body language reveals. In many cases, the characters' dialogue and body language tell us that they are coming to important insights or are experiencing some kind of inner change. Because these insights or inner changes of the central characters are not readily apparent on a first reading, the endings of most of the stories seem inconclusive or even surprising.

However, the surprise endings of "A Perfect Day for Bananafish" and "Teddy" are not merely narrative tricks as in some of Salinger's apprentice pieces. Instead, these surprise endings seem to be designed to make us re-read the stories in order to find explanations for the unexpected behavior of the central characters.

At the end of "Bananafish," the suicide of Seymour Glass comes as a total surprise. But when we re-read the story, we will find that Seymour's decision to kill himself is the resolution of a conflict between Seymour and his wife Muriel. This conflict is easy to miss because the only time we see the couple together is in the last paragraph of the story when Seymour enters the hotel room where Muriel is asleep. He pulls a pistol from a suitcase, sits down on the unoccupied twin bed, and fires a bullet through his right temple. However, the conflict is developed indirectly in a phone conversation that Muriel has with her mother. From that phone conversation we find out that Seymour has called Muriel "Miss Spiritual Tramp of 1948" because she reads magazine article about sex rather than the poetry of Seymour's favorite poet. Moreover, we also learn that Seymour has just been released from the psychiatric ward of an Army hospital and that he has attempted to commit suicide before. Also, a second reading will alert us to the importance of the bananafish story that Seymour tells the three-year-old Sybil Carpenter just before he kills himself. That story is about greedy fish who swim into a banana hole and eat so many bananas that they can't get back out through the narrow entrance. Trapped in the banana hole, they contract banana fever and die. After we re-read the story, Seymour's suicide no longer seems unmotivated, even if we cannot immediately identify the cause of his despair.

The surprise ending of "Teddy" also makes us want to re-read the story in search of clues. At the end of that story, the ten-year-old child prodigy Teddy McArdle fractures his skull and dies instantaneously when his six-year-old sister Booper pushes him into an empty swimming pool. When we re-read the story, we will find that Teddy's death is actually a suicide. From Teddy's conversation with the education professor Bob Nicholson, we learn that Teddy is a child prodigy, that he can foresee the future, and that he believes in reincarnation. For instance, he knows when his death will occur, for he writes in his diary: "It will either happen today or February 14, 1958 when I am sixteen" (182). He also knows how his death will occur, for he tells Nicholson that his sister might push him into the empty swimming pool. Therefore, when Teddy walks toward the empty pool, we realize that he deliberately chose the earlier of the two dates for his death. A re-reading of the story will also reveal the reason for Teddy's suicide. He wants to move on to his next incarnation because he finds that "it's very hard to meditate and live a spiritual life in America. People think you're a freak if you try to" (188).

Two stories that seem to be character sketches rather than stories proper are "Uncle Wiggily in Connecticut" and "Pretty Mouth and Green My Eyes." "Uncle Wiggily" is the account of a drunken afternoon that two former college roommates, Eloise and Mary Jane, spend together. Mary Jane is divorced and Eloise feels trapped in an unhappy marriage. They reminisce about their college days, and Eloise talks at length about her relationship with a soldier whom she found unusually sweet, funny, and very different from her husband Lew. The soldier's name was Walt, and he was killed in an accident at the end of World War II. The reminiscences of the two women are interrupted three times, twice when Eloise's small daughter Ramona comes into the house from playing outside, and a third time when Eloise goes to Ramona's bedroom later on to see if she's asleep. Throughout, Eloise is unkind to her daughter (probably because Ramona looks a lot like her father whom Eloise despises), but after she yells at Ramona in her bedroom, Eloise recognizes her own unkindness and starts to cry. The story ends when Eloise wakes up Mary Jane, who has passed out in the living room, and asks her what she, Eloise, was like when she was in college: "'I was a nice girl,' she pleaded, 'wasn't I?'" (38). This ending doesn't resolve any conflict, nor is it clear whether or not it signals an inner change in Eloise. This apparent open-endedness forces us to re-read the story in order to make sense of it.

Upon re-reading "Uncle Wiggily in Connecticut," we find that Eloise comes to the realization that she has indeed become "hard as nails," as Mary Jane puts it (23). Re-reading the story also makes us realize—but it is questionable if Eloise shares this insight—that Eloise's negative attitude toward her husband Lew and her daughter Ramona is due to her inability to let go of her dead lover Walt.

In "Pretty Mouth and Green My Eyes," we are also likely to miss the subtle inner change of the central character at a first reading. The story consists almost entirely of two phone conversations between two colleagues in a New York City law firm, Lee and Arthur. Lee, the older of the two, is in bed with Arthur's wife, Joan. Arthur calls Lee because Joan has disappeared from a party that the three attended together, and Arthur is worried about her. Lee tries to reassure Arthur by saying that Joan probably went home with another couple to have a few more drinks. Having overheard Lee's end of the conversation, Joan tells him that she feels "like an absolute dog" but that Lee was "marvelous" in reassuring Arthur. While Joan is still in bed with Lee, Arthur calls back to report that Joan just came home.

When we first read this story, we have a hard time deciding who the central character is. It could be any one of the three, Lee, Arthur, or Joan. No matter whom we pick, the story still seems primarily concerned in developing the central character as a negative model of behavior. However, when we re-read the story, we will find that Lee is the central character because he seems to come to an insight while Arthur and Joan do not. Lee's responses to both Arthur and Joan show that he is disgusted with his own adulterous behavior. The most obvious clue is that he gets quite brusque with Joan and that he tells her he doesn't think he was so "marvelous" on the phone with Arthur.

Three stories whose narrative structure is conventional are "Just Before the War with the Eskimos," "Down at the Dinghy," and "De Daumier-Smith's Blue Period." In "Just Before the War," the fifteen-year-old Ginnie insists that her tennis partner Selena owes her money for cab fare back from the tennis courts. She follows Selena into her parents' apartment and waits for Selena to wake up her mother from her afternoon nap so she can get the money from her. While Ginnie is waiting, she has two conversations, one with Selena's brother Franklin and another with Franklin's friend Eric. During her conversation with Franklin, Ginnie develops a crush on him. This becomes obvious when she refuses to take the cab money from Selena and invites herself over to Selena's house for that evening instead of going to the movies as she had originally planned. Thus Ginnie's infatuation with Franklin resolves her conflict with Selena. However, the resolution of the conflict is ironic for two reasons. One reason is that when Ginnie says good-bye to Selena, she finds out that Franklin is twenty-four-years old and will probably not be interested in a fifteen-year-old girl. The other reason is that Ginnie's infatuation with Franklin makes her unable to see that Franklin's friend Eric is a homosexual and that Franklin might be his lover.

In "Down at the Dinghy," the core of the narrative structure is the conflict between Boo Boo Tannenbaum and her four-year-old son Lionel. Lionel is sitting in the family's small sailboat that is tied to a dock, and he is pretending to be running away from home. Boo Boo tries to discover why he wants to run away and to console him, but Lionel rebuffs her. Boo Boo finally finds out that Lionel wants to run away because he overheard Sandra, the family's maid, refer to his father as "a big—sloppy—kike." But Boo Boo also finds out that Lionel thinks a "kike" is "one of those things that go up in the *air*.... With *string* you hold" (86). As the conflict between Boo Boo and her son Lionel is resolved, we realize that in addition to the central conflict between Boo Boo and Lionel, there is a more subtle and unresolved minor conflict between the Tannenbaums and their anti-Semitic maid Sandra.

The narrative structure of "De Daumier-Smith's Blue Period" is even more conventional than that of "Just Before the War with the Eskimos" and "Down at the Dinghy." The plot in "De Daumier" culminates in a clearly-marked climax, a moment when the central character experiences an epiphany, a moment of transcendent insight. In fact, the narrator-protagonist John Smith even talks about having had an "extraordinary experience, one that still strikes me as having been quite transcendent" (163). John Smith works as an instructor for a correspondence art school and becomes romantically interested in one of his students, a nun by the name of Sister Irma. He plots to meet her and seduce her, but he changes his mind after his transcendent experience. That experience occurs as he looks into the show window of an orthopedic appliance store and watches a woman changing a truss on a wooden dummy. When the woman sees him watching her, she stumbles and falls down. As she gets back up to finish her task, Smith experiences a flash of light and says in retrospect: "Blinded and frightened—I had to put my hand on the glass to keep my balance" (164). When Smith gets his sight back, the woman is gone from the show window "leaving behind her a shimmering field of exquisite, twice-blessed, enamel flowers" (164). After this Experience (Smith capitalizes the word), he writes in his diary: "I am giving Sister Irma her freedom to follow her own destiny" (164). While the narrative structure of "De Daumier-Smith's Blue Period" is conventional because the plot development culminates in an epiphany, it is still far from clear what that epiphany means, and—as with most of Salinger's stories—we find ourselves compelled to re-read it in order to get a better understanding than a first reading can provide.

In terms of point of view, three of the nine stories are unusual. They are "The Laughing Man," "De Daumier-Smith's Blue Period," and "For Esmé—with Love and Squalor." In "Laughing Man" and "Daumier-Smith" we get two different points of view, and in "Esmé" we get three.

Although "The Laughing Man" and "De Daumier-Smith's Blue Period" are both told from a first person point of view, we get a double perspective because the adult narrators tell us about events that happened when they were younger. Both narrators report on how they reacted to the events when they first occurred, and they also comment on them in retrospect, as adults.

"The Laughing Man" takes us back to 1928 when the anonymous narrator was nine years old (as were J.D. Salinger and Buddy Glass who were also born in 1919). Back then, the narrator of the story and 24 other young boys called themselves the "Comanche Club" and worshipped their Chief, a young law student by the name of John Gedsudski. Gedsudski was working his way through law school by organizing after-school and weekend activities for middle-class boys from Manhattan. On weekends he took the boys hiking in Van Cortlandt Park or camping in the Palisades in New Jersey. On weekdays he divided the boys into baseball or football teams in Central Park. But most importantly, after every outing, he told them installments of a story he made up as he went along, and that is the story of the Laughing Man. The Laughing Man is a hideously deformed master criminal with whom the boys all identify passionately.

The boys are terribly shocked one day when Gedsudski—without any apparent provocation—suddenly starts swearing at them and ends the ongoing story by making the Laughing Man die a gruesome death. In retrospect, the narrator understands that Gedsudski's apparent personality change and the sudden death of the Laughing Man in his serial story were due to Gedsudski's break-up with his girlfriend Mary Hudson.

In this story, Salinger handles the point of view in such a way that the reader can tell that John and Mary were lovers even though the narrator says, "I had no idea what was going on between the Chief and Mary Hudson" (70). When the narrator was a nine-year-old, he accepted Mary in the baseball line-up of the Comanches because she was a spectacular hitter. It was not clear to him that she meant much more to John Gedsudski. Therefore, after Mary ended her relationship with John, the nine-year-old boy couldn't see any connection between the death of that relationship and the death of the Laughing Man in Gedsudski's story. Looking back as an adult, he sees the connection and so does the reader.

In "De Daumier-Smith's Blue Period," the distance between the adult narrator and his younger self is not as great as it is in "The Laughing Man" because John Smith was nineteen at the time the events of the story took place. We sense that John Smith was tempted to begin his story with the first words from F. Scott Fitzgerald's *The Great Gatsby,* "In my younger and more vulnerable years..." (5). Instead, he begins his story by explaining that he was an art student in France, that he applied for a job at a correspondence art school in Montreal, Canada, and that he passed himself off as the twenty-nine-year-old cousin of the French painter Honoré Daumier.

The adult narrator delights in reporting his naive thoughts and lack of perceptiveness as a nineteen-year-old. For instance, he tried to ingratiate himself with his Japanese employers, Mr. and Mrs. Yashoto, by claiming that he was a student of Buddhism only to find that they were Presbyterians. He also reports that night after night, "one or the other of the Yashotos began to moan in his or her sleep, just the other side of [his] wall." He didn't realize that the Yashotos were making love, and he says that what he heard was "a high broken moan" which seemed to come "less from an adult than from either a tragic, subnormal infant or a small malformed animal" (141).

After the narrator very seriously tells us of the "transcendent experience" he had in front of the orthopedic appliance store, he undercuts the effect that this experience had on him by telling us that after the correspondence art school closed down, he spent the next six or eight weeks "investigating that most interesting of all summer-active animals, the American Girl in Shorts" (165).

The most unusual of the *Nine Stories* in terms of point of view is "For Esmé—with Love and Squalor." In that story, we get three points of view. The first half of the story is told in the first person by a narrator who has been invited to attend the wedding of Esmé, a British girl whom he met when she was thirteen and he was stationed at an American army base in England. In this part of the story, we already get two points of view, that of the middle-aged civilian narrator and that of the young soldier. The story of the narrator's wartime meeting with Esmé, whose father had recently been killed in the war, ends with Esmé telling the narrator: "I hope you return from the war with all your faculties intact" (103).

In the second half of the story, which takes place in the South of Germany after the end of the war, the point of view changes again. At the beginning of this part of the story, the narrator says: "I'm still around, but from here on in, for reasons I'm not at liberty to disclose, I've disguised myself so cunningly that even the cleverest reader will fail to recognize me" (103). The narrator not only disguises himself as "Staff Sergeant X" but he also switches to a third person omniscient point of view.

The reason for the disguise and the switch in point of view is that the narrator has not come through the war with all his faculties intact. He has suffered a nervous breakdown and he apparently doesn't want to talk about that experience in the first person. Although Sergeant X has been treated at an Army hospital, his hands are still shaking, one side of his face is still twitching, and he is afraid he will have another nervous collapse. But when Esmé sends him her dead father's military wristwatch and wants him to wear it as "a lucky talis-man," Sergeant X believes he stands a good chance of overcoming the trauma he has suffered.

The rest of the nine stories are more conventional in their narrative perspec-tive than "Esmé." In fact, in this respect they are less daring than such uncol-lected stories as "The Varioni Brothers," "The Inverted Forest," and "Blue Mel-ody." For the record: six of the nine stories are told in the third person, two in the first person, and one shifts from first to third. It is important to note that four of the third person narratives are told from a mostly objective point of view. These four stories are "A Perfect Day for Bananafish," "Uncle Wiggily in Connecticut," "Pretty Mouth and Blue My Eyes," and "Teddy."

Salinger was attracted to the third person objective point of view from the very beginning of his writing career and was then quite obviously imitating the grand master of that type of storytelling, Ernest Hemingway. One of the hall-marks of the way in which Hemingway handled this point of view was to tell us that a character in a dialogue was unresponsive to something the other person said. In Hemingway's Nick Adams stories, for example, the phrase "Nick said nothing" usually means that Nick doesn't agree with or is upset about what the other person has just said. We get echoes of this third person objective tech-nique in *Nine Stories*. For instance, in "A Perfect Day for Bananafish," Seymour Glass tells the three-year-old Sybil Carpenter that he likes her friend Sharon Lipschutz because she never uses balloon sticks to poke little dogs as Sybil does. The narrator describes Sybil's reaction by saying, "Sybil was si-lent" (15). Like Hemingway in many of his stories, Salinger here forces us to interpret a character's silence. And, as in Hemingway's stories, such silences usually are signs of negative reactions. Similarly, in the story "Teddy," the title character, a famous child prodigy, explains to the education professor Bob Nicholson that according to Hindu philosophy everything is God and that when his little sister was drinking milk, "all she was doing was pouring God into God." The narrator then tells us, "Nicholson didn't say anything" (189). Again the silence indicates a negative reaction.

By using the third person objective point of view, Salinger makes us partici-pate in creating the meaning of his stories. Rather than having his narrators tell us what his characters are thinking or feeling, Salinger makes us interpret the characters' body language, examine the way they express their thoughts, and guess at the thoughts they are trying to keep to themselves.

CHARACTERIZATION AND STYLE

At a first glance, *Nine Stories* seems to deal mostly with children and adolescents. There's the three-year-old Sybil Carpenter in "A Perfect Day for Bananafish," the four-year-old Ramona Wengler in "Uncle Wiggily in Connecticut," the fifteen-year-old Ginnie Maddox in "Just before the War with the Eskimos," the unnamed adult narrator recalling his experiences as a nine-year-old in "The Laughing Man," the four-year-old Lionel Tannenbaum in "Down at the Dinghy," the thirteen-year-old Esmé and her five-year-old brother Charles in "For Esmé—With Love and Squalor," the nineteen-year-old John Smith in "De Daumier-Smith's Blue Period," and the ten-year-old Teddy McArdle and his six-year-old sister Booper in "Teddy."

However, only one child and two adolescents—the ten-year-old Teddy McArdle, the fifteen-year-old Ginnie Mannox and the nineteen-year-old John Smith—are actually the central characters in their stories. The other children and adolescents function as sounding boards for the protagonists, as younger versions of the narrator's selves, or as the catalysts for the protagonist's character change just as Phoebe does for Holden in *The Catcher in the Rye*. This is particularly obvious in "A Perfect Day for Bananafish" when Seymour Glass tells the three-year-old Sybil Carpenter the story of the bananafish who die because of their own greed; in "Uncle Wiggily in Connecticut" when the four-year-old Ramona makes her mother realize that she, the mother, is no longer a "nice girl" but has become "hard as nails;" and in "For Esmé—with Love and Squalor" when the spontaneous affection of the thirteen-year-old Esmé and her five-year-old brother Charles give Sergeant X the hope that he may once again become a man "with all his faculties intact."

The six central characters who are adults are a mixed group. Four of them are males and two are females, and they range in age from the twenty-five-year old Boo Boo Tannenbaum in "Down at the Dinghy" to the gray-haired lawyer Lee in "Pretty Mouth and Green My Eyes." But what they have in common is that they all come from the upper middle class.

Among the central characters in *Nine Stories,* four stand out because they are extraordinary people. They are at odds with those around them because they are exceptionally sensitive or exceptionally spiritual or both. This is true for Seymour Glass in "Bananafish," Sergeant X in "For Esmé," John Smith in "Daumier-Smith," and Teddy McArdle in "Teddy."

However, over half of the characters in *Nine Stories* are average individuals whose experiences are shown to be representative rather than exceptional. This is true for Eloise Wengler in "Uncle Wiggily," Ginnie Mannox in "Just Before the War," John Gedsudski in "The Laughing Man," Boo Boo Tannenbaum in "Down at the Dinghy," and the lawyer Lee in "Pretty Mouth." The experiences of these characters are exemplary, and—as I will show later—this makes the themes in their stories quite different from those in the stories with central characters who are extraordinary individuals.

As far as the techniques of characterization in *Nine Stories* are concerned, they vary according to the narrative perspective in each story. But it seems that when he wrote *Nine Stories,* Salinger still believed that a storyteller should be *showing* rather than *telling* the reader what the personalities of his characters are like.

There are very few instances in *Nine Stories* where the narrator *tells* us what the personality traits of a character are. These instances occur in the stories that use a third person omniscient point of view. For example, in "Just Before the War with the Eskimos," the narrator describes the large hands of a character named Eric by saying: "They looked neither strong nor competent nor sensitive. Yet he used them as if they had some not easily controllable aesthetic drive of their own" (51). Later it turns out that Eric is a homosexual. And in "Down at the Dinghy," the narrator allows himself to say about Boo Boo Tannenbaum that "her general unprettiness aside, she was—in terms of permanently memorable, immoderately perceptive, small area faces—a stunning and final girl" (77).

The characterization in the third person objective stories is more convincing than that in the third person omniscient ones because we are allowed to make up our own minds about the personalities of the characters on the basis of the descriptive detail that Salinger provides. The first paragraph of "A Perfect Day for Bananafish" is perhaps the finest example of the skill with which Salinger uses such detail to shape our response to a character. He begins by telling us that the "girl" he is describing has been waiting for a long distance phone call for over two hours. He does not tell us yet that she is Muriel, the wife of Seymour Glass, but he does tell us what she is doing while she is waiting:

She read an article in a women's pocket-size magazine, called "Sex is Fun—or Hell." She washed her comb and brush. She took the spot out of the skirt of her beige suit. She moved the button of her Saks blouse. She tweezed out two freshly surfaced hairs in her mole. When the operator rang her room, she was sitting on the window seat and had almost finished putting nail lacquer on the nails of her left hand. (3)

Five of the six sentences in this passage describe activities that have to do with Muriel's physical appearance and one has to do with the physical act of sexual intercourse. Salinger's selection of the descriptive detail not only suggests that he wants us to see Muriel as a very shallow person, it also prepares us for Muriel's admission that Seymour has called her "Miss Spiritual Tramp of 1948."

In the two stories that are told in the first person, "The Laughing Man" and "De Daumier-Smith's Blue Period," we find that Salinger has gone quite a bit beyond Ring Lardner and Sherwood Anderson whose first-person narratives he admired. While Lardner's and Anderson's narrators tend to be unaware of their own shortsightedness, Salinger's first person narrators describe their own younger selves critically and with amused detachment. Here, for instance, is how the thirty-year-old narrator in "Laughing Man" describes his conviction, as a nine-year-old, that he is the Laughing Man's only legitimate son:

I was not even my parents' son in 1928 but a devilishly smooth impostor, awaiting their slightest blunder as an excuse to move in—preferably without violence, but not necessarily—to assert my true identity. As a precaution against breaking my bogus mother's heart, I planned to take her into my underworld employ in some undefined but appropriately regal capacity. (62)

In this passage the adult narrator provides a characterization of himself as a typical nine-year-old who dreams of living a life of crime but also wants to make sure that he doesn't hurt his mother's feelings.

The style in *Nine Stories* is mixed. We still see a definite Hemingway influence, but we also see Salinger taking further steps toward the whimsical and digressive style of the later Glass Family Series. The stories that use an objective point of view consist almost entirely of dialogue, and the narrative passages are brief and so are the sentences. Here for instance, is a narrative passage from "A Perfect Day for Bananafish." Its short, objective, and matter of fact sentences illustrate the Hemingway influence: "The young man put on his robe, closed the lapels tight, and jammed the towel in his pocket. He picked up the slimy wet, cumbersome float and put it under his arm. He plodded alone through the soft, hot sand toward the hotel" (17).

The first person narratives and the two stories that use a third person omniscient point of view are characterized by a much more complex style than the three stories that use a third person objective point of view. The complexity and subjectivity of this style is due to the narrator's strategy of delineating the personality of a character by revealing his or her secret opinions. Here is one example from the first page of "Just Before the War with the Eskimos": "Ginnie openly considered Selena the biggest drip at Miss Basehoar's—a school ostensibly abounding with fair-sized drips—but at the same time she had never known anyone like Selena for bringing fresh cans of tennis balls" (39). The style in this passage is very different from that of "A Perfect Day for Bananafish," "Uncle Wiggily in Connecticut," and "Teddy," but it does not yet anticipate the digressive style of Buddy Glass in the later Glass series. However in "The Laughing Man" and "De Daumier-Smith's Blue Period," there are passages whose style sounds quite a bit like that of Buddy Glass. Here for instance is the opening sentence of "De Daumier-Smith's Blue Period":

If it made any real sense—and it doesn't even begin to—I think I might be inclined to dedicate this account, for whatever it's worth, especially if it's the least bit ribald in parts, to the memory of my late, ribald stepfather, Robert Agadganian, Jr. (130)

The core idea of this sentence is that the narrator wants to dedicate his story to his late stepfather. This core idea is expanded and embellished by four modifying and qualifying phrases; five if we count the man's name. This piling up of digressive modifiers and qualifiers, which slow down the pace of the sentence, is one of the hallmarks of the style in Salinger's later fiction.

SETTINGS AND SYMBOLS

As far as the settings in time are concerned, the events in most of the nine stories occur in the now time, that is, at the approximate time that the stories were published. However, in none of the stories do we get exact dates as we do in some of Salinger's early stories, for instance, in the novella "The Inverted Forest." However, in two stories we get the kind of double time frame that Salinger used in some earlier stories, for instance in "Blue Melody." Like "Blue Melody," both "The Laughing Man" and "De Daumier-Smith's Blue Period" are told by adult narrators who tell of events that happened to them when they were younger. "Laughing Man" takes us back to when the narrator was nine, and "Daumier-Smith" to the time when the narrator was nineteen.

In terms of the locations, there is more variety in *Nine Stories* than in terms of their temporal settings. Three of the stories are set in New York City: "Just Before the War with the Eskimos," "The Laughing Man," and "Pretty Mouth and Green My Eyes." In the rest of Nine *Stories* we get different locations. For instance, "A Perfect Day for Bananafish" is set in Florida; "Uncle Wiggily" is set in suburban Connecticut; "Down at the Dinghy" is set on a lake in Upstate New York; "For Esmé—with Love and Squalor" is set in England and Germany; "De Daumier-Smith's Blue Period" is set in Montreal, Canada; and "Teddy" is set on an ocean liner en route from England to America.

However, the social environment of the nine stories is the same as in *The Catcher in the Rye*, that is, upper middle class. In fact, in three of the stories ("Uncle Wiggily," "Just Before the War," and "Down at the Dinghy") we find that the families are so well off that they have live-in maids just like the Caulfields in *The Catcher in the Rye*.

In most of the nine stories, the settings do not play an important role in developing the meaning, but in some instances they cast little flashes of light on the personalities of the characters. For example, in "A Perfect Day for Bananafish," Muriel Glass reports to her mother that she has been discussing her husband Seymour with a psychiatrist whom she met at their hotel in Florida. She wants to talk to this psychiatrist some more, and she knows exactly where she can find him. As she tells her mother, "He's in the bar all day long" (8). Made in passing, this little comment casts doubt on the trustworthiness of this psychiatrist who spends all day in a bar.

In another scene in "Bananafish," the setting also tells us something about the personality of a character, in this case Muriel Glass. When Seymour returns to his and Muriel's hotel room, we get this laconic statement: "The room smelled of new calfskin luggage and nail-lacquer remover" (18). The smell that pervades the room—that of new, expensive luggage and of freshly painted nails—points to Muriel's dominant character trait, her concern for appearances.

In three of the nine stories, the meaning depends to a large degree on the setting. The most obvious example is "Down at the Dinghy" where young Lionel has been sitting in the family's small sailboat for over four hours, pretending that he is running away from home. The story would not work as well if Lionel had, for instance, locked himself in the family car because then he could not defy his mother by tossing his uncle Seymour's goggles and his mother's key chain into the lake. But most importantly, the dinghy is docked at the edge of the family's property, while a car would probably be closer to the house and thus closer to the maid Sandra whose ethnic slur about Lionel's father makes Lionel want to run away.

The setting is even more important to the meaning in "For Esmé—with Love and Squalor." Here it is not the locations or the details of the physical setting that are important but the historical background, namely World War II and its aftermath. That the war is indeed to blame for Sergeant X's nervous breakdown is confirmed by two passages. In one of them the narrator tells us that Sergeant X "had not come through the war with all his faculties intact" (104). In the other passage, we learn that Sergeant X had been in the European Theater of Operations "from D-Day straight through five campaigns of the war" (106).

The third story in which the setting is crucial to the meaning is "De Daumier-Smith's Blue Period." Before the narrator-protagonist tells us of his transcendent experience, he describes the setting where this experience takes place. One evening, as he returns to his room in the correspondence art school in Montreal, Smith stops and looks into the display window of an orthopedic appliance store. He comments:

The thought was forced on me that no matter how coolly or sensibly or gracefully I might one day learn to live my life, I would always at best be a visitor in a garden of enamel urinals and bedpans, with a sightless, wooden dummy-deity standing by in a marked down rupture-truss. (157)

These pessimistic thoughts and negative images (which seem inspired by Nathanael West's novel *Miss Lonelyhearts*) later give way to a hopeful outlook when Smith has his transcendent experience. He is once again looking into the display window of the orthopedic appliance store, but this time a hefty girl of about thirty is changing the truss on the wooden dummy. She sees Smith staring at her, drops the truss, steps back on a stack of irrigation basins, and falls down. Smith reaches out to her as if to steady her through the glass of the display window and then experiences a flash of light that blinds him for a moment. When he regains his sight, Smith finds the setting transformed and tells us, "the girl had gone from the window, leaving behind her a shimmering field of exquisite, twice-blessed enamel flowers" (164). Thus the change in Smith's perception of the setting reflects the change in his outlook. His sudden empathy for the embarrassment of the girl in the display window has pulled him out of his shell of egotism. He no longer feels superior to others; he no longer feels that he is an outsider who will only be a visitor in the world. Most importantly, the world now seems shimmering and twice-blessed rather than hopelessly depressing.

The symbolism in *Nine Stories* is of two kinds, allegorical and natural. Salinger indulges his bent toward the allegorical not only in "Daumier-Smith" but also in three other stories. In the remaining five stories the symbols are natural ones and are open to as many interpretations as the ducks in Central Park in *The Catcher in the Rye*.

Two obvious and artificial symbols—allegorical signs, really—are the greedy fish in "A Perfect Day for Bananafish" and Esmé's military wristwatch in "For Esmé—with Love and Squalor."

That the bananafish represent greed and material values is apparent from their description. Seymour tells Sybil Carpenter that the bananafish are very ordinary fish when they swim into a hole where there are a lot of bananas, but "once they get in, they behave like pigs." Seymour says he's seen some bananafish who eat as many as 78 bananas. As a result they get so fat that they can't get out of the hole again, and they die of "banana fever" (16). The allegorical meaning of Seymour's bananafish story emerges when we consider the yellow (golden) color and the phallic shape of the bananas that the fish crave. Seen this way, the bananafish represent people who are greedy for money and sex. The banana fever is their materialism—that is, their desire for things physical—which causes their spiritual death.

Another allegorical use of symbolism occurs in "For Esmé—with Love and Squalor." The allegorical object is the military watch that used to belong to Esmé's father. She sends it to Sergeant X as "a lucky talisman," but the watch arrives with its crystal broken. When Sergeant X can't muster the courage to wind the watch and find out if it still works, we realize that the watch represents Sergeant X himself who has recently had a nervous breakdown and who doesn't know if he has a chance of again becoming a man with all his faculties intact.

The symbolism in "Uncle Wiggily in Connecticut" is more difficult to interpret than that in the other stories. "Uncle Wiggily" presents us with two characters who seem to be symbolic. They are the four-year-old Ramona's imaginary friends, Jimmy Jimmereeno and Mickey Mickeranno. Ramona makes Jimmy die in an accident (her mother Eloise's lover Walt also died in an accident), and Ramona replaces Jimmy with a new imaginary friend, Mickey Mickeranno. When Ramona sleeps far over on the side of her bed so as not to hurt her new friend, Eloise shrieks at her and bodily drags her to the middle of the bed. It seems that she is angry because Ramona can let go of her love for the dead Jimmy and transfer it to her new friend Mickey while she, Eloise, has not been able to let go of her dead lover Walt and is therefore not allowing herself to love her husband Lew and her daughter Ramona, who looks a lot like Lew. That Eloise is indeed thinking of Walt when she drags Ramona to the middle of her bed is made clear a moment later when Eloise starts to cry, picks up Ramona's glasses, presses them to her cheek, and says over and over again, "Poor Uncle Wiggily." "Poor Uncle Wiggily" is what Walt once said when Eloise stumbled and twisted her ankle. The symbolism in the story therefore suggest that Ramona is unwittingly teaching her mother how to deal with the loss of her lover.

In "Just Before the War with the Eskimos" the symbolism isn't quite as subtle as in "Uncle Wiggily," but it is more ambiguous. The symbol is half of a chicken sandwich that Ginnie Mannox is offered by Franklin, the brother of her classmate Selena Graff. During Ginnie's conversation with Franklin, it becomes obvious that she is developing a crush on him. He offers her the sandwich in a clumsy gesture of concern: "You just played tennis, for Chrissake. Aren'tcha hungry?" (46). Ginnie at first refuses the sandwich but then reluctantly takes a bite. As Ginnie says good-bye to Selena, she learns that Franklin is much older than she thought. She is fifteen and Franklin is twenty-four. A moment later, as she is leaving Selena's apartment house, Ginnie finds the chicken sandwich in her coat pocket, and the narrator tells us: "She took it out and started to bring her arm down, to drop the sandwich into the street, but instead she put it back into her pocket" (55). Ginnie's decision to keep the sandwich could mean that she is still infatuated with Franklin, despite the age difference, and wants to keep the sandwich as a memento of him. On the other hand, the narrator also tells us: "A few years before, it had taken her three days to dispose of the Easter chick she had found dead on the sawdust in the bottom of her wastebasket" (55). The comparison of the chicken sandwich to the dead Easter chick suggests that the sandwich might have a negative meaning for Ginnie. The comparison might mean that her budding love for Franklin died a premature death just like the Easter chick. In short, the symbolism of the chicken sandwich can be used to develop two very different statements about the theme of adolescent infatuation.

THEMES AND INTERPRETATIONS

Some critics have treated *Nine Stories* as a short story cycle such as Sherwood Anderson's *Winesburg, Ohio*, Ernest Hemingway's *In Our Time*, or William Faulkner's *Go Down, Moses*. Such an approach does not make sense in light of Salinger's development as a writer. During the five years between the composition of the first and the last of the nine stories, Salinger's vision of life changed drastically, and this change is reflected in stark differences between the themes and the vision of life of the earlier and later of the nine stories.

The pieces in *Nine Stories* are arranged in the chronological order of their composition, and the differences between the first and last story are stunning. When Salinger wrote "A Perfect Day for Bananafish" (1948), his vision of life was still quite unspiritual and pessimistic because he had not yet become interested in Eastern philosophy. But when he wrote "Teddy" (1953), he had already begun to study Advaita Vedanta at the Ramakrishna-Vivekananda Center in New York, and his new religious interest is reflected in the story. Teddy McArdle's Socratic dialogue with the education professor Bob Nicholson is essentially an exposition of the core ideas of Vedanta Hinduism. The shift in Salinger's outlook is apparent when we compare the deaths of Seymour Glass in the first story, "A Perfect Day for Bananafish," and that of Teddy McArdle in the last story, "Teddy." Seymour's suicide is depicted as an act of despair and Teddy's as an act of hope.

The first four stories reveal a pessimistic vision of life, the middle story, "Down at the Dinghy" seems optimistic, and the last four stories, with the exception of "Pretty Mouth and Green My Eyes," also develop an optimistic outlook. Moreover, the dominant themes in the first six stories are psychological and sociological and those in the last three are philosophical or even religious.

"A Perfect Day for Bananafish" (1948)

There are basically two types of interpretations of "A Perfect Day for Bananafish," psychological interpretations that are based exclusively on close readings of the story, and philosophical or religious ones that consider information about

Seymour Glass from later stories. One type of interpretation tends to see Seymour Glass as a psychotic, the other as a victim or even a saint.

Two readings of the story that see Seymour as a negative character with severe psychological problems are those of Gwynn and Blotner and Frank Metcalf. Gwynn and Blotner, the authors of the 1958 book, *The Fiction of J.D. Salinger*, say that "Seymour is destroyed by his own hypersensitivity pathetically heightened by lack of love." And by love they mean sexual love, for they identify "Seymour's sexual inadequacy" as the story's "underlying motif" (19-20). Frank Metcalf also explains Seymour's suicide in terms of a sexual problem. In his 1972 essay "The Suicide of Seymour Glass," Metcalf interprets the bananafish as being the three-year-old Sybil Carpenter because she wears a yellow bathing suit, and he explains Seymour's suicide as the result of his guilty feeling about his "sublimated pedophilic desires" (245). Metcalf concludes: "The nearly conscious desires expressed in his bananafish story and his erotic pretense with the girl are made fully conscious to him by Sybil's innocent responses to his story and to the kiss on her foot. The only solution ... is suicide" (246).

By contrast, Ihab Hassan and James Bryan describe Seymour as a positive character. Hassan and Bryan's interpretations are based not only on the text of "A Perfect Day for Bananafish" but also on additional information about Seymour from the stories "Raise High the Roof Beam, Carpenters" (1955), "Zooey" (1957), and "Seymour—An Introduction" (1959). In these stories, Seymour is developed as a person whose principal aim in life was to make spiritual progress toward oneness with God. With the later Seymour stories in mind, Hassan calls Seymour's suicide "a cleansing act," for what drives Seymour into suicide is a world that is "ruthless ... with the power of spiritual vulgarity" (145). In the same vein, James Bryan says that Seymour kills himself because he is "depressed by his own concupiscence and Muriel's sexual hold upon him, by the stupefying and despritualizing bonds ... which Seymour sees as inescapable and fatal to his spiritual progress" (229).

Two controversies among the critics who have written about "A Perfect Day for Bananafish" concern the interpretation of the central symbol of the bananafish and the interpretation of Seymour's reasons for killing himself. Most critics share William Wiegand's view that Seymour himself is the bananafish because "he has become so glutted with sensation that he cannot swim out into society again" (125). According to Wiegand, Seymour's banana fever is caused by "the weight of his experience" and by "a psychological conflict between the desire to participate in and the need to withdraw from society" (130). Wiegand concludes that "the 'perfect day' is the day when the bananafish is able to end all his suffering by killing himself" (126). A minority of critics, among them Alfred Kazin, Kenneth Hamilton, and Eberhard Alsen, disagree with Wiegand and identify the bananafish (plural) of the title as the materialistic people who surround Seymour and their banana fever as the materialism which kills their souls.

As far as the motivation for Seymour's suicide is concerned, critics have offered both negative and positive interpretations. Some—like Hassan, Bryan, and Wiegand—have described his self-inflicted death as an act of despair, as an escape from a life that no longer seems worth living. Others have argued that Seymour died as a saint who had made as much spiritual progress in this particular lifetime as he could and therefore had no more reason to live. In his essay, "Seymour: A Clarification," Gordon Slethaugh puts it this way: "Seymour's suicide is the utmost commitment to God; he acts according to God's wishes. It has little to do with inability to live in this world; it has nothing to do with escapism; it has everything to do with acceptance of spiritual responsibility" (127).

"Uncle Wiggily in Connecticut" (1948)

Critics have commented on sociological, psychological, and philosophical themes in this story. One of the most thoughtful interpretations of "Uncle Wiggily in Connecticut" is by Warren French in his 1963 book *J.D. Salinger*. French takes a philosophical approach and comments both on the values of the protagonist, Eloise Wengler, and on the vision of life implied in the story. French compares "Uncle Wiggily" to *The Catcher in the Rye*, which also contrasts the "nice world" to the "phony world," and he says that the story is "the only one of Salinger's works that offers, in a few pages, visions of both worlds with which he is concerned" (38). In the story, the phony world is symbolized by Eloise's husband Lew and the nice world by Eloise's dead lover Walt. The story is about Eloise's realization that she is no longer a "nice" person but belongs to the world of the phonies. This becomes apparent after Eloise forces her daughter Ramona to deny the existence of her imaginary friend Mickey Mickeranno. She suddenly breaks down and cries because she recognizes that she is no longer a "nice" person. As French sees it, the story dramatizes the plight of the person who is sensitive enough to recognize the nice world and its values even if that person lives by the values of the phony world. French digs even deeper into the story when he explains that it was the "loss of this 'nice' world [that] has turned Eloise into a bitch" (40). Describing Walt's accidental death as the turning point in Eloise's life, French says that the story implies a belief in an "absurd universe" in which "man is simply at the mercy of the chaotic forces of blind chance" (42).

"Just Before the War with the Eskimos" (1948)

The few critics who have commented on "Just Before the War with the Eskimos" have chiefly dealt with its psychological implications and treated it as a love story. However, James Lundquist has analyzed the story in terms of its vision of life, and he has concluded that it is very pessimistic. Lundquist believes that at the story's climax, the central character, Ginnie Mannox, comes to the realization that she has been too self-centered in her relationship with her tennis partner Selena. He suggests that by changing her mind and refusing to take the money for cab fare she asked Selena for, Ginnie shows that she has undergone a character change for the better. However, when Lundquist focuses on the role of Selena's brother Franklin who brings about the change in Ginnie, he concludes that Franklin is "in such despair over the absurdity of human existence, that he sees no end to the continuing cycle of mortal foolishness. One

war has ended, but people are running to the draft boards to sign up for another." Franklin's pessimistic attitude is revealed in his sarcastic prophecy that
the next war will probably be fought against the Eskimos. "Life is that absurd,"
concludes Lundquist, but he admits that at least Ginnie and Franklin, through
their contact with each other, have recognized this "essential absurdity" (92).

"The Laughing Man" (1949)

Early interpretations of "The Laughing Man" have seen it chiefly as a com-
ing-of-age story and have therefore dealt with its psychological themes. However, more recent interpretations have examined its philosophical meaning and
have related it to the pessimistic vision of life in the earlier of the *Nine Stories*.

The reading of "The Laughing Man" that forms the basis of all later interpretations is that of Gwynn and Blotner in *The Fiction of J.D. Salinger* (1958).
Gwynn and Blotner identify the core of the story when they say that it is "the
recollection by a mature man of a crucial experience at the age of nine: the end
of a hero-worship-laden relationship with an idealized older man who, preoccupied with his own romance, killed off the fictional projection of himself [the
Laughing Man] to which the boy had given unabashed and imitative devotion"
(24-25). Gwynn and Blotner point out that the Laughing Man, the hero in the
continuing story that John Gedsudski tells the pre-adolescent boys of the Comanche Club every Saturday, is "an unconscious wish-fulfillment projection of
himself" (25). When Gedsudski's romance with his girlfriend Mary Hudson
breaks up, Gwynn and Blotner surmise that the break-up is due to the differences in their social background, because Gedsudski comes from Eastern European immigrant stock and Mary Hudson comes from an aristocratic Long Island
family. The break-up makes Gedsudski kill off the Laughing Man and thus
ends the serial story he has been telling. Gedsudski destroys the positive relationship between himself and the boys and deprives the nine-year-old narrator
and his fellow Comanches of two role models, himself and the Laughing Man.

Gwynn and Blotner's analysis does not wind up with a thesis that explains
what universal meaning the story suggests, but Paul Strong takes their analysis
to a logical conclusion. In his article, "Black Wing, Black Heart—Betrayal in
J.D. Salinger's 'The Laughing Man'," Strong argues that the betrayal of the
Laughing Man by the detective Marcel Dufarge and his daughter in the last installment John Gedsudski's story reflects Gedsudski's own sense of having been
betrayed by Mary Hudson and her father. Strong writes: "No doubt, we are to
assume from all this that the 'detective,' Mary's father, has learned of his daughter's interest in the Staten Islander [Gedsudski] and forced the romance to its
unceremonious end" (94). This interpretation of Mary Hudson's reason for ending her relationship with John Gedsudski leads Strong to conclude that Salinger's abortive love story "demonstrates how the denial of love can twist, even
destroy a life. Indeed, like Seymour's bananafish story, John's [about the
Laughing Man] is a cautionary tale, a warning to the young about the dangers of
entrapment in a deceptive world" (95).

"Down at the Dinghy" (1949)

Coming in the exact middle of *Nine Stories,* "Down at the Dinghy" is the first of the nine to have an upbeat ending (despite the anti-Semitism of a minor character). Most interpretations of the story have dealt with psychological and sociological themes and focused on whatever it is that the four year old Lionel learns or doesn't learn about dealing with unpleasant adults and/or with ethnic prejudice.

So far the most detailed reading of "Down at the Dinghy" is a psychological interpretation by Martin Dolch and John Hagopian. The two critics identify Boo Boo Tannenbaum, rather than her son Lionel, as the central character because the story's central concern is "how an intelligent modern mother copes with a precociously sensitive-four-year-old son" (226).

Dolch and Hagopian stress two circumstances in the story: One is that ever since Lionel was two-and-a-half years old, he has been reacting to insults and fears by running away, and the other is that in trying to find out what has upset Lionel this time, his mother "offers no threats, no 'reasoning'—but a gay plunge into the spirit of play" (227). To get Lionel out of the dinghy, Boo Boo pretends to be "Vice-Admiral Tannenbaum. Née Glass. Come to inspect the stermaphors." Lionel says she's no admiral, but his mother stuns him into open-mouthed admiration by forming one of her hands into a sort of funnel and sounding an elaborate a bugle call, a mixture of "Taps" and "Reveille." When Lionel flips his uncle Seymour's diving goggles into the lake, Dolch and Hagopian believe that Lionel is testing his mother's love: "If she does not scold him or punish him, then he can safely repeat to her the dangerous expression he has heard" (27). Instead of punishing Lionel, Boo Boo pretends that she is going to toss into the lake a present she has brought him, a key chain with even more keys on it than his Daddy has. But when she gives the keys to Lionel, he himself flicks them into the water in what Dolch and Hagopian call "an apparent gesture of self punishment" (227). A moment later Lionel begins to cry heartrendingly, and this gives Boo Boo the opportunity resolve her conflict with Lionel by taking him on her lap and consoling him with hugs and kisses. Without being prompted, Lionel then explains that he wanted to run away because he overheard Sandra, the maid, refer to his father as "a big—sloppy—kike." Boo Boo flinches but is relieved when she finds out that Lionel doesn't know that "kike" is an anti-Semitic epithet. Then she races Lionel back to the house and lets him win, and Dolch and Hagopian conclude that "the mother wins the more important contest against the vague but ugly cruelty that her child is doomed to suffer" (228).

"For Esmé—with Love and Squalor" (1950)

Most Salinger scholars agree that "For Esmé—with Love and Squalor" is, as Frederick Gywnn and Joseph Blotner termed it, "the high point of Salinger's art" (143). One of the few dissenters was Leslie Fiedler who dismissed "For Esmé" as "a popular little tear-jerker" (59). The most convincing case for the excellence of the story is made by Brother Fidelian Burke in his essay "Salinger's 'Esmé': Some Matters of Balance." Burke points pout that the story is not only divided in two major parts—one dealing with love, the other with squalor—but that its structure contains "a number of balances among thematic and other strands . . . that cut across the basic contrast, as well as echoes of specific situations and images" (342). For instance, there is a basic dialectic in the relationships that Sergeant X has with other characters, and Burke points out the contrast between Sergeant's X's positive relationship with Esmé on the one hand and the negative relationships he has his wife, his mother in law, and Corporal Clay on the other hand. Burke also points out the squalid parallels between the lives of Sergeant X and Esmé, particularly the isolation of the two characters. Burke notes that Esmé's relationship with Sergeant X "involves an undercurrent for contrasts that operate elsewhere in the story —between male and female, youth and age, civilian and military, inferior and superior, but most particularly between naiveté and experience" (344). Concerning the ending of the story—Sergeant X receiving Esmé's gift of her father's watch—Burke points out that it parallels the addendum to the first part of the story in which Esmé drags her little brother Charles back into the tea-room to kiss Sergeant X good-bye, his wet smacker in the first section parallels his HelloHelloHello note at the end of the letter that accompanies the watch. As far as the meaning of the story goes, Burke says that it offers "a deep insight into the nature and necessity of love" (341). Burke therefore hews close to the standard interpretation of he story.

That standard interpretation sees the central theme of the story as a psychological one because the narrator-protagonist has had a nervous breakdown as a result of his squalid war experiences, and he is helped in his recovery by the love of the title character, the thirteen-tear-old Esmé. Two interpretations that depart slightly from the standard view of the story are those of James Bryan and John Wenke.

In his 1967 essay "A Reading of Salinger's 'For Esmé—with Love and Squalor'," James Bryan agrees with the view that the story recounts "a man's miraculous salvation from war and squalor by the love of a child," but he points out tat previous interpretations haven't paid enough attention to the squalor in the story. He days: "A careful reading of 'For Esmé' reveals beneath the lyricism ... an unsentimental and even philosophical attitude toward love and squalor, as the young protagonist comes to recognize their complexities—and interdependency—in his life" (275-276). According to Bryan, the protagonist, Sergeant X, achieves a "moral growth" because he learns from Esmé that "love is impossible without squalor" (287).

More recently, John Wenke took a new tack and examined the theme of communication as suggested by the many instances in which the characters' language—both written and spoken—obstructs mutual understanding. In his essay "Sergeant X, Esmé, and the Meaning of Words" (1981), Wenke comes to the conclusion that "For Esmé—with Love an Squalor" is indeed the high point of Salinger's art because "it addresses one of the central problems in Salinger's fiction in particular and in modern literature in general—the problem of finding valid forms of communication—at the same time that the story suggests that

love is the force which animates expression." Wenke winds up his article with
this statement about the story's meaning:

In a story in which love ultimately triumphs, the relationship between the narrator
and Esmé embodies a beautiful, if tenuous, example of how individuals might pass
through squalor to love, achieving meaningful, redemptive expression, even though
the successful uses of language are a constant reminder of its general failure. (259)

Finally, there has been some controversy concerning the character of Sergeant
X in "For Esmé—with Love and Squalor." Many critics have noted similarities
between the characterization of Sergeant X and the characterizations of both
Seymour Glass and Buddy Glass in "A Perfect Day for Bananafish," "Raise
High the Roof Beam Carpenters," and "Seymour—An Introduction." After all,
both Seymour and Buddy were stationed in Germany at the end of the war, and
both were sergeants. Moreover, like Sergeant X, Buddy is a short story writer
and, like Sergeant X, Seymour had a nervous breakdown while in the army.
Such similarities and others led Dan Wakefield to declare in his essay "Salinger
and the Search for Love," that Buddy Glass is "the writer who appeared as Sergeant X in 'For Esmé—with Love and Squalor'" (186). Disagreeing with
Wakefield, Tom Davis argued in his essay "The Identity of Sergeant X" that
"thematic parallels between 'For Esmé' and the Seymour stories ... help us establish the identity of Sergeant X as Seymour Glass" (262). Neither Wakefield
nor Davis makes a convincing case because we would have to sweep under the
carpet a number of facts in the story to argue that Sergeant X is either Buddy or
Seymour Glass in disguise. Nevertheless, "For Esmé" sheds light on the Glass
Family Series because it illustrates the kinds of experiences that both Buddy
and Seymour might have had at the end of World War II.

"Pretty Mouth and Green My Eyes" (1951)

"Pretty Mouth and Green My Eyes" was published after "Down at the Dinghy" and "For Esmé—with Love and Squalor," but it presents such a negative
view of human nature that it seems it must have been written before those two
other, more upbeat stories. Although the theme of marital infidelity invites
moral and psychological interpretations, some commentators also deal with the
philosophical theme of human nature because that topic comes up in the conversation between Lee, the older man, and Arthur, the husband of the woman with
whom Lee is in bed.
    The most thoughtful reading of the story is the essay by John Hagopian enti-
tled "'Pretty Mouth and Green My Eyes': Salinger's Paolo and Francesca in
New York." Hagopian's title refers to two adulterous lovers who are being pun-
ished for their sins of the flesh in the second circle of hell in Dante's *Inferno*.
As the Dante allusion in the essay's title suggests, Hagopian sees he story as
having primarily a "moral message" with "profoundly religious overtones" (352-
353). He argues convincingly that the story's central character is the older lawyer Lee who is having and affair with Joan, the wife of a younger colleague.
Hagopian presents convincing evidence to show that by the end of the story

"Lee is deeply shaken with remorse and has a new contempt for himself and for the girl in bed with him" (353). Lee's insight occurs during his phone conversation with Arthur when Arthur says about his wife that she is "an animal." Lee replies, "We're all animals.... Basically, we're all animals." But Arthur disagrees and says that he may be a "stupid, fouled-up twentieth-century son-of-a bitch" but that he is no animal. Having overheard the phone conversation between her lover and her husband, Joan says: "I feel like an absolute dog." She thus underlines what Hagopian takes to be the story's pessimistic message about the human nature: Humans are no better than animals.

"De Daumier-Smith's Blue Period" (1952)

Interpretations of "De Daumier-Smith's Blue Period" have gone in several different directions. The story has been read as being about education, adolescent psychology, art, and religion. An interpretation that sees a connection between all of these themes, especially the latter two, is John Russell's article, "J.D. Salinger: From Daumier to Smith" (1963). For one thing, Russell points out that "Daumier-Smith" is "the first of Salinger's stories to present a dramatized and so-named 'transcendent' experience" and that the story can be seen "as a kind of companion piece to 'Teddy'" (70-71). Russell believes that the central concern in "De Daumier-Smith's Blue Period" comes out when the protagonist "denies his art for the sake of cultivating non-possessive love" (80). Russell is here referring to the change in Jean De Daumier-Smith as a result of the blinding flash of light he experiences when looking in the display window of the orthopedic appliance store. This change makes him give up the bogus identity of Jean De Daumier-Smith and transforms him back into plain John Smith. The change is manifested when Smith abandons his plan to seduce one of his students and decides on "giving Sister Irma her freedom" because "everybody is a nun." Russell interprets this cryptic statement as meaning that "the boy has been brought to see every person as sacred" (79). When Smith gives up not only Sister Irma but also his fantasy of becoming a great artist and teacher of other artists, he does so, Russell argues, because he has recognized that "others are holy and not to be appropriated" (86).

"Teddy" (1953)

Some early interpretations saw the title character of the story "Teddy" as an obnoxious, psychotic brat and didn't take the religious ideas in the story seriously. One reviewer of *Nine Stories* even suggested that at the end of the story it is Teddy who pushes his sister Booper into the empty pool and not vice-versa. However, some astute readers recognized right away that Salinger was sympathetic to Teddy's Vedantic vision of life, and later critics recognized that the God-seeker Teddy McArdle is the prototype for the re-designed Seymour in the Glass Family Series.

The most detailed discussion of the story along religious lines is William Bysshe Stein's essay "Salinger's 'Teddy': *Tat Tvam Asi* or That Thou Art."

Stein explains that Teddy "has achieved the state of *jivana-mukta* (release from the egotistical desires induced by the attachment to external things)" and that he has therefore come to the realization of the central truth of Hinduism, *Tat Tvam Asi*, "the assertion of 'That Thou Art,' [which] affirms the identity of 'That' (the Supreme Spirit) and 'Thou' (the individual Spirit)" (254).

After explaining Teddy's belief in reincarnation, in the physical world as mere appearance, and in several other Hindu concepts, Stein concentrates on Teddy's opposition to Western logic because it causes the unity of the cosmos to fall apart: "Logic separates and divides, setting up systems of opposites that exist only in the mind." Stein points out that Teddy and Salinger's opposition to Western logic is based on their Vedantic vision of life:

To be sure, [logic] is the curse of God that implants this vision of phenomenal existence. But for Teddy (and Salinger) this is the supreme irony. In the Hindu world of process and eternal duration, despite periodic creations and dissolutions, there is no beginning and no end, there is no good and no evil, there is no life and no death. To think otherwise is to submit to the illusion of time and relativity and to accept the belief that the body can destroy the spirit. Vedantic wisdom decrees that such is not the case, and that is why Teddy is able to take his death without protest. (261)

CONCLUSION

Anyone who reads through *Nine Stories* for the first time will be struck by how varied the pieces in this collection are. Once we realize that the stories are arranged in the chronological order of their original magazine publication, with "A Perfect Day for Bananafish" (1948) being the earliest story and "Teddy" (1953) the most recent, we understand that the earlier and the later stories must have been written in two different phases of Salinger's development as a writer.

The stories that Salinger wrote in the earlier phase still have much in common with the work he did during his apprenticeship years. Like many of Salinger's uncollected pieces, four of the *Nine Stories* deal with the effect that World War II had on soldiers and civilians ("Bananafish," "Uncle Wiggily," "Just Before the War," and "For Esmé"). Moreover, some of the earlier pieces in *Nine Stories* still show the influence of Ernest Hemingway in their laconic style and in their use of the third person objective point of view. Most importantly, the stories of the earlier phase all develop a pessimistic of view of the world as being chaotic and a negative view of man as being essentially an animal.

The vision of life and the view of human nature becomes more optimistic in the middle of *Nine Stories*, beginning with "Down at the Dinghy" (1949), and the last two stories, "De Daumier-Smith's Blue Period" (1952) and "Teddy" (1953) foreshadow the religious worldview of Salinger's later work. "Teddy" still uses a third person objective point of view and has a few Hemingwayesque passages in its dialogue, but "De Daumier-Smith's Blue Period" is written in the first person, and the narrator's style is almost as whimsical and digressive as that of Buddy Glass in the Glass Family Series. And while both stories reveal a consciousness of the negative capabilities in human nature, the worldview in both stories is a religious one that is based on a belief in the existence of an eternal spiritual world beyond the appearances of the temporal physical world.

The radical differences between the worldview of Salinger's earlier and the later phase is best illustrated in the different reasons for the suicides of Seymour Glass in "A Perfect Day for Bananafish" and of Teddy McArdle in "Teddy." While Seymour kills himself out of despair over the rampant greed of the bananafish—the materialistic people that surround him—Teddy McArdle chooses to die on the earlier of two possible dates because he finds it too hard to lead a spiritual life in America and he wants to move on to a new incarnation in which he can make better spiritual advancement toward union with God.

For a reader who is totally unfamiliar with Salinger's fiction, *Nine Stories* will serve as a better introduction than *The Catcher in the Rye.* First of all, *Nine Stories* represents what is arguably Salinger's best work because in their thematic concerns these stories are less dated and more universal than *The Catcher in the Rye.* Secondly, *Nine Stories* also provides a better introduction to Salinger's work than *The Catcher in the Rye* because it reflects two different phases of Salinger's development as a writer. On the one hand, the collection contains stories that reveal both his earlier pessimistic outlook and his artistic debt to Ernest Hemingway, on the other hand it contains stories that demonstrate his later religious outlook and his emergence as a writer with a distinctly original voice.

And finally, most of the stories in the collection have not yet been over-analyzed as *The Catcher in the Rye* has been. Although dozens of critical analyses have been published on "A Perfect Day for Bananafish" and "For Esmé—with Love and Squalor," not very much criticism exists about the rest of the nine stories. Especially "Just Before the War with the Eskimos," "The Laughing Man," and "De Daumier-Smith's Blue Period" deserve more attention than they have received so far.

WORKS CITED

Baro, Gene. "Some Suave and Impressive Slices of Life" [Review of *Nine Stories*]. *New York Herald Tribune Book Review* (12 April 1953): 6.

Bryan, James E. "A Reading of Salinger's 'For Esmé—with Love and Squalor'." *Criticism* 9 (1967): 275-288.

___ . "Salinger's Seymour's Suicide." *College English* 24 (December 1962): 226-229.

Burke, Brother Fidelian. "Salinger's 'Esmé': Some Matters of Balance." *Modern Fiction Studies* 12 (Autumn 1966): 341-347.

Davis, Tom. "J.D. Salinger: The Identity of Sergeant X." *Western Humanities Review* 16 (Spring 1962): 181-83. Rpt. in *Studies in J.D. Salinger.* Ed. Marvin Laser and Norman Fruman. New York: Odyssey, 1963, 261-264.

Dolch, Martin, and John Hagopian. "Down at the Dinghy." In *Insight I: Analyses of American Literature.* Frankfurt: Hirschgraben, 1975, 225-228.

Fitzgerald, F. Scott. *The Great Gatsby* [1925]. New York: Scribner, 1995.

French, Warren. *J.D. Salinger.* Boston: Twayne, 1963.

Grunwald, Henry A., ed. *Salinger: A Critical and Personal Portrait.* New York: Harper, 1962.

Gwynn, Frederick L., and Joseph L. Blotner. *The Fiction of J.D. Salinger.* Pittsburgh: U of Pittsburgh P, 1958.

Hagopian, John V. "'Pretty Mouth and Green My Eyes': Salinger's Paolo and Francesca in New York." *Modern Fiction Studies* 12 (Autumn 1966): 349-354.

Hassan, Ihab. "Rare Quixotic Gesture: The Fiction of J.D. Salinger." *Western Review* 21 (Summer 1957): 261-280. Rpt. in Grunwald 138-163.

Krim, Seymour. "Surface and Substance in a Major Talent" [Review of *Nine Stories*]. *Commonweal* 58 (24 April 1953): 78. Rpt. in Grunwald 64-69.

Lundquist, James. *J.D. Salinger.* New York: Ungar, 1979.

Metcalf, Frank. "The Suicide of Salinger's Seymour Glass." *Studies in Short Fiction* 9 (Summer 1972): 243-246.

Mizener, Arthur. "In Genteel Traditions" [Review of *Nine Stories*]. *New Republic* (23 May 1953): 19-20.

"Nine By Salinger" [Review of *Nine Stories*]. *Newsweek* (6 April 1953): 98.

Russell, John. "Salinger: From Daumier to Smith." *Wisconsin Studies in Contemporary Literature* 4 (Winter 1963): 70-87.

Salinger, J.D. *Nine Stories* [1953]. New York: Bantam, 1964.

Slethaugh, Gordon E. "Seymour: A Clarification." *Renascence* 23 (1971): 115-128.

Stein, William Bysshe. "Salinger's 'Teddy': *Tat Tvam Asi* or That Thou Art." *Arizona Quarterly* 29 (Autumn 1973): 253-265.

Strong, Paul. "Black Wing, Black Heart—Betrayal in J.D. Salinger's 'The Laughing Man'." *West Virginia University Philological Papers* 24 (March 1988): 91-96.

Wakefield, Dan. "Salinger and the Search for Love." *New World Writing* No. 14. New York: New American Library, 1958: 68-85. Rpt. as "The Search for Love" in Grunwald 176-191.

Welty, Eudora. "Threads of Innocence" [Review of *Nine Stories*]. *New York Times Book Review* (5 April 1953): 1. Rpt. in Eudora Welty, *A Writer's Eye: Collected Book Reviews.* Jackson, MS: UP of Mississippi, 1974, 109-110.

Wenke, John. "Sergeant X, Esmé, and the Meaning of Words." *Studies in Short Fiction* 18 (1981): 251-259.

West, Nathanael. *Miss Lonelyhearts* [1933]. New York: Avon, 1964.

Wiegand, William. "Seventy-eight Bananas." *Chicago Review* 11 (1959): 3-19. Rpt. in Grunwald 123-136.

SUGGESTIONS FOR FURTHER READING

Alsen, Eberhard. "A Perfect Day for Bananafish." In *Salinger's Glass Stories as a Composite Novel.* Troy, NY: Whitston, 1983, 9-20.

Antico, John. "The Parody of J.D. Salinger: Esmé and the Fat Lady Exposed." *Modern Fiction Studies* 12 (Autumn 1966): 325-340.

Bryan, James. "The Admiral and Her Sailor in Salinger's 'Down at the Dinghy'." *Studies in Short Fiction* 17 (Spring 1980): 174-178.

Davison, Richard Allen. "Salinger Criticism and 'The Laughing Man': A Case of Arrested Development." *Studies in Short Fiction* 18 (Winter 1981): 1-9.

Genthe, Charles V. "Six, Sex, Sick: Seymour, Some Comments." *Twentieth Century Literature* 10 (January 1965): 170-171.

Hamilton, Kenneth. "Hell in New York: J.D. Salinger's 'Pretty Mouth and Green My Eyes'." *Dalhousie Review* 47 (1967): 394-399.

Kazin, Alfred. "J.D. Salinger: Everybody's Favorite." *Atlantic* 208 (August 1961): 27-31. Rpt. in Grunwald 43-52.

Kaufman, Anthony. "'Along this road goes no one': Salinger's 'Teddy' and the Failure of Love." *Studies in Short Fiction* 35 (1998): 129-140.

Korte, Barbara. "Narrative Perspective in the Works of J.D. Salinger." *Literatur in Wissenschaft und Unterricht* 2 (1987): 343-351.

Piwinski, David. J. "Salinger's 'De Daumier-Smith's Blue Period': Pseudonym as Cryptogram." *Notes on Contemporary Literature* 15 (October 1985): 32-39.

Prigozy, Ruth. "*Nine Stories*: Salinger's Linked Mysteries." In *Modern American Short Story Sequences*. Ed. J. Gerald Kennedy. Cambridge, England: Cambridge UP, 1995, 114-132.

Russell, John. "Salinger's Feat." *Modern Fiction Studies* 12 (Fall 1966): 299-311.

Chapter 5

"Franny"

I'm sick of not having the courage to be an absolute nobody.

Franny

"Franny" was first published in the *New Yorker* on January 29, 1955. In 1961, it was re-published between hard covers as part of *Franny and Zooey*. Internal evidence shows that when Salinger wrote the story, he had not yet decided to make Franny a member of the Glass family. Franny's last name is never mentioned, and there is no reference to her six siblings Seymour, Buddy, Boo Boo, Walter, Waker, and Zooey. Nor is there a reference to Franny in the three earlier stories that deal with other members of the Glass family, "A Perfect Day for Bananafish," "Uncle Wiggily in Connecticut," and "Down at the Dinghy."

Further indications that Salinger changed his mind about Franny can be found in "Zooey." That novella contains a number of statements which contradict what we are told in "Franny." One contradiction concerns Franny's religious background and the little green book she is carrying with her. In "Franny," we are told that she is taking a "Religion Survey" course at college and that she got the little green book, *The Way of a Pilgrim,* out of her college library after her instructor mentioned it to her. But in "Zooey" we find that Franny would probably not take a survey course in religion because she had received years of advanced religious training from her older brothers Seymour and Buddy. Also, Zooey tells us that Franny got *The Way of a Pilgrim* and its sequel *The Pilgrim Continues His Way* not from her college library but from Seymour's room in the Glass family's apartment. And finally, there is a discrepancy concerning the date of Franny's nervous breakdown as it is reported in "Franny" and in "Zooey." In "Franny," the events that are being described must have taken place before January 1955, because that is when the story was first published. But in "Zooey," we get November of 1955 as the time of Franny's nervous collapse ("Zooey" 50).

When Salinger combined the two stories to form the book *Franny and Zooey* (1961), the novelist John Updike noted that "the Franny of 'Franny' and the Franny of 'Zooey' are not the same person." For this reason, so Updike said, "these two stories, so apparently complementary, distinctly jangle as components of one book" (228).

Biographical information explains why the Franny of "Franny" and the Franny of "Zooey" are not the same person. In her memoir *Dream Catcher,* Salinger's daughter Margaret reports that her father wrote "Franny" as a wedding present for her mother, Claire Douglas, and that he deliberately gave Franny some of Claire's traits. Margaret quotes her mother as saying that "it wasn't even Franny's story, it was mine.... In real life, the girl in a blue dress, with the blue-and-white overnight bag slung over her shoulder was named Claire." Margaret also reports that her mother "still has the order slip from Brentano's Bookbinding Department for 'Franny's' book *The Way of a Pilgrim*" (84).

To sum up, the central character in "Franny" is different from the Franny in the later Glass stories because Salinger originally wrote "Franny" as a story for and about his new bride Claire, and he later made subtle changes in order to turn Franny into a member of the Glass family.

CRITICAL RECEPTION

Two notable things about the reception of the story "Franny" are that some readers concluded that Franny's collapse is due to her being pregnant and that others believed the narrator wanted us to identify with Lane Coutell rather than with Franny. However, the publication of the sequel "Zooey" laid those misconceptions to rest.

Almost all the reviewers and critics of "Franny" praised the story and compared it favorably to its sequel "Zooey." For instance, Gwynn and Blotner said that "Franny" is "the best chapter in the Glass history" (46). Granville Hicks noted that even though the story is "conventional in form," it shows that "Salinger's eye and ear are magnificent," especially in his description of the college students waiting for their dates at the train station and in his rendition of the conversation between Franny and Lane (26). And Leslie Fiedler observed that "Franny" is "an eminently satisfactory piece of reportage" because it is "scarcely ever 'cute' like much of 'Zooey'" (57). Above all, Fiedler liked the story because "it ends ambiguously before its author, whose resolutions are often disasters, can manage to be either sentimental or sage" (58).

One of the few negative assessments of "Franny" was that of Maxwell Geismar who found that the story "leaves an unpleasant or disagreeable impression." Geismar said that "the descriptions of Western materialism and Eastern spiritualism ... are hardly convincing," that the story is full of "obscurities," and that "both the central characters become almost equally unpleasant toward the close" (96).

NARRATIVE STRUCTURE AND POINT OF VIEW

In its narrative structure and narrative perspective, "Franny" is a transitional story between *Nine Stories* and the novellas of the Glass Family Series. In its length of 10,600, words "Franny" falls between the longest of the *Nine Stories* and the shortest of the Glass family novellas, but in its structure it is closer to the tight patterns of the earlier pieces than to the more loosely woven webs of the later ones. In its narrative point of view "Franny" also shares elements of Salinger's earlier and later fiction. In the beginning, the narrator uses the very subjective omniscient perspective of Salinger's later fiction, and toward the end, the narrative perspective reverts back to the third person objective point of such earlier stories as "A Perfect Day for Bananafish" and "Pretty Mouth and Green my Eyes."

Another peculiarity of the story is that initially the protagonist and the an-tagonist are given equal importance so that we cannot tell for a while who the central character actually is. In that respect "Franny" is reminiscent of the earlier story "The Varioni Brothers" and the later novellas "Raise High the Roof Beam, Carpenters" and "Seymour—An Introduction." But while the other pieces actu-ally have dual protagonists, in "Franny" it eventually becomes clear that the title character is indeed the protagonist.

Four spaces in the layout of the text of "Franny" reveal a division into five parts that correspond to the five acts of conventional drama: an exposition, a three-part complication, and a resolution. What is less conventional is that the complication part consists of a double conflict, one of them external and the other internal. However, both conflicts are resolved in a clearly marked climax.

The exposition takes place on the platform of a train station where Franny's boyfriend Lane Coutell is waiting for Franny's train. Both are seniors at Ivy League colleges, and Franny is about to join Lane for a football weekend. Right from the start, we see that all is not well in their relationship. This be-comes apparent when Lane re-reads a letter from Franny. Although Franny says five times that she loves Lane, she also hopes that when they meet he won't again analyze everything to death, especially not her. And although one mo-ment she claims that she loves him to pieces, the next moment she says that she hates him when he is being "hopelessly super-male."

More of Franny's negative feelings toward Lane are revealed after her train arrives. She and Lane kiss, and she says that it's lovely to see him and that she missed him. But the narrator tells us that she didn't really mean what she said. Feeling guilty about lying to Lane, Franny gives his arm a little squeeze that is supposed to show her affection. Right from the beginning, the narrator raises the expectation that something is going to happen to bring the conflict between Franny and Lane out into the open.

The complication part of the story consists of a long conversation that Franny and Lane have at a fashionable restaurant. During this conversation, the external conflict between Franny and Lane is paralleled by an internal conflict that Franny experiences. The external conflict is a clash between Lane and Franny's different views on education, poetry, and religion, and the internal conflict is between Franny's worldly and her spiritual aspirations.

The external conflict arises when Lane brags on and on about a literature term paper for which he has received an "A." Franny finally tells him that he talks

like a section man. A section man is a graduate assistant who takes over a professor's literature class and ruins things for the class by tearing down the work
of the author under discussion. Franny realizes that Lane is offended, but she
continues to speak her mind "with equal parts of self-disapproval and malice."
This is where Franny's inner conflict begins. She doesn't want to be malicious,
but she can't help herself. Even though Franny admits that she has felt destructive all week, Lane's irritation with her increases as she tells him she almost
dropped out of college because she doesn't respect any of her professors. When
Lane reminds her that two of her professors are well-known poets, Franny says
their work isn't real poetry but just "syntax droppings."

All through this argument, the external conflict escalates, and the narrator
tells us that Lane is becoming worried that Franny might not be in the mood to
have sex with him later on. Meanwhile, Franny's inner conflict also intensifies,
and as a result she begins to perspire and to get very pale. Franny ignore Lane's
question if she feels all right and suddenly excuses herself to go to the ladies'
room.

The middle part of the complication section begins in the ladies' room where
Franny locks herself in a stall, sits down in a fetal position, and cries for a full
five minutes. Then she takes a small pea-green book from her purse, looks at it
for a short time, and presses it to her chest. This little ritual gives her the
strength to wash her tear-stained face, brush her hair, and face Lane Coutell
again.

The external conflict between Franny and Lane continues when Lane orders
frog legs and objects to Franny ordering only a chicken sandwich and a glass of
milk. And Franny, in turn, objects when Lane talks about his plans to meet his
friend Wally Campbell for drinks before the football game. Franny doesn't
want to see Wally because he represents everything she dislikes about Ivy
League students. After complaining about how conceited and status-conscious
people like Wally Campbell are, Franny concludes her tirade by saying that everything the people around her aspire to do seems insignificant and sad-making
to her.

As Franny is talking, her internal conflict intensifies and she feels "a wave of
self-hatred that, quite literally, made her forehead begin to perspire again" (25).
Also, she turns so pale that Lane notices it and comments on it. The nature of
Franny's internal conflict becomes clear when she explains that what has been
bothering her for some weeks is not only the self-centeredness of other people
but also her own ego. In fact, she quit the play she was cast in because she
suddenly felt that her motives for wanting to be on the stage were utterly selfish
and that she was being a nasty egomaniac. She explains that she is sick of her
own and everybody else's ego. Although she admits that she likes it when people rave about her performance as an actress, she says that she is also ashamed of
herself, and she concludes, "I'm sick of not having the courage to be an absolute
nobody"(30).

At this point, the emphasis has shifted from the external conflict between
Franny and Lane to Franny's internal conflict. In fact, the external conflict gets
damped down when Lane shows concern for Franny's physical condition and
offers her his handkerchief to wipe the perspiration from her forehead.

The third part of the complication section begins when Lane asks Franny

about the little green book she is carrying around with her. In that section of
the narrative, the internal and external conflicts intensify further and eventually
result in Franny's nervous collapse. At first Franny is reluctant to talk about
the little green book. Then she explains that its title is *The Way of a Pilgrim*
and that it was written by an anonymous Russian peasant. The peasant went on
a quest to find out what the Bible means when it gives us the advice to pray
incessantly. The peasant met a *starets*, an advanced religious person, who directed him to a book called the *Philokalia.* The book advocates praying the so-
called Jesus Prayer, "Lord Jesus Christ, have mercy on me," in such a way as to
synchronize the prayer with the heart beat. The effect of this prayer will be to
purify the person's mind and give him or her a totally new outlook on life. We
now begin to see why Franny loves the little green book. She hopes that with
the help of the Jesus Prayer she can resolve her inner conflict and overcome her
selfishness and her critical attitude toward others. But we soon find out that
this is not all she hopes to gain from the Jesus Prayer.

While Franny summarizes of *The Way of a Pilgrim*, the external conflict between her and Lane comes back to the surface. At first this conflict takes the
form of comments by Lane that reveal his lack of interest in what Franny is
telling him. As he is eating his frogs' legs, he interrupts Franny several times
by commenting that he will be reeking of garlic, by asking her if she wants her
butter or if he can have it, and by observing that she hasn't touched her food
yet.

The external conflict comes to a head when Lane has finished eating and has
no choice but to concentrate on what Franny is saying. The result is that he
rides roughshod over her enthusiasm. What excites Franny about the Russian
Orthodox practice of saying the Jesus Prayer incessantly is that it has parallels
in Buddhism and Hinduism. In all three religions there is a belief that if a person keeps saying the name of God over and over again, the person will have a
mystical experience. But when Franny asks Lane if he ever heard anything so
fascinating in his life, Lane can only ask if she actually believes that stuff.
Franny doesn't quite dare to admit that she believes it, but she says it can't be
coincidence that in several religions there are spiritually advanced people who
tell us that if we keep repeating the name of God continuously, something will
happen. Lane now asks what the result is that is supposed to follow from of all
this synchronization mumbo-jumbo. Still unperturbed, Franny now spells out
what she is really after: "You get to see God. Something happens ... and you
see God, that's all" (39). Here Franny reveals her innermost desire to Lane, and
Lane's response is to ask her whether she wants desert or coffee.

Lane's insensitivity and condescension toward Franny precipitate the resolution of both the external and internal conflict. Oblivious to how deep Franny's
religious feelings are, Lane dismisses them as being symptoms of mental instability. He tells Franny that she leaves no margin for elementary psychology and
that there's an obvious psychological explanation for all religious experiences.
After this demonstration of his lack of concern for what's important to Franny,
Lane adds insult to injury when he says: "Anyway. Just in case I forgot to
mention it. I love you. Did I get around to mentioning that?" (40). Because
Lane has literally made Franny sick, Franny excuses herself to go the ladies'
room once more, but on the way she staggers, faints, and collapses. Franny's

collapse is the climax of the story because it ends both the external and the internal conflict.

The short resolution section of the story finds Franny regaining consciousness on a couch in the restaurant manager's office. Some critics have called the story's ending ambiguous, but we can tell from Franny's behavior that she has decided to resolve her conflict with Lane and her inner conflict by withdrawing into the Jesus Prayer. This seems clear from her final interaction with Lane. After Lane has expressed a perfunctory concern for Franny's condition, he once more demonstrates his crassness when he tells Franny that she should go to her rooming house and get a good rest, and later on he would find a way of sneaking into her room. He reminds her that they haven't had sex for over a month, and that's too long for him. Instead of encouraging or discouraging Lane, Franny simply sends him out of the room to get her a glass of water. When she is alone, Franny looks at the ceiling and begins to say the Jesus Prayer under her breath.

The narrative perspective in "Franny" starts out as a third person omniscient point of view, then gradually shifts to a less and less subjective perspective, and finally winds up being totally objective. To put it differently, at the beginning of the story the narrator tells us what Franny and Lane are thinking and feeling, in the middle of the story, he makes guesses as to what their thoughts and feelings are, and at the end he only tells us what they do and say and no longer what they think and feel.

The initial third person omniscient point of view is well illustrated in a paragraph near the beginning of the story which reveals the thoughts and feelings of both Franny and Lane. As the two are ready to order lunch at Sickler's Restaurant, the narrator tells us that Lane looks around the room with a great sense of well-being because he is proud to be "in the right place with an unimpeachably right looking girl" (11). The narrator also tells us that Franny notices Lane's pride and that she not only understands it but that she feels guilty for noticing it. She therefore decides to punish herself by pretending to listen to Lane's conversation with great interest.

As the story progresses, the narrator gets more selective in his omniscience, and he claims that he is not sure what Franny and Lane are thinking. For instance, he says that Lane is watching Franny with mounting irritation and that Lane "quite probably" resents that Franny isn't as absorbed by his conversation as he expects her to be. Similarly, the narrator claims that he doesn't know what causes the glistening perspiration on Franny's forehead. He says the perspiration might only be a sign that the heat in the restaurant is turned up to high, or that Franny has an upset stomach, or that her Martini is too strong. In short, the reader is now invited to help the narrator guess what Franny and Lane's thoughts and feelings are.

In the resolution section of the story, the narrator steps back completely and presents what happens from a third person objective point of view, a point of view that is reminiscent of the short stories of Hemingway and of some of Salinger's own earlier work. That the narrator is now totally objective is especially obvious when Franny regains consciousness while lying on the couch in the restaurant manager's office. Almost as soon as she comes to, Lane tells her about his plan to sneak into her room at the boarding house so they can have sex. When Lane says that there is a back staircase he can use, the narrator tells us that "Franny didn't say anything. She looked at the ceiling." The narrator here forces us to draw our own conclusion from Franny's reaction. If we have felt empathy for Franny in her spiritual crisis, then we understand that her silence means disapproval of Lane's plan. Similarly, in the final paragraph of the story, the narrator leaves us outside of Franny's mind and tells us only that she is still lying on her back, staring and the ceiling, and that her lips are forming soundless words. Most readers of the story will understand that the soundless words on Franny's lips are those of the Jesus Prayer and that she has decided to pray incessantly as advocated in her little green book, *The Way of a Pilgrim*.

CHARACTERIZATION AND STYLE

Franny and Lane represent two recurring character types in Salinger's later fiction, the spiritual person and the unspiritual person. Ralph Waldo Emerson once described these two different types of people when he said that "mankind have ever divided into two sects, Materialists and Idealists" ("Transcendentalist" 87).

Lane follows in the footsteps of such earlier unspiritual characters as Muriel in "A Perfect Day for Bananafish" and Corporal Clay in "For Esmé—With Love and Squalor." Like these forerunners, Lane is self-absorbed, vain, and overly concerned with appearances. But worst of all, Lane thinks that those who value spiritual over material things ought to have their heads examined. Lane expresses his contempt for spiritual matters in two places. When Franny explains that it was her concern about her own selfishness that made her decide to drop out of a play, Lane suggests that Franny might just be afraid to compete and that a really competent psychoanalyst could probably straighten her out. And later when Franny tells Lane that in several religions there are accounts of people achieving visions of God after synchronizing their prayers with their heartbeat, Lane facetiously suggests that such practices might give people heart trouble. Then he tells Franny that he can't take her accounts of people having divine visions seriously because there is an obvious psychological explanation for all mystical experiences. In short, Salinger doesn't want us to like Lane Coutell because Lane is, as the critic Alfred Kazin has observed, "a spiritual enemy" (47).

By contrast, Salinger wants us to like Franny, for she is a spiritual person who follows in the footsteps of such earlier Salinger characters as Sergeant X in "For Esmé—With Love and Squalor" and Teddy McArdle in "Teddy." The most important trait that Franny has in common with these other idealists is that her values make her feel at odds with the materialism of most of the people around her.

At first glance Franny doesn't seem to be so different from Lane Coutell. After all, Lane Coutell is proud to be seen with her because she is such an unimpeachably right-looking girl. But as the story progresses, we find out that Franny is not a typical Ivy League co-ed. In fact, she hates belonging to that particular social and financial bracket because, as she says, everybody in that bracket desperately wants to be interesting and do something terribly distinguished. Eventually, we find out that it is Franny's religious preoccupation that makes her character so different from Lane's.

Despite her attempts to conform to Ivy League undergraduate culture, Franny is aware of a spiritual dimension beyond the appearances of the world of physical objects, and she feels more connected to that spiritual dimension than to the physical and social reality around her. Like Teddy McArdle in the story "Teddy," Franny finds that it is very difficult to lead a spiritual life in America, and like Teddy, she finds that people think she's a freak because she tries to.

As far as Salinger's techniques of characterization in "Franny" are concerned, he uses a mixture telling and showing. In the exposition of the story, the narrator makes a number of statements that tell us explicitly what the personalities of Franny and Lane are like, but as the story progresses, he relies more and more on showing us their character traits through the way they react to one another and above all on the way they speak.

"Franny" begins with a long narrative passage which anticipates the digressive and parenthetical style of later Glass novellas such as "Raise High the Roof Beam, Carpenters" and "Seymour—An Introduction." But the style of the dialogue in the complication part of the story and the narrative sections in the resolution is definitely more like the terse and laconic one of such earlier stories as "A Perfect Day for Bananafish."

We get a whiff of Salinger's later style in the beginning of the story, when Lane and Franny have arrived at a fashionable restaurant. Note the length of the sentence and the digressive qualifying statements that interrupt its flow:

> About an hour later, the two were sitting at a comparatively isolated table in a restaurant called Sickler's, downtown, a highly favored place among, chiefly, the intellectual fringe of students at the college—the same students, more or less, who, had they been Yale or Harvard men, might rather too casually have steered their dates away from Mory's or Cronin's. (10)

One of the typical traits of the style in the narrative sections of "Franny" is that it tends to qualify many of its adjectives with adverbs, as in the phrases "comparatively" isolated and "highly" favored in the quotation above, or when the narrator describes the voices of the students in the train station as "collegiately" dogmatic, or when he describes Franny as "unimpeachably" right-looking and "extraordinarily" pretty.

During the long conversation between Franny and Lane, the style changes as the narrator keeps his analysis of the characters' thoughts, feelings, and motivations to a minimum and instead concentrates on their speech mannerisms and body language. When Lane explains that the professor who gave him an "A" for his term paper on Flaubert is a "big Flaubert man," Franny's response is a monosyllabic "Oh." And then the narrator tells us: "She smiled. She sipped her Martini. 'This is marvelous,' she said, looking at the glass" (12). Here Franny shows her disinterest in Lane's paper by avoiding eye contact with Lane and by not commenting on Lane's professor being a Flaubert specialist and instead praising the quality of her martini. In this and several other instances in the story, Salinger is employing Hemingway's iceberg principle because the most important part of the conversation is not above but below the surface. It is not what Franny says but what she does not say that shows she is not interested in Lane's term paper.

The ending of the story is also written in this sparse style which seems to place more emphasis on what is not being said rather than on what is being said. For instance, when Franny regains consciousness in the restaurant manager's office, Lane asks her if she feels better, and the narrator reports: "Franny nodded. She closed her eyes for a second against the overhead light, then reopened them" (41). The story's last paragraph, which consists of only two sentences, is marked by the same laconic style: "Alone, Franny lay quite still, looking at the ceiling. Her lips began to move, forming soundless words, and they continued to move" (44).

Salinger also uses smaller units of style, such as word choice, as an important tool in delineating the differences between the personalities of Franny and Lane. While Lane's manner of expressing himself is crude, brash, and pretentious, Franny's is emotional, tentative, and apologetic. And while Franny's style exposes her feelings and tries to hide her ideas, Lane's style does the opposite, it overexposes his ideas and tries to hide his feelings.

The first thing we notice about Lane's speech mannerisms is that he uses the adjective "goddam" in almost every other sentence. When we examine the contexts in which he uses the word, we find that for Lane, "goddam" can have both positive and negative connotations. For example, he asks Franny to stop talking about the "goddam" section men that she is comparing him to, but he also wonders if he should publish the "goddam" paper that he received an "A" for. In short, for Lane "goddam" is simply an all-purpose adjective that he uses to create emphasis in a way that is supposed to show how tough and superior he is.

Lane has such a high opinion of himself that he dismisses unimportant detail with the rhetorical phrase "or what"? When he notices that Franny is getting pale and is starting to perspire, he asks if there is anything wrong with her, "or what?" Later on, he again asks her is she is o.k., "or what?" And after Franny has explained the effects of the Jesus Prayer to him, he asks her if she actually believes that stuff, "or what?" The "or what" is rhetorical because Lane isn't really interested in having Franny answer him.

Another aspect of Lane's style is his use of the word "boys" for men who have won universal respect. For instance, Lane refers to classic writers of world literature as "all the real good boys, Tolstoy, Dostoevsky, *Shake*speare"(13). By calling these writers "boys," Lane signals his belief that he is a superior intellect because he is not as impressed by them as everybody else is.

Finally, Lane is given to demonstrating his Ivy League education by using pretentious jargon. The best example of this quality of Lane's style is his assertion that Flaubert's fiction lacks "testicularity." When Franny asks Lane what he means by that, Lane says he means "masculinity." Also, Lane talks about the "motif" of his Flaubert paper and about Flaubert being "neurotically attracted to the *mot juste*" (12). This quality of Lane's style is another indication of his need to convince others that he is a superior individual.

By contrast, Franny's style shows her to be a very insecure and emotional person. For one thing, she is often tentative and even apologetic in expressing her ideas. In her letter to Lane, she apologizes for making spelling mistakes and for sounding "unintelligent and dimwitted." Also, during her conversation with Lane, she says so frequently she is sorry that Lane tells her, "Stop saying you're sorry—do you mind?" (17). And when Franny tells Lane what it is that excites her about the Jesus Prayer, she is afraid to let that excitement show too plainly and adds two qualifiers to the rather tame word "interesting." She says it is "sort of" interesting, "in a way" (36). In response to Lane's question if she really believes that stuff, Franny won't admit that she does and instead says that she didn't say she believed it or she didn't believe it, she only said that it was "fascinating."

The words that Franny keeps repeating also tell us something about her character, namely that she is a person who gives her emotions free reign. When she likes something, she isn't ashamed to call it "lovely" or "marvelous"; and when she wants to give emphasis to words, she uses the words or "terrible" or "terribly" to create both negative and positive emphasis, much as Lane does with the word "goddam." On the one hand, Fanny says that typical college students don't talk about others unless they can say something "terribly" disparaging; on the other hand, she explains that a Russian *starets* is a "terribly" advanced religious person. The difference between Lane and Franny is that the indiscriminate use of "goddam" hides the speaker's feelings while the equally indiscriminate use of "terribly" reveals the speaker's feelings.

SETTINGS AND SYMBOLS

As in most Salinger stories, the general geographical location is the Eastern Seaboard, and the social milieu is upper middle class. There is a reference to the football game between Lane Coutell's college and Yale University, and one critic has speculated that Lane's school must be Princeton. Also, as in most Salinger stories, we get very little information about the physical appearance of the setting, neither of the train station in the exposition, nor of the restaurant and its ladies' room in the complication, nor of the manager's office in the resolution.

Salinger's descriptions of his settings are sketchy, but they provide information that is more important that the visual details. For instance, in the opening paragraph of "Franny," Salinger tells us in his first sentence that the time is the Saturday morning before the big football game against Yale, that the day is brilliantly sunny, but that it is already "overcoat weather." In the second sentence, he tells us that of the 20 or so students who are waiting at the train station for their dates, "no more than six or seven were out on the cold open platform. The rest were standing around in hatless, smoky little groups of twos and threes and fours inside the heated waiting room"(3). So, instead of giving us a description of the physical setting, the train station, Salinger tells us what's more important, the time of year, the day of the week, the time of day, the weather, and the social and emotional ambiance.

Similarly, Salinger does not give us a physical description of Sickler's restaurant where Franny and Lane go for lunch, but he lets us know what the social environment is. He tells us that Sickler's does not specialize in inch-thick steaks but instead is known for its French fare of snails and frog legs. When Lane and Franny have been served their drinks, Lane looks around the restaurant, and we still don't get a description of the place. Instead, the narrator tells us that Lane was brimming over with a sense of well being because he was in the right place with a right-looking girl. The indirect description of the setting tells us that Sickler's is a paradise for people that Holden Caulfield would call "phonies."

However, the setting might have symbolic significance because the name "Sickler's" has several ominous connotations. For one thing, Franny does get physically *sick* at that restaurant. For another thing, one might argue that much of the clientele of the restaurant, the would-be intellectuals among the students at the college, might be spiritually as *sick* as Lane Coutell. More ominously still, a "sickler" is a person who works with a sickle, and that person would be Mr. Death. So the restaurant's name suggests that it is a place of spiritual death or simply the place where Franny and Lane's relationship dies.

The negative connotations of the restaurant's name are amplified by the time of year it is. It seems to be late fall or early winter because there are references to the weather being very cold. It is the season when organic things in nature decay and die—much like Franny's feelings for Lane. The story would have a more hopeful feel if its events took place in spring. However, the negative feeling created by the season also casts doubt on Franny's attempt to solve her spiritual crisis with the help of the Jesus Prayer.

"Franny" is a story so devoid of obvious, contrived symbols that we almost feel guilty looking for symbolism. Perhaps there are indeed no symbols in the conventional sense, but the narrator uses several objects and metaphors to clarify the personalities of Franny and Lane and the nature of their conflict.

When Lane uses of the word "testicularity" instead of "masculinity" in describing what he thinks Flaubert's fiction lacks, the word takes on a metaphoric quality because it describes the excess testosterone that seems to be driving Lane. Franny addresses that aspect of Lane's character when she says in her letter that she hates him when he is being "hopelessly super-male." Lane's "testicularity" asserts itself again at the end of the story when Franny is just regaining consciousness after her nervous collapse and Lane wastes no time in telling her of his plans to have sex with her.

Additional light is shed on Lane's character by his choice of frogs' legs at the restaurant. When Franny is "intensely interested in the way Lane was dismembering his frogs' legs," it almost seems as if she is watching herself being dismembered. After all, in her letter she had complained about Lane analyzing her too much. And a moment later, Lane's interaction with the frogs' legs has an almost sexual connotation when he interrupts Franny's story of the Jesus Prayer by saying to a pair of frogs' legs, "Hold still."

Franny's choice of food also has symbolic connotations. Instead of ordering frogs' legs or snails, as Lane expects her to, she orders a chicken sandwich and a glass of milk. First of all, her choice reveals that she doesn't care to make a status statement with her order. But more importantly, the very humbleness of a chicken sandwich and a glass of milk is in keeping with the story of the Russian pilgrim that she is telling, for she explains that the only food the pilgrim carries in his knapsack is some bread and some salt. Therefore, Franny's order of an extremely simple meal foreshadows her decision to emulate the Russian peasant in the book *The Way of a Pilgrim*.

There are two other aspects of Franny's behavior that are symbolic, and both foreshadow the story's ending, Franny's withdrawal into the Jesus Prayer. This withdrawal in foreshadowed the first time when Lane asks Franny a question about her letter and Franny doesn't answer because she has blocked him out and is concentrating on a small speck of sunshine on the table. Instead of answering Lane's question, Franny stares at the little circle of sunshine so intensely that it seems to the narrator that Franny would like to become very small and lie down in that circle of sunlight. The second time, Franny physically withdraws from Lane not only by going to the ladies' room, but by sitting down and pulling her legs up to her chin so as to assume what the narrator calls a "fetal position."

Finally, there is the symbolism of Franny's little pea-green, cloth bound book, *The Way of a Pilgrim*. The book takes on symbolic significance because Franny is initially very defensive and later very effusive about it, and in between she treats it like an amulet with mystical powers.

Lane notices the book for the first time as he greets Franny on the platform of the railroad station. When he asks what the book is, Franny doesn't want to tell him, and she quickly stuffs it into her handbag. Later, after Franny has begun to perspire profusely because her conflict with Lane and her inner conflict have made her physically ill, she takes the book to the ladies' room with her. There, she engages in the ritual of looking at the book for a while and then pressing it to her chest. This gives her the strength to wash her face, brush her hair, and come walking out of the ladies' room looking as stunning as ever. It seems therefore that the little green book has magic powers because it helps Franny to temporarily pull out of her depression.

The full symbolic importance of the book becomes apparent in the last third of the story when Lane asks Franny about it and she explains its content, at first reluctantly and later enthusiastically. Franny explains that the book contains instructions on how to pray without ceasing so that one will see God. Unaware of Lane's disinterest in the book, she asks him if he has ever heard anything so fascinating in his entire life. To Franny the little book is the most fascinating thing she has ever encountered. She believes it can cure her of her selfishness.

The little green book can therefore be seen to represent Franny's hope for spiritual advancement. Green is, of course, the color of hope. But the book is ultimately an ambivalent symbol because it is questionable if the kind of spiritual practice that it advocates will enlighten Franny and make her as happy and peaceful as she expects to be.

THEMES AND INTERPRETATIONS

Some early commentaries on the story treated "Franny" essentially as a social satire on academia and Lane Coutell as a personification of what's wrong with higher education. Several of these interpretations quote a passage from "Zooey" as expressing the message of "Franny." In that passage, Franny complains that colleges are places dedicated to knowledge for knowledge's sake, and she says what she misses in college is the notion that "knowledge *should* lead to *wisdom*, and if it *doesn't*, it's just a disgusting waste of time" ("Zooey" 146).

Very few critics have interpreted "Franny" as an independent story and not as the "prequel" to "Zooey." One of these critics is Klaus Karlstetter who says that "Franny" illustrates "the frustrations common to many young people of today who become so involved with the teachings of various forms of mysticism that they fail to perceive the fundamental idea present in all of them" (231). That fundamental idea is the belief in "the divinity present in all mankind," a belief shared by J.D. Salinger, Vedanta Hinduism, Aldous Huxley's "perennial philosophy," and Emersonian Transcendentalism (226-227). Another critic who has looked at "Franny" as a self-contained story is William Wiegand. He says that when Franny silently recites the Jesus Prayer at the end of the story, "Franny is using it, evidently, as a narcotic, so that it carries her away." Franny's behavior therefore illustrates an observation of the Danish philosopher Søren Kierkegaard who said: "The God-relation infinitizes; but this may so carry a man away that it becomes an inebriation" (Wiegand 143).

Other critics have interpreted "Franny" in the context of themes familiar from Salinger's previous work. Franny has been likened to Holden Caulfield in her irritation with the "phoniness" of people such as Lane Coutell and his friend Wally Campbell; or she has been likened to Sergeant X in "For Esmé—with Love and Squalor" who had a nervous breakdown because of his inability to love; or she has been compared to the God-seeker Teddy McArdle in the story "Teddy" who, like Franny, swims against the materialist mainstream of American culture because he wants to lead a spiritual life.

By far the most common approach to interpreting the meaning of "Franny" has been to discuss it in the context of the later Glass stories and treat it as a prologue to "Zooey." Seen this way, Franny's nervous breakdown is the result of the religious training she received from her older brothers Buddy and Seymour. This approach is taken by Robert Detweiler in his book *Four Spiritual Crises in Mid-Century American Fiction*. Detweiler says that Franny's crisis "is the result of a confused concept of sainthood" (37). Franny has worshipped her older brother Seymour as though he were a saint, and his suicide has "shaken her faith." Moreover, her disgust for "normal society," which stems from the religious education she received from Seymour and Buddy, is taking on pathological proportions. What drives her over the brink and into a nervous breakdown is the two pilgrim books which she got from Seymour's desk. Through the Jesus Prayer, Franny intends to "force a vision of God," but she fails, and the reason for her failure is that Seymour has become "her surrogate for Jesus" and therefore "her prayer is directed more toward Seymour than toward Christ" (38-39). Ultimately, Franny "wishes to have the holy life without the distractions of the crude, unenlightened worldly society" that surrounds her. This, so Detweiler says, is "a dangerous desire and the one which caused Seymour himself to founder" (39).

CONCLUSION

"Franny" (1955) is the second installment of the Glass Family Series, the first being "A Perfect Day for Bananafish" (1948). Like "A Perfect Day for Bananafish," "Franny" was apparently written before Salinger had decided to write a narrative series about the Glass family. Also like "A Perfect Day for Bananafish," "Franny" is a short story while the next four installments of the Glass Family Series are all novellas. The narrative structure of "Franny" is conventional, but the narrative perspective is not because it shifts from an initial third person omniscient point of view to a third person objective point of view near the end. The central conflict in "Franny" parallels that in "A Perfect Day for Bananafish" because it is a conflict between two familiar types of Salinger characters, the spiritual and the unspiritual person, the idealist and the materialist. Franny's boy friend Lane Coutell is a totally unspiritual person who believes that psychiatrists can explain all there is to know about human motivation and behavior. By contrast, Franny is a deeply spiritual person who is consumed by the belief that by saying the Jesus Prayer incessantly and by synchronizing it with her heartbeat, she may get to see God.

The most important difference between "Franny" and "A Perfect Day for Bananafish" is that its central concern is religious while no religious ideas are mentioned in "Bananafish." In that respect, "Franny" is similar to the story "Teddy" (1953) which also has a central character who finds it difficult to lead a spiritual life in mid-twentieth-century America.

For the reader who would like to become acquainted with Salinger's Glass Family Series, "Franny" would make an ideal introduction. It is not only shorter and easier to read than the later novellas, but it also provides a better introduction to the religious ideas in the Glass Family Series because in "Franny" these religious ideas come mostly from a familiar Christian context rather than from Advaita Vedanta, classical Taoism, and Zen Buddhism as they do in the later parts of the Glass Family Series.

The themes that are developed in "Franny" are familiar ones from Salinger's previous work: the theme of the general phoniness of middle-class American life (*The Catcher in the Rye*), the theme of the conflict between the sensitive idealist and the assertive materialist ("The Inverted Forest"), and above all, the related themes of the near-impossibility to lead a spiritual life in America ("Teddy") and of the conflict between spiritual and material values ("A Perfect Day for Bananafish").

What has not yet been sufficiently explored in analyses of "Franny" is the story's psychological and sociological implications. For instance, although Franny and Lane are supposedly lovers, their conversation is full of deliberate miscommunication and even hostility. A study of their motivations for keeping their hopeless relationship going might reveal valuable insights into the dynamics of young male-female relationships. And although the story has been analyzed as a satire on collegiate life in the Ivy League, much more can be done in analyzing the degree to which Franny and Lane's different values reflect trends in American upper middle-class culture of the 1950s.

WORKS CITED

Detweiler, Robert. "J.D. Salinger and the Quest for Sainthood." In *Four Spiritual Crises in Mid-Century American Fiction.* Coral Gables: U of Florida P, 1963, 36-41.

Emerson, Ralph Waldo. "The Transcendentalist." In *The Selected Writings of Ralph Waldo Emerson.* Ed. Brooks Atkinson. New York: Modern Library, 1950, 87-103.

Fiedler, Leslie. "Up From Adolescence." *Partisan Review* 29 (Winter 1962): 127-131. Rpt. in Grunwald 57-62."

Geismar, Maxwell. "The Wise Child and the *New Yorker* School of Fiction." In *American Moderns: From Rebellion to Conformity.* New York: Hill and Wang, 1958, 195-209. Rpt. in Grunwald 87-101.

Grunwald, Henry A., ed. *Salinger: A Critical and Personal Portrait.* New York: Harper, 1962.

Gwynn, Frederick L., and Joseph L. Blotner. "Franny." In *The Fiction of J.D. Salinger.* Pittsburgh: U of Pittsburgh P, 1958, 46-48.

Hicks, Granville. "Sisters, Sons, and Lovers" [Review of *Franny and Zooey*]. *Saturday Review* 44 (September 1961): 26.

Karlstetter, Klaus. "J.D. Salinger, R.W. Emerson and the Perennial Philosophy." *Moderna Sprak* 63 (1969): 224-236.

Kazin, Alfred. "J.D. Salinger: Everybody's Favorite." *Atlantic* 208 (Aug. 1961): 27-31. Rpt. in Grunwald 43-52.

Salinger, J.D. *Franny and Zooey* [1961]. New York: Bantam, 1964.

Salinger, Margaret. *Dream Catcher.* New York: Washington Square, 2000.

Updike, John. "Anxious Days for the Glass Family" [Review of *Franny and Zooey*]. *New York Times Book Review* 17 Sepember 1961: 1, 52. Rpt. in Grunwald 53-56.

Wiegand, William. "Salinger and Kierkegaard." *Minnesota Review* 5 (1965): 137-156.

SUGGESTIONS FOR FURTHER READING

Chester, Alfred. "Salinger: How to Love Without Love." *Commentary* 35 (June 1963): 467-474.

French, R.M., trans. *The Way of a Pilgrim and The Pilgrim Continues His Way.* New York: Seabury, 1965.

French, Warren. "Franny." In *J.D. Salinger, Revisited.* Boston: G.K. Hall, 1988, 89-93.

Hamilton, Kenneth. "One Way to Use the Bible: The Example of J.D. Salinger." *Christian Scholar* 47 (1964): 243-251.

McIntyre, John P. "A Preface for 'Franny and Zooey'." *Critic* 20 (1962): 25-28.

Panichas, George A. "J.D. Salinger and the Russian Pilgrim." In *The Reverent Disciple.* Knoxville: U of Tennessee P, 1974, 372-387.

Seitzman, Daniel. "Salinger's 'Franny': Homoerotic Imagery." *American Imago* 22 (1965): 57-76.

Chapter 6

"Raise High the Roof Beam, Carpenters"

He threw [the stone] at her because she looked so beautiful.

Buddy Glass

"Raise High the Roof Beam, Carpenters" first came out in the *New Yorker* on 19 November 1955, 10 months after "Franny." In 1963, it was reprinted in a book with the unusually long title *Raise High the Roof Beam, Carpenters and Seymour—An Introduction.* It is in "Carpenters" that all nine members of the Glass family are mentioned for the first time. Since Salinger's previous story, "Franny," doesn't mention Franny's family name or the names of any of her siblings, Salinger must have formulated his plan for a narrative series about the Glass family between the time he wrote "Franny" and the time he wrote "Carpenters."

"Raise High the Roof Beam, Carpenters" is told by Buddy Glass, and it is his account of the events on his brother Seymour's wedding day in 1942. World War II is going on, and Buddy is in the military, but he gets a three-day pass to travel from Fort Benning, Georgia, to New York for the wedding. However, Buddy and the rest of the wedding party wait in vain for Seymour to arrive. Eventually, the parents of Muriel, the bride, announce that they will give a reception at their apartment, wedding or no wedding. Buddy winds up in a limousine with four other wedding guests, the Matron of Honor and her husband, an aunt of Muriel's, and Muriel's great uncle, a tiny old gentleman in a tuxedo and top hat. During the limousine ride, the Matron of Honor is boiling with anger about Seymour's failure to show up for the wedding, and Buddy unsuccessfully tries to withhold the information that he is the brother of the absentee bridegroom. When the limousine gets held up indefinitely by a parade, Buddy invites the four other occupants to telephone the bride's parents from his and Seymour's nearby apartment. The apartment is now occupied by their sister Beatrice, a.k.a Boo Boo, who hardly ever uses it because she is in the Navy. At the apartment, the Matron of Honor continues to attack Seymour, and Buddy finally explodes with an irrational defense of his brother. Thereafter, the Matron of Honor makes her phone call and reports that Seymour and Muriel have eloped. Meanwhile Buddy has found Seymour's diary, and in its most recent entry he discovers information that explains why Seymour stood up Muriel at the wedding ceremony.

CRITICAL RECEPTION

"Raise High the Roof Beam, Carpenters" drew mixed reviews. Some critics appreciated the new ground that Salinger was breaking in terms of narrative structure, style, and subject matter, but others deplored not only his departure from the terse style and tight structure of the pieces in *Nine Stories* but also his decision to pursue further the religious themes of stories such as "De Daumier-Smith's Blue Period," "Teddy," and "Franny."

The most enthusiastic praise of "Carpenters" came from novelist John Updike and critic Alfred Kazin. Updike said about "Carpenters" that it is "the best of the Glass pieces: A magic and hilarious prose-poem with an enchanting end effect of mysterious clarity" (229). Kazin focused on the sociological aspects of the Glass stories which most other critics neglected. Kazin said that "the whole charm of Salinger's fiction lies in his gift for comedy, his ability to represent society as it is, for telltale gestures and social manners." Kazin concluded that "Raise High the Roof Beam, Carpenters" is probably Salinger's "best story" and that it is a "beautifully spun-out account" full of "meticulous telling of every detail" and "light ironic allusions to the contrasts of the shifting social groupings in the obviously but not explicitly Jewish bourgeoisie" (115-116).

"Carpenters" received the harshest comments from the reviewers of *Newsweek* and *Commentary* magazines. The anonymous reviewer for *Newsweek* granted that there is a "comic exhilaration" and an "emotional daring" in "Carpenters" which "sets Salinger quite apart from other living writers." But those traits are "a momentary flash, unfortunately, obscured by the whole tone and accenting of the story, which is far less a paean to Seymour than a merely boastful tale of Buddy's entitled 'How I Slew the Philistines And Found Love in my Brother's Diary'" (90). Even more negative was Alfred Chester's review in *Commentary*. Chester deplored Salinger's religious preoccupation and said about "Raise High the Roof Beam, Carpenters" that it is the "fakest and most trivial kind of hagiography" and that Seymour, the saint who is the subject of this hagiography, "is nothing but a mixture of cold blood and confectioner's sugar," in other words "a sopping fraud" (471-472). Moreover, in "Carpenters," so Chester said, "Salinger becomes desperate in his style" because he "must use a thousand abstract words to describe what once took ten concrete ones. For his lost charm, he substitutes archaisms, cutenesses, coynesses, leaden mannerisms" (471). It is an indication of Chester's total rejection of Salinger's outlook that he considers Muriel Fedder and Lane Coutell to be the most sympathetic characters in all of his work.

NARRATIVE STRUCTURE AND POINT OF VIEW

While its immediate predecessor, "Franny," is a short story, "Raise High the Roof Beam, Carpenters" is a novella. For one thing, "Carpenters" is more than twice as long (23,350 vs. 10,700 words); for another thing, "Franny" doesn't have a subplot and "Carpenters" does. Moreover, "Carpenters" is more complex in its narrative perspective than "Franny." It is told in the first person by Buddy Glass, but Buddy not only makes self-reflexive comments on the way he tells his story, but he also varies the narrative perspective and the narrative distance.

Despite its other differences from "Franny," "Raise High the Roof Beam, Carpenters" also begins with an external conflict which eventually gives way to a more important internal one. Moreover, as in "Franny," we initially can't tell who the protagonist is. But while this question is settled in the climax of "Franny," "Carpenters" doesn't have a clearly marked climactic scene, and it really has not one but two central characters.

"Raise High the Roof Beam, Carpenters" begins with an anecdote that demonstrates Buddy's high opinion of Seymour. In this anecdote, Buddy tells of a time some 20 years earlier, when he was fifteen and Seymour seventeen, and the ten-month-old Franny couldn't go to sleep because she had the mumps. Seymour therefore read her a Taoist tale. The tale was about a Duke Mu whose horse trainer Po Lo was too old to travel around and scout for good horses, so the duke sent Chiu-fang Kao in Po Lo's stead to find a horse for him that was truly exceptional. Chiu-fang Kao returned from his mission with a perfect animal, but he could not tell whether the horse was a mare or a stallion and what color it was. Duke Mu was taken aback, but Po Lo realized that Kao was indeed a superlative judge of horses because he paid attention only to a horse's "spiritual mechanism" and not to such unimportant details as color and gender. Buddy concludes the anecdote by comparing Seymour to Chiu-fang Kao and by saying that despite Seymour's suicide he cannot think of anyone whom he would care to send out looking for horses in Seymour's stead.

The anecdote about Seymour reading the Taoist tale to Franny forms the prologue to "Raise High the Roof Beam, Carpenters." In the exposition proper, Buddy provides information about his family. This information explains why Buddy is the only member of the Glass family who shows up for Seymour's wedding in 1942. At that time, the family is flung all over the United States. The parents—the former vaudeville team of Les Glass and Bessie Gallagher—are currently in California and have their two youngest children Zooey (Zachary) and Franny (Frances) with them. They can't come to New York because Franny is sick. Walter is in the Army, somewhere in the Pacific; his twin brother Waker is interned in a conscientious objectors' camp; and Boo Boo (Beatrice), a Navy ensign on the staff of an admiral, is on a trip with her boss. In this part of the exposition, Buddy also informs us that the seven Glass children all were, or still are, regulars on a national radio quiz show called "It's a Wise Child," and that Seymour was the brightest of the bunch.

As the story of Seymour's wedding day unfolds, it is initially the external conflict between the Matron of Honor and the absent Seymour that keeps us reading. The woman is so angry that she says she would like to strangle

Seymour, and two of the other passengers in the limousine, the woman's husband and Muriel's aunt, a Mrs. Silsburn, seem to share her feelings. However, the fourth passenger, the tiny old gentleman in the tuxedo and top hat keeps silent and stares straight ahead. When the Matron of Honor asks Buddy what his connection with Seymour is, Buddy only tells her that he and Seymour were boys together. At this point, Buddy becomes involved in the conflict as the Matron of Honor's secondary antagonist because we are made to wonder if the Matron of Honor will find out that he is Seymour's brother and what she will say to him when she does.

The conflict escalates when the Matron of Honor reports that the mother of the bride, Mrs. Fedder, is convinced that Seymour is a latent homosexual and a schizoid personality. She also reports that Seymour begged Muriel to postpone the wedding because he was "too *happy* to get married." The Matron of Honor says that Seymour should be "stuck in some booby hatch" because he is "an absolute raving maniac" (39-40). To support her opinion, she mentions that the crooked smile on the face of Charlotte Mayhew, a well-known movie actress, is due to a childhood incident when she had to have nine stitches in her face because Seymour hit her.

The external conflict intensifies further after the Matron of Honor makes Buddy admit that he is indeed Seymour's brother, and when she begins to attack not only Seymour but also Buddy and his other siblings. She refers to the notoriety that the Glass children achieved as the stars of the radio show "It's a Wise Child," and she says that they all led freakish lives when they were kids and that they never learned to relate to normal people.

There is a short respite in the conflict when the limousine gets held up by an interminable parade and the Matron of Honor decides that they should all walk to the nearby Schrafft's restaurant on 79th Street and call Muriel's parents from there. When it turns out that the restaurant is closed, Buddy invites the other wedding guests to come to his and Seymour's nearby apartment and make their phone call from there.

At Seymour and Buddy's apartment, the external conflict is renewed when the Matron of Honor brings up the Charlotte Mayhew incident again and says to Buddy that Seymour doesn't know how to relate to anybody because all he can do is hurt people so they need stitches in their faces. Seymour is therefore totally unfit for marriage. The Matron of Honor concludes her new tirade by revealing that all this is exactly what the bride's mother, Mrs. Fedder, had said about Seymour earlier that day.

At this point the external conflict is resolved when Buddy blows up. He calls Mrs. Fedder a professional dilettante and amateur bitch and lumps her together with all the small-minded people who have analyzed Seymour ever since he was ten years old. He says that Seymour never was a nasty little egomaniac who wanted to show off his high-I.Q., and he adds that nobody outside his family has ever seen him for what he really was: "A poet, for God" sake" (60). Buddy's defense of Seymour on the grounds that he is a poet cannot possibly make any sense to the Matron of Honor because she is not the kind of person who would value poetry. Before the Matron of Honor can respond to Buddy, he announces that he will fix cold drinks for everybody.

Although the external conflict is now resolved, Buddy's inner conflict is not. This inner conflict is between Buddy's admiration of Seymour and three very unadmirable choices Seymour made. These choices are his cruelty to Charlotte Mayhew way back when he was twelve years old, his choice of Muriel as a marriage partner, and his decision to stand up Muriel at the altar. In short, what happens to Buddy on Seymour's wedding day is that his high opinion of his brother is put to a severe test.

We get the first inkling of Buddy's inner conflict early on in the story when Buddy realizes that the Matron of Honor's anger at Seymour is justified. She says that a person can't just go around hurting other people's feelings whenever he or she feels like it, and Buddy admits that the Matron of Honor made him feel a touch of prejudice against Seymour for being so unkind to Muriel and her parents.

Buddy's slight irritation with Seymour's behavior turns into inner turmoil after the Matron of Honor brings up the injury that Seymour caused Charlotte Mayhew by deliberately hitting her in the face with a stone. When the Matron of Honor reminds him of the Charlotte Mayhew incident, Buddy apparently thinks that Seymour's failure to show up for his own wedding is another one of his inexplicable acts of cruelty. Buddy is therefore relieved when the Matron of Honor makes a phone call to the parents of the bride and reports that Seymour and Muriel have eloped to get married privately. But this does not resolve Buddy's inner conflict. It merely shifts Buddy's attention to the question of why Seymour would want to get married to someone as superficial as Muriel in the first place.

This aspect of Buddy's inner conflict is a worry that was placed in his mind by his sister Boo Boo when she wrote him a letter asking him to attend Seymour's wedding. Because Buddy has never met Muriel, he relies on Boo Boo's judgment of her personality, and this judgment is negative. Boo Boo says that Muriel is intellectually a zero but that she is extremely good-looking.

Buddy's worry about Seymour marrying the wrong kind of person is intensified after he finds Seymour's diary and retreats to the bathroom to read it. This diary makes up the subplot and accounts for over 10% of the novella's length. The entries record Seymour's courtship of Muriel from December 1941 up to the day before the wedding on 4 June 1942, and they all deal with visits that Seymour made to meet Muriel's parents and with dates on which Seymour and Muriel went together. These diary entries show not only that Muriel is simpleminded but also that she is selfish and materialistic. However, Seymour says that he worships and needs Muriel's simplicity, and he is even willing to see a psychiatrist for her sake.

After Buddy learns that Seymour has agreed to have himself psychoanalyzed, he cannot bear to continue reading and slams the diary shut. It seems that he is angry because Seymour plans to see a psychiatrist in order to become more "normal" like Muriel.

Buddy's anger about Seymour's choice of Muriel as a marriage partner manifests itself in his agitated behavior. After he slams the diary shut, he flings it into a laundry hamper with a vicious movement of his wrist. Then he storms out of the bathroom and slams the door behind him. He goes to the kitchen to pour himself a tall drink of Scotch while whimpering softly to himself. And because Buddy is a non-drinker, he swigs the Scotch down in one huge gulp.

Buddy's inner turmoil increases when he finds out that Muriel looks a lot like Charlotte Mayhew. This happens when Muriel's aunt, Mrs. Silsburn, looks at a photograph of Charlotte Mayhew from "It's a Wise Child" and observes that Charlotte could have been Muriel's double when they were children. The information leaves Buddy stunned and unable to consider its many ramifications. When Mrs. Silsburn asks Buddy if Seymour meant to hurt Charlotte Mayhew when he hit her in the face with a stone or if it was an accident, Buddy can only stammer, "Oh, God, Mrs. Silsburn" (84). Buddy is saved from having to give an answer when the Matron of Honor announces the news of Seymour and Muriel's elopement. At that point all of Buddy's guests leave, except for Muriel's great uncle, the little deaf-mute gentleman.

Seymour's elopement with Muriel resolves part of Buddy's inner conflict, but he is still so troubled by the Charlotte Mayhew incident that he feels compelled to lie about it to the deaf-mute. Buddy tells him that Seymour threw the stone at Charlotte "because she looked so beautiful sitting there in the middle of the driveway with Boo Boo's cat" (89). Everyone, so Buddy tells the deaf-mute, understood Seymour's behavior, even Charlotte herself. But then Buddy admits to us, his readers, that he is a liar and that Charlotte never understood why Seymour threw that stone at her. Buddy here implies that he did not understand Seymour's behavior either and that he still doesn't. It is possible that Buddy is so agitated because he sees Seymour's throwing a stone at Charlotte and his extreme unkindness to Charlotte's look-alike, Muriel, as signs of a cruel side to Seymour's character that he does not want to acknowledge.

Buddy resolves his inner conflict when he retrieves Seymour's diary and reads the rest of it. The diary shows that Seymour asked Muriel several times to elope with him. On the day before the wedding, Seymour begged Muriel for the last time to just go off alone with him and get married privately because he was too excited to be with a lot of people. And then he explains that he feels as though he were about to be re-born: "Sacred, sacred day." Seymour's sacramental view of marriage comes from a miscellany of Vedanta that he has been reading all day. According to the Vedanta view of marriage, marriage partners should serve each other: "Elevate, help, teach, strengthen each other, but above all *serve*." Seymour ends his last diary entry with the words: "The joy of responsibility for the first time" (90-91)

This last diary entry explains two things that were not clear before. One is that the reason Seymour did not show up for the wedding ceremony was not that he was afraid of marriage, as Mrs. Fedder assumed, or that he wanted to hurt Muriel, as Buddy apparently assumed. Instead, the reason was that he was so unbearably happy to be entering a new stage of his life that he did not want to share this moment with anyone but his bride. The other problem that the last diary entry clarifies is that Seymour married Muriel because he felt that he could be spiritually elevated by her simplicity just as much as she could by his erudition.

After Buddy reads Seymour's last diary entry, he goes to sleep (or passes out from too much Scotch), and when he wakes up, he is reconciled to Seymour's choice of Muriel. He even thinks of sending the couple a wedding gift, albeit one so strange that even Seymour might have trouble understanding it. That wedding gift—which Buddy does not send—is the butt-end of the old deaf-mute's cigar in a nice gift box, accompanied by a blank page of paper "by way of explanation."

Although "Raise High the Roof Beam, Carpenters" is told from a first person point of view and could therefore be expected to be an extremely subjective narrative, the narrator, Buddy Glass, uses two narrative techniques to mitigate the subjectivity of his account. The first of these techniques is to insert pieces of writing composed by other writers, and the second is to vary the narrative distance, that is, the distance from which we, the readers, are made to perceive what happens in his narrative. These shifts in narrative distance include three passages in which Buddy makes self-reflexive comments on the way in which he is telling the story.

Right from the start, Buddy varies the narrative perspective when he invites another writer into his narrative by reprinting the Taoist tale that Seymour read to the ten-month-old Franny. This tale is immediately followed by the first instance of self-reflexiveness in the novella which is also the first shift in narrative distance. It occurs as Buddy explains to us why he begins his account of Seymour's wedding day with this Taoist tale. The reason is to assure us from the start that Seymour—his suicide notwithstanding—was as perceptive a judge of people as Chiu-fang Kao was a judge of horses.

Before Buddy starts his account of Seymour's wedding day, he again shifts the narrative perspective when he reproduces a second piece of writing by someone else. This second piece of writing is the letter from his sister Boo Boo who urges him to attend Seymour's wedding because no one else in the Glass family is able to. In this letter, Boo Boo tells Buddy that she thinks Muriel is a zero and her mother is insufferable.

Buddy varies the narrative distance a second time by inserting a self-reflexive paragraph into the story right after the Matron of Honor has begun her verbal attacks on Seymour. Buddy begins this self-reflexive section by saying that he thinks a paragraph should be wedged in at this point to answer two questions: One is why he, Buddy, got into the limousine to ride to a reception where he knew he would not be welcome, and the other question is why he didn't get out of the limousine when it was stopped? The lame answers Buddy gives to these two questions are that the army had trained him to keep close to the herd and that he was lonely.

Buddy again varies the narrative perspective when he reproduces a second piece of writing by his sister Boo Boo. This happens after the conflict between Buddy and the Matron of Honor has been after the Matron of Honor had labeled Seymour a schizoid personality and a latent homosexual and Buddy had risen to Seymour's defense. The piece of writing that Buddy reproduces at this point is a message that Boo Boo wrote on the bathroom mirror for Seymour. It begins with these two lines from a poem by the classical Greek poet Sappho: "Raise high the roof beam, carpenters. Like Ares comes the bridegroom, taller far than a tall man" (65). What is crucial about Boo Boo's message is that she considers Seymour to be spiritually head and shoulders above other humans. The purpose of inserting Boo Boo's mirror message at this point in the narrative seems to be chiefly to lend support to Buddy's positive view of Seymour as opposed to the negative view of the Matron of Honor and Mrs. Fedder.

The most important shifts in narrative perspective occur near the end of the novella when Buddy reproduces the two sections of Seymour's diary that deal with his courtship of Muriel. But before Buddy reproduces the first entry from Seymour's diary, he indulges in his third self-reflexive comment and explains that what follows will be an "exact reproduction" of Seymour's diary entries. He also tells us that he will leave out the dates for the individual entries but that they are all from late 1941 and early 1942.

The first and longer of the two diary excerpts—it takes up almost ten pages—contains two bits of information that Buddy Glass apparently finds disturbing. One concerns Seymour's choice of Muriel as a marriage partner, and the other concerns Seymour's cruelty in hurting Charlotte Mayhew by throwing a stone at her. The diary reveals that Seymour knew Buddy would despise Muriel for being a very simple-minded person, but Seymour says that he worships Muriel's simplicity. The other bit of information that apparently upsets Buddy is that Seymour claims that the Charlotte Mayhew incident is "old finished business" but that he admits he still can't discuss his hurting Charlotte Mayhew, at least "not over just one drink" (74).

When Buddy stops reading the diary, we not only get a shift back from Seymour's to Buddy's point of view but also a shift in narrative distance. Because Buddy is so upset about what he just read in Seymour's diary, he no longer tells us what he thinks and feels, and we have to deduce his thoughts and emotions from his behavior as if the story were being told by a third person objective narrator. We notice how upset Buddy is when he slams the bathroom door behind him and whimpers softly as he fixes Tom Collinses for his guests.

This brief passage of third person objective narration comes to an end when Buddy reports that, like a cartoon character, he suddenly saw a light bulb being turned on above his head. The bright idea that occurs to Buddy is to pour himself a large drink of Scotch even though he is a non-drinker. Here he is emulating Seymour in trying to anesthetize himself with alcohol.

Right after Buddy reports drinking the tall glass of Scotch in one huge gulp, there is another brief passage of self-reflexiveness in which Buddy comments on his storytelling. He says that it is with a definite shudder that he has told us about gulping down four fingers of Scotch.

The narrative perspective shifts again from Buddy's to Seymour's point of view when Buddy reproduces Seymour's last diary entry. This entry lays to rest Buddy's fear that Seymour's standing up Muriel at the altar was a deliberate act of cruelty. Buddy is reassured when Seymour reveals that he sees his wedding day as so "sacred" that he wants to spend it only with Muriel and not with a lot of strangers. Moreover, Seymour sees marriage as a new beginning in his spiritual quest, and he thinks that he needs Muriel's simplicity as much as she needs his spirituality.

When we return to Buddy's point of view in the last three paragraphs of the novella, he is again sharing his thoughts and feelings. We find that he is not overjoyed about Seymour's marriage to Muriel but he is no longer upset about it. Like Boo Boo, he seems to feel that maybe the marriage will work out all right.

CHARACTERIZATION AND STYLE

The most curious thing about the characterization in "Raise High the Roof Beam, Carpenters" has to do with the names of the nine members of the Glass family. No previous story mentions all nine names. When Buddy lists those names in the exposition of "Carpenters," it is striking that more than half of them have double vowels or double consonants in them: Bessie, Buddy, Boo Boo, Zooey, and Franny. So does their last name, Glass, and Bessie's maiden name, Gallagher. This doubling of letters in his characters' names is a peculiarity in Salinger's fiction that goes back to apprentice stories such as "The Hang of It" where the double letters in the names of Harry and Bobby Pettit point to a theme of doubling because during basic training in the Army, Harry Pettit is just as inept a recruit as his father, the Colonel Bobby Pettit, was in his younger days. In "Carpenters" and in the other later Glass family novellas, the double letters in the names also point to doubling motifs. The most obvious one in "Carpenters" is a revelation that stuns Buddy, namely that as a child Charlotte Mayhew "could *double* for Muriel." A less obvious doubling in "Carpenters" has to do with the external conflict. In that conflict, the Matron of Honor serves as a proxy for Mrs. Fedder, the mother of the bride, and Buddy Glass serves as a proxy for his brother Seymour, the absentee bridegroom. And finally, as in apprentice piece such as "The Varioni Brothers" and "The Inverted Forest," Salinger develops "Carpenters" as a narrative that does not focuses on one single central characters but on two.

As far as character types in "Carpenters" are concerned, we encounter further developments of three that are familiar from previous Salinger stories. Seymour is the same character type as the protagonists in "Teddy" and "Franny" who are also on spiritual quests and are at odds with the unspiritual people around them. The Matron of Honor and Mrs. Fedder are character types similar to previous unspiritual antagonists such as the education professor Bob Nicholson in "Teddy" and Lane Coutell in "Franny." And finally, the narrator Buddy Glass is reminiscent of Robert Waner, one of the narrators in "The Inverted Forest" who—like Buddy—also can't be objective toward the people in the story he is telling.

The most notable thing about the characterization in "Raise High the Roof Beam, Carpenters" is that Seymour—who is the thematic focus of the novella—doesn't make a physical appearance and is characterized only by what others say about him and by the entries in his diary. Similarly, we see Seymour's principal antagonists, his bride and her mother, only briefly and from a distance when they get into a limousine and drive away. Therefore, Muriel and Mrs. Fedder are also characterized only by what other people say and write about them. The intriguing thing about this type of characterization is that we get contradictory opinions about Seymour, Muriel, and Mrs. Fedder so that we must make up our minds about whose opinion we want to trust.

In the case of Seymour, we find out from the very beginning that what Buddy Glass tells us about him is colored by his admiration. At the conclusion of the anecdote about Seymour reading the Taoist tale to the ten-month-old Franny, Buddy says that like Chiu-fang Kao in the Taoist tale, Seymour has an unusual perceptiveness that allows him to see the spiritual mechanism beneath the homely details. We tend to accept Buddy's view of Seymour because he mentions that Seymour was a child prodigy, that he became a regular on the national radio quiz show "It's a Wise Child" when he was ten, that he was a freshman at Columbia University when he had just turned fifteen, and that he was a professor at the age of twenty-five. This information about Seymour explains why Boo Boo compares him to Ares who is taller far than a tall man.

Buddy and Boo Boo's exalted opinion of Seymour's personality stands in sharp contrast to the negative opinion of the Matron of Honor and the bride's mother, Mrs. Fedder. Initially, it seems that this negative opinion is only due to Seymour's failure to show up for the wedding. The Matron of Honor is understandably angry with Seymour and says that he embarrassed Muriel's parents half to death and broke Muriel's spirit. And because Seymour's excuse for not showing for the wedding ceremony was that he was "too happy to get married," the Matron of Honor calls him a "raving maniac" who should be "stuck in some booby hatch" (39-40). But then we learn from the Matron of Honor that Mrs. Fedder had a negative opinion of Seymour even before he stood Muriel up at the altar. After discussing Seymour with her psychiatrist, Mrs. Fedder had decided that he is not only a "schizoid personality" but also a "latent homosexual" who is afraid of marriage. In support of this opinion, the Matron of Honor mentions Seymour's hitting the beautiful Charlotte Mayhew in the face with a stone.

When we get to Seymour's self-characterization in his diary, we discover additional positive and negative traits. On the positive side, we find that Seymour is as erudite as we would expect someone to be who was a child prodigy. He quotes for Muriel the definition of sentimentality by the Zen scholar R.H. Blyth; he quotes a haiku poem by the Japanese poet Saigyo; he discusses with Mrs. Fedder's psychiatrist the Taoist concept of indiscrimination; he explains a Zen story for Muriel; and he summarizes the Vedanta view of marriage. Moreover, we also find out that Seymour is not afraid of marriage but that he considers his wedding day a "sacred day," that he worships Muriel's simplicity, and that he says loves and needs her undiscriminating heart.

In addition to these positive traits, Seymour's self characterization in his diary also reveals some negative traits. First of all, we notice that in spiritual terms he is a bull in a china shop. He is so engrossed in his studies of Eastern philosophy that he forgets that not many Westerners would recognize a koan when they saw or heard one (a koan is a puzzling action or paradoxical statement that a Zen master wants his students to meditate on). Seymour's radio audience did not understand that he was talking about a hypothetical koan when he said on "It's a Wise Child" that President Lincoln shouldn't have given the Gettysburg Address. Instead he should have silently shaken his fist at his audience. Similarly, Seymour baffles Mrs. Fedder when she asks him what he wants to be when the war is over and he says that he would like to be a dead cat. When Muriel later brings the matter up, Seymour explains that he was referring to a famous koan. A student asked a Zen master what the most valuable thing in the world is, and the master said that it is a dead cat because no one can put a price on it. Most importantly, it doesn't occur to Seymour that Muriel, her parents, and the wedding guests cannot possibly understand that he considers marriage a new phase in his spiritual advancement and that he doesn't want to share his excitement about this important step with anyone but Muriel.

Seymour's thoughtlessness seems a minor shortcoming compared to three other faults. One of these more serious faults is his cruelty in hurting Charlotte (although he may thrown that stone at her because of some obscure religious impulse). Another negative trait of Seymour's is his need to have more than one drink before he can discuss the Charlotte Mayhew incident. But the most troubling detail of Seymour's self-characterization in his diary is the revelation that he tried to commit suicide some time before he met Muriel. This comes out when Seymour regrets that Muriel was naïve enough to mention to her mother where he got the scars on his wrists.

The overall picture that the characterization of Seymour in "Carpenters" creates is that of a troubled genius. Even if we don't share Mrs. Fedder's view that Seymour is a schizoid personality and a latent homosexual, we also cannot share Buddy's unconditional admiration of Seymour at the beginning of the novella, especially since by the end Buddy himself is very disturbed by some of Seymour's character traits.

Before I analyze the characterization of Seymour's antagonists, I want to comment briefly on the difference between the characterization of the Seymour in "Raise High the Roof Beam, Carpenters" (1955) and the earlier Seymour in "A Perfect Day for Bananafish" (1948). Like the Seymour in "Carpenters," his name-sake in "Bananafish" is extremely well-educated (for example, he quotes from T.S. Eliot's "The Waste Land") and he is also a lover of poetry (he expects Muriel to read the poetry of his favorite poet who happens to be German). But there is no mention in "Bananafish" of Seymour having been a child prodigy and, even more importantly, there are no references in "A Perfect Day for Bananafish" to Seymour's deep interest in Buddhism and Hinduism.

The most common-sense explanation of the difference between the personalities of the earlier and the later Seymour is that when Salinger wrote "A Perfect Day for Bananafish" (1948), he had not yet decided to make Seymour the focus of a narrative series. After all, "Bananafish" doesn't mention any other members of the Glass family. The first story to reveal that Seymour had siblings is "Down at the Dinghy" (1949). The protagonist of that story is Seymour's sister Boo Boo, and the story mentions Seymour and his brother Webb (probably Buddy) only in passing. Moreover, when Salinger wrote "A Perfect Day for Bananafish," he was not yet involved in Eastern philosophy in general and in Vedanta Hinduism in particular. This new interest in Eastern religion begins to show up in "De Daumier-Smith's Blue Period" (1952), and it dominates "Teddy" (1953) which is designed as an introduction to the core ideas of Advaita Vedanta. In fact, Teddy McArdle is the prototype for the reconceived Seymour in "Carpenters." After all, both Teddy and Seymour were child prodigies, and both derive their religious beliefs from Vedanta.

But if we disregard outside information and look only at "A Perfect Day for Bananafish" and "Raise High the Roof Beam, Carpenters" as installments of the

Glass Family Series, then a more compelling thematic explanation offers itself
for why the Seymour in the earlier story is different from the Seymour in the
later one. The reason for the difference is simply that Seymour changed in the
six years between the time the two stories take place, that is, between the time
he married Muriel and the time he killed himself. In 1942, when he married
Muriel, Seymour was in the Army, and there was a war going on. In 1948,
when he killed himself, he had just been released from an Army hospital. It
may therefore have been Seymour's war experiences that brought about the
change in his personality. Support for this assumption is a comment by Mrs.
Fedder's psychiatrist in "Bananafish." Dr. Sivetski says that it was criminal of
the Army to release Seymour from the hospital because "Seymour may com-
*plete*ly lose control of himself" (6). Dr. Sivetski's comment has two ramifications. One is that Seymour was in the psychiatric ward of an Army hospital;
the other is that Seymour was not released from the Army hospital until 1948,
three years after the war ended. This might mean that his case was so severe
that the Army kept him locked up for three years.

It doesn't seem to be too far fetched to assume that Seymour's war experiences brought out the mean streak that he first manifested when he deliberately
hit Charlotte Mayhew in the face with a stone. We see this same cruelty in his
decision to blow his brains out in a hotel room in Florida while sitting on a bed
near the sleeping Muriel. The point I am making here is that the Seymour in
"Bananafish" is not really a different person from the Seymour in "Carpenters"
but the same person, only six years older and spiritually run-down.

Now back to the characterization of Seymour's antagonists in "Raise High the
Roof Beam, Carpenters." The characterization of two of them, Muriel and Mrs.
Fedder, is accomplished through indirect means—just like the characterization
of Seymour—that is, through what others say and write about them. However,
the characterization of the most vocal antagonist, the Matron of Honor, is direct
and conventional; but even so, it still contains both positive and negative traits.

The first impression we get of Muriel is created in Boo Boo's letter to
Buddy. It is a negative impression because Boo Boo says that Muriel is terri-
fic-looking but that she seems to be a zero. Boo Boo reports that when she met
her, Muriel didn't say more than two words and just smiled and smoked. The
next description of Muriel comes from Buddy who describes her as "fragile" and
"invalided" looking when her parents helped into the bridal car that whisked her
away from the place where she had been stood up by Seymour. Thereafter, the
Matron of Honor makes three comments that add to Muriel's characterization.
She says that Muriel is "just darling enough" to be pushed around by everybody, that Seymour had her "buffaloed" so that she didn't know whether she
was coming or going, and that Seymour broke her spirit by not showing up for
the wedding ceremony.

So far, what little information about Muriel's character we have gotten has
been both positive and negative. We get more information about Muriel's personality from Seymour's diary, and most of it is unflattering, even though
Seymour doesn't intend it to be read that way.

From Seymour's diary entries we can tell that Muriel is not only unspiritual
and superficial but also materialistic and self-absorbed. Her superficiality comes
out when Seymour reports watching a Greer Garson movie with her. The film

(probably *Mrs. Miniver,* MGM, 1942), is about a British family's hardships while living through the German air raids. But all that Muriel can find to talk about afterwards is the lost kitten that the children in the movie bring to their mother. In addition to her simplemindedness and sentimentality, the diary entries also reveal Muriel's materialism and her preoccupation with her appearance. These traits are illustrated when Seymour says that on some days when he leaves their house, Seymour feels that Muriel and her mother have stuffed his pockets "with little bottles and tubes containing lipstick, rouge, hair nets, deodorants, and so on." Later he reports that one of Muriel's marital goals is that she wants to get a very deep tan and go up to the desk in a very expensive resort hotel and ask the desk clerk if her Husband (capital "H") has stopped by yet to pick up the mail. Another one of Muriel's marital goals is that she wants have good-looking children, with her features, not Seymour's.

The indirect characterization of Muriel's mother, Mrs. Fedder, also contains both positive and negative traits, including comments that are intended as compliments but have the opposite effect. As in the case of Muriel, we get our first impression of Mrs. Fedder from what Boo Boo Glass says in her letter to Buddy. That impression is again a negative one. When Boo Boo first met her, Mrs. Fedder told her Seymour's problem is that he doesn't relate to people. Mrs. Fedder also mentioned that she herself sees a good Jungian psychiatrist twice a week and she asked if Boo Boo had ever been in psychoanalysis. Furthermore, Mrs. Fedder apparently bragged about being a patron of the arts, and she stressed that Muriel's wedding would be non-sectarian and emancipated, which means it would be a totally unspiritual ceremony performed by a judge and not by a rabbi or a minister.

As an antidote to Boo Boo's negative portrayal of Mrs. Fedder, Salinger offers the opinion of the Matron of Honor. The Matron of Honor adores Mrs. Fedder and says that she is one of the most brilliant people she has ever met. The Matron of Honor reports that Mrs. Fedder used to teach, that she worked on a newspaper, and that she designs all her clothes herself. Not only has Mrs. Fedder read almost everything that has ever been printed, she also does her own housework and is a fabulous cook. And when Mrs. Fedder expressed her opinion of Seymour to the Matron of Honor, she didn't say anything derogatory or small-minded, she "only" said that Seymour was a schizoid personality and a latent homosexual.

Although the Matron of Honor adores Mrs. Fedder, we still remember that Boo Boo had a negative impression of her, and this impression is confirmed by what Seymour says about Mrs. Fedder in his diary. Seymour notes how close Mrs. Fedder and Muriel are, and he therefore makes the comment that their household seems to be a secular two-woman convent. He also says that Mrs. Fedder is irritating and opinionated, that she has no understanding of the current of poetry that runs beneath the surface of everyday reality, and he concludes that "she might as well be dead" (72).

While the characterization of Mrs. Fedder is developed in terms of what others say about her, the characterization of Seymour's most outspoken antagonist, the Matron of Honor, is developed in terms of the way she acts and the way she speaks.

The Matron of Honor is Seymour and Buddy's antagonist—and thus the villain of the piece—but Salinger still gives her both positive and negative traits. Her name is Edie Burwick, and Buddy describes her as a stout person who is twenty-four or twenty-five and looks as if she had been a physical education major in college. The initial impression that the characterization creates is negative. The Matron of Honor is shown to have bad taste when she admits that she copied a "darling idea" from Mrs. Fedder. She reports that she had matchbook covers printed to read, "These Matches Were Stolen From the House of Bob and Edie Burwick" (34). Moreover, like Mrs. Fedder, the Matron of Honor accepts the opinions of psychiatrists as gospel and is intolerant of anyone whose behavior she doesn't consider normal. She not only refers to Seymour as a raving lunatic, but she also questions the sanity of the old deaf-mute gentleman when she asks Buddy if he thinks the old man is crazy.

However, the characterization of the Matron of Honor isn't one-sided because Buddy Glass acknowledges some of her positive traits. Buddy respects the Matron of Honor's basic sense of decency when she says about Seymour standing up his bride and the wedding guests that "you can't just *barge* through life hurting people's feelings whenever you feel like it" (21). Secondly, Buddy recognizes her as a born leader when the limousine gets held up by the parade and she takes the initiative and decides how to deal with the delay. Thirdly, when the Matron of Honor inadvertently hurts the feelings of Muriel's aunt, Mrs. Silsburn, by talking about all of Muriel's "crazy aunts and uncles," she impresses Buddy by apologizing without being obsequious. At this point, Buddy grudgingly admits that the Matron of Honor is "not altogether unadmirable" (29). And finally, even though Buddy recently yelled at the Matron of Honor, when she takes her leave, she is gracious enough to thank him for the cold drinks he served. In short, unlike some earlier unspiritual people in Salinger's fiction, the Matron of Honor is no two-dimensional cardboard villain. Although she is a recognizable type, she does come across as a believable, flesh-and-blood person.

A third character type familiar from Salinger's earlier fiction is the narrator Buddy Glass. Buddy is a more complex version of the narrator Robert Waner in "The Inverted Forest." Although Buddy Glass feels at odds with the rest of the wedding party, and although he functions as a surrogate for Seymour in the external conflict with the Matron of Honor, he is not an outsider type like Seymour. Instead, he is more of a joiner. First of all, he instinctively jumps into a limousine that's headed for a reception where he really has no business after Seymour stood up the bride. Secondly, Buddy not only accepts the invitation to join the Matron of Honor and the other limousine passengers at the Schrafft's restaurant, but when that restaurant is closed, he even invites that woman to his and Seymour's nearby apartment.

By the end of the novella, when it becomes clear that Seymour is never going to show up, we realize that in terms of the narrative structure, Buddy and not Seymour is the protagonist. If this surprise makes us re-read the novella to find out more about Buddy, then we will find that the information Buddy provides about himself is very sketchy.

We learn that Buddy is the second oldest of the Glass children and was born in 1919, two years after Seymour but the same year as J.D. Salinger. He was eight and Seymour ten when the two of them began to appear on the radio quiz show "It's a Wise Child," and they performed on that show for six years.   In 1933, when Seymour was kicked off the show, Buddy—who was then 14—also left.   We do not find out what Buddy did between the time he left "It's a Wise Child" and the time he was drafted, except that he must have gone to college because he says the seven Glass children's income from "It's a Wise Child" was enough to pay for all of their college expenses.   We do know, however, that before Buddy went into the military, he shared an apartment in Manhattan with Seymour.

More important than the biographical data are Buddy's attitudes and beliefs. These attitudes and beliefs show him to be Seymour's disciple.   In the anecdote about Seymour reading the Taoist tale to the ten-month-old Franny, Buddy initially questions Seymour's judgment in trying to calm down the baby by reading the Taoist tale to her, but later Buddy admits that he now goes out of his way to recommend prose pacifiers to parents or siblings of ten-month-old infants.   Buddy concludes the anecdote by suggesting that Seymour is spiritually as perceptive as Chiu-fang Kao, the superlative judge of horses in the Taoist tale.

Moreover, Buddy must have studied the same oriental religious texts as Seymour, because when the Matron of Honor invites Buddy to join her and the other wedding guests at the Schrafft's restaurant, Buddy says that his acceptance of the invitation was a religious impulse.   Then he explains that in certain Zen monasteries it is a basic rule that a monk must instantly reply "Hi!" without thinking when another monk calls out to him.

The passage in "Carpenters" that best illustrates Buddy's discipleship is his impassioned but irrational defense of Seymour after the Matron of Honor reports Mrs. Fedder's judgment that Seymour is a sick person unfit for marriage because all he can do is hurt others so that they need stitches in their faces. Buddy doesn't address the question of Seymour's cruelty to Charlotte.   Instead he denounces Mrs. Fedder and all the other people who have analyzed Seymour and failed to see that he was a true poet and that he should therefore not be judged by the standards we apply to normal people.   In short, Buddy's self-characterization makes it clear that he has been worshipping Seymour all his life and that he still thinks Seymour is a saint and seer, the disturbing revelations of his diary notwithstanding.

Buddy's unusual style rounds out his characterization as an extraordinary individual.   The sentence construction and vocabulary in "Raise High the Roof Beam, Carpenters" are very different from what we find in *Nine Stories*.   While the style in most of the pieces of *Nine Stories* is direct and terse with short sentences and a word choice guided by everyday colloquial speech, the style in "Carpenters" is indirect and convoluted, and the word choice is too erudite to be colloquial.

Buddy's vocabulary includes quite a few words that the average person would have to look up in a dictionary.   He says, for instance, that his story has a "mortality" all its own, that the Fedders' invitation to a non-wedding reception was a "*beau geste*," that he helped the wedding guests into the limousines with a bogus "puissance" while trying to act exceptionally "adroit," that the year 1942 was "crapulous," and that an "effulgent" intuition told him the Matron of Honor had recognized him as Seymour's brother.

Buddy's style is especially unusual as far as his sentence structure is concerned. The hallmark of this style is Buddy's habit of loading up his sentences with qualifying phrases. In the sentence below, the basic information (which I have underlined) accounts for only one-third of its bulk (19 words). Two-thirds of the sentence consists of qualifying phrases (40 words):

At twenty minutes past four—or, to put it another, blunter way, an hour and twenty minutes past what seemed to be all reasonable hope—the unmarried bride, her head down, a parent stationed on either side of her—was helped out of the building and conducted, fragilely, down a long flight of stone steps to the sidewalk. (13)

As far as the level of style in this sample sentence is concerned, it is words such as "stationed," "conducted," and "fragilely," which elevate the language above what most people would consider colloquial and comfortable.

The overall effect of the long sentences, packed full of qualifiers, is that they give Buddy's storytelling a leisurely, contemplative quality. It is very fitting that "Raise High the Roof Beam, Carpenters" should have this quality because it is 1955 when Buddy gives us his account of the events on Seymour's wedding day in 1942, and he had over a decade to ponder the significance of these events. And the overall effect of the slightly elevated diction is that it reminds the reader that Buddy not only used to be a child prodigy himself but that he is now the chronicler of the life of a nationally-celebrated genius.

SETTINGS AND SYMBOLS

"Raise High the Roof Beam, Carpenters" provides precise information about the setting in time and place and about the social environment but not much visual description. Instead we get only a few impressionistic details that create the ambiance of a location. As far as the symbolism is concerned, it plays almost as important a role and is handled just as unobtrusively as in *The Catcher in the Rye*. Moreover, two related metaphors are part of the symbolic meaning of the novella, and they shed light on two key questions in "Carpenters" and the rest of the Glass Family Series, the question of why Seymour married Muriel and the question of why Seymour killed himself six years later. The new thing about the symbolism in "Carpenters" is that some incidents are portents, or signs from fate, and that some of the symbolism has the quality of Zen koans.

Buddy Glass tells us that Seymour's wedding day was 4 June 1942. The events of the main plot all occur on that day. However, in the prologue Buddy takes us back to 1922, and in the subplot Seymour takes us back to December of 1941. We also get the exact time of day of the events in the main plot, because Buddy tells us that he arrived at Penn Station in New York at 2:10 p.m., that he barely made it to the wedding ceremony which was scheduled to begin at 3:00 p.m., and that at 4:20 p.m. the family of the bride canceled the ceremony because the groom did not shown up. Moreover, Buddy tells us that it was so hot on the day of the wedding that the asphalt in the streets was soft and gummy and that everyone was perspiring profusely.

The three locations where the action of the main plot takes place can be located on the city map of New York. The wedding guests assemble at the apartment of the bride's grandparents which is on 63rd Street, two blocks east of Madison Avenue. The limousine that carries Buddy and four other wedding guests goes north on Madison Avenue until it is stopped by a parade in the upper Eighties. When the passengers abandon the limousine, they walk south on the east side of Madison Avenue until they get to the Schrafft's restaurant on the corner of 79th Street. Because they find that restaurant closed, they walk east, just down the block to Buddy and Seymour's apartment. The rest of the events take place at this apartment which is located on the north side of 79th Street, one block east of Madison Avenue.

Although Buddy is very specific about the locations, he does not describe them in much detail. He mentions that the apartment of the bride's grandparents, where the wedding ceremony is supposed to take place, is in an enormous old brownstone building with a canvas canopy in front, but he doesn't provide any physical details of the interior. All Buddy mentions is that the room is oversize, that it is jam-packed, that is stifling hot, and that there is an organ playing directly behind him. While these details are sparse, they are enough to convey the feeling of the place.

Salinger's impressionistic handling of his settings is even more evident in the part of the narrative which takes place in Buddy and Seymour's apartment. Again we don't get much physical detail, but what we get is well-chosen to develop an ambiance. One such detail is that the only noise in the apartment is the purring of the second-hand refrigerator in the kitchen. Another telling detail is that the current occupant of the apartment, Buddy's sister Boo Boo, has left all the ashtrays in the living room blossoming with Kleenex tissues and cigarette ends that have lipstick on them. And the third unique detail is the easy chair that Buddy's deceased Boston bull terrier used to sleep in. The chair is upholstered in corduroy, and its arms have been thoroughly chewed and slobbered on during the dog's nightmares. These details give the apartment and extremely lived-in feeling.

Perhaps the most important aspect of the setting in "Carpenters" is the social environment. This social environment is not only upper middle class, as in most of Salinger's fiction, it is Jewish upper middle class. First of all, there can be no doubt that the Fedder family is well-off. After all, they can afford to rent limousines for all the wedding guests, and Mrs. Fedder strikes Buddy's sister Boo Boo as a caricature of a Jewish society matron who is a patron of all the arts. Moreover, Mrs. Fedder is certifiably sane and normal because she sees a good Jungian psychiatrist twice a week. She has planned a wedding for her daughter that is going to be a civil ceremony performed by a judge. It is to be an affair that Boo Boo calls not only non-sectarian but also emancipated, with a capital "E." And indeed, as we later find out, the Fedders belong to that part of the Jewish bourgeoisie who are out of touch with their ethnic heritage because, like the Christian majority in America, they celebrate Christmas by decorating a tree and giving each other presents.

Even though Buddy Glass says that Seymour's wedding day was a day of rampant "signs and symbols," the symbolism in "Carpenters" is not at all rampant but is handled just as subtly as it is in *The Catcher in the Rye*. First of all, Buddy makes the intriguing comment that on Seymour's wedding day, "Fate took circuitous pains" to send him signs (64). The first such sign is that—against all common sense—Buddy leaps into a limousine that is bound for a reception where no relative of Seymour's is going to be welcome. The second sign is that a parade prevents the limousine from getting to the reception. The next sign is that the restaurant from which the wedding guests want to telephone the Fedders is closed. A further sign is that Buddy and Seymour's apartment happens to be just down the block from the restaurant. And the final sign is that Buddy discovers Seymour's diary on top of Seymour's open canvas valise before the Matron of Honor can find it. All of these signs suggest that Buddy and the wedding guests were destined to wind up at Buddy and Seymour's apartment to discuss the dark side of Seymour's character and that Buddy was destined to find the diary which reveals that all is not well with Seymour.

As far as the symbols in "Raise High the Roof Beam, Carpenters" go, three stand out: Charlotte's nine stitches, the old deaf-mute gentleman, and the wedding present that Buddy wants to send Seymour. In addition to these three symbols, "Carpenters" contains a number of symbolic actions that are reminiscent of Zen koans.

The nine stitches that Charlotte Mayhew had to have in her face after Seymour threw a stone at her have symbolic significance because they are mentioned five times in the novella: twice by the Matron of Honor, once by Mrs. Silsburn, once by Buddy, and once by Seymour. Charlotte's nine stitches mean different things to different people. To the Matron of Honor they are a symbol of Seymour's latent homosexuality. To Mrs. Silsburn—who loved to listen to Seymour when he was on "It's a Wise Child"—they are a sign of childish mischief, of Seymour hitting Charlotte by accident. To Seymour and Buddy, the nine stitches represent a serious flaw in Seymour's character which Seymour doesn't want to discuss even though he claims the Charlotte Mayhew incident is "old finished business." Thus the most important thing about Charlotte's nine stitches is that they symbolize something Seymour and Buddy don't want to face, the fact that Seymour is not as far advanced spiritually as they both would like to think.

Another symbol in "Raise High the Roof Beam, Carpenters" is the tiny gentleman in the tuxedo and the top hat, Muriel's deaf-mute great-uncle. He stands out because he is such a bizarre-looking person and because he is, of all the people that Buddy meets on Seymour's wedding day, the only one that Buddy likes. He can be seen as serving two symbolic purposes in the novella.

First of all, the little deaf-mute personifies the sense of isolation that Buddy feels among the other wedding guests. This becomes clear when Buddy admires the little old man's "insularity" and says that he is "sublimely out of touch" with those around him (42). Like Holden Caulfield in *The Catcher in the Rye*, Buddy feels so alienated that he wishes he were a deaf-mute so he doesn't have to participate in any useless conversations, especially not conversations with people who don't respect his brother Seymour.

Secondly, the bizarre little gentleman can be seen as representing the uncommonplace. Because of his diminutive size, his great age (he is over 80), and the emphatic way he grins and gesticulates, he is just as far removed from the normalcy represented by the Matron of Honor and her husband, Lieutenant Burwick, as Seymour is. For instance, the Matron of Honor calls Seymour a "raving lunatic," and she also refers to the little old deaf-mute as "crazy." Moreover, before Buddy knows that the old gentleman is a deaf-mute, he credits him with the inner peace of a truly spiritual person, a person like Seymour. And then there is a third similarity between the little old man and Seymour. Buddy says that Seymour would be a poet even if he never wrote any poems, and Buddy also considers the deaf-mute a poet because when the little gentleman writes the word "Delighted" on his note pad, Buddy says that he recognized a poem when he saw one.

The little old deaf-mute is therefore a symbolic figure that serves to clarify Buddy's personality. Buddy projects onto the tiny gentleman qualities and attitudes which he, Buddy, admires in Seymour and which he shares to a certain extent with Seymour, but they are qualities that are very rare among people outside the Glass family.

The most puzzling symbol in "Raise High the Roof Beam, Carpenters" is the strange wedding gift that Buddy thinks he should send Seymour but doesn't. After the old deaf-mute gentleman has left and Buddy finds his cigar butt in an ashtray, Buddy says that he is thinking of sending the cigar end to Seymour as a wedding present. At first he wants to send only the cigar end in a nice gift box. Then he wonders if he shouldn't send along a blank page of paper. Eventually, he decides against sending this strange gift.

Buddy seems to intend this odd wedding present as a koan. He is apparently thinking of the koan with which Seymour mystified Mrs. Fedder, the statement by the Zen master that the most valuable thing in the world is a dead cat because nobody can put a price on it. Similarly, no one can put a price on a cigar end. The other part of the wedding gift, the blank sheet of paper, is also reminiscent of one of Seymour's koans. It is the equivalent of President Lincoln being silent instead of giving the Gettysburg Address.

However, Buddy decides not to send this gift to Seymour. Perhaps he realizes that the gift could be taken as a sign that he still isn't reconciled to Seymour's choice of Muriel. The blank sheet of paper might represent Buddy's unwillingness to say anything to Seymour, and the cigar butt might also be taken as a negative symbol. After all, a cigar is what a young father hands out to his friends in celebration of the birth of a child. And the burned-down cigar end might be interpreted as a sign that Buddy hopes Seymour will never have children with a person as superficial, selfish, and materialistic as Muriel.

Ultimately, then, the cigar end and the blank sheet of paper symbolize the ambivalence of Buddy's attitude toward Seymour's marriage motives and Seymour's marriage partner.

In addition to the symbols, there are two related metaphors that enrich the figurative meaning in "Raise High the Roof Beam, Carpenters." They are the metaphor of poetry and that of perception/discrimination. These metaphors play an important role because they point even more directly to the unique vision of life in Salinger's fiction than do the symbols.

The first time we encounter the metaphor of perception is in the prologue when Chiu-fang Kao is able to perceive the superlative horse's spiritual mechanism beyond the homely details of the animal's color and gender and when Buddy suggests that Seymour is just as perceptive as Kao. The metaphor of extreme perceptiveness recurs in connection with the metaphor of poetry when Seymour discusses discrimination and indiscrimination with Mrs. Fedder's psychiatrist, Dr. Sims. Seymour refers to the core idea of Chinese Taoism when he explains that the highest form of discrimination—the way of the Tao—is indistinguishable from indiscrimination. He says that this kind of pure perception is extremely difficult to acquire, especially for someone who is already capable of a high degree of discrimination. Such a discriminating person "would have to dispossess himself of poetry, go *beyond* poetry. That is, he couldn't possibly learn or drive himself to *like* bad poetry in the abstract, let alone equate it with good poetry. He would have to drop poetry altogether" (74).

Here Seymour is not talking about written poetry. He is using the word poetry as a metaphor for the ineffable divine essence that permeates all things, the spiritual entity that is called the Tao by the Taoists and *Brahman* by the Vedantists. That this is indeed what Seymour means by poetry becomes clear when he says about Mrs. Fedder that she is a person who is "deprived, for life, of any understanding or taste for the main current of poetry that flows through things, all things" (72).

Once we understand that Seymour and Buddy use the word poetry as a metaphor for the divine essence that is immanent in all things, we can understand Buddy's apparently absurd comment about Seymour that no one outside of the Glass family has been able to see him for what he really was, namely a poet, and that even "if he never wrote a line of poetry, he could still flash what he had at you with the back of his ear" (60). In this statement, a poet is not someone who writes poems but someone who has a higher degree of perception or discrimination than normal people, and Seymour's ability as a Seer is of course what sets him apart from other people.

Seymour's comments about discrimination and indiscrimination can explain not only why he married Muriel but also why he killed himself. Seymour speaks of himself as a discriminating man, but he does not seem to be content with the degree of discrimination he has attained. Instead, he hankers after what he calls "pure discrimination" which is almost indistinguishable from indiscrimination. This is one reason why he says he loves and needs Muriel's undiscriminating heart. However, after he married Muriel, he may have realized that by adoring her indiscrimination, he was mistaking bad poetry for good poetry, naiveté and superficiality for sublime wisdom. He therefore may have decided to "dispossess himself of poetry, go beyond poetry," by dropping poetry altogether, that is, by committing suicide.

THEMES AND INTERPRETATIONS

The commentaries on "Raise High the Roof Beam, Carpenters" fall into two categories, those that see the novella merely as an explanation of Seymour's character and/or suicide and those that look for more universal thematic concerns.

Irving Howe is one of several critics who have interpreted "Carpenters" as an explanation of Seymour's suicide as reported in "A Perfect Day for Bananafish." Howe focuses on "the mid-Manhattan philistinism to which Seymour links himself in *Carpenters*," and he says that Seymour's marriage to Muriel Fedder "can only lead to the disaster of *Bananafish*" (95).

William Wiegand offers an explanation of Seymour's suicide that is very different from that of critics such as Irving Howe and Ihab Hassan who consider Seymour a victim of Muriel's vulgarity and materialism. Wiegand says:

Without "Carpenters" the suicide which closes "Bananafish" appears motivated chiefly by Seymour's inability to put up with his bourgeois wife. With "Carpenters," however, we see Seymour as a man not deprived of, but rather surfeited with, the joy of life. Salinger's sole excuse for Seymour's desperate social irresponsibility is this same curious surfeit of sensation. (123).

Two studies explore specific religious ideas in "Carpenters." Dennis O'Connor analyzes the novella chiefly in terms of its Taoist ideas and explains Seymour's questionable decision to marry Muriel in this way: "Seymour marries Muriel, this Aphrodite-zero, and thereby embraces the Taoist life of indiscrimination, mirroring its essential formlessness, its egolessness that seems foolishness but is truly wisdom" (134). And Eberhard Alsen believes that Seymour's acceptance of the Vedanta view of marriage holds the key to an understanding of his decision to marry Muriel. Having pursued his spiritual development for many years along the paths of knowledge and meditation, *jnana yoga* and *raja yoga*, Seymour came to the realization that he has become estranged from common humanity and that his spiritual advancement has stopped. In order to resume his progress toward oneness with God, Seymour "joyfully gave up the paths of study and meditation in order to become a householder and *karma yogin*" (199).

Critics who have looked for universal themes in "Raise High the Roof Beam, Carpenters" have offered different ways of defining the conflict between the outlook of people like the Matron of Honor and the Fedders on the one hand and that of Seymour and Buddy on the other. In his book *Radical Innocence*, Ihab Hassan provides a catalog of opposite ideas to describe the multiple layers of themes in "Carpenters." They are the ideas of "normality and alienation, of imperviousness and vulnerability, of assertiveness and responsiveness, of squalid purpose and lovely inutility, or irreverent prejudice and holy indiscrimination" (280).

Three interpretations that wind up with different conclusions about the novella's universal meaning are those of Arthur Schwartz, Theodore Gross, and James Lundquist. Schwartz says that in "Carpenters," Salinger tries to shock us into "an awed acceptance of some kind of 'saintliness' and, ultimately, the grudging admission on our part that we just haven't [Seymour's] eye for the superlative horse" (88). Schwartz's discussion of Seymour as a "holy man" adds up to this universal statement: "The world's lover, the selfless man, is an aberration in our culture so that we are conditioned to be wary of the large-hearted and the great-souled" (89).

The interpretation of Theodore Gross focuses on the conflict between the idealistic artist and the materialist society in which he has to live. Gross points out that we all tend to identify with the doomed idealism of the artist. He says: "Salinger touches upon our collective desire and need to salvage whatever idealism we can in a country increasingly dominated by authority." Just like Buddy, who tries to ignore Seymour's suicide which is "the fate of the exceptional man, of the artist-seer, so Salinger's readers seek a survival that is not altogether one that compromises ideals" (462).

And, finally, James Lundquist acknowledges Seymour's high ideals but also points out the danger of embracing them. He describes Seymour as "a Zen master, mystic, seer, and Christ figure," who has "standards so high, so out-of-this-world that he cannot survive." Seymour's fatal example teaches all those who come in contact with him, "that they must move toward compromise if they are to have a philosophy they can live by" (142).

CONCLUSION

"Raise High the Roof Beam, Carpenters" stands out in Salinger's fiction because of five firsts. It is the first story in which Salinger mentions all the members of the Glass family; it is the first story in which Buddy Glass identifies himself as the narrator; it is the first story that refers back to another part of the Glass Family Series ("A Perfect Day for Bananafish"); it is the fist story to introduce a reinvented Seymour, a Seymour quite different from the central character in "A Perfect Day for Bananafish"; and it is the first story which suggests a reason for Seymour's suicide.

Unlike the previous two parts of the Glass Family Series—"A Perfect Day for Bananafish" and "Franny"—which are short stories, "Raise High the Roof Beam, Carpenters" is a novella. The heart of its main plot is the conflict between Buddy's view that his brother Seymour is a highly spiritual person, a near-saint, and the view of the other wedding guests that Seymour is "a raving maniac of some crazy kind" because he didn't show up for his own wedding. The sub-plot, told in diary form by Seymour himself, is the story of Seymour's courtship of Muriel. This sub-plot helps resolve Buddy's conflict, but it also modifies Buddy's view of his brother.

In retrospect, Buddy still can't think of anybody whom he'd care to send out looking for horses in Seymour's stead, because like the supreme judge of horses, Chiu-fang Kao in the Taoist tale, Seymour is so intent on a person's spiritual qualities that he ignores the homely details. However, in reading Seymour's diary, Buddy is reminded of three flaws in his brother's character, of his mean streak which made him hit Charlotte Mayhew in the face with a stone, of his mental instability which made him try to commit suicide by slashing his wrists, and of his drinking to avoid facing his spiritual problems

By making us aware of Seymour's mean streak, "Raise High the Roof Beam, Carpenters" explains the cruelty of Seymour's decision to blow his brains out in his Florida hotel room while sitting on a bed near the sleeping Muriel. Moreover, Seymour's diary also offers a reason for the suicide. In his conversation with the psychiatrist Dr. Sims, Seymour makes a comment that implies that at least part of his reason for killing himself may have been his choice of Muriel as a marriage partner. He says that for a discriminating man it would be near impossible to "learn or drive himself to *like* bad poetry, let alone equate it with good poetry. He would have to drop poetry altogether." In short, "Raise High the Roof Beam, Carpenters" suggests that Seymour mistook Muriel's simple-mindedness for spiritual indiscrimination, and when he realized his mistake, he killed himself.

For a reader who is unfamiliar with Salinger's fiction, it would not be a good idea to start with "Raise High the Roof Beam, Carpenters." At the very least, such a reader should first read "A Perfect Day for Bananafish," the account of Seymour's suicide. But the early story that best explains Seymour's strange behavior in "Raise High the Roof Beam, Carpenters" is "Teddy" because Teddy McArdle's goal in life was to make spiritual progress toward union with God, and that was also Seymour's goal. Moreover, "Teddy" contains an exposition of the key ideas of Teddy and Seymour's belief system, Advaita Vedanta, the most abstract and eclectic branch of Hindu thought.

Those who have read "A Perfect Day for Bananafish" will find "Raise High the Roof Beam, Carpenters" interesting because they will learn more about three of the characters in that story, Muriel Fedder, her mother, and Seymour Glass. Above all, they will find that "Carpenters" sheds light on the mystery of Seymour's suicide, and they will discover that Seymour's despair over his marriage was only one of several reasons for his suicide because he already tried to kill himself by slashing his wrists before he ever met Muriel.

And finally, readers who are familiar with the later parts of the Glass Family Series, with "Zooey," or "Seymour—An Introduction," or "Hapworth 16, 1924," will find that "Raise High the Roof Beam, Carpenters" is easier to read because it has a more eventful plot than the later novellas, because its content is less religious, and because the style is not quite as elliptical and digressive.

Although much has been written on "Raise High the Roof Beam, Carpenters," there are still some aspects of the novella that have not yet been well enough explored. First of all, almost all articles and book chapters on "Carpenters" use information from the later novellas to interpret it rather than analyzing it as it stood when it was first published in 1955. Second, there has not yet been any comparative analysis of Buddy's attitude toward Seymour in 1942, the year of the wedding, and in 1955, the year when Buddy tells the story. Third, there has not been any analysis of the contradiction between Buddy's claim that Seymour is as spiritually advanced as Chiu-fang Kao in the Taoist tale and Buddy's discovery, in Seymour's diary, that he is a very flawed human being. A related fourth problem is that while there have been plenty of psychological analyses of Seymour's character, there haven't been any of Buddy's. And finally, there hasn't been sufficient analysis of the important role that the women characters play in "Raise High the Roof Beam, Carpenters."

WORKS CITED

Alsen, Eberhard. "A New Beginning." In *Salinger's Glass Stories as a Composite Novel.* Troy, NY: Whitston, 1983, 186-201.

Barrett, William. "Reader's Choice" [Review]. *Atlantic Monthly* 211 (February 1963): 128-130.

Chester, Alfred. "Salinger: How to Love Without Love" [Review Article]. *Commentary* 35 (June 1963): 467-474.

Gross, Theodore. "Suicide and Survival in the Modern World." *South Atlantic Quarterly* 68 (1969): 454-462.

Grunwald, Henry A., ed. *Salinger: A Critical and Personal Portrait.* New York: Harper, 1962.

Hassan, Ihab. *Radical Innocence.* Princeton: Princeton UP, 1961.

Howe, Irving. "More Reflections in the Glass Mirror" [Review]. *New York Times Book Review* (7 April 1963): 4-5, 34. Rpt. in Irving Howe, *Celebrations and Attacks.* New York: Horizon, 1979, 93-96.

"In Place of the New, A Reissue of the Old" [Review]. *Newsweek* (28 January 1963): 90, 92.

Kazin, Alfred. *Bright Book of Life.* Boston: Little & Brown, 1973.

Lundquist, James. "A Cloister of Reality: The Glass Family." In *J.D. Salinger.* New York: Ungar, 1979, 115-150.

O'Connor, Dennis. "Salinger's Religious Pluralism: The Example of 'Raise High the Roof Beam, Carpenters'." *Southern Review* 20 (April 1984): 316-332. Rpt. in *Modern Critical Views: J.D. Salinger.* Ed. Harold Bloom. New York: Chelsea House, 1987, 119-134.

Salinger, J.D. *The Catcher in the Rye* [1951]. New York: Bantam, 1964.

_____ . "A Perfect Day for Bananafish." In *Nine Stories* [1953]. New York: Bantam, 1964, 3-18.

_____ . *Raise High the Roof Beam, Carpenters and Seymour—An Introduction* [1963]. New York: Bantam, 1965.

Schwartz, Arthur. "For Seymour—With Love and Judgment." *Wisconsin Studies in Contemporary Literature* 4 (Winter 1963): 88-99.

Updike, John. "Anxious Days for the Glass Family." *New York Times Book Review* (17 September 1961): 1, 52. Rpt. in Grunwald 53-56.

Wiegand, William. "Seventy-eight Bananas." *Chicago Review* 11 (1958): 3-19. Rpt. in Grunwald 123-136.

SUGGESTIONS FOR FURTHER READING

Baskett, Sam. "The Splendid/Squalid World of J.D. Salinger." *Wisconsin Studies in Contemporary Literature* 4 (Winter 1963): 48-61.

Chuang-Tzu. *The Texts of Taoism.* Trans. James Legge. Intro. D.T. Suzuki. New York: Julian, 1959.

French, Warren. "Recollection." In *J.D. Salinger.* Boston: Twayne, 1963, 148-153.

Gwynn, Frederick L., and Joseph L. Blotner. "Raise High the Roof Beam, Carpenters." In *The Fiction of J.D. Salinger.* Pittsburgh: U of Pittsburgh P, 1958, 45-46.

Hassan, Ihab. "Almost the Voice of Silence: The Later Novelettes of J.D. Salinger." *Wisconsin Studies in Contemporary Literature* 4 (Winter 1963): 5-20.

Vivekananda, Swami. *Karma Yoga and Bhakti Yoga.* New York: Ramakrishna-Vivekananda Center, 1955.

Wenke, John. *J.D. Salinger: A Study of the Short Fiction.* Boston: Twayne, 1991.

Chapter 7

"Zooey"

All legitimate religious study *must* lead to the unlearning of the differences, the imaginary differences, between boys and girls, animals and stones, day and night, hot and cold.

Seymour Glass

"Zooey" first appeared in the *New Yorker* on 4 May 1957. It is a sequel to the story "Franny" (1955), and in 1961, the two companion pieces were reprinted between hard covers as *Franny and Zooey*. With 41,130 words, "Zooey" is the longest part of Salinger's narrative series about the Glass family. It is told in the first person by the garrulous Buddy Glass, who made his first appearance as a narrator in the previous installment of the Glass Family Series, "Raise High the Roof Beam, Carpenters" (1955). Buddy's new narrative is about Zooey's efforts to help Franny recover from the nervous breakdown she suffered two days earlier during her date with her college boyfriend Lane Coutell. In addition to Buddy, Zooey, and Franny, we meet their mother, Bessie Glass, who has two conversations with Zooey in the bathroom. We also get new information about the life and beliefs of Seymour Glass who is the subject of much of the conversations between Zooey and his mother and between Zooey and Franny.

Aside from its great length, the unique thing about "Zooey" is its departure from conventional patterns of storytelling. Like "Raise High the Roof Beam, Carpenters," "Zooey" has not one central character but two. Moreover, Buddy warns us right at the beginning that what he is about to offer is not a short story at all, but a "prose home movie" (47) and that we should not expect "brevity of detail or compression of incident." Buddy also says about the plot of his new narrative that it is really "a compound, or multiple, love story, pure and complicated" (49).

CRITICAL RECEPTION

When "Zooey" came out in book form together with "Franny," this was a much-anticipated literary event. *Time* magazine celebrated this event by putting Salinger's face on its cover and by printing a six-page feature story on Salinger's life and work. Moreover, bookstores received so many advance orders for *Franny and Zooey* that the book became a bestseller even before it was actually published and even though Salinger had refused to sell the rights to any of the book clubs.

Despite the book's great popularity with the book-buying public, the publication of *Franny and Zooey* marked the end of the critics' honeymoon with J.D. Salinger. While there were plenty of positive reviews in popular magazines and newspapers, most of the criticism in highbrow magazines and scholarly journals was negative, and most of it was directed at "Zooey" rather than "Franny." Salinger anticipated the critics' chief objection when he made Zooey tell the narrator Buddy Glass that his plot hinges on a religious theme, and that Buddy's religious preoccupation can only precipitate his undoing as a professional writer. And indeed, it was chiefly the religious message of "Zooey" that most critics found objectionable.

In his review for the *New Statesman*, Frank Kermode expressed a widely-held opinion when he said that while "Franny" is "irreproachably written," "Zooey" is "an almost total disaster" because its religious message is "so simple and so untrue" (382). Mary McCarthy found even harsher words for the content of "Zooey.' Writing for *Harper's Magazine*, McCarthy complained that the Glass family is a "closed corporation" whose members exhale "an ineffable breath of gentle superiority" (248). The Fat Lady, for whom Seymour tells Zooey to shine his shoes, is not just "the average ordinary humanity with varicose veins" but "the kind of everybody that the wonderful Glass kids tolerantly approve of" (247). McCarthy concluded by relating Seymour's Fat Lady advice to his suicide, and she asked why Seymour killed himself: "Because he had married a phony, whom he worshipped for her 'simplicity, her terrible honesty'? Or because he was so happy and the Fat Lady's world was so wonderful? Or because he had been lying, his author had been lying ... and it was all terrible, and he was a fake?" (250).

Points of criticism that recurred in several reviews were spelled out by the novelist John Updike. In his essay for the *New York Times Book Review,* Updike said that "'Zooey' is just too long; there are too many cigarettes, too many goddams, too much verbal ado about not quite enough" (55). In addition, Updike felt that the R.H. Blyth definition of sentimentality, which Seymour quotes in "Raise High the Roof Beam, Carpenters," fits "Zooey" to a T. We are sentimental, so Blyth said, "when we give to a thing more tenderness than God gives to it." It was Updike's opinion that "Salinger loves the Glasses more than God loves them.... He loves them to the detriment of artistic moderation." And lastly, Updike objected to what he called the novella's "vehement editorializing" which makes it seem that in "Zooey," "a lecturer has usurped the writing stand" (56).

By contrast, the reviewers for *Newsweek, Time,* and the *New York Herald Tribune* had high praise for *Franny and Zooey* in general and for "Zooey" in particular. *Newsweek* called "Zooey" "a remarkable tour de force of characteriza-tion" and said that "Salinger has been able to make his story not merely contain but evolve before our eyes a boldly explicit statement of personal philosophy, which boils down to Remember Thy Neighbor, and love him if you can" (109). In *Time* magazine, John Skow defended "Zooey" against those critics who ob-jected to its "italicized talkiness." He said that the talk, "like the book itself, is dazzling, joyous, and satisfying" because Salinger has given his characters "an astonishing degree of life and a stunning and detailed air of presence" (9). And Robert Phelps, the reviewer for the *New York Herald Tribune,* said about the two pieces in *Franny and Zooey:* "In concept, they are extraordinary, and in execution they are as inspired as anything published today." Phelps concluded his review by calling Salinger "a writer who can reveal his knowledge dramati-cally, in terms of the walking, talking, densely documented lives of particular people" (3).

One of the few academics that joined this popular chorus of praise was Martin Green. In his book, *Re-Appraisals,* Green argued that the themes in *Franny and Zooey* "are among the most ambitiously highbrow, and its craftsmanship most uncompromisingly virtuoso" (197). According to Green, Salinger's greatest strength is apparent in the characterization of Zooey because Zooey is one of Salinger's two most successful characters; the other one is Holden Caulfield in *The Catcher in the Rye.* Green said about Zooey and Holden that "they bulk so large in the worlds in which they appear that they create a new balance, a new order in the writer's meaning" (209). In Zooey's case this is because his person-ality crowds out even that of the family saint, Seymour, and because Zooey expresses "exactly the criticism of Salinger's religiosity one has felt oneself" (209). According to Green, the extraordinary achievement in the characterization of Zooey is that "Salinger has not merely built self-criticism into a story, he has let it take over" (210).

NARRATIVE STRUCTURE AND POINT OF VIEW

"Zooey" is much too long to be a short story and a bit too short to be a novel. If we absolutely want to classify it, we might call it a novella. How-ever, it is a very unconventional novella because not much happens in the plot aside from two conversations between Zooey and his mother Bessie and two conversations between Zooey and his sister Franny. Also, unlike most novel-las, "Zooey" does not have a subplot, and the events take up only as much time as it takes to read about them.

"Zooey" shares two typical traits with Salinger's previous fiction. One has to do with narrative structure and the other with narrative perspective. One familiar trait is that "Zooey" is structured in such a way that we again have two central characters rather than one. We see this trait in several previous stories. Two examples are "The Inverted Forest" and "Raise High the Roof Beam, Carpen-ters." In "Zooey," we get the feeling that the title character may not be the pro-tagonist because the focus of the narrative is Franny's spiritual crisis and be-cause both Franny and Zooey experience epiphanies that are likely to change their lives. This structural peculiarity is signaled by the doubling of letters in

Franny's and Zooey's names, and it is accompanied by two other instances of doubling, the two pairs of conversations Zooey has with his mother and his sister, and Zooey's impersonation of Buddy in his phone conversation with Franny.

The other typical Salingeresque trait in "Zooey" is a shifting narrative perspective. This is also reminiscent of "The Inverted Forest" and "Raise High the Roof Beam, Carpenters." In "Zooey," the shifts in point of view are due partly to Buddy's self-reflexive comments on the progress of his narrative and partly to another familiar trait of Salinger's fiction, the inclusion of a long letter, of diary entries, and of a series of quotations from Seymour and Buddy's favorite books.

"Zooey" begins with a conventional introduction in which the narrator, Buddy Glass, introduces himself and the two principals in the story, Franny and Zooey. In addition, Buddy adds a long footnote in which he presents information about Franny and Zooey and his other five siblings. And finally, Buddy also warns us that what he is about to present isn't a short story and that we should therefore not expect it to be brief and compact.

The plot of the narrative is clearly divided into three major parts because what little action there is takes place in three different settings. The setting for the first part is the bathroom of the Glass family's apartment, and this segment of the novella consists chiefly of two conversations between Zooey and his mother, Bessie Glass. The setting for the second part is the living room where Zooey and Franny have a long face-to-face conversation. And the setting for the third part is Seymour and Buddy's old room where Zooey uses Seymour's telephone to call up Franny for a second conversation.

In the first part of the narrative, Franny is not physically present, but she is discussed in the two conversations between Zooey and Mrs. Glass. They are talking about Franny because she had a nervous breakdown during a football weekend at college, and she has come to seek refuge in her parents' apartment. This part of the novella actually begins with Zooey reading a long letter that Buddy wrote to him four years earlier. The core of that letter is Buddy's advice to Zooey not to go out for a Ph.D. degree, as his parents want him to, but to fulfill his heart's desire and become an actor: Buddy's advice is this: "*Act*, Zachary Martin Glass, when and where you want to, since you feel you must, but do it *with all your might*" (68). Zooey re-reads this letter because he is looking for advice he might give to Franny who has decided to abandon her career as an actress.

In his two conversations with his mother, Zooey first reports what he found out about Franny's nervous breakdown when he talked to her the night before. Next, he analyzes the causes of the breakdown. And finally, he reveals that he has been struggling with problems very similar to Franny's.

Zooey explains that what Franny is experiencing is a religious crisis. Unable to cope with normal, unspiritual people, she is trying to retreat into the so-called Jesus Prayer, "Lord Jesus Christ, have mercy on me." By saying this prayer incessantly, Franny hopes to achieve enlightenment and to actually see God. Franny's nervous breakdown, so Zooey believes, is chiefly due to the religious education that he and Franny received from their older brothers Seymour and Buddy. Zooey gets quite vehement when he says that Seymour and Buddy are responsible for turning him and Franny into freaks by giving them home seminars in various Eastern religions from an early age on. The result is that he can't have lunch with a normal person because he either gets bored to death or he gets so preachy that the other person would probably like to break a chair over his head. Listening to Zooey, Mrs. Glass recognizes that he is just as profoundly unhappy as Franny, and she adds her own indirect criticism of Seymour and Buddy when she asks what good all their religious education did Zooey and Franny if it didn't make them happy.

The middle part of the narrative consists of a long conversation in the living room where Zooey tries to convince Franny that retreating into the Jesus Prayer is not going to resolve her crisis. Initially, the conversation goes well as Zooey tells Franny that he has the same problem as she in dealing with people whose values are less spiritual than his own. Then Zooey repeats his attack on Seymour and Buddy. He calls them "bastards" and says they turned him and Franny into "freaks" with freakish standards. Moreover, Zooey confesses that his conflicts with unspiritual people have given him an ulcer and that he sometimes feels that it would be a happy release if he could just lie down and die.

While Zooey is talking, he gets more and more tense and agitated, and he starts to perspire profusely. It seems that he hadn't realized how serious his own problem was until Franny's crisis made him confront it. It also seems that while he thinks he has a solution for Franny's crisis, he has no solution for his own. In his frustration, Zooey starts to get abusive and tells Franny that by saying the Jesus Prayer, she is beginning to give off the disagreeable smell of piousness. Moreover, to top it all off, she is not saying the prayer to the real Jesus but to a Jesus of her own invention who is a combination of Heidi's grandfather, St. Francis of Assisi, and her older brother Seymour.

When Zooey begins to get abusive, Franny at first tries to tune him out by silently saying the Jesus Prayer to herself. When that doesn't work, Franny starts sobbing and eventually shrieks at Zooey to stop talking. She is therefore not in a receptive mood at all when Zooey relents and tells her it's o.k. for her to say the Jesus Prayer as long as she is not using it to avoid doing her duty in life or simply her daily duty. Aware of his failure to reach Franny, Zooey stops talking at her, apologizes, and leaves the living room.

In the third part of the narrative, Zooey draws on his talent as an actor when he pretends to be Buddy and calls Franny on the telephone from Seymour and Buddy's old room. But before he picks up the phone, he prepares himself spiritually by doing three things. He first reads a random entry in a diary of Seymour's, then he reads two pages worth of quotations from sources such as the *Bhagavad Gita*, Tolstoy, Kafka, and *The Gospel of Sri Ramakrishna* which Seymour and Buddy had posted on the door of their room, and finally he closes his eyes and meditates for half an hour.

Zooey's impersonation of Buddy fools his mother when she takes the call in the living room, and after she hands the phone to Franny, it takes Franny quite some time to see through Zooey's act. While Franny still thinks she is talking to Buddy, she complains about Zooey and his destructive attitude toward her. Despite these complaints, Franny shows that she fully understands why Zooey was so destructive. She says that Zooey is very bitter about a number of things, among them his work as a television actor and the freakish religious education that he and Franny received from their older brothers Seymour and Buddy.

When Franny suddenly realizes that she is talking to Zooey and not to Buddy, she doesn't hang up the phone but allows Zooey to pick up their conversation where they left it off in the living room. Zooey is now much gentler than he was before and lets Franny do much of the talking.

In the climactic section of the novella, Zooey leads Franny to an epiphany and in the process comes to an important insight himself. Zooey remembers that when he was seven years old and was about to leave for the broadcast studio to perform on the show "It's a Wise Child," Seymour stopped him and told him to shine his shoes. Zooey argued that no one would see his shoes where he sat, and Seymour told him to shine them anyway, to shine them for the Fat Lady. Zooey didn't understand what Seymour meant, but ever after he shined his shoes for the Fat Lady out of respect for Seymour.

As he is relating this anecdote to Franny, Zooey comes to understand that what Seymour meant when he told him to shine his shoes for the Fat Lady was the same thing Buddy meant when he told him to act "with all his might." Zooey passes this insight along to Franny when he says: "An artist's only concern is to shoot for some kind of perfection." (199). But that is only one part of the insight to which Zooey comes. The other part has to do with who the Fat Lady is. Zooey tells his sister that originally he had imagined the Fat Lady sitting on her porch all day swatting flies and listening to the radio. He also imagined that the heat was terrible and that she had cancer. At this point, Franny chimes in and says that Seymour once told her to be funny for the Fat Lady. She imagined that her Fat Lady sat in an awful wicker chair, that she had very thick and varicose legs, and that she also had cancer.

Now Zooey gets very excited because he finally comprehends what Seymour's Fat Lady stands for. He shouts with excitement when explains to Franny: *"There isn't anyone out there who isn't Seymour's Fat Lady."* And then Zooey asks, *"don't you know who that Fat Lady really is?...* It's Christ Himself" (201-202).

With Zooey's interpretation of Seymour's advice ringing in her ears, Franny also experiences an epiphany. She joyfully holds on to the phone long after Zooey has hung up. Then she gets into the bed she has been sitting on, pulls up the covers, smiles at the ceiling for a few minutes, and falls into a dreamless sleep.

This ending parallels the ending of the story "Franny" where an earlier Franny also lies alone in a room and stares at the ceiling. However, in the earlier story, Franny doesn't smile, and she doesn't fall asleep. Instead, the earlier story ends with Franny silently moving her lips to the Jesus Prayer.

But now Franny doesn't need the Jesus Prayer anymore, and we can be fairly certain that she is going to resume her acting career and that she will be acting with all her might so as not to disappoint Seymour's Fat Lady. In addition, we can also assume that Zooey is going to have an easier time from now on when dealing with all the ego-obsessed and unspiritual people in the television business because he has recognized that there isn't anyone among them who isn't Christ Himself.

The narrative perspective in "Zooey" keeps shifting back and forth between the first and the third person. The narrator begins by identifying himself as Buddy Glass and addressing us in the first person, but at the end of the introduction, he says about himself, "we will ... leave this Buddy Glass in the third person from here on in" (50). However, right at the beginning of the narrative proper, he has Zooey read a 13 page letter (almost 10% of the total length of "Zooey") which he, Buddy, wrote four years earlier and in which he, of course, speaks in the first person.

Buddy narrates most of "Zooey" from a third person point of view but occasionally shifts the narrative distance and the degree of objectivity with which he tells the story. He increases the distance between his audience and the events in his story when lets us in on the process of story telling or when he expresses his own opinions. For instance, before he describes Zooey's personality, Buddy comments on the way he is telling the story and says that Zooey's complex character demands that he, Buddy, insert two paragraphs of information before he launches into the story. Shortly thereafter, Buddy forgets his intention to stay in the third person and expresses his personal opinion that Zooey's face is an almost perfectly beautiful face. And a few paragraphs later, after talking about Zooey's career as a panelist on the radio quiz show "It's a Wise Child," Buddy again comments on his storytelling in the first person when he says that the information about Zooey's performing on the radio quiz show is not a digression but is indeed relevant to the story we are about to read.

In the main part of the narrative, the point of view is fairly objective so that we must deduce the states of mind and feelings of the characters from their body language and from the way they speak. For instance, we can tell that Franny is extremely nervous when she tries to take a match out of a matchbox and spills the matches on the floor. Also, we can tell that she is getting excited about what Zooey is telling her over the phone wen she suddenly stands up and begins to hold the phone with both hands.

As in previous Salinger stories, the way the characters talk reveals if they are calm or excited. To indicate his characters' agitated state of mind, Buddy italicizes words that they are speaking more loudly than the rest. For instance, Franny tells her Mother to "*please*" stop offering her chicken soup, and Zooey tells Franny that he has no authority to speak like a "*seer*." Having become aware of this stylistic peculiarity of Salinger's, we therefore understand that Zooey is extremely excited in the climactic scene when he italicizes two whole statements. One of these statements is that everyone out there in the radio audience is Seymour's Fat Lady and the other one is the rhetorical question if Franny knows who Seymour's Fat Lady really is.

Near the end of "Zooey," Buddy seems tempted to abandon the objectivity of the third person point of view and to state explicitly that Zooey's spiritual counseling of his sister has finally been successful. But he keeps his distance—even if just barely—by using such words as "apparently," "appeared," "seemed," and "as if." For instance, Buddy describes Franny's first reaction to the news that the Fat Lady is Christ by saying that is was "apparently" for joy that Franny held the phone with both her hands. Then he tells us that after Zooey hangs up the phone, Franny "appeared" to find the sound of the dial tone extremely beautiful to listen to. And finally, Buddy comments that it "seemed" as though Franny knew when she should stop listening to the dial tone and hang up, and that it was "as if" she suddenly felt that all the wisdom in the world were hers.

To sum up, in narrating "Zooey," Buddy Glass uses a flexible point of view that shifts back and forth between subjectivity and objectivity. He mostly makes us interpret his characters' states of mind for ourselves, but he occasionally interprets them for us.

CHARACTERIZATION AND STYLE

As far as the characterization in "Zooey" is concerned, it is a departure from what we are used to in Salinger's fiction because Buddy provides us with more description of physical attributes than in any previous story. In addition, we still get the customary characterization through behavior, speech patterns, and opinions. However, "Zooey" also stands out among the other parts of the Glass Family Series because the character of Zooey is developed in greater detail than any character in Salinger's previous fiction, with the exception of Holden Caulfield in *The Catcher in the Rye*. And finally, the novella also gives us new information about three characters we have met before in the Glass Family Series—Seymour, Franny, and Buddy—and it introduces us to a character we haven't met before, the matriarch Bessie Glass, née Gallagher. We also get a more varied style in "Zooey" than in any other part of the Glass Family Series because Buddy, Zooey, Mrs. Glass, and Franny are all speaking for extended periods of time, and each one has different speech mannerisms.

When critics say that in "Zooey" Salinger shows too much love for the Glasses, they probably base that judgment on his glowing descriptions of Zooey's handsomeness and Franny's beauty. But they don't pay attention to Zooey and Franny's unlovely traits which Salinger develops in even more detail, and they don't pay attention to Salinger's characterization of Mrs. Glass as both a caricature and as the representative of common sense in the Glass family.

True enough, there is something excessive about the description of Zooey's physical attributes. After telling us that Zooey is a small person who is extremely thin, Buddy describes Zooey's face as spectacularly handsome. In fact, so Buddy adds, Zooey's face only misses being too handsome and even gorgeous because one of his ears sticks out a bit more than the other. To Buddy it seems, therefore, that Zooey's face is an almost perfectly beautiful face.

What mitigates Buddy's effusive praise of Zooey's handsomeness is Zooey's fight against narcissism which began when Zooey was seven or eight. Zooey made a habit not to look at his body when drying himself in front of a full-length mirror after a bath.and not to look at his face but at his eyes when shaving or combing his hair. Another strategy in Zooey's battle against narcissism is to joke about his handsomeness. At one point, while he is talking to his mother, he asks her if she is listening to him or if she is only staring at his gorgeous face.

Moreover, Zooey's handsomeness is balanced by his negative character traits, especially his unkindness and his condescending attitude toward people he doesn't like. Even his mother tells Zooey that he is not kind at all. Zooey's unkindness is illustrated when he gets abusive while talking to Franny and when he doesn't quit even after Franny shrieks at him to stop talking. In fact, Franny later complains that she's never met anyone so completely destructive in her life. While Zooey himself doesn't seem to be aware of his unkindness, he is aware of his condescension to others. He even reports to his mother that one of his colleagues at the television studio told him that he is "a *superior* son of a bitch."

Another negative aspect of Zooey's personality that counteracts Buddy's praise of his handsomeness is his coarse speech mannerisms. At the age of twenty-five, Zooey still hasn't outgrown the false bravado of Joe College-types like Lane Coutell in "Franny." Like Lane, Zooey liberally sprinkles his speech with the adjective "goddam," the noun "bastard," and the phrase "like hell." When Zooey blames Seymour and Buddy for the freakish education they gave him, Zooey calls them both "bastards" and says: "This whole goddam house stinks of ghosts. I don't mind so much being haunted by a dead ghost, but I resent like *hell* being haunted by a half-dead one" (103). Then he asks rhetorically "why the hell" Buddy doesn't kill himself like Seymour did. But what is perhaps most objectionable is the way Zooey talks to his mother. He not only calls her "Bessie girl" and "buddy" but also "fatty" and "you fat old Druid." And on three different occasions, he tells her, "You're so stupid, Bessie." Buddy Glass tries to excuse Zooey's verbal abuse of his mother by saying it is a kind of "doting brutality" which Mrs. Glass understands.

More important in Zooey's characterization than his handsomeness or his unkindness or his coarse speech is his superior intelligence and his preoccupation with religion. Since 1927, when he was seven years old, Zooey had been exhibiting his precociousness on the radio quiz show "It's a Wise Child." In 1942, when Zooey was twelve, a Boston research group analyzed Zooey on five different occasions to find out why he was so intelligent. They reached no conclusion, but they found that at the age of twelve, Zooey already had a vocabulary equal to the adult vocabulary of the famous spiritualist Mary Baker Eddy. In college, Zooey majored in Mathematics and Greek and went on to earn an M.A. To get over an unhappy love affair, Zooey once translated the Mundaka Upanishad, a Hindu text, from Sanskrit into Classical Greek. When Zooey got his M.A. degree in 1951, his parents wanted him to continue for a Ph.D., but instead Zooey decided to become an actor. In November of 1955, when the events of the novella take place, Zooey is a much sought-after leading man in television movies and has been offered to star in a movie that will be shot in France. Despite his professional success, Zooey is not happy. A sign of his unhappiness is an ulcer that he has developed because of his anger about the shoddy values of the people he is working with in the TV industry.

In his description of Franny, Buddy doesn't indulge in quite as many superlatives as in his description of Zooey, but he exhibits a similar fondness. Buddy calls Franny "a first-class beauty," and he says: "Her skin was lovely, and her features were delicate and most distinctive. Her eyes were very nearly the same quite astonishing shade of blue as Zooey's" (126). As far as more specific attributes of Franny's appearance are concerned, we learn that her jet-black hair is cut fashionably short and parted in the middle and that she wears a beige silk dressing gown with a pattern of tiny pink tea roses.

As several critics have pointed out, the personality of Franny in the novella "Zooey" is slightly different from what it is in the short story "Franny." One reason is that their religious background is different. The Franny in the earlier story did not know as much about religion as the later Franny. The earlier Franny was taking a religion survey course in college and she found the Jesus Prayer in a copy of *The Way of a Pilgrim* that she got out of her college library. The Franny in "Zooey" knows quite a bit more about religion because from grade-school-age on, she participated in the religious "home seminars" in which Seymour and Buddy introduced their younger siblings to the lives and writings of such holy men as Gautama Buddha, Shankaracharya, Hui-neng, and Sri Ramakrishna. This is why she is not taking a religion survey course—as the original Franny did—but an advanced religion seminar taught by a professor from Oxford. Therefore, Franny's religious crisis, which seems to be of her own making in "Franny," has a much different cause in "Zooey." Like Zooey's ulcer, it is caused by the "freakish" religious education that she and Zooey received from Seymour and Buddy.

Although Buddy wants us to feel sorry for Franny, he also makes both her mother Bessie and her brother Zooey express the opinion that Franny is taking herself and her religious crisis too seriously. For instance, Mrs. Glass puts Franny's behavior in perspective when she says that Franny is simply over-wrought by having read too many books on religion. And Zooey tells Franny that she is having "a tenth-rate nervous breakdown" because of a "snotty little crusade" she is leading against everybody. And then he tells her that her withdrawal into the Jesus Prayer is inexcusable and that she should know better because of the religious philosophy that Seymour and Buddy funnel-fed her with.

While Franny's personality is slightly different in "Franny" and in "Zooey," her emotional style of speaking is not. She often uses the word "absolutely" to exaggerate ideas, and she often raises her voice (indicated by italics) to emphasize parts of words or whole words. A typical sample of her style is her description of how she prevented her college boyfriend Lane Coutell from having a good time. She says that she totally *"ruined"* the day for Lane because she passed *"out"* on him and because she contradicted him so much that he could not have "a *nor*mal and *happy*" football weekend. Like other characters whom Salinger wants us to like, Franny gets to say a line that's a great non-sequitur. It is a complaint about Zooey making tactless comments about her nervous breakdown. She tells him to try and get sick sometime and visit himself, and he will discover just how tactless he is.

The matriarch of the family, Bessie Glass, also gets a line that's a priceless non-sequitur. However, hers is a non-sequitur not because there is an internal lack of logic but because the statement doesn't follow logically from a previous statement she made about Zooey. After Zooey tells his mother she is stupid because she doesn't know that the religious books which she thinks caused Franny's nervous breakdown came from Seymour's desk, Mrs. Glass tells Zooey that his main problem is that he isn't kind. She ponders that pronouncement for a moment, and then tells Zooey she wishes he'd get married. This remark—which the narrator actually labels a non-sequitur—isn't as illogical as it seems (105). If Zooey were married, he wouldn't be as preoccupied with himself and he would probably learn how get along better with others than he now does.

Buddy's description of Mrs. Glass's physical attributes reveals great fondness even though he eventually turns her into a caricature. We encounter Mrs. Glass as she enters the bathroom to talk to Zooey. Buddy initially only describes her as a medium-stout person of indeterminate age who is wearing a hairnet. Later on, Buddy adds telling details when he says that his mother's hands are extremely slender, that her legs are very shapely, and that she used to be a dancer and vaudevillian who was well-known for her great beauty

Aside from the doting detail, the description of Mrs. Glass also contains a whimsical tour de force in which Buddy characterizes her via his description of the bizarre kimono she is wearing around the house. This kimono is extremely baggy and gives Mrs. Glass a faintly "marsupial" appearance. The kimono is so baggy because Mrs. Glass has added two enormous pockets in which she carries around a collection of objects which range from packs of cigarettes and matches to household tools such as a screwdriver, a hammer, and a Boy Scout knife, as well as screws, nails, hinges, and faucet handles. The description of Mrs. Glass becomes preposterous when Buddy adds that the contents of her kimono pockets make his mother clink and rattle as she goes about her business in the apartment.

Buddy develops the caricature further when he stresses his mother's Irish descent. He says that she seems to be wearing an invisible "Dublin-black-shawl," and he has Zooey call Mrs. Glass a "fat Irish rose" and a "fat old Druid." When Mrs. Glass leaves the building in the fashionable neighborhood where the Glasses are living, so Buddy says, she looks like a "refreshing eyesore." On such occasions she always gives the impression that she is on her way to O'Connell street in order to bring home the body of one of her sons whom the Black and Tans have just shot dead.

Mrs. Glass's style of speaking completes the caricature. She keeps addressing Zooey as "young man," and she refers to Franny as "that child." Two of her favorite adjectives are "lovely" and "crazy." For instance, she doesn't want Zooey to brush his teeth with his "crazy" tooth powder because the powder will take all the "lovely" enamel off his "lovely" teeth. Two other speech habits of Mrs. Glass's are to refer to herself as "nobody" and to preface her remarks with the phrase "for your information." A typical sample of Mrs. Glass's way of speaking is her reply to Zooey when he suggests she talk to Buddy about Franny's crisis: "Just kindly lower that voice of yours, please, young man. Nobody's deaf. For your information, I have called the college" (79).

Even though Mrs. Glass comes across as a caricature, she also represents common sense in a household full of high-strung people. Three of her statements go right to the heart of Zooey's problem. For one thing, she says that neither Zooey nor Buddy are able to talk to people they don't like. She also says that Zooey finds it so hard to get along with people because he has extremely strong likes and dislikes. And finally, she says that it doesn't do Zooey any good to be so smart and know so much since it doesn't make him happy. These common sense statements suggest that one of the functions of Mrs. Glass in the novella is similar to that of the chorus in Greek tragedy because she puts the events of the plot and the opinions of Zooey and Franny in an objective perspective.

The fourth major character in "Zooey" is the narrator Buddy Glass. Born in 1919 (the same year as J.D. Salinger), Buddy is the second oldest of the Glass children. Readers who are familiar with previous Glass stories will remember him as the narrator of "Raise High the Roof Beam, Carpenters." In that novella, we get a good sense of Buddy's personality from the way he interacts with the wedding guests on Seymour's wedding day, but we do not get much information about his life. For instance, we are not told what Buddy did for a living before was inducted in the Army in 1941. In "Zooey," we learn that Buddy has been writing fiction since the age of fifteen, that he was an English major in college, that he taught writing at several colleges even though he never got a college degree himself, and that he is currently (in 1957) a writer-in-residence at a girls' junior college in Upstate New York. At that college, he teaches two advanced writing courses, and on Friday evenings, he gives lectures on Mahayana and Zen Buddhism to his colleagues, their wives, and a few brainy undergraduates.

We also learn that Buddy thinks of his brother Seymour as a wise man and near-saint even though Seymour committed suicide. Moreover, in his letter to Zooey, Buddy makes a negative comment about the vanity and phoniness of Seymour's wife Muriel, and this comment suggests that he holds her responsible for Seymour's death. Two external signs of Buddy's worshipful attitude toward Seymour are that he insists on preserving his and Seymour's old room as it was before he and Seymour moved to their own apartment and that he insists on keeping their old telephone listed in Seymour's name even though he himself doesn't have a phone in his house in Upstate New York.

Perhaps the most important new information about Buddy Glass is that Salinger considers him his "alter-ego." This information is not contained in the novella "Zooey" itself but in the dust jacket notes for the book *Franny and Zooey*. In those notes, Salinger reveals that "Franny" and "Zooey" are parts of a "narrative series" about the Glass family, but he says he doesn't know when the next installment will come out because while he, J.D. Salinger, works "like greased lightning," his "alter-ego and collaborator, Buddy Glass, is insufferably slow."

The style in "Zooey" is a further development of the style in "Raise High the Roof Beam, Carpenters." It is still as elliptical as before, but it has become even more whimsical. In the introduction of "Zooey" there is a sentence that refers to Buddy's worry that his introduction might be too personal to be effective. Buddy writes: "If, with the right kind of luck, it comes off, it should be comparable in effect to a compulsory guided tour through the engine room, with myself, as guide, leading the way in an old one-piece Jantzen bathing suit" (47). As has by now become typical of Salinger's style, there are again several qualifying phrases that slow down the pace of the sentence. What's new is the strange comparison of the introduction to a guided tour of the engine room of an ocean liner and the bizarre image of Buddy in a silent-movie bathing suit.

Buddy's style in "Zooey" is very similar to Salinger's style in the dust jacket blurb for *Franny and Zooey*. For instance, when Salinger admits that he is worried about the progress of his narrative series, he says that "there is a real-enough danger, I suppose, that sooner or later I'll bog down, perhaps disappear entirely, in my own methods, locutions, and mannerisms." Here we notice two qualifying phrases—"I suppose" and "perhaps disappear entirely"—that slow down the pace, and we also notice the extravagant image of the author disappearing in the morass of his swampy style. Both are stylistic traits typical of Buddy. Salinger's reference to Buddy as his alter ego can therefore be seen as his acknowledgement that his and Buddy's writing styles are identical.

SETTINGS AND SYMBOLS

In "Zooey," Salinger spells out the setting in time in somewhat less detail than in "Raise High the Roof Beam, Carpenters" where he gives us an exact date for Seymour's wedding. In "Zooey," we don't get the date, but we are told that the story begins at 10:30 in the morning, and that it is a Monday in November of 1955. "Zooey" also differs from "Carpenters" in that the events of the plot take up only as much time as it takes to read about them.

Moreover, in "Zooey" Salinger gives us more detailed descriptions of his settings than in "Carpenters" or any other previous story. All the events of the novella take place in the fifth-floor apartment of the Glass family which is located in the East Seventies between 2nd Avenue and 3rd Avenue in New York City. The three major settings are the bathroom, the living room, and Seymour and Buddy's old room.

The first setting, the bathroom, isn't described as to its size or shape, but it receives its character from the design on the shower curtain and the contents of the medicine cabinet. The shower curtain is made of nylon, is scarlet in color, and has a canary-yellow design of musical clefs, sharps, and flats on it. The color scheme is ghastly, but the design denotes the family's cultural interests even though we don't find out which ones among the Glass children play the Steinway in the living room. The medicine cabinet tells us even more about the Glass family. It contains what Buddy romantically calls "a host of golden pharmaceuticals." In a page-long, Whitmanesque catalog, Buddy enumerates over 40 objects in the medicine cabinet, among them several different brands of pain killer tablets, antacids, face creams, and hair oils, as well as hair brushes, tweezers, nail files and scissors, and a half dozen unrelated items such as a snapshot of a cat, two sea shells, three ticket stubs from a Broadway show, a blue marble, a class ring, and the broken chassis of a lady's wrist watch. The contents of the medicine cabinet speak volumes. Fans of the Glasses can go through this catalog and assign almost every item to a specific family member. More importantly, in view of this "host of golden pharmaceuticals," we understand why Zooey sarcastically refers to the bathroom as a "chapel." As the contents of the medicine cabinet show, the bathroom is a place for narcissism and ego worship.

By contrast, the Glass living room is a place of family interaction. Buddy Glass gives us a two-and-a-half page inventory of the furniture that includes such items as a Steinway grand piano, three radios, a 21 inch television set, a marble coffee table, an eider down sofa, a 12 gallon fish tank, overflowing bookcases on three walls, and a plethora of framed show business photographs and mementos on the walls. Three telling details stand out. They give the room an even more lived-in quality than we get in the description of Seymour and Buddy's apartment in "Raise High the Roof Beam, Carpenters." One detail is that most of the legs on the furniture are badly marred or nicked. Another is that the port-wine-red carpet sports several pancreas-shaped stains that were obviously made by the family's various pets. And the third telling detail is a large brown stain on the ceiling that Zooey once made with a water pistol filled with root beer.

The third setting in the novella, Seymour and Buddy's old room, is also described in great detail. Buddy says that the room is "unsunny and unlarge," and that its two small windows look out on an "unpicturesque brick-and-concrete valley." Again we get an inventory of the furniture. In this case, the furniture consists mostly of a maple set of twin day beds, a night table, and two small, boy-size desks. Above all, there are books everywhere, on the desks, overflowing from tall bookshelves, and in stacks on the floor. But the two most important items in the room are the telephone on Seymour's desk that is still listed in his name, seven years after his suicide, and the large piece of white beaver board nailed to the door on which are inscribed two columns of quotations from Seymour and Buddy's favorite books. As readers of Salinger's previous fiction would expect, these 12 quotations are reprinted in full.

There are four major symbols in "Zooey." One is the figure of the wise little girl which appears in three different episodes, a second is Mrs. Glass's bowl of chicken soup, a third is Seymour's telephone, and the most important one is Seymour's Fat Lady.

The first recurring symbol in "Zooey" is that of the little girl who brings an adult to an insight. This is a favorite Salinger symbol which occurs in much of his fiction. He first developed it as the character of Mattie Gladwaller in the story "Last Day of the Last Furlough" (1944), and he perfected it in the character of Phoebe in *The Catcher in the Rye* (1951).

The first little girl is mentioned in Buddy's letter to Zooey. She is someone that Seymour saw while he was traveling on a commercial airliner. Seymour wrote a double haiku poem about the girl, and Buddy found the poem when he went to Florida to bring Seymour's body home after his suicide. The haiku runs like this: "The little girl on the plane/ That turned her doll's head around/ To look at me" (64). Like a Zen koan, this haiku does not yield up its meaning easily. Instead of trying to explain the poem, Buddy relates it to his own meeting with a little girl at the meat counter in a supermarket.

Buddy's little girl is a four-year-old that was staring up at him in a supermarket. When Buddy complimented her on how pretty she was and asked her if she had many boyfriends, the girl held up two fingers. Buddy asked what their names were, and the little girl shouted: "*Bobby and Dorothy*." Buddy was overwhelmed by this answer because Seymour once told him that it is the goal of all advanced religious study to make the student learn that there are no differences between heat and cold, day and night, animals and stones, boys and girls. What Seymour here alludes to is one of the central ideas of Hinduism, Taoism, and Buddhism. That idea is expressed in Sanskrit as "Tat Tvam Asi," or "you are that," which means that there is ultimately no difference between the individual and all the things he or she observes because *Brahman*, the Supreme Spirit, is in all things organic and inorganic. Buddy is amazed at the little girl in the supermarket because he credits her with the kind of wisdom that most people lose as they grow up.

The third little girl is someone whom Zooey observes while he is talking to Franny in the living room. As Zooey looks out of a window of his parents' fifth-floor apartment, he sees a girl of seven or eight playing hide-and-seek with her little dachshund. Zooey notes the despair of the little dog when it can't find the girl right away and the immense joy of both when they are reunited. Zooey is delighted and shares his reaction with Franny. He says that we often fail to notice what nice things there are in the world because we always refer everything back to our insignificant egos. In this tiny episode, the little girl seems to represent the simple joys that come from unconditional love, joys which we are incapable of experiencing when we get as self-absorbed as Franny and Zooey are. Zooey's little girl therefore helps Zooey to become aware of his self-centeredness.

The common denominator that connects the three little girls in "Zooey" to the other little girls in Salinger's fiction is the romantic belief that children are wiser than adults because they can see the essence of things untrammeled by the corrupting influence of socialization and education. No matter whether this is wishful thinking or not, Buddy's attitude is similar to that which the British romantic poet William Wordsworth expressed in his "Ode: Intimations of Immortality." In that poem, Wordsworth says that we are all born "trailing clouds of glory" because "we come from God, who is our home" (ll. 64-65). Like William Wordsworth, J.D. Salinger apparently believes that the child is closer to God than the adult, and that the child is therefore a "Mighty Prophet! Seer blest!" (l. 114). In short, Salinger's little girls represent the wisdom beyond knowledge that most adults are no longer able to grasp.

Another symbol in "Zooey" is the bowl of chicken soup that Bessie Glass offers to her daughter Franny on five different occasions and that Franny rejects each time. Zooey tells Franny that if it is the religious life she wants, she needs to be able to recognize genuine religious behavior when she encounters it. He tells her that she doesn't even recognize "a bowl of consecrated chicken broth" when someone offers it to her. Here Zooey reflects the spirit of the *Bhagavad Gita* when he suggests that the most religious thing we can do is what Mrs. Glass does, namely to do our daily duty and to do it with all our might. In a less Vedantic sense, the symbol of Bessie's bowl of chicken broth suggests that we all need to recognize that the cups of soup which others offer us when we are sick are "consecrated" by the concern and compassion with which they are offered.

Yet another symbol in "Zooey" is Seymour's telephone. It is a symbol for two reasons. One is that while Mrs. Glass wants it disconnected, Buddy says hat he loves that old phone because it is essential to his inner peace to have Seymour's name listed in the phone book year after year. On this level of meaning, Seymour's phone represents Buddy's inability to cope with Seymour's death.

A second level of meaning becomes apparent when Zooey uses Seymour's phone to get through to Franny, something he had not been able to do face-to-face. Before Zooey calls Franny up on this telephone, he rereads an old diary entry of Seymour's plus some quotations from books that Seymour loved, books such as the *Bhagavad Gita* and *The Gospel of Sri Ramakrishna*. Then, when Zooey approaches Seymour's desk to pick up the phone, the narrator tells us that he moved as if someone had attached marionette strings to him and yanked them vigorously. Here the suggestion is that after Zooey has immersed himself in Seymour's mind-set, his marionette strings are being pulled by Seymour, and this is why Zooey is finally able to connect with Franny and talk her out of the Jesus Prayer and back into her career as an actress. Seymour's old phone therefore comes across as a mystical object, a conduit through which Seymour's spirit continues to affect his siblings.

But the most important symbol in "Zooey" is Seymour's Fat Lady. That symbol has at least two levels of meaning. When Seymour told the seven-year-old Zooey to shine his shoes for the Fat Lady before he went to the broadcast studio, young Zooey understood the first level of meaning because he imagined the Fat Lady to be a woman with cancer who needed the entertainment that he, Zooey, and his siblings were providing for her by performing on the radio show "It's a Wise Child." It isn't until Zooey is twenty-five years old and tries to help Franny overcome her religious crisis that he comes to understand a second level of meaning, namely that the Fat Lady is really "Christ Himself." This statement allows a number of interpretations. The most obvious is the one suggested in the Bible by Matthew 15: 25, "What you do to the least of these my brethren you do unto me."

THEMES AND INTERPRETATIONS

The major themes that reviewers and critics have pointed out in "Zooey" are religious, psychological, and sociological. Carl Bode said about "Zooey" that "essentially it is a theological tract" (68). Leslie Fiedler believed that "Zooey" is about "madness as the chief temptation of modern life, especially for the intelligent young" (59-60). And according to Alfred Kazin, the central concern in "Zooey" is the problem of how to tolerate or even love the people who represent our "unbearably shallow culture" (46). Each of these three major themes has been explored from a variety of perspectives.

A number of critics who have dealt with the religious meaning of "Zooey" have pointed out that its message is non-Christian, even though it depends on an understanding that Seymour's Fat Lady represents "Christ Himself."

The Christian theologian Kenneth Hamilton examines Salinger's use of the Bible in "Zooey" and comes to the conclusion that Buddy Glass classifies the Bible as "a sub-type of Eastern philosophy and believes that it may be placed alongside Advaita Vedanta and Taoism" (40). Hamilton concludes that whoever or whatever Seymour, Buddy, Zooey, and Franny see in the Fat Lady, "they never see the Holy One of Israel" (45).

Similarly, James Lundquist urges us "not to assume that Salinger is naively advocating the acceptance of Christianity" (132-133). He argues that in "Zooey," "Salinger is still writing with the Zen ideas found in *Nine Stories* in mind" (133). Lundquist therefore believes that "Franny gets over her breakdown by the very absurdity of Zooey's equation of Christ and the Fat Lady" (133). Lundquist concludes that this "is quite in keeping with Zen teachings" because "Zen enlightenment is often the result of a ridiculous gesture of the master or an absurd answer to a serious question" (133).

Like Hamilton and Lundquist, Som P. Ranchan Sharma also argues that the religious meaning of "Zooey" is essentially non-Christian. In the article "Echoes of the *Gita* in Salinger's 'Franny and Zooey'," Sharma reminds us that Salinger studied Vedanta Hinduism at the Ramakrishna-Vivekananda Center in New York. But the main purpose of the article is to stress the importance of the long quotation from the *Bhagavad Gita* in "Zooey." Sharma notes that Zooey points out to Franny that she can't escape her karma "because her desires have turned her into an actress just as Krishna [in the *Bhagavad Gita*] points out to Arjuna that he has to be a warrior" (216). According to Sharma, Zooey manages to set Franny straight by convincing her to accept the "Gita credo of Karma-Yoga" (215). This credo is expressed by one of the statements in the long quotation from the *Bhagavad Gita* that Seymour and Buddy inscribed on the door of their room: "Perform every action with your heart fixed on the Supreme Lord. Renounce the attachment to the fruits" (Prabhavananda 34; "Zooey" 177).

A combined religious and esthetic interpretation is advanced by John Wenke who stresses that both Zooey and Franny are artists. Wenke interprets the Fat Lady as "that person out there who needs the performance to get through the day." The message that "Zooey" holds for the artist is that "one performs in the service of art and thereby enacts the dictates of religion." Wenke concludes: "The actor pursues the possibility of 'Christ Consciousness' not through detachment but through engagement—the self redemptive act of playing to a crowd of Fat Ladies" (88).

Of the several psychological interpretations of "Zooey," the most detailed one is that of Daniel Seitzman who is not a literary scholar but a clinical psychologist. Seitzman acknowledges the primacy of the religious meaning in the novella but points out that the plot can be seen as Zooey's administering "wild" psychiatric therapy to Franny, and that his efforts take up three separate "sessions." Seitzman identifies Franny's "illness" as "severe depression" combined with an "identity crisis" and "feelings of worthlessness" (140). Zooey's therapeutic method consists of a "destructive" and an "integrative" phase. Seitzman explains that Zooey's "bullying, his venom, his very gaucherie are actually expressions of his devotion," but that it is his phone call which is "of central importance in the recovery" (157). Before Zooey makes the phone call, so Seitzman explains, he steeps himself in Seymour and Buddy's memorabilia: "One has the feeling that as he communes with the spirits of those savants, the one dead, the other living, he inhales them and becomes possessed. Through his voice speak the voices, Dybbuk-fashion, of the awesome brothers" (158). Zooey's efforts to cure Franny are successful because "the transference love of Seymour has come down through Buddy by means of Zooeys voice and talent" (160).

Quite a few interpretations have considered the sociological and cultural implications of "Zooey." Most of them analyze the novella in terms of the conflict between the values of Seymour, Buddy, Zooey, and Franny on the one hand and those of their less-cultured and less-spiritual contemporaries on the other. Several of these studies express doubts that Zooey's notion of the Fat Lady being "Christ Himself" can really help him and Franny overcome their estrangement from American mainstream culture. Paul Phillips goes even further in his skepticism when he says that "at the end, Zooey, Franny, and Salinger are just as alienated as before from the world they have repudiated" (38). In fact, Phillips believes that in *Franny and Zooey*, Salinger has become "even more despairing and pessimistic" than in his earlier work. Because of the bitterness he perceives in Salinger and his characters, Phillips says that Salinger "is best to be understood as a satirist" and that the target of his satire is "the vulgarity, the rampant selfishness, the fundamental hypocrisy and foulness of bourgeois conventions" (38-39).

CONCLUSION

"Zooey" stands out in the Glass Family Series because it is much longer than any of the other parts; because its settings are described in unusual detail; because the narrator is extremely fond of his two main characters, Franny and Zooey; and because the novella presents one of the most memorable symbols in the Glass Family Series, that of Seymour's Fat Lady.

What "Zooey" shares with its predecessor in the series, "Raise High the Roof Beam, Carpenters," is a whimsical style, an intrusive and self-reflexive narrator, a flexible point of view, and two protagonists rather than one. But above all, "Zooey" shares two themes with "Carpenters," that of the quest for spiritual advancement and that of the conflict between the spiritual Glasses and their unspiritual contemporaries.

As a self-contained work of art, "Zooey" may not display Salinger's craftsmanship to its best advantage, but as a part of the Glass Family Series, it is of eminent importance because it defuses many of the objections of critics. It does that by making Zooey criticize the ideas of the family saint, Seymour, who instilled impossibly high spiritual standards in his siblings. But the novella also points out the positive aspects of Seymour's teachings. And Seymour's teachings are summed up memorably when Seymour asks Zooey to shine his shoes for the Fat Lady and when Zooey realizes that the Fat Lady is Jesus Christ.

Another reason why "Zooey" is such an important part of the Glass Family Series is the non-sectarian nature of its religious message. This message is couched in Christian terms—the Fat Lady is Jesus Christ—but it incorporates Eastern ideas, especially the core idea of the *Bhagavad Gita* which is that the most religious thing we can do is to do our everyday duty with all our might.

A reader who has never read anything by Salinger would probably not be able to appreciate and understand "Zooey." Having read "Franny" beforehand would help, but having first read "A Perfect Day for Bananafish" and "Raise High the Roof Beam, Carpenters" would help even more.

While a lot has been written about "Zooey," most of this commentary has been imbedded in articles or book chapters about all of Salinger's work or about the Glass Family Series. In short, there have been very few studies of "Zooey" as a self-contained work of art and even fewer studies that consider the novella's unusual structure and narrative technique. As far as themes are concerned, there have been too few explorations of what "Zooey" says about the nature of art and the role of the artist in society, even fewer studies of the family dynamics in the novella, and none of the mother-daughter relationship in "Zooey."

WORKS CITED

Bode, Carl. "Salinger, J.D. *Franny and Zooey*" [Review]. *Wisconsin Studies in Contemporary Literature* 3 (Winter 1961): 65-71.

Fiedler, Leslie. "Up From Adolescence." *Partisan Review* 29 (Winter 1962): 127-131. Rpt. in Grunwald 57-62.

Green, Martin. "Franny and Zooey." In *Reappraisals: Some Common-Sense Readings in American Literature.* New York: Norton, 1965, 197-210.

Grunwald, Henry A., ed. *Salinger: A Critical and Personal Portrait.* New York: Harper, 1962.

Hamilton, Kenneth. *J.D. Salinger: A Critical Essay.* Grand Rapids, MI: Eerdmans, 1967.

Kazin, Alfred. "J.D. Salinger: Everybody's Favorite." *Atlantic Monthly* 208 (August 1961): 27-31. Rpt. in Grunwald 43-52.

Kermode, Frank. "One Hand Clapping" [Review of *Franny and Zooey*]. *New Statesman* (8 June 1962): 831-832.

Lundquist, James. *J.D. Salinger.* New York: Ungar, 1979.

McCarthy, Mary. "J.D. Salinger's Closed Circuit." *Harpe's Magazine* 225 (October 1962): 45-48. Rpt. in *Studies in J.D. Salinger.* Ed. Marvin Laser and Norman Fruman. New York: Odyssey, 1963, 245-250.

Mizener, Arthur. "The American Hero as Poet: Seymour Glass." In *The Sense of Life in the Modern Novel.* Boston: Houghton Mifflin, 1963, 227-246.

Phelps, John. "A Writer Who Talks To, and Of the Young" [Review of *Franny and Zooey*]. *New York Herald Tribune Book Review* (17 September 1961): 3, 14.

Phillips, Paul. "A Look at a Best-Seller: Salinger's *Franny and Zooey*" [Review]. *Mainstream* 15 (1962): 32-39.

"Plain and Fancy" [Review of *Franny and Zooey*]. *Newsweek* (18 September 1961): 109-110.

Prabhavananda, Swami, and Christopher Isherwood, trans. *The Song of God: Bhagavad Gita* [1944]. New York: Signet, 1972.

Salinger, J.D. *Franny and Zooey* [1961]. New York: Bantam: 1964.

Seitzman, Daniel. "Therapy and Antitherapy in Salinger's 'Zooey'." *American Imago* 25 (Summer 1968): 140-162.

Sharma, Som P. Ranchan. "Echoes of the *Gita* in Salinger's 'Franny and Zooey'." In *The Gita in World Literature.* Ed. C.D. Verma. New Delhi: Sterling, 1990, 214-219.

Skow, John. "Sonny: An Introduction." *Time* (15 September 1961): 84-90. Rpt. in Grunwald 3-18.

Updike, John. "Anxious Days for the Glass Family" [Review of *Franny and Zooey*]. *New York Times Book Review* (17 September 1961): 1, 52. Rpt. in Grunwald 53-56.

Wenke, John. *J.D. Salinger. A Study of the Short Fiction.* Boston: Twayne, 1991.

Wordsworth, William. "Ode: Intimations of Immortality." In *The Norton Anthology of British Literature.* 7th ed. Vol. 2. Ed. M.H. Abrams et al. New York: Norton, 2000, 287-292.

SUGGESTIONS FOR FURTHER READING

Aitkant, Satish C. "From Alienation to Accommodation: Salinger's 'Franny and Zooey'." *Kyushu American Literature* 28 (October 1987): 39-44.
French, Warren. "The House of Glass." In *J.D. Salinger, Revisited.* Boston: G.K. Hall, 1988, 89-98.
Galloway, David D. "The Love Ethic." In *The Absurd Hero in American Fiction.* Austin, TX: U of Texas P, 1966, 140-169. Rpt. in *Modern Critical Views: J.D. Salinger.* Ed. Harold Bloom. New York: Chelsea House, 1987, 29-51.
Hassan, Ihab. "Almost the Voice of Silence: The Later Novelettes of J.D. Salinger." *Wisconsin Studies in Contemporary Literature* 4 (Winter 1963): 5-20.
McIntyre, John P., S.J. "A Preface for 'Franny and Zooey'." *Critic* 20 (1962): 25-28.
Nikhilananda, Swami. *Hinduism: Its Meaning for the Liberation of the Spirit* [1958]. New York: Ramakrishna-Vivekananda Center, 1992.

Chapter 8

"Seymour—An Introduction"

[He] competently blundered his way to the heart of the matter.

Buddy Glass

"Seymour—An Introduction" was first published in the *New Yorker* on 6 June 1959, and it was reprinted between hard covers in 1963 as part of *Raise High the Roof Beam, Carpenters and Seymour—An Introduction.* With 31,300 words, "Seymour—An Introduction" is the second longest of Salinger's Glass Family stories, some 10,000 words shorter than "Zooey."

As the title "Seymour—An Introduction" suggests, the subject of the novella is the life and personality of Seymour Glass, the genius and poet whose quest for spiritual perfection and oneness with God ended when he committed suicide at the age of thirty-one. The narrator of the "Introduction" is Seymour's brother, Buddy Glass, and one of the tasks that Buddy sets for himself is to convince us and himself that despite his suicide, Seymour was a near-saint. In the process, Buddy engages in a considerable amount of introspection concerning his relationship with Seymour and his problems in writing about him.

In "Seymour—An Introduction," Salinger takes another step away from his earlier, more conventional fiction such as the novel *The Catcher in the Rye* and the short story collection *Nine Stories.* As in "Zooey," the narrator, Buddy Glass, again tells us that he is not considering himself a short-story writer. Instead, he sees himself as "a thesaurus of undetached prefatory remarks" about Seymour. Moreover, Buddy warns us that in writing about his brother he can't be "moderate, or temperate, or brief" and that he will happily stray away from his subject when he sees "something off the beaten plot line that looks exciting or interesting." And he also admits that he cannot be "detached" because he is a narrator "with extremely pressing personal needs." And indeed, at a first glance the "Introduction" seems overly long, poorly organized, and excessively introspective.

CRITICAL RECEPTION

"Seymour—An Introduction" received more negative reviews than any of Salinger's previous work, even "Zooey." Most of the negative as well as the few positive evaluations came from the academic critics, while the reviews in the newspapers and popular magazines occupied a noncommittal middle ground. Also, this time around, most of the negative criticism concerned not the content, as in the case of "Zooey," but the form.

The two critics who were hardest on "Seymour—An Introduction" were Warren French and Stanley Edgar Hyman. French found the characterization of Seymour unconvincing and considered "Seymour—An Introduction" a "crashing bore." Moreover, he said that the novella is not serious art but "*kitsch*." French defined *kitsch* "as that which describes feelings no one actually feels" (160). Stanley Edgar Hyman also found fault with the characterization of the title character and said: "The Seymour of all this turgid hagiography is preposterous." Seymour's poems as paraphrased by Buddy are, according to Hyman, "hogwash," and Seymour's statements about the creative process are "sentimental misadvice." Although Hyman believed that "Salinger is the most talented fiction writer in America," he also said that the decline of Salinger's fiction from "one of the finest short stories in our time, 'A Perfect Day for Bananafish,' to one of the most boring ever written, 'Seymour—An Introduction,' is appalling" (126-127).

Two of the few critics who had positive things to say about the "Introduction" are Henry Grunwald and Arthur Schwartz. Grunwald argued that the focus of the novella is less on Seymour than on Buddy and that Buddy is cracking under the strain of convincing us and himself that Seymour was a saint. To involve the audience in Buddy's crack-up, Salinger attempts "to destroy the proscenium" in the manner of the playwright Pirandello and "to bring the audience completely into the action, to make them forget what is real and what is not" (xxiv). Grunwald admitted that it is debatable whether or not this method works, but he said: "I for one feel that the method works hair-raisingly well." Therefore, in Grunwald's judgment, "Seymour—An Introduction" is Salinger's "most impressive story" (xxiv). Unlike Grunwald, Arthur Schwartz believed that the focus of "Seymour—An Introduction" is not on Buddy but on Seymour and that the task that Salinger set for himself was to create the first American protagonist who is "a holy man." Schwartz sensed that Salinger felt nervous about his effort "to purify [Seymour] into sainthood" and that Salinger's style shows this nervousness. To do justice to his topic, Salinger "has deliberately struck out for a new style that is somehow more expressive" (94). What Salinger has done with this style is "to meld wit and emotion, hoping the cleverness will guard the sentiment. Salinger's strategy, to deflect the thrust of the intellect by exploiting its weakness for ingenuity, is ingenuity itself" (95).

NARRATIVE STRUCTURE AND POINT OF VIEW

"Seymour—An Introduction" has a unique structure which weaves a chronological narrative into what is essentially an expository essay, and the resulting web is interlaced with anecdotes. The "Introduction" therefore defies generic categories, but since the narrator emphatically tells us that what he is presenting is not a short story and since the "Introduction" is not long enough to be a novel, most critics have referred to it as a novella.

Although the "Introduction" represents a further advance in Salinger's experimentation with narrative form and technique, it does share some typical traits with his previous work. One of these traits is that we again have two central characters instead of one. And again we get doubling motifs, for instance when Buddy tells us that his family thinks the Seymour who commits suicide in "A Perfect Day for Bananafish" has a striking resemblance to Buddy himself and when Seymour tells Buddy not to be upset that the two of them occasionally sound like each other.

As far as its narrative perspective is concerned, "Seymour—An Introduction" differs from previous installments of the Glass Family Series in two ways. For one thing, it has the most intrusive and self-reflexive narrator in all of Salinger's fiction. For another thing, it is told by an unreliable narrator who confesses that he sometimes misrepresents his subject. But as in previous Salinger stories, the point of view is again not fixed but flexible because the narrative is broken up by four footnotes—three of them quite lengthy—a string of memos, a five page letter from Seymour, and a page of quotations from two of Buddy's favorite authors, Søren Kierkegaard and Franz Kafka.

"Seymour—An Introduction" begins with apologies. The first apology has to do with the content of the "Introduction." It is presented in the form of the two long quotations from Kierkegaard and Kafka which both have to do with an author misrepresenting the subject he is writing about. This is Buddy's way of preparing us for presenting Seymour as he wants us to see him rather than as the rest of his family saw him.

The second apology has to do with the form of the "Introduction." Buddy Glass warns us that what he is going to offer will be a very unconventional piece of fiction. He explains that he wants to follow his whims and that he therefore cannot be expected to accommodate readers who want him tell his story with detachment, moderation, and brevity. And then Buddy uses one of his extravagant metaphors to describe what will happen to us, the readers, when we keep reading. He says that from time to time, when something interesting occurs to him, he intends to jump on the reader's back and steer him or her away from the beaten path of the plot line.

However, the structure of "Seymour—An Introduction" is not as haphazard as Buddy's comments suggest. This becomes apparent when we construct a topic outline and when we take into consideration that the "Introduction" consists of two layers, one expository and the other narrative. The layout of the text shows a division into six major sections:

I. Seymour as a Sick Man/Buddy's Artistic Credo
II. Seymour as God-knower
III. Seymour's Poetry
IV. Seymour's Vaudeville Background
V. Seymour as Buddy's Artistic Mentor
VI. Physical Description of Seymour

The longest of these sections—the last one—is in turn subdivided into eight parts which are separated by indentations and bullets:

1. Seymour's Hair Jumping in the Barber Shop
2. Seymour's Hair and Teeth
3. Seymour's Height, Smile, and Ears
4. Seymour's Eyes, Nose, and Chin
5. Seymour's Hands, Voice, and Skin
6. Seymour's Clothes
7. Seymour as Athlete and Gamesman
8. Seymour as Buddy's Gift to the Reader

What this outline does not reveal is that Buddy again and again uses anecdotes to illustrate his ideas. What the outline does reveal, though, is that Buddy goes against expository practice because he does not move from the least important to the most important aspects of Seymour's personality. Instead of moving from appearance to essence, he moves from essence to appearance. However, at the end of the section on the physical aspects of Seymour's personality, Buddy suddenly circles back to make what he acknowledges to be a metaphysical point.

Buddy begins the "Introduction" by stressing his brother's closeness to God and by suggesting that even though Seymour was a Sick Man, a mystic, and an unbalanced type, he may well have been a saint. References to such concepts as karma and reincarnation show that Seymour's religious beliefs were shaped by Hindu-Buddhist ideas. Next, Buddy focuses on Seymour as a poet and describes his unpublished poems, most of which were in a double haiku form. Then Buddy considers the influence on Seymour of the parents, grandparents, and great grandparents who were all vaudeville or circus performers. After that, Buddy talks about Seymour's constructive criticism of his, Buddy's, short stories and about Seymour's influence on him in general. This topic remains an undercurrent through the last and longest section about Seymour's physical appearance. The last section includes the marble-shooting anecdote which brings Buddy to an insight about Seymour's spiritual and artistic legacy.

The second layer of structure in "Seymour—An Introduction" is the narrative which culminates in an epiphany. It is the story of Buddy's struggle to write an account of the life and personality of Seymour that will lay to rest his own and the reader's doubts about Seymour's character. What looms behind this narrative is Seymour's suicide.

The narrative structure of the "Introduction" is marked by a series of time references which establish a chronological framework. We find that Buddy writes the first four sections in two sittings, apparently on a weekend. Then Buddy gets sick and spends nine weeks in bed with acute hepatitis. After Buddy re-reads seven memos and an old letter from Seymour, he resumes his work on a Thursday night and writes section V ("Seymour as Buddy's Artistic Mentor") in one sitting. The next section, the eight-part description of Seymour's physical appearance, takes up seven consecutive nights of composition. Buddy writes one part each night and two parts on the last night and the following morning. He begins these last two parts of Section VI at ten o'clock on a Sunday night and stops sometime after midnight when he arrives at a sudden realization which makes him perspire from head to foot. He decides to take a half-hour rest and stretches out on the floor. When he wakes up three hours later, he continues his work by describing the realization that turned him into a dripping wreck. Buddy finishes "Seymour—An Introduction" at 7:30 on Monday morning, an hour-and-a-half before he is due in Room 307 at his college to teach the first of his two writing classes.

In addition to this overarching narrative structure, there are anecdotes interspersed to illustrate ideas in the expository sections. These small narratives come in three sizes: Mini anecdotes that take up only two or three sentences; medium-size anecdotes that concentrate on one incident and take up a full paragraph or two; and double anecdotes that deal with two related incidents and occupy over one page. These anecdotes illustrate specific facets of Seymour's personality. They are the meat on the skeleton of the expository structure.

Two mini anecdotes concern Seymour's physical appearance and his lack of vanity. In the first of these anecdotes, the eleven-year-old Waker points at Seymour's hairy arms and tells him to take off his sweater because it's so warm in the apartment. Seymour loved this kind of horseplay from his siblings even though it was at his expense. In another mini anecdote, the four-year-old Franny sits on Seymour's lap, stares at his teeth, and then tells him how nice and yellow they are. This comment about his tobacco-stained teeth delighted Seymour immensely. It, too, reveals that Seymour was not the least bit vain about his physical appearance.

Two medium-size anecdotes illustrate the special nature of Seymour's intellect. In the first of these two, Seymour is eight years old, and his parents are giving a party for some 60 guests. Around two o'clock in the morning, when the party breaks up, Seymour asks permission to bring the guests their coats. Buddy reports that Seymour—without asking any questions—brought almost all the guests, with one or two exceptions, their proper coats and hats. In another medium-size anecdote, young Seymour wakes Buddy up in the middle of the night to tell him that he had finally figured out why Christ tells us to call no man a fool. This was a problem that had been troubling Seymour for a whole week, and now he had come up with a solution. He explains to Buddy that Christ said not to call anyone a fool because there really are no fools, only dopes. Although Seymour doesn't explain what the difference between fools and dopes is, this distinction is so important to him that it merits waking up Buddy in the middle of the night.

But the most interesting anecdotes in "Seymour—An Introduction" are the ones which deal with two related incidents. One of them serves to illustrate the legacy of Seymour's circus and vaudeville ancestors. It begins as an anecdote about Les Glass paying a visit to his sons, Seymour and Buddy, after they had moved to their own apartment. Les was in a bad mood because all afternoon he had been holding bad cards in a pinochle game. He scowled at the furnishings of the apartment, he criticized both Seymour and Buddy for smoking too much, and he even claimed that there was a fly in his highball. Then, after looking at a photo of himself and Bessie on the wall, he suddenly asked Seymour if he remembered the time in 1922, in Brisbane, Australia, when Seymour was five years old and Joe Jackson gave him a ride on his nickel-plated trick bicycle all

over the stage of a vaudeville theater. Seymour was extremely pleased to be
asked this question and answered that it seemed to him he had never got off that
beautiful bicycle. Seymour's answer expands Buddy's earlier comment that
Seymour's poetry is literate vaudeville of a high order.

Another double anecdote serves the purpose of clarifying the epiphany that
Buddy Glass has at the end of "Seymour—An Introduction." It is the story of
Seymour resolving a family crisis that the nine-year-old Waker Glass caused
when he gave away his bicycle to an unknown boy who asked him for it. It was
Waker's ninth birthday, and his parents had just bought him the bike at
Davega's Sports Store. They were therefore very angry when he told them he
gave it away because a boy he didn't even know asked him for it. Waker should
just have given the boy a nice long ride, they said; but Waker responded that the
boy didn't want a ride, the boy wanted the bike. Seymour was excited about
Waker's generosity, and Buddy reports that Seymour blundered his way to the
heart of the controversy so competently that it took only a few minutes before
Waker and his parents made up and kissed. This anecdote not only illustrates
Seymour's intuitive way of dealing with human problems, it also provides
Buddy with the metaphor of the gift bicycle which he later uses to explain what
he has learned in the process of writing "Seymour—An Introduction."

Buddy has his epiphany after he relates the most important anecdote in the
novella. In this anecdote, the ten-year-old Seymour watches the eight-year-old
Buddy lose at curb marbles for a while and then gives him the advice not to aim
so much. Seymour explains to Buddy that if his marble hits that of his opponent because he aimed for it, it will only be luck. Buddy disagrees and asks
how it can be luck if he aims. Seymour answers that Buddy will be glad if he
hits his opponent's marble, and if he is glad if he hits somebody's marble, then
he secretly doesn't expect to hit it. Therefore it would have to be by luck or by
accident that he actually hit the marble. At that point, Buddy's pride rises up,
and before Seymour can give him any more advice, Buddy breaks up the game
by saying that it is getting too dark.

After finishing this anecdote, Buddy comes to a double insight. One is that
with his marble-shooting advice, Seymour was instinctively getting at something similar to the principle of "Aiming but no aiming" which Japanese master
archers try to instill in their archery students. The other insight, Buddy says, is
that he was "at long last being presented with a Davega bicycle of [his] own to
give away" and that this Davega bicycle was Seymour. In short, like his little
brother Waker, Buddy has just received a valuable gift, and he is now giving it
away to his readers. That valuable gift is Seymour's belief in "Aiming but no
aiming," in aiming to make perfect shots and not to win marbles, or, to put it
differently, to do things not for a tangible reward but for spiritual satisfaction.

In "Seymour—An Introduction," there is no trace left of the objective point
of view we find in some of the pieces in *Nine Stories*. Now the point of view
is highly subjective because Buddy Glass not only keeps intruding into the narrative to address the reader and to comment on the progress of his narrative, he
also keeps intruding to question his own motivations and to reveal his untrust-

worthiness as a storyteller, that is, his tendency to write things about Seymour that are false.

Right from the beginning of the "Introduction," Buddy addresses himself to a general reader. But Buddy's general reader is really an ideal reader. This becomes apparent when Buddy tells this reader that he or she, the reader, must be a great bird lover who is fascinated by birds because of all creatures they seem to be the ones who are closest to pure spirit. In short, the reader whom Buddy has in mind is a person who is as interested in things spiritual as Buddy is himself. In addition, Buddy gives us a catalogue of the kinds of people for whom he does not write. They are "the grounded everywhere," the people incapable of spiritual flight. Also, Buddy says he is not writing for readers who want him to get on with his story as expeditiously as possible, and he suggests that such readers stop reading before they get any farther into the "Introduction."

As the narrative progresses, Buddy again and again intrudes to address his readers directly and to worry about their response to what he is writing. On one occasion, Buddy wishes his readers could talk to him, even if they had something negative to say. On another occasion, Buddy actually imagines that his readers might respond to what he has written and that they might remind him in a shrill and unpleasant voice that he was going to tell them what Seymour looked like and that they don't want to hear all the analysis and "gluey" emotional stuff Buddy has been presenting. Buddy responds by admitting that he is overdoing the analysis a bit but that he wants every bit of the "gluey stuff."

Buddy's response to an imaginary objection from his readers is one of the many instances in the "Introduction" in which Buddy talks about the way he is composing his narrative. In another passage, Buddy asks if he is going on about his brother's poetry too long and if he is being garrulous. He admits that, yes, he is going on about Seymour's poetry too long, and yes, he is being garrulous. Then, after Buddy describes Seymour's face, he takes stock of what he has written so far and admits that his writing methods lack total perfection and that he is perhaps going a bit overboard with his physical description of Seymour.

The most fascinating aspect of the narrative perspective in "Seymour—An Introduction" is Buddy's self-confessed unreliability as a narrator. Buddy even begins with two quotations that are supposed to forestall attacks on his unreliability. In one quotation Franz Kafka says he finds himself misrepresenting people's personalities even though and perhaps because he is writing about them with "steadfast love." In the other quotation, Søren Kierkegaard says that when he makes a slip of the pen while describing a character, it sometimes seems as if this "clerical error were to revolt against the author," assume a life of its own, and stand up and tell his creator, "thou art a very poor writer." The purpose of these two quotations seems to be to prepare us for Buddy's later admission that he misrepresented Seymour in "A Perfect Day for Bananafish."

Buddy admits his untrustworthiness as a narrator for the first time when he says that in writing "Seymour—An Introduction" he has been too panegyric and that he has not come to criticize but to praise Seymour, in short, that he will only deal with Seymour's positive traits. Buddy states even more clearly that he is an unreliable narrator when he admits that he misrepresented Seymour in "A Perfect Day for Bananafish," the story of Seymour's suicide. After Buddy takes credit for having written that story, he reports that his family has pointed out to him that the Seymour in that story is not Seymour at all but a person with a striking resemblance to Buddy himself. Buddy admits that this is true and that it makes him feel a craftsman's twinge of reproof. Buddy's admission suggests that his portrait of his brother in the "Introduction" may be yet another distorted picture of the Seymour his family knew.

CHARACTERIZATION AND STYLE

In "Seymour—An Introduction," we see a further stage in Salinger's changing conception of Seymour's character and also in Salinger's increasing identification with his narrator Buddy Glass. Most importantly, Salinger avoids discussing Seymour's flaws so that he can depict him as a person who is spiritually so far advanced that he has acquired supernatural mental powers. He also explains Seymour's complex belief system and thereby lays to rest the popular misconception that the vision of life in the Glass Family Series is derived exclusively from Zen Buddhism. And finally, Salinger provides us with the first description of the physical appearance of both Seymour and Buddy, and he gives additional support to his comment—on the dust jacket of *Franny and Zooey*—that Buddy Glass is his alter ego.

In previous stories, Salinger did not tell us much about what Seymour looked like. In "A Perfect Day for Bananafish," all we learn about Seymour's appearance is that he was a pale young man whose shoulders were white and narrow and whose swimming trunks were royal blue. In "Raise High the Roof Beam, Carpenters," Seymour doesn't make a physical appearance, but his sister Boo Boo says in a letter that he has an ecstatic look on his face and that he doesn't weigh much more than a cat.

"Seymour—An Introduction" makes up for Salinger's early reticence in describing Seymour because Buddy Glass now gives us an exhaustive description. According to Buddy, Seymour was an "Attractively Ugly Man" (179). But while Buddy might find Seymour's ugliness attractive, the reader is more likely to find it grotesque or even clownish.

Seymour was five foot ten-and-a-half, had very hairy arms, and originally had black, wiry hair, but was getting very bald by the age of twenty-eight. He had hardly any chin at all, a feature of his face which emphasized his large nose and his large ears. Buddy says that Seymour's nose was not only big and drooping but also that it was slightly lopsided because it had been broken at the bridge. Buddy also compares Seymour's ears to those of an old Buddha because they had extremely long, fleshy lobes. And finally, Buddy tells us that when Seymour smiled, he revealed teeth that were yellow with tobacco stains.

In addition to being very homely, Seymour always wore ill-fitting clothes. He simply didn't care about his appearance and didn't seem to notice that his sleeves either stopped above his wrists or came down to the middle of his thumbs and that the seats of his pants always drooped as if the pants were six sizes too large for him.

Buddy doesn't give us as much information about his own appearance as about Seymour's, but he says that he was proud of the physical resemblance between him and Seymour. In particular, he mentions that, like Seymour, he too doesn't have much of a chin and that he shares Seymour's large nose. However, Buddy says that in contrast to Seymour, he himself is a very sharp dresser. He also mentions that he is slightly shorter than Seymour and that while Seymour was always thin as a rail, he, Buddy, is slightly paunchy.

More important than the physical differences between Seymour and Buddy are the differences in their temperaments. Buddy illustrates this difference when he says that if Seymour told his younger siblings to take off their galoshes when they came into the apartment, they all knew that Seymour meant they would track up the floor and Bessie would have to mop up the mess. But if Buddy told them to take off their galoshes, they knew that he meant that people who didn't take off their galoshes were slobs. Buddy here suggests that Seymour was a much kinder and more even-tempered person than he himself was. This is confirmed by several anecdotes in the "Introduction." In one of them, Buddy complains that Seymour's "damn hair" always jumps all over him when they get their haircuts. In another anecdote, Buddy ends a game of curb marbles rather than take marble shooting advice from Seymour.

Buddy knew all his life that Seymour was spiritually farther advanced than he was, and he even says that Seymour was the only person he ever knew who "more frequently than not tallied with the classical conception, as I saw it, of a *mukta,* a ringding enlightened man, a God-knower" (106). Here it is important to note that Buddy qualifies his statement with the phrases "more frequently than not" and "as I saw it." In short, Buddy does not claim that Seymour was actually a *mukta.* The term *mukta* comes from the Sanskrit word *mukti* which has a meaning similar to that of the Zen Buddhist word *satori.* Salinger's teacher, Swami Nikhilananda of the Ramakrishna-Vivekananda Center in New York, explains the term *mukti* as follows:

The goal of spiritual life is *mukti,* or liberation—liberation from imperfection, bondage, separateness, misery, and death. It is the ultimate blessedness, the outcome of the realization of man's unity with the universal Consciousness.... The man who realizes the state of God-consciousness in this life is called a jivanmukta.... Realizing all souls in himself and himself in all souls, he loves all beings. (70-72)

Upon his death, a *mukta* is liberated from the wheel of *samsara,* the cycle of death and rebirth. As Teddy McArdle explains it in an earlier Salinger story, a *mukta* is spiritually so far advanced that when he dies, he goes "straight to Brahma and never again [has] to come back to earth" ("Teddy" 188).

Even though Buddy admits that Seymour was not quite a *mukta,* he refuses to answer his own question if Seymour had no grievous faults, no vices, and no meannesses, and if he was perhaps a saint. Buddy here sweeps all of Seymour's negative character traits under the carpet and even tries to excuse his suicide by saying that like many great artists, Seymour was a "Sick Man" who was done in by the scruples of his sacred conscience.

Even if Seymour had some faults and vices, the "Introduction" suggests that he was spiritually as far advanced as the title character in the story "Teddy." Like Teddy McArdle, Seymour had achieved a limited clairvoyance which allowed him to remember previous incarnations. This comes out in Seymour's long letter to Buddy when he explains why the two of them are so close. Seymour reports that two summers ago, during meditation, he lost consciousness for a long time, and during that trance he was able to trace that he and Buddy and Zooey had been brothers for at least four incarnations.   When Seymour refers to his loss of consciousness, he suggests that he had been practicing *raja yoga* meditation because during that type of meditation a person can reach a state of trance called *samadhi.* It is in this state of *samadhi,* so Vivekananda explains, that one may have "glimpses" of previous lifetimes (*Raja Yoga* 25-26). Like Seymour, Teddy McArdle also has glimpses of previous incarnations during meditation, and he admonishes himself in his diary not to "lose consciousness" during dinner because it makes his father furious when he does ("Teddy" 180).

Near the end of "Seymour—An Introduction," Buddy makes an explicit statement of his and Seymour's religious beliefs. After comparing Seymour's marble-shooting advice to Zen Archery, Buddy stresses that he and Seymour were never Zen Buddhists. He says that their "roots in Eastern Philosophy ... are planted in the New and Old Testaments, Advaita Vedanta, and classical Taoism" (208). People who know about Vedanta Hinduism will not be surprised to find Buddy classifying the New and Old Testaments as part of Eastern philosophy because Vedanta Hinduism considers Jesus Christ to be not the only son of God but one of several incarnations of the Creator. Other divine incarnations are Gautama Buddha and Sri Ramakrishna.

That Vedanta Hinduism is indeed the foundation of Seymour and Buddy's eclectic religious beliefs comes out in the statement that immediately follows Buddy's explanation of his and Seymour's roots in Eastern philosophy.   Buddy says that he regards himself "as a fourth-class Karma Yogin," and he also admits to a fascination with Jnana Yoga. Buddy is here referring to the Vedanta concept of the four *yogas* or paths of spiritual advancement. The four paths are *karma yoga*, the path of fulfillment of everyday duties; *bhakti yoga*, the path of worship and prayer; *jnana yoga,* the path of study and learning; and *raja yoga*, the "royal" path of asceticism and meditation. Buddy's chosen path is that of *karma yoga*, the fulfillment of his duties as a teacher and writer, but he also spends some of his efforts on the path of *jnana yoga*, study and learning.

When Buddy calls himself a "fourth-class" Karma Yogin, he is referring to the four *asramas,* or stages of life. As explained by Vivekananda, the first stage is *brahmacharya*, the student stage (mentioned by Buddy in reference to young Seymour on page 113). The second stage is *garhasthya,* the stage of the married householder. The third stage is *vanaprasthya*, the stage of the retired person; and the fourth stage is *sannyasa,* the stage of the hermit and teacher (*Karma Yoga* 20). Thus Buddy's description of himself as a "fourth-class Karma Yogin" takes into consideration not only his dedication to his teaching and to his writing but also to his life as a hermit in the woods of Upstate New York.

Buddy's self-characterization in the "Introduction" invites us to draw even further parallels between him and J.D. Salinger than in previous stories. Just as Buddy is a "literary shut-in" in the woods of Upstate New York, so Salinger is a hermit in the woods of New Hampshire. More importantly, Buddy takes credit for some of Salinger's most important earlier work. Buddy says, for example, that some people have told him he put a lot of Seymour into the protagonist of the only novel he has published. That novel is, of course, Salinger's *The Catcher in the Rye*. Next Buddy tells us that he has written two short stories that were directly about Seymour. He identifies one of them as the story of the events on Seymour's wedding day in 1942, and he says about the other one that in it, Seymour committed suicide by shooting himself through the head. Here Buddy is referring to "Raise High the Roof Beam, Carpenters" and "A Perfect Day for Bananafish." And later on, when discussing Seymour's eyes, Buddy compares them to those of the central character in an earlier story of his about a child prodigy traveling on an ocean liner, and this is a clear reference to the story "Teddy" in *Nine Stories*.

The identification between Salinger and Buddy Glass extends not only to their religious beliefs but also to their views of art. The similarities between Buddy and Salinger's philosophy of composition are reflected in the unconventional form of "Seymour—An Introduction." It seems possible that in writing this novella, Salinger actually followed the Zen Archery principle of "Aiming but no aiming" and that Buddy's running commentary on the process of composition is actually Salinger's own record of how he composed "Introduction."

Several critics have pointed out that the style of "Seymour—An Introduction" is even more "prolix" than that of Salinger's previous two novellas, "Zooey" and "Raise High the Roof Beam, Carpenters." Actually, "prolix" isn't quite the right word. The style of "Seymour–An Introduction" is *extra-vagant* in the true sense of the word: It wanders beyond the boundaries of the ordinary. It is exactly as extra-ordinary as its subject requires it to be. After all, Seymour Glass is no ordinary person, nor is the narrator, Buddy Glass, who tries to emulate him.

Buddy is aware that his unusual style will strike some of his readers as self-indulgent, and he therefore tries to forestall criticism by conceding that his style is "wordy," by apologizing for his "verbiage" and his overly long sentences, and by admitting that he loves "digressions" and "parenthetical comments." What he does not admit is that he loves foreign and unusual words and that he often reveals his insecurity about his style with the interpolated phrase "I'm afraid."

The following passage is a good sample of the extravagant style of "Seymour—An Introduction." The passage begins with a reference to Buddy's assumption that his reader is a kindred spirit:

In this *entre-nous* spirit, then, old confidant, before we join the others, the grounded everywhere, including, I'm sure, the middle-aged hot-rodders who insist on zooming us to the moon, the Dharma Bums, the makers of cigarette filters for thinking men, the Beat and the Sloppy and the Petulant, the chosen cultists, all the lofty experts who know so well what we should or shouldn't do with our poor little sex organs, all the bearded, proud, unlettered young men and unskilled guitarists and Zen-killers and incorporated aesthetic Teddy boys, who look down their thoroughly unenlightened noses at this splendid planet where (please don't shut me up) Kilroy, Christ, and Shakespeare all stopped—before we join these others, I privately say to you old

friend (unto you, really, I'm afraid) please accept from me this unpretentious bouquet of early blooming parentheses: (((()))). (97-98)

What is stylistically most striking about this passage—and the style of
"Seymour—An Introduction" in general—is two things, the length of the sentence and the reason for the length, the many parenthetical phrases. While not
all sentences in the "Introduction" are as long as the one above, several are even
longer and run on for a page and a half. The parenthetical interruptions that
make the quoted sentence so long are of two kinds. One kind of interruption is
addressed directly to the reader as in "old confidant," "please don't shut me up,"
and "unto you, really, I'm afraid." The other kind of parenthetical interruption
is a word or phrase used to slow down the flow of speech such as the "then" and
the "I'm sure" in the first two lines of the quotation or the "really" in the last
parenthetical comment.

Two other less-noticeable idiosyncrasies of the style are Buddy's use of foreign words and his use of the apologetic phrase, "I'm afraid." It makes sense
that the vocabulary in the novella should be erudite. After all, the narrator is a
college English instructor and his subject was a genius, a poet, and a professor
at Columbia University. However, some of the foreign words seem better justified than others.

Foreign words that are well justified are the Sanskrit ones.   When Buddy
uses the words *mukta* (fully enlightened person), *brahmacharya* (person in the
student stage of life), *karma yogin* (person who follows the path of the scrupulous performance of everyday duties), and *jnana yoga* (path of study and knowledge), he lets us know that the basis of Seymour and his own belief system is
Vedanta Hinduism.

Less well-justified are Buddy's choices of the German words *echt* (true),
Dichter (poet), *verstaendlich* (understandable), and *Kollegen* (colleagues), and of
the French words *entre nous* (among ourselves), zut (damn it), *trompe* (trunk),
gaffe (blunder), and *cher maitre* (dear master). But then again, these German
and French words remind us that Seymour and Buddy were/are able to read and
speak several foreign languages.

Another distinctive trait of the style in "Seymour—An Introduction" is
Buddy's repeated use of the phrase "I'm afraid." He uses it to apologize for
what he fears might be the reader's objections to his style. In the long quotation that ends with the bouquet of parentheses, Buddy apologizes for saying
something that his reader might find preachy. He therefore admits that he is
really saying it "unto you, really, I'm afraid." The "unto you" is a reference to
the New Testament where Jesus Christ often prefaces his sermons with the
phrase "I say unto you," and the "I'm afraid" means that Buddy is here apologizing for being too preachy. The phrase "I'm afraid" again pops up when Buddy
admits that in "A Perfect Day for Bananafish," he described a Seymour who was
not at all the Seymour his family knew but "someone with a striking resemblance to—alley oop, I'm afraid—myself" (113). Here again, the phrase "I'm
afraid" signals Buddy's apology to the reader not only for his idiosyncratic
style—in this case the use of the vaudeville phrase "alley oop"—but also for
pulling a vaudeville stunt by impersonating Seymour.

A final comment that needs to be made about the style in "Seymour—An Introduction" is that there is less stylistic variety than in previous stories. In "Raise High the Roof Beam, Carpenters" and "Zooey," for example, we get a variety of styles because there is a considerable amount of dialogue between people who have different speech mannerisms. But in "Seymour—An Introduction," there is only Buddy Glass talking to us. We don't even get much respite from Buddy's style when he reproduces seven brief memos and one long letter from Seymour because Seymour's style is only a less extreme form of Buddy's. Even Seymour himself mentions that their styles are similar when he tells Buddy not to worry that the two of them sometimes sound alike.

SETTINGS AND SYMBOLS

With one exception, the anecdotes in "Seymour—An Introduction" are all set in Manhattan between 1923 and 1940, when Seymour was between the ages of six and twenty-three. The one exception is the anecdote set on the stage of a theater in Brisbane, Australia, where a vaudeville performer named Joe Jackson gave the five-year-old Seymour a ride on his trick bicycle.

As far as the Manhattan settings are concerned, Buddy Glass gives us street names so that we could actually visit the locations if we wanted to. Until 1929, when Seymour was twelve and Buddy was ten, the Glass family lived in an apartment building on the corner of 110th Street and Riverside Drive. Several anecdotes take place in that neighborhood. For instance, it is in Mario and Victor's barbershop on 108th Street and Broadway that Seymour's hair jumps all over Buddy. It is on his way to the drug store on Broadway and 113th Street that Buddy becomes the Second Fastest Boy Runner in the World when Seymour overtakes him. It is in the Columbia University branch of the public library, on 114th street near Broadway, that Miss Overman works and that young Seymour discovers oriental poetry. And it is in front of the Glass's apartment building on 110th Street and Riverside Drive that Seymour gives Buddy advice on how to shoot marbles.

After the Glasses moved to an apartment in the East Seventies in 1929, we get several anecdotes that are set in that new neighborhood. For instance, it is in nearby Central Park that Waker gave away his new bicycle. That bicycle was purchased from Davega's Sports Store on 86th Street between Lexington and Third Avenue. And it is at the Glass's new apartment that Seymour arbitrates the family dispute about Waker giving the new bicycle away. And when Seymour borrows a necktie that Buddy keeps stored in cellophane, this happens in the apartment on 79th Street that the two of them moved to in 1940. This apartment is also the location of the anecdote concerning the visit of the grouchy Les Glass and his reminiscing about Seymour's ride on Joe Jackson's trick bicycle.

"Seymour—An Introduction" contains no detailed descriptions of settings, such as the catalogue of the furnishings of the Glass' living room and of Seymour and Buddy's room in "Zooey." However, in the case of the marble-shooting anecdote, Buddy presents us with an impressionistic description of the late afternoon ambiance in which that incident was steeped. Buddy calls the time of day "that magic quarter hour" when the street lights and the parking lights of cars have just been turned on and when boys in New York City are not so different from boys in Tiffin, Ohio, who hear a train whistle in the distance as they drive the last cows into the barn. By calling the time of this episode a "magic quarter hour," Buddy prepares us for the ten-year-old Seymour to deliver magical advice which Buddy later recognizes to have been about much more than marble-shooting.

Since "Seymour—An Introduction" is written largely in an expository rather than a narrative mode, it depends more on metaphors and similes than on symbolism in communicating its meaning. As Buddy Glass tells us, his most important symbol is Seymour himself. In addition, the novella contains four major metaphors: The curlew sandpiper, the bouquet of parentheses, the Davega bicycle, and one glass marble striking another. While the meaning of these metaphors is pretty much spelled out for us, Buddy makes one major metaphorical statement relating to Seymour's suicide which is so opaque that it allows any number of interpretations.

Near the beginning of the novella, Buddy Glass tells us that while he lived, Seymour represented many different things to different people but that he represented all *real* things to him and his sibling. Among other things, Seymour was the family's "consultant genius," their "one full poet," their "notorious 'mystic'," and their "'unbalanced type'" (106).

By writing about Seymour, Buddy has made him grow in stature not only as a genius, poet, and mystic, but also as an unbalanced type. In fact, in the opening section of the "Introduction," Buddy makes Seymour into the prototype of the kind of "artist-seer" who is also a "Sick Man," a classical neurotic who is "curiously-productive-though-ailing" (102). To clarify this point, Buddy compares Seymour to other specimens of this type, Søren Kierkegaard, Vincent Van Gogh, and Franz Kafka.

Buddy gives an added symbolic dimension to the personality of Seymour by comparing him to a curlew sandpiper. Buddy says about birds in general that they are of all created beings the nearest to pure spirit. Then he talks about the curlew sandpiper which breeds close to the Arctic Circle and then flies to New Zealand for the winter. Later, in the section on Seymour's poetry, Buddy compares the curlew sandpiper to the true poet in general and to Seymour in particular. Buddy addresses his reader directly and says about Seymour that he is a curlew sandpiper and that he, Buddy, will tell us whatever he knows about this bird's flights, his unusually high body temperature, and his astonishing heart.

Another major metaphor appears in the opening section when Buddy asks us, the readers, to accept from him a bouquet of "early blooming parentheses: (((()))))." As we continue reading, Buddy warns us that his narrative will be full of digressions and asides even though he is aware that most readers don't like it when narrators indulge in parenthetical comments while they are purportedly telling a story. In short, the bouquet of parentheses is a symbolic representation of one of the most distinctive traits of Buddy's style, his love of parenthetical comments.

A third important metaphor in the novella is that of Seymour being Buddy's Davega bicycle. The reference is to a bicycle from Davega's Sports Store on 86th Street that Buddy's brother Waker received for his ninth birthday and then gave away to an unknown boy in Central Park. At the climax of the "Introduction," Buddy says that he was struck "by the sudden realization that Seymour is [his] Davega bicycle" and that he, Buddy, has been waiting most of his life for the chance to give away a Davega bicycle of his own (204). A few pages later, Buddy explains that the Davega bicycle that he has at last been presented with to give away is Seymour's marble-shooting advice, "Could you try not aiming so much." Buddy did not understand the meaning of this advice until he began writing down the marble-shooting anecdote, and at that point he also understood that Seymour's advice applies to much more than shooting marbles, that it reflects a special attitude toward life and also toward art. Buddy therefore feels that, just like Waker, he has received a valuable present, and just like Waker, he feels compelled to give it away to someone else who may need it more than he does.

But the most complex metaphoric statement in "Seymour—An Introduction" is a statement by Buddy which concerns Seymour's suicide. After comparing Seymour to another genius who also took his own life, the Dutch painter Vincent Van Gogh, Buddy says: "I say that the true artist-seer, the heavenly fool who can and does produce beauty, is mainly dazzled to death by his own scruples, the blinding shapes and colors of his own sacred human conscience" (105). The visual metaphor of being dazzled to death by blinding shapes is very fitting when applied to the painter Vincent Van Gogh. Van Gogh was dazzled to death by the unbearable beauty of the world to which he felt his paintings could not do justice. However, Seymour Glass was dazzled to death not by visual shapes but by the moral shapes of his conscience. Buddy's phrase suggests that Seymour's conscience may have dazzled him, that is, disoriented him, because his spirituality had become both a refracting prism and a solipsistic mirror. What good is it to be an artist-seer only to see more glass?

No matter how we interpret Buddy's statement that Seymour was dazzled to death by his conscience, it confirms what "Raise High the Roof Beam, Carpenters" suggested four years earlier, namely that Salinger wants us to see Seymour's suicide as a positive choice rather than as an act of despair or vindictiveness as it seems to be in "A Perfect Day for Bananafish."

THEMES AND INTERPRETATIONS

Critics have identified three major thematic concerns in "Seymour—An Introduction." Most have concentrated on the personality of Seymour Glass as either an artist or a saint or both. Others have investigated Seymour's Christian, Zen Buddhist, and Vedanta ideas. A third group of critics have focused more on Buddy than on Seymour and have dealt with what the novella has to say about creative processes in general and storytelling in particular.

Sam Baskett is one of those critics who have treated Seymour primarily as a modern holy man. Baskett's essay "The Splendid/Squalid World of J.D. Salinger" makes the point that "Seymour is quite possibly Salinger's idea of a Zen saint" (56). Contrary to other critics who believe that Seymour has achieved only partial *satori*, Baskett says that Seymour should be seen as a fully enlightened person and "a model of saintly qualities with resemblances to both Buddha and Christ" (57). This claim of course raises the question of why Seymour would commit suicide if he were really a saint. Baskett answers this question as follows: "He has some of the qualities of the Zen saint who has nothing further to do, of the husband at cross purposes with his wife, of the visionary stultified by his materialistic environment, of the Christ figure who is inevitably crucified" (58). Unfortunately, Baskett does not offer an explanation of what he means when he says that Seymour "is crucified ... and dies so that others may live" (57).

Bernice and Sanford Goldstein have also analyzed the Zen ideas in "Seymour—An Introduction," but they present a different view of Seymour than does Sam Baskett. Besides, they consider Buddy and not Seymour to be the protagonist of the "Introduction." In their article "Zen and Salinger," they say that the novella is about the "partial enlightenment" of Buddy Glass. To explain what the kind of enlightenment it is that all the Glass siblings strive for, the Goldsteins quote the Zen master Yashutani-Roshi: "'When I heard the temple bell ring, suddenly there was no bell and no I, just sound.' In other words, he no longer was aware of a distinction between himself, the bell, the sound, and the universe" (314). The Goldsteins believe that all the Glass siblings strive for this kind of "liberated moment, that is, experiences fully lived in which there is no separation between self and other" (314). Buddy's "final growth" toward such enlightenment occurs "when he recognizes the wisdom of his Zen Master brother," the dead Seymour (321). This happens when he recounts the marble shooting anecdote. While narrating that incident, Buddy realizes that Seymour's advice of "Aiming but no aiming" also applies to his, Buddy's, writing: "The separation of the self which strives after something, in this instance publication and success, the foolishness of such striving, and the non-separated self which does not strive but 'writes with all his stars out' is the wisdom Buddy attains from Seymour's advice recalled almost thirty years after the event" (321).

Finally, there are a number of interpretations of "Seymour—An Introduction" which focus on what Buddy Glass calls "modern artistic processes." A representative reading of this kind is the chapter "'Seymour—An Introduction': 'A Thesaurus of Undetached Prefatory Remarks'" in John Wenke's book *J.D. Salinger: A Study of the Short Fiction* (1991). Like the Goldsteins, Wenke treats Buddy Glass as the protagonist and says that the novella is "an introduction to the *process* of writing an introduction of Seymour" (100). In this introduction, Buddy "records the improvisational unfolding of his thoughts," and as he writes about Seymour, Buddy "presents his mind in the act of thinking" (102). This approach produces an unprecedented kind of fiction, and "Seymour—An Introduction" therefore has to be seen as an experiment: "Rather than being a story, it depicts a literary activity in which the mind making the words is literally the subject of the tale" (105). What Buddy's narrative process ultimately celebrates, so Wenke concludes, is "the randomness and vagaries of the creative imagination" (106).

CONCLUSION

In "Seymour—An Introduction," Salinger carries further the experiments in narrative structure of "Raise High the Roof Beam, Carpenters" and "Zooey." Again he uses not one protagonist but two because Buddy, the narrator, can't suppress his lust to share top billing with Seymour. The "Introduction" is also unconventional in its structure because it combines an expository and a narrative framework and because it reinforces both with anecdotes. The expository framework consists of the traits of Seymour's personality and his physical appearance, and the narrative framework consists of a running account of Buddy's struggle to present Seymour as a near-saint despite his suicide. Ultimately, Buddy decides that, suicide or not, what is important about Seymour is his positive influence on others, especially on himself.

In terms of narrative perspective, "Seymour—An Introduction" is also more complex than any of the previous installments of the Glass Family Series. As in "Raise High the Roof Beam, Carpenters" and "Zooey," Salinger again varies the point of view by including written communications by writers other than the narrator, in this case a string of memos and a long letter by Seymour. But more importantly, Buddy Glass is more self-reflexive than he ever was before; that is, in this novella, he talks more about the process of writing than previously. Also, he admits for the first time that he is an unreliable narrator where Seymour is concerned. He confesses that he misrepresented Seymour's personality in "A Perfect Day for Bananafish" and that he is determined to tell us only positive things about Seymour in the "Introduction."

While the characterization of Seymour's personality in the "Introduction" is "graphically panegyric, Buddy's description of Seymour's physical appearance is not flattering at all. As Buddy describes him, Seymour was a hairy-armed but balding person with a fleeing chin, a fleshy nose, huge ears, and tobacco-stained teeth. Moreover, he cared nothing about his clothes and often sported jackets with arms that were too short and trousers that were too baggy.

The "Introduction" also gives us a better picture of Buddy than any previous installment of the Glass Family Series. Buddy tells us that he has the same receding chin, big nose, and big ears as Seymour. However, Buddy is slightly shorter than Seymour. and while Seymour was always very thin, Buddy admits that he himself is getting a bit paunchy in his middle age.

In terms of his intellectual and spiritual achievements, Buddy cannot hold a candle to Seymour. While Seymour was a professor at Columbia University at the age of twenty-five, Buddy never got a college degree and wound up with a part-time job teaching writing courses at a girls' junior college in Upstate New York. More importantly, while Seymour is almost "a *mukta*, a ringding enlightened man," Buddy is spiritually less advanced because he lacks Seymour's forbearance and even temper. The spiritual differences between Seymour and Buddy have made one critic suggest that the two represent two sides of Salinger's personality, Seymour the spirit and Buddy the body.

The extravagant style of "Seymour—An Introduction" is a further development the whimsical and parenthetical one in "Raise High the Roof Beam, Carpenters" and "Zooey." The sentences are even longer now with even more modifying phrases than earlier. In addition, we get a word choice that seems more erudite than before, with sprinklings of words and phrases in German, French, and even Sanskrit.

The settings in "Seymour—An Introduction" are familiar from Salinger's previous work. Almost all the locations are in Manhattan, in the neighborhoods where J.D. Salinger grew up. Moreover, most of the events take place between 1925 and 1941, when Seymour was between eight and twenty-four years old. Also, because much of the "Introduction" is descriptive rather than narrative, the novella contains more metaphors than symbols. One of the memorable metaphors compares poets such as Seymour to birds who are "of all created beings the nearest to pure spirit." Another compares Seymour's advice that Buddy should "try not aiming so much" when playing marbles to one marble hitting another, to "glass hitting glass."

And finally, "Seymour—An Introduction" is slightly different from previous installments of the Glass Family Series because a perennial theme in Salinger's fiction, that of the conflict between spiritual and unspiritual people, idealists and materialists, is of very little importance. Instead, the novella focuses on aesthetic and religious themes. One cluster of themes is concerned with the nature of poetry and the personality of the poet. Another is concerned with the nature of religion and the personality of the enlightened person.

The overall importance of "Seymour—An Introduction" in Salinger's work is threefold. First of all, when the novella was published in 1959, it was the most experimental piece of fiction that Salinger had written so far. It anticipated by a decade the self-reflexive trend in American postmodernist fiction, a trend that became fashionable in the late sixties and early seventies (See John Barth, *Lost in the Funhouse* 1967, and Robert Coover, *Pricksongs & Descants* 1969). Secondly, the novella carries further the identification between J.D. Salinger and his alter ego, the narrator Buddy Glass, so that Buddy's statements about his religious beliefs and about artistic processes and storytelling can be taken to represent Salinger's own opinions. And thirdly, "Seymour—An Introduction" redefines Seymour as a near-saint whose suicide should not be seen as an act of despair but as an attempt to move on to a new incarnation in which—like the central character in the story "Teddy"—he can make better progress toward oneness with God than in his present appearance.

Despite its title, "Seymour—An Introduction" would not be a good first story to read for someone who is interested in the Glass Family Series. Its lack of a suspenseful plot and its great length are formidable obstacles for new readers. Even someone who has already become acquainted with Salinger through *The Catcher in the Rye* would be better off entering the world of Seymour Glass via a different story than the "Introduction." As I have suggested in previous chapters, the best way to approach the Glass Family Series is to read first "A Perfect Day for Bananafish" (1948) and then "Teddy" (1953), the story which anticipates Salinger's redefinition of Seymour's character in such later stories as "Raise High the Roof Beam, Carpenters" (1955) and "Zooey" (1957). The story "Teddy" explains one of the crucial concepts in "Seymour—An Introduction," namely that Seymour's life-long goal was to make progress toward spiritual perfection and oneness with God.

In addition to reading "Teddy" and previous Glass stories, a reader of "Seymour—An Introduction" would do well to browse through some of the outside sources that Buddy Glass mentions or alludes to.   Seymour and Buddy's spiritual quests for *mukti,* oneness with God, will become more under-standable for the reader who reads an introduction to Vedanta such as Swami Nikhilananda's *The Essence of Hinduism.*   Similarly, the importance of the marble shooting anecdote and its impact on Buddy Glass will become much clearer to readers who take the trouble to read Eugen Herrigel's little book, *Zen in the Art of Archery.*

Since "Seymour—An Introduction" is such a difficult text, it is not surpris-ing that some things have been written about it that plainly contradict state-ments by the narrator Buddy Glass.   The most prevalent error that critics have made is the contention that before his death Seymour had achieved full enlight-enment and oneness with God.   This is clearly contradicted by Buddy's state-ment that Seymour came close to being a *mukta,* a fully enlightened man, but that he did not actually achieve *mukti.*   This is an important point which has a bearing on Seymour's suicide and on his relationship with his siblings.   An-other point that Buddy makes and that has been largely ignored is that he ad-mits to being an unreliable narrator.   After all, Buddy's family pointed out to him that the Seymour in "A Perfect Day for Bananafish" is very different from the Seymour they knew and that this Seymour bears a strong resemblance to Buddy himself.   The implications of this admission still have not been taken into consideration in discussions of Seymour's suicide and of his relationship with his wife Muriel.

Additional aspects of "Seymour—An Introduction" that have been insuffi-ciently explored include the sibling rivalry between Buddy and Seymour, the relationship between Seymour and his parents and between geniuses and their parents in general, the role of karma and reincarnation in Seymour's life, and, last but not least, we need a better explication than has been provided so far of Buddy's puzzling statement that Seymour was "dazzled to death by his own scruples, by the blinding shapes and colors of his own sacred human con-science."

WORKS CITED

Baskett, Sam S. "The Splendid/Squalid   World of J.D. Salinger." *Wisconsin Studies in Contemporary Literature* 4 (1963): 48-61.

French, Warren. *J.D. Salinger.* New York: Twayne, 1963.

Goldstein, Bernice, and Sanford Goldstein.   "Zen and Salinger." *Modern Fiction Studies* 12 (1966): 313-324.

Grunwald, Henry A. "Introduction." In *Salinger: A Critical and Personal Portrait.* New York: Harper, 1962, ix-xxviii.

Hyman, Stanley Edgar. "J.D. Salinger's House of Glass." In *Standards: A Chronicle of Books of Our Time.* New York: Horizon, 1966, 123-127.

Nikhilananda, Swami.   *The Essence of Hinduism.*   New York: Ramakrishna-Vivekananda Center, 1946.

Salinger, J.D. *Raise High the Roof Beam, Carpenters and Seymour—An Introduction* [1963]. New York: Bantam, 1965.

___ . "Teddy." In *Nine Stories* [1953]. New York: Bantam, 1964, 166-198.

Schwartz, Arthur. "For Seymour—With Love and Judgment." *Wisconsin Studies in Contemporary Literature* 4 (Winter 1963): 88-99.
Vivekananda, Swami. *Karma Yoga and Bhakti Yoga.* New York: Ramakrishna-Vivekananda Center, 1955.
___ . *Raja Yoga.* New York: Ramakrishna-Vivekananda Center, 1955.
Wenke, John. *J.D. Salinger: A Study of the Short Fiction.* Boston: Twayne, 1991.

SUGGESTIONS FOR FURTHER READING

Chuang-tzu. *The Texts of Taoism.* Trans. James Legge. Intro. D.T. Suzuki. New York: Julian, 1959.
Goldstein, Bernice and Sanford. "'Seymour—An Introduction': Writing as Discovery." *Studies in Short Fiction* 7 (1970): 248-256.
Hassan, Ihab. "Almost the Voice of Silence: The Later Novelettes of J.D. Salinger." *Wisconsin Studies in Contemporary Literature* 4 (Winter 1963): 5-20.
Herrigel, Eugen. *Zen in the Art of Archery.* Trans. R.F.C. Hull. New York: Pantheon, 1953.
Lyons, John O. "The Romantic Style of Salinger's 'Seymour—An Introduction'." *Wisconsin Studies in Contemporary Literature* 4 (Winter 1963): 62-69.
M. [Mahendranath Gupta]. *The Gospel of Sri Ramakrishna.* Trans. Swami Nikhilananda. New York: Ramakrishna-Vivekananda Center, 1942.
Suzuki, Daisetz Teitaro. *Essays in Zen Buddhism* [1949]. New York: Grove, 1986.
Weinberg, Helen. "J.D. Salinger's Holden and Seymour and the Spiritual Activist Hero." In *The New American Novel: The Kafkan Mode in Contemporary Fiction.* Ithaca, NY: Cornell UP, 1970, 141-164.
Yutang, Lin, ed. *The Wisdom of Laotse.* New York: Modern Library, 1948.

Chapter 9

"Hapworth 16, 1924"

> Even our magnificent God's perfection allows for a touch-
> ing amount of maddening leeway.
>
> Seymour Glass

"Hapworth 16, 1924" was published in the *New Yorker* on 19 June 1965. With 28,000 words it is, after "Zooey" and "Seymour—An Introduction," the third longest installment of Salinger's narrative series about the Glass family. In 1997, the *New York Times* reported that Orchises Press of Alexandria, Virginia, was going to publish "Hapworth" as a small book, and the Internet bookstore amazon.com started taking orders. But the publication date kept being moved up and has now been postponed indefinitely.

"Hapworth" is a letter that the seven-year-old Seymour wrote home from Camp Simon Hapworth in Maine. The letter reveals that Seymour was an even more astonishing child prodigy and passionate God-seeker than Buddy had told us in "Seymour—An Introduction." We also find that Seymour was troubled by his sensuality, his emotional instability, and the malice he felt toward un-spiritual people. Because of his obsession with spiritual advancement and his emotional instability, Seymour got into two major fights, one with a counselor and the other with the camp director. These conflicts made him decide to with-draw from the world of normal, unspiritual people, and this decision is a turn-ing point in Seymour's life.

CRITICAL RECEPTION

The publication of "Hapworth 16, 1924" in the *New Yorker* was all but ig-nored by the newspapers and popular magazines. One exception was *Time* magazine, which printed a one-paragraph notice in the "People" section of its 25 June 1965 issue. After judging "Hapworth" to be inferior to *The Catcher in the Rye* and *Franny and Zooey*, the anonymous reviewer described young Seymour as a "perfervid scholar, linguist, spiritual genius and altogether verbose little man." Then the reviewer took out of context two salacious passages and re-printed them without comment. In one passage, the seven-year-old Seymour mentions that the wife of the camp director, Mrs. Happy, has "quite perfect legs, ankles, saucy bosoms, very fresh, cute hindquarters." In the other passage, Seymour asks his parents to tell him "what imaginary sensual acts gave lively, unmentionable entertainment to your minds" (52).

The reaction of the academic critics to "Hapworth" was generally negative. One of the first critics to comment on "Hapworth" was James E. Miller in a 1965 University of Minnesota Pamphlet on American Writers. Even though Miller is one of Salinger's most steadfast admirers, the only positive thing he found to say about "Hapworth" is that "the story was an important addition to the life of the Glasses, particularly as it shed new light on the remarkable charac-ter of Seymour" (43). Miller admitted that "Hapworth" accentuates "those char-acteristics of the later work which most readers found disturbing—a tedious length, a humor often self-consciously cute, a muting of narrative in favor of philosophical asides" (42). For Miller himself the major problem with "Hap-worth" was that he found Seymour's uncanny mental powers and superhuman erudition unbelievable. As an example, Miller cited the enormous number of books that Seymour has already read and wants to have sent to camp for re-reading: "Few men could get through this interminable list in a lifetime, let alone in a summer" (44). Miller predicts that "Hapworth" will damage Salin-ger's reputation and he says "most readers are likely to be disturbed by the dif-fuseness and miscellaneousness of all the materials in this story, elements which seem to confirm the deterioration of talent detected in "Seymour—An Introduc-tion" (45).

An even more negative assessment of "Hapworth" was that of Max Schulz in his article "Epilogue to 'Seymour—An Introduction': Salinger and the Crisis of Consciousness." Schulz said that "Hapworth" is "more inchoate in structure and cute in tone than any of the stories that preceded it" (60). According to Schulz, the chief flaw of the novella is that "the child as saint grows somewhat stale in repetition" (61). Schulz therefore believed that with the Glass series Salinger has written himself into a thematic cul-de-sac, and he suggested that he write himself out of it by "turning his attention to one of the non-Zen Glasses." Schulz said about these other members of the Glass Family: "If their outlook is not the route to spiritual salvation, it may prove the turn to esthetic redemption, for they too are artists of a sort, with a practical idea of what does not 'go' with audiences" (61).

In 1975, after Salinger had not published for 10 years, the British critic and novelist David Lodge wrote a retrospective article for the London *Times Liter-ary Supplement*. In that article, entitled "Family Romances," Lodge put "Hap-worth 16, 1924" in the context of the rest of Salinger's work. In the Glass se-ries, Lodge observed, Salinger is playing "an elaborate game with his audience and with the conventions of his art." Lodge called it "the game of assent." As the content of the stories became less and less credible, Salinger tried to make his readers suspend their disbelief by cozying up to them. He did this by gradually revealing more and more about the storyteller, Buddy Glass, and by dropping hints that he himself is Buddy Glass: "With each successive story,

Salinger has raised the stakes in the game of assent, and each time more and more readers have dropped out, unable to take the mysticism, the ESP, the God-knowingness at their face value" (642). By the time he wrote "Hapworth," so Lodge believed, Salinger demanded a suspension of disbelief which most readers were not capable of.

Lodge explained Salinger's apparent unconcern with this loss of readership by citing a comment that Salinger made to *New York Times* reporter Lacey Fosburgh. In a 1974 telephone interview, Salinger complained about the unauthorized publication of *The Complete Uncollected Short Stories of J.D. Salinger*. He was equally concerned with the invasion of his privacy as with the theft of his work, and he said: "There is a marvelous peace in not publishing. It's peaceful. Still Publishing is a terrible invasion of my privacy. I like to write. I love to write. But I write just for myself and my own pleasure" (Fosburgh 1). Lodge used this comment to explain what he considers to be one of the disappointments of "Hapworth": "Instead of the dialogue between the writer and the reader that animates the three preceding stories ["Seymour—An Introduction," "Zooey," and "Raise High the Roof Beam, Carpenters"], we seem to be overhearing a self-congratulatory dialogue of the writer with himself. That is why ... one feels misgivings at the reported words, 'I write just for myself and my own pleasure'" (642).

In 1997, when the *New York Times* ran the story that Salinger was planning to re-publish "Hapworth" in hard cover, that article included another assessment of "Hapworth 16, 1924" in the overall context of Salinger's career. The author of the article, Michiko Kakutani, analyzed "Hapworth" and called it "a logical, if disappointing culmination of Mr. Salinger's published work to date." She said that "Hapworth" is not of much interest to anyone except to "ardent Glass-ites" and even for those readers "it is likely to prove a disillusioning, if perversely fascinating, experience, an experience that will forever change their perception of Seymour and his siblings" (C15). Salinger fans will be disillusioned, Kakutani said, because in "Hapworth," the saintly Seymour comes across as "an obnoxious child, given to angry outbursts" and as "a hero who is deeply distasteful" (C19). Kakutani summed up "Hapworth" as "a sour, implausible, and sad to say, completely charmless story," and she speculated that "this falling off in [Salinger's] work, perhaps, is a palpable consequence of Mr. Salinger's own Glass-like withdrawal from the public world: withdrawal feeding self-absorption and self-absorption feeding tetchy disdain" (C19).

Fortunately such *ad-hominem* criticism has not stopped Salinger scholars from taking "Hapworth" seriously and analyzing it objectively. Unfortunately, however, the negative criticism seems to have disturbed Salinger so much that he keeps postponing the republication of "Hapworth."

NARRATIVE STRUCTURE AND POINT OF VIEW

Like "Seymour—An Introduction" before it, "Hapworth 16, 1924" combines expository and narrative elements and therefore does not fit into any conventional genre of fiction. In addition to an arbitrary expository structure, there are two narrative strands in "Hapworth." As in "Franny" and "Raise High the Roof

Beam, Carpenters," one narrative strand develops an external conflict and the other an internal one. However, the narrative perspective is more consistent than in previous installments of the Glass series because there are no interpolated memos, diary entries, footnotes, and lengthy quotations from favorite authors.

"Hapworth" begins with a four-paragraph preface by Buddy Glass. In that preface, Buddy explains that what we are about to read is a forty-year-old letter that he just received from his mother, Bessie Glass. Buddy explains that the letter was written by Seymour back in 1924 when Seymour was seven years old; that he, Buddy, had never seen the letter before; and that he will type up an exact copy for us. I will discuss this preface later on, in the context of the narrative perspective in "Hapworth."

The letter itself is conventional in its structure, with an introduction, a three-part body section, and a conclusion, plus a postscript. The topics of the three body sections are life at Camp Hapworth, advice to parents and siblings, and a long list of books which Seymour discusses to explain why he wants to have them sent to him at camp:

The Events at Camp Hapworth

Advice to the Family

Book List

The arrangement of these topics shows an inward movement because the focus of the letter moves from the public events at the camp to the private sphere of the Glass family, and from there to the inner world of Seymour's intellectual and spiritual pursuits.

Parallel to this expository structure run two narrative strands. The exterior conflict pits Seymour against the other boys and the staff at Camp Hapworth. This conflict is resolved near the end of the first and longest section of the body—two-thirds into the letter—when Seymour is laid up with a leg injury and thus escapes from the routine activities of the camp. The parallel inner conflict concerns Seymour's relationship with God. It is caused by Seymour's emotional instability and by the difficulty he has in getting along with normal, unspiritual people. This inner conflict is not resolved until near the end of the letter when Seymour decides to withdraw from the world of normal people and to pursue his quest for spiritual advancement via the self-directed paths of study and meditation.

At a first glance, "Hapworth" seems to contain much redundant material, and it therefore seems much longer than necessary. But there is a good reason why the letter is so long. Seymour has a lot of time on his hands because he is in bed, recuperating from a leg injury. He begins writing the letter shortly after dawn, and he does not finish it until some time after supper on that same day. Since Seymour is alone during most of that time, he has ample opportunity to reflect on his experiences at camp. These experiences have been very upsetting to Seymour, and his writing the letter is really not so much an act of communication as an act of self-analysis.

Seymour's account of camp life shows that he and his five-year-old brother,

Buddy, are not happy to be at Camp Hapworth. There are three reasons for their unhappiness. One is that Seymour and Buddy did not want to go to summer camp in the first place. Another reason is that they both object to the way the camp is run because it interferes with their studies. But the most important reason for Seymour and Buddy's unhappiness is that they simply do not fit in because their values and interests are radically different from those of everybody else at the camp.

Although Seymour protests several times that he and Buddy are regular boys, he can't help feeling contemptuous of most of the other campers, and especially of the counselors. It is Seymour's harsh judgment that few of his fellow campers will mature in the true sense of the word; most of them will just "senesce." And about the counselors, Seymour says that they are incapable of counseling because they have picayune attitudes and are totally indifferent to the concerns of the campers.

Because Seymour and Buddy's interests are so different from those of everyone else at camp, Seymour admits that neither he nor Buddy is very popular with their fellow campers. In fact, the only people they are getting along with are the lisping and bed-wetting Griffith Hammersmith who is even more despised than Seymour and Buddy; the intrepid John Kolb who is secure enough so that he doesn't have to shun the unpopular Glass boys; and the lonely and unloved Mrs. Happy, who is a big fan of Seymour and Buddy's parents, the Gallagher-Glass vaudeville team. Otherwise, so Seymour admits, "we are currently being ostracized" (55).

Moreover, Seymour and Buddy submit only grudgingly to the camp's routine. They have therefore received quite a few demerits during their first 16 days at camp, most of them because they haven't been tidying up their bungalow, because they haven't been singing at pow wow, and because they have been leaving pow wow without permission. Rather than taking an interest in the camp's scheduled activities, Seymour and Buddy use every chance they get to study, write, and meditate. Since their arrival, Seymour has composed 51 poems and Buddy has written six short stories.

Seymour and Buddy's unwillingness to fit in eventually leads to confrontations with members of the staff, and during these confrontations Seymour's emotional instability makes him to lose his temper. Seymour says that since his arrival at the camp he has been trying very hard "to leave a wide margin for human ill will, fear, jealousy, and gnawing dislike of the uncommonplace" (44), but his hostility toward those who don't respect his values eventually spills out.

The first incident occurs on Tuesday, after Buddy has won a bet with Mr. Nelson, the cook. In order to be allowed to use the mess hall for study and meditation during off-hours, Buddy memorizes a sizable book, *The Hardwoods of North America*, in less than half an hour. News of Buddy's amazing feat quickly spreads all over the camp, and later that day, Roger Pittman, the head counselor, asks Buddy a question, and when Buddy doesn't know the answer, Pittman makes a sarcastic remark to the effect that Buddy should know because he is supposed to be such a genius. Seymour is enraged and reports that he told Pittman he would either kill Pittman or kill himself if Pittman ever again spoke to Buddy in such an insulting manner.

The second confrontation is between Seymour and the camp's director, Mr.

Happy, and it occurs on Wednesday during a strawberrying expedition. While helping to push the camp's horse-drawn wagon out of a mud hole, Seymour severely injures his leg on a piece of iron sticking out of the vehicle. Seymour holds Mr. Happy responsible for the accident and tells him that his father, Les Glass, will sue him for every cent he has if Seymour were to lose his leg due to loss of blood, infection, or gangrene.

In both confrontations, that with Roger Pittman and that with Mr. Happy, Seymour is unable to control the contempt he feels for people whose attitudes he considers to be picayune and devoid of spirituality. Seymour's major problem is not that he cannot suppress his contempt for people like Roger Pittman and Mr. Happy but that he feels this contempt in the first place. After all, he claims to be a regular boy and to feel sympathetic toward human folly in all its forms. It seems, however, that his experiences at Camp Hapworth make him realize that he is not a regular boy and that he does not really want to be one, either.

Seymour resolves his external conflict with the people at Camp Hapworth by showing them that he is a very special person and must be treated differently than the other campers. He does this by refusing to accept any anesthesia while the doctor is preparing to sew up his leg. When he declines the anesthesia, the doctor and Mr. Happy think he is just trying to show off and will not be able to stand the pain, but Seymour demonstrates that he is able to cut the nerve communication between his leg and his brain. By taking 11 stitches without anesthesia, Seymour shows that he has some very special abilities which regular boys do not have. He therefore violates his agreement with Buddy not to reveal their extraordinary endowments. Buddy, as we have seen, also violated this agreement when he proved to Mr. Nelson that he has a photographic memory. As these two incidents show, Seymour and Buddy have given up trying to convince themselves and others that they are average boys.

But even though Seymour's demonstration of his special powers resolves his external conflict, it intensifies his internal one. This is apparent in his continued agitation and in a number of explicit statements. At the end of the section about camp life, for instance, Seymour comments on "the constant turmoil in [his] ridiculous breast," and near the conclusion, he admits that his nerves are still "quite raw." Moreover, on five separate occasions, he confesses that he can't help weeping while writing the letter. All this indicates that Seymour is experiencing an inner crisis, a crisis that is brought on by his inability to relate to the people at Camp Hapworth.

The expository structure of the letter suggests that the difficulties Seymour has in getting along with normal people eventually make him withdraw from the physical world. In this withdrawal, the world of the Glass family serves as a transitional stage. For after Seymour has spent two-thirds of his letter describing his relationships with the other campers and the staff at Camp Hapworth, he devotes the remainder to giving advice to his family and to commenting on some 30 authors whose works he wants to have sent to him. This shift in focus reveals the outcome of Seymour's inner struggle, his decision to withdraw from the world of ordinary people and to devote himself and to the spiritual guidance of his family and to intellectual pursuits. The ideas that Seymour develops in the last two sections of the letter bear out what its structure suggests.

Although the advice that Seymour gives to his family is in part very practical, this section does represent a withdrawal from everyday reality, for the Glasses are certainly not average people. Some of Seymour's advice concerns his family's activities as professional entertainers. He knows, for instance, that his father is tortured by his desire to record a smash hit, and he therefore gives him and his mother some tips on how to improve their singing when they record their next song, "Bambalina." He also advises his brothers Walter and Waker, who plan to become entertainers like their parents, to practice their tap dancing and juggling constantly and to wear their tap shoes and carry with them their juggling objects for at least a couple of hours each day. For his sister Boo Boo, however, Seymour provides chiefly spiritual advice. She has come to dislike her old bedtime prayer because it is addressed to a humanoid God. Seymour therefore gives her a new prayer which addresses God as "the nameless hallmark" who has been guiding Boo Boo's destiny both during and between her various incarnations on this planet.

In the third part of the letter, Seymour retreats even farther from average, everyday life and from the problems at Camp Hapworth. He discusses books by over 30 authors that he would like to have sent to camp so he can re-read them. But he does not just list these books; he also talks about the personalities and ideas of the authors. For example, he comments on John Bunyan's objectionable conception of God's perfection, on the sex life of the French writer Guy de Maupassant, on two disgusting scholarly books written by professors who are motivated by self-aggrandizement rather than scholarly curiosity, and on the Sherlock Holmes novels of Sir Arthur Conan Doyle, whom he likes better than he celebrated German poet, playwright, and novelist Johann Wolfgang von Goethe. Because his parents, Les and Bessie, would have to be quite well-read in order to understand Seymour's ideas, it appears that in this section Seymour is really no longer talking to his parents and siblings but only to himself.

Near the end of the book list, Seymour resolves this inner conflict between the demands of the physical and the spiritual world. This is apparent in the section where he discusses what his duty in life is and how to discharge it. After requesting some books on Chinese religion after Lao-tse and Chuang-tse, Seymour concedes that his intense admiration of God might have a negative effect on his poetry. He reports that a librarian who read his poems told him that he may be on his way to becoming a splendid poet but that his religious preoccupation might be damaging to his poetry and ultimately turn him into a literary failure. Seymour acknowledges that possibility but explains that he feels obliged to continue his quest for God and to remain absorbed in his own special methods of pursuing enlightenment. These methods involve the study of literature and religion, the best records of the workings of the human heart and brain. In short, Seymour decides to withdraw even more into the spiritual world, to concentrate even more on his studies than he did before coming to Camp Hapworth.

In the conclusion of the letter, Seymour expresses his awareness that his stay at Camp Hapworth marks a significant change, a turning point in his life. Earlier in the letter, he referred to his sixteenth day at camp as a memorable day in his life, and in the conclusion he once more implies that some extraordinary change has occurred. This becomes clear when he tells his parents that they will be paying an "exorbitant price" for having made him and Buddy go to summer camp. What this means becomes clear when we consider how Seymour's changed notion of his duty in life is going to affect his family. His father Les, so Seymour told us earlier, takes it very hard as it is that his two eldest sons are so different from other regular boys. And now Seymour is not even going to try any longer to be a regular boy. Instead he is going to withdraw even more deeply into his studies, and he is going to pull Buddy along with him. This is indeed an exorbitant price to pay for sending Seymour and Buddy to summer camp against their wishes.

The narrative perspective in "Hapworth 16, 1924" is a straightforward first person point of view. The only peculiarity in the novella's point of view has to do with Seymour's relationship to his audience because there is a gradual and unconscious shift in whom he is talking to.

The salutation identifies the audience as Seymour's parents Les and Bessie Glass and his siblings Beatrice, Walter, and Waker. Again and again, Seymour addresses the members of his family individually by prefacing his remarks with such phrases as "Bessie, sweetheart" or "Les, old man." This gives the false impression that Seymour is keeping his audience in mind.

In the third part of the letter—the long book list—Seymour is not talking to his family anymore but to himself and to God. Discussing the books he loves and hates gives him so much pleasure that he forgets that his audience doesn't share his erudition and intellectual excitement. Although he knows that he can't really expect his parents to ask the library to send him all the books he discusses—among them the complete works of Jane Austen, Charles Dickens, Leo Tolstoy, and Marcel Proust—he continues adding to the book list because he loves to talk about the personalities and ideas of the authors. But Seymour is not only indulging himself in a monologue.

Near the end of the letter, there is a long passage in which Seymour addresses God Himself. This passage begins with the words, "If you have the stomach to read this letter, dear God..." (105). In this passage, Seymour wonders what direct communication with God would be like, especially what it would be like to receive personal orders from God. Seymour thinks it would amount to rank favoritism if God gave a person such direct commands. Seymour thanks God for not prescribing to him what form his worship should take, and he ends the passage by telling God that he is glad God is so hard to figure out. This is one reason why he, Seymour, loves God so much and will forever be God's servant.

After Seymour is done talking to God, he addresses his parents again and adds a few more titles to the list of books he wants to have sent to camp. But near the end of the letter, he realizes how ridiculously long his list is, and he says that he doesn't really expect that Mr. Fraser at the library can send him more than two or three books. That Seymour has returned to the real world is also signaled by his passing along to his parents Buddy's request to send him writing tablets without lines as well as "middle bunny" to replace "big bunny" which Buddy lost on the train.

If we accept the letter in "Hapworth" as written by Seymour, then the only unusual thing about the point of view in the novella is that the writer is gradually losing touch with the audience for whom he writes and that he winds up talking only to himself and to God until he remembers to address his family again at the end of the letter. This shift parallels Seymour's withdrawal from the everyday reality of Camp Hapworth that is revealed by the expository structure of the letter

However, the preface to "Hapworth" suggests the possibility that the letter was not written by Seymour but by his brother Buddy. Buddy arouses this suspicion because he says twice that he is about to type up "an exact copy" of the letter. If he had said it only once, there would be no reason to doubt him.

But why would Buddy forge a letter by Seymour? His motivation is not hard to understand once we realize that "Hapworth" contains more negative information about Seymour's personality than any other installment of the Glass Family Series since "A Perfect Day for Banana-fish." Since Buddy worships Seymour, it is understandable that he does not want to be the one to tell us about Seymour's character flaws. So instead of telling the story of the events at Camp Hapworth from his, Buddy's, point of view, Buddy makes Seymour himself tell us about those events and about the negative character traits they bring out in him.

Another reason for Buddy to impersonate Seymour may be that in pondering the failure of Seymour's spiritual quest, Buddy may have realized that Seymour's problems began in the summer of 1924, at Camp Hapworth. But Buddy may not have been sure what the exact nature of these problems was. Therefore—so we may speculate—he decided to find out what these problems were by writing the kind of letter that Seymour would have written back then, at the age of seven. By allowing the process of composition to become a process of discovery, Buddy may have come to understand that Seymour doomed his quest for God to failure when he decided to avoid interaction with unspiritual people as much as possible because such people bring out his instability and his malice. And we see this instability and malice in "A Perfect Day for Bananafish" when Seymour yells at a lady in the elevator not to stare at his feet and when he blows his brains out in his hotel room while sitting on a bed near his sleeping wife.

CHARACTERIZATION AND STYLE

"Hapworth 16, 1924" is a tour de force of self-characterization by a letter writer. It is such an unusual piece of writing both in its content and its style because the letter writer is one of the most extraordinary characters in all of literature, and his style is just as unusual.

In the course of reading the letter, we find out that the seven-year-old Seymour is not only extremely erudite and religious, but that he has occasional glimpses into the future and into his own and other people's past incarnations. These traits of Seymour's personality had already been mentioned in "Seymour—An Introduction," but now they are illustrated in detail. Moreover, we now also find out about three negative character traits of Seymour's that had only been hinted at in "A Perfect Day for Bananafish" and "Raise High the Roof Beam, Carpenters." They are Seymour's sensuality, his emotional instability, and his latent malice. These three traits stand out in "Hapworth" because Seymour worries about them as major obstacles to his spiritual advancement.

In three previous installments of the Glass series, we were told that Seymour was a child prodigy who was a regular for six years on the radio quiz show "It's a Wise Child." The book list in "Hapworth" is the best illustration so far of Seymour's astounding erudition. We find out that at the age of seven, Seymour has not only read more classics of European literature than most adult academics, but he has read such writers as Balzac and Maupassant in the original French and Cervantes in the original Spanish. In addition to French and Spanish, Seymour has also been studying Italian. Moreover, he has not only read widely in Western literature, he is also familiar with Taoism and Hinduism as is shown by his references to Lao-tse, Chuang-tse, and Vivekananda (there are no references to Zen Buddhism in the letter).

"Hapworth" also illustrates in detail the nature and intensity of Seymour's religious preoccupation. The letter reveals that Seymour's religious aspirations began to take shape when he was six and started his systematic reading in a neighborhood branch of the New York Public Library. He mentions in his letter that he has exhausted all of that library's books written on religion and God by authors with names beginning with letters from A to H. However, young Seymour's consuming preoccupation with God is not, as we might expect, an emotional infatuation with a divine father figure. Such an anthropomorphic conception of God, so Seymour says, "stinks to high heaven." Instead, his interest in God is very intellectual and abstract, for he prefers to see his God as a shapeless entity quite unlike the bearded grandfather figure depicted in religious books for children. Moreover, although Seymour has great respect for Jesus Christ, he does not think of Jesus as the only Son of God but merely as a human being who was spiritually farther advanced than anyone else.

In short, Seymour's religious outlook is not Christian. The over 20 references to reincarnation and the familiarity he demonstrates with Taoism and Hinduism indicate that his outlook has been shaped by his readings in Eastern philosophy. For instance, Seymour says that in his opinion Judgment Day "quite regularly occurs between human bodies" (94). Moreover, Seymour discusses Swami Vivekananda's *Raja Yoga*, a meditation manual which mentions that advanced practitioners of raja yoga meditation will acquire special *siddhis* or supernatural powers, among them the ability to have "glimpses" into the future and into past incarnations. Seymour borrows the term "glimpses" from Vivekananda when referring to his own clairvoyance.

We already know from "Seymour—An Introduction" that during meditation Seymour was able to trace his and his family's previous incarnations. In "Hapworth" we find out more about these quasi-supernatural powers. Seymour mentions a number of glimpses he has had of incidents in his own and other people's previous lifetimes. He says, for instance, that in his previous incarnation, the camp director, Mr. Happy, made ropes in Turkey or Greece, and that he was executed because he made some defective ropes that resulted in the deaths of influential mountain climbers. Seymour also mentions that in his and Buddy's previous incarnation, their relationship with their father Les was not a harmonious one.

Several of Seymour's glimpses concern the future. He predicts that some time during the next winter, his parents will give a party and that during this party, he and Buddy will be made a business offer. He also predicts that many years later, Buddy will be writing a short story about this very party. As we know from the preface, Buddy had indeed been working on a story about this very party when his mother sent him Seymour's old letter from Camp Hapworth. And from information in "Seymour—An Introduction," we know that as a result of the business offer that Seymour and Buddy were made, they became regulars on the radio quiz show "It's a Wise Child."

Some of Seymour's glimpses into the future are less clear than others. He predicts correctly that he will "live a generous matter of thirty (30) years or more" (he was 31 when he killed himself), but he makes what seems an incorrect prediction about his and Buddy's deaths. He says that one of them will be present at the other's death, and we know that Buddy was not present when Seymour shot himself. However, it is still possible that in a future story a reincarnated Seymour will be present at Buddy's death.

Contrary to what we might expect, Seymour does not enjoy his clairvoyance. He feels his glimpses are not worth the wear and tear on his normalcy and on his peace of mind. Referring to the two tiny "portals" in his mind through which his glimpses come, he says that if it were up to him, he would happily shut those portals himself.

Another one of Seymour's extraordinary powers is his ability to control his nervous system. This is illustrated after he has injured his leg and takes 11 stitches without anesthesia. As he explains, he simply shut down the nerve connection between his leg and his brain.

Although Seymour insists that he and Buddy are "exceedingly regular boys" and that they are "every bit as decent, foolish, and human" as all the other boys and counselors at the camp, their extraordinary mental powers set them apart from average, normal people and create difficulties for them at camp. At the beginning of their stay at Camp Hapworth, Seymour and Buddy make a pact to keep their mouths shut about their special powers and abilities, but later both of them violate this agreement, and as a result they are no longer considered regular boys by the staff and the other campers.

While previous Glass stories only hinted at flaws in Seymour's character, "Hapworth" illustrates three of them, his sensuality, his emotional instability, and his malice. Seymour calls his sensuality a "karmic responsibility" and says that he does not look forward to "being distracted quite day-in and day-out by charming lusts of the body for the few remaining blissful years allotted to me in this appearance" (36). One of these distractions is the young wife of the camp director, Mrs. Happy, who arouses all of Seymour's "unlimited sensuality." The lonely young woman often invites Seymour to stop by and chat with her, and Seymour says that he looks forward to the unlikely possibility that one day when he comes to visit her, she will open the door stark naked. From his conversations with her, Seymour knows that Mrs. Happy does not feel close to her husband. Seymour believes their problem is that that the two of them have "failed to become one flesh quite to perfection" (38). He wonders therefore if he should give them advice. But he doesn't think that verbal advice would help, and he says he would be willing to demonstrate if his friend, the eight-year-old Désirée Green, were here.

A less preposterous problem is Seymour's emotional instability. Seymour is fully aware of this obstacle to his spiritual advancement. He admits that "a vein of instability runs through [him] quite like some turbulent river" (48) and that he has left this problem uncorrected in his previous two incarnations. He adds that this instability is a problem which cannot be corrected by prayer, that it can only be corrected by serious and sustained effort on his part. Then Seymour explains that this problem manifests itself particularly in his inability to control his tongue when talking to people whom he despises. He says that his emotional instability may well turn out to be "the cause of [his] utter dégringolade [downfall] in this appearance, unless [he gets] a move on" (44). What he means here is that his instability might prevent him from making any spiritual advancement in his present incarnation.

But the most serious problem lying in the path of Seymour's spiritual advancement is his latent malice. When talking about his relationship with the camp director Mr. Happy, Seymour says about him that this man brings out "supplies of hidden malice" (66) that Seymour thought he had worked out of his system long ago. This malice comes out after Seymour hurts his leg on a jagged piece of metal that is sticking out of a wagon and he threatens Mr. Happy that is father, Les Glass, would sue him for every penny he has. Reporting that incident, Seymour uses a Biblical simile when he says, "my malice shot forward like a snake" (66). This comment reveals that Seymour is fully aware that there is evil hidden in his soul and that he has to deal with this problem before he can reach his goal of full enlightenment and oneness with God.

The style of Seymour's letter from camp is just what one would expect from an emotionally unstable seven-year-old genius who has just gone through a traumatic experience. Right from the start, we notice the stilted and unnatural sentence construction and the mixture of erudition and slang in the word choice. Seymour is aware of his shortcomings as a writer and says that his instability and emotionality will always be apparent in the way he writes. He also knows that his style is marked by "fustian," by bad taste, and by his desire to show off.

The "fustian" to which Seymour refers is his use of recondite words and his unnecessarily complex sentence constructions. Both contrast ludicrously with his often colloquial and even slangy diction. Seymour likes to show off by using such rare words as "dégringolade," "feculent," "nemophilous," and "pauciloquent," and he often gets himself entangled in such unnatural construction as, "I am far from above hoping the case is vice versa," or, "I was born without any great support in the event of continued absence of loved ones." Yet a moment later, he will slip back into the more natural speech patterns of a seven-year-old when he tells his parents that he misses them "like sheer hell" or when mentions his leg injury and says he will tell them about the whole "crappy incident" later or, when he says that "Mr. Happy is no prize package."

Another peculiarity of Seymour's style has to do with his choice of adjectives. Most of his adjectives carry connotations that reveal his strong emotional responses to the persons, objects, or ideas he describes. His favorites are "moving," "touching," "stirring," "thrilling," and "heartrending." In addition, he often uses superlatives such as "superb," "magnificent," and "excellent." Adjectives of this kind are largely responsible for the emotional tone of the letter.

What further contributes to the emotionality of Seymour's style is his frequent use of exclamations such as "Jesus," "Oh, my God," and "God Almighty," and of such emphatic vulgarities as "damn," "hell," and "crap." These elements of his style suggest that Seymour is in a very agitated state of mind when he writes the letter.

Whenever Seymour becomes aware of his emotional attitude toward what he describes, he tries to be more objective and detached. This is why he likes to use the pronoun "one" instead of "I" when he refers to himself. A good example of Seymour's stilted use of the pronoun "one" is the following sentence in which he talks about his struggle to overcome his sensuality. He says that "one meets it, one conquers it, or if one does not conquer it, one enters into honorable contest with it, seeking and giving no quarter" (36).

Another typical element of Seymour's style is his use of multiple adjectives with conflicting connotations. For instance, he calls another camper "this excellent, droll, touching, intelligent lad"; he calls his own homesickness "a simple, nagging, humorous fact"; and he describes a discussion as "helpful, quite spooky, or openly distasteful." Seymour's piling up of adjectives suggests that he tries to look at the things he describes from more than one angle. This is particularly apparent when he chooses adjectives that express amused detachment, as for instance when he discusses his own state of mind and refers to his despair as "humorous" and to his inner turmoil as "ridiculous." But as the emotionality of the style shows, Seymour does not manage to achieve the desired distance from the events, people, and ideas that he is writing about.

The style of the letter tells us two things about Seymour's character which are of great importance to an understanding of his inner turmoil. The verbal sophistication and complex sentence construction show that he is an extremely precocious seven-year-old, and the contrast between pretentiousness and slanginess and between adjectives suggesting enthusiasm and detachment reveal that Seymour is torn between two desires. On the one hand he wants to be a regular boy who responds uncritically to the world, and on the other hand he wants to be a "young poet, and private scholar" (32) who maintains a detached attitude toward everything around him.

SETTINGS AND SYMBOLISM

The location where the action of the novella takes place is imaginary. There is no town named Hapworth in Maine. However, the camp seems to be modeled after Camp Wigwam on Bear Lake, near Waterford, Maine, where J.D. Salinger spent the summer of 1930, when he was eleven years old.

The physical location plays no role in this novella except that Seymour and Buddy don't want to be at camp to begin with. There are two reasons why we don't get a description of the place. One reason is that Seymour uses his letter writing to get away from the camp—at least in spirit. The other reason is that

Seymour is in bed with a leg injury. Thus his visual horizon is limited to the inside of the "Intermediate" bungalow.

We learn more about the setting in time in "Hapworth 16, 1924" than about the location. As the title tells us, the year is 1924, and the day on which Seymour writes his letter is the sixteenth day of camp. If we consult a calendar of the year 1924, and if we examine the various time references in the letter, we will find that Seymour and Buddy came to Camp Hapworth on the first of July; that Seymour had his fight with Roger Pittman on Tuesday, the 15th of July; that he injured his leg and had his conflict with Mr. Happy on Wednesday, the 16th of July; and that he spent all day writing the long letter on Wednesday, the 17th of July.

As it turns out, then, the number 16 in the title of the novella has a double meaning. It refers to both the sixteenth day of Seymour and Buddy's stay at the camp and to the sixteenth day of the month of July when Seymour had the traumatic experience that changed his life. That traumatic event is the injury to his leg which made him blow up at Mr. Happy and decide to demonstrate that he is not an ordinary boy but an individual with extraordinary powers.

As in "Seymour—An Introduction," we again don't get much symbolism in "Hapworth 16, 1924" because the dominant mode of writing is expository rather than narrative, and in expository writing metaphors and similes tend to take the place of symbols. While Buddy, the narrator of "Seymour—An Introduction," favors metaphors, Seymour's figurative language in "Hapworth" tends more toward similes. Some of Seymour's similes are inept while others are quite memorable. For instance, when Seymour says that he and Buddy have certain powers and abilities that are "warmly attached to [them] like cement from previous appearances" (40), this is a clumsy simile. It does not conjure up the kind of compelling image that we get when Seymour says that his instability runs through him "like a turbulent river" (44) or when he reports that while talking to Mr. Happy, his "malice shot forward like a snake" (66).

The most important among the few metaphors in "Hapworth" is the "light" that Seymour mentions several times. It is a metaphor rather than a symbol because a symbol is something concrete that can represent several abstract ideas. While Seymour says that the light is something that he actually perceives, its meaning is narrowly circumscribed and not open to multiple interpretations as a symbol would be. Seymour began to see the light for the first time—so he reminds his mother—a year earlier, in May of 1923, and he now sees it regularly during meditation when his mind stops racing around and becomes absolutely still. In connection with the light he sees during meditation, Seymour discusses Vivekananda of India, the author of the meditation manual *Raja Yoga*. Seymour says about Vivekananda that "he was fully acquainted with the lights I mentioned earlier, far more than I" (92). In *Raja Yoga*, Vivekananda makes several references to lights that we will see when we successfully practice *raja yoga* meditation. He explains that through this kind of meditation we can free our coiled *kundalini* energy and make it travel upward through the five *chakras*, or energy centers, that are situated along the spine: "And when it reaches the metropolis of all sensations, the brain, the whole brain, as it were, reacts, and the result is the full blaze of illumination" (*Raja Yoga* 57). This illumination is both literal and figurative. We will literally experience our brain filled with light, and we will attain "divine wisdom, super-conscious perception, and realization of the Spirit" (*Raja Yoga* 58). However, Vivekananda says that we will not always experience the "full blaze." In the beginning, when we have just started to practice *raja yoga,* we will only see "little specks of light floating and becoming bigger and bigger" (*Raja Yoga* 71). Similarly, when Seymour mentions the lights, he does not always mean full illumination. For instance, when he discusses books on the structure of the heart in general and pictures of the heart in particular, he says that the crucial, "uncharted" parts of the heart—that is, the non-physical parts—can be visualized only at brief moments "when one's lights are quite definitely turned on" (107). In short, the lights represent the moments of temporary enlightenment that Seymour achieves or, more generally, his ability to see more than less spiritual people.

If we look for symbolic objects in "Hapworth," the only things that come to mind are the many books that Seymour discusses near the end of the letter. There is something unreal about the books; they are not physical objects but ideas. They are what Franny Glass calls "treasure" ("Zooey" 146), intellectual and spiritual treasure that Seymour has piled up. These books can represent three different things. They can be seen as symbolizing Seymour's astonishing intellect and erudition; they can also represent Seymour's withdrawal from the world of the normal, unspiritual people at Camp Hapworth; and they can represent the path of study and acquisition of knowledge, the means Seymour has chosen for his spiritual development.

In his letter from camp, Seymour also mentions two things that he and Buddy did which have symbolic significance. These symbolic incidents are Buddy's memorizing a whole book in half an hour and Seymour's taking 11 stitches in his leg without anesthesia. Both are violations of the agreement Seymour and Buddy had made not to show off their unusual extraordinary powers. When Buddy demonstrates to the cook, Mr. Nelson, that he can memorize *The Hardwoods of North America* in half an hour, he sets himself apart from the other campers and serves notice that he is not a regular boy. Seymour does the same when he simply cuts the communication of pain between his brain and his leg and has his leg injury sewn up without anesthesia. These two incidents are the two most important things that happen during Seymour and Buddy's stay at Camp Hapworth. They mark watersheds in the two boys' relationships with normal people because it seems that from now on, Seymour and Buddy will no longer try to make themselves and others believe that they are average, regular boys.

THEMES AND INTERPRETATIONS

In "Hapworth 16, 1924," the religious ideas form an even more important part of the meaning than in any previous work by J.D. Salinger. For instance, the word "God" appears over 70 times; that is, more than once per page. It is therefore not surprising that the published commentary on the novella deals chiefly with religious themes, especially with Seymour's quest for spiritual advancement and with the wrongness or rightness of his suicide.

There are three different directions in which critics have gone in interpreting "Hapworth." Most analyses of the novella examine it for clues that would explain Seymour's suicide. Of those, the majority use "Hapworth" to interpret Seymour's suicide as a positive act while a few dissenters suggest that Seymour's instability and malice led to his failure as a God-seeker. Rare are interpretations that look for a universal meaning in "Hapworth."

Gordon Slethaugh's article, "Seymour: A Clarification," is one of several interpretations that sees an explanation of Seymour's suicide in "Hapworth." Slethaugh is struck by the many times that Seymour refers to his previous lives or, as Seymour calls them, his previous "appearances." Slethaugh says:

Most important to an understanding of Salinger's fiction is this concept that Seymour, by thinking in terms of appearances, of a limited time in this appearance, and of his obligations to fulfill the plan of God, does not act stupidly but wisely. This wisdom is not the wisdom of Western logic that means the rejection of the idea of transmigration of the soul, but the wisdom of the Glass's intuition based on Oriental religion and the Romantic tradition. (120)

What Slethaugh finds most important in "Hapworth" is that Seymour's glimpses into the future tell him that he has very little time to fulfill his spiritual obligations: "Since he always foresaw the time of his own death, he acts in accordance with the divine dictate" (127). Seymour's several suicide attempts suggest that he thought "this 'appearance' is finished, this incarnation is done, and he must hasten along to another incarnation." Slethaugh therefore believes that "Seymour's suicide is the utmost commitment to God" (127). According to Slethaugh, "Hapworth" shows that Seymour's suicide "has nothing to do with inability to live in this world; it has nothing to do with escapism; it has everything to do with acceptance of spiritual responsibility" (127).

Another interpretation that suggests "Hapworth" can explain Seymour's suicide is Arthur Quagliano's article, "'Hapworth 16, 1924': A Problem in Hagiography." Quagliano points out that the novella allows two different types of interpretations. According to one, Seymour is a saint; according to the other, he is a spiritual failure. Quagliano thinks that "Salinger is urging us to opt for the halo" (41). But Quagliano also develops the more interesting negative interpretation and suggests that "Hapworth" can be seen to illustrate a "crisis of perfectionism ... so real that it may have been the cause of Seymour's suicide" (36). He points out that in "Hapworth" Seymour is "still bound to earthly, human desires," he quotes the passage in which Seymour talks about the "vein of instability which runs through [him] quite like some turbulent river," and he comments on Seymour's "murderous urge toward Roger Pittman" (37). Quagliano sums up this negative interpretation of "Hapworth" when he says that it is based on the assumption that between the ages of seven and thirty-one, Seymour was unable to overcome the obstacles to his spiritual advancement that are illustrated in "Hapworth." He finds this conclusion plausible, but he stresses that it bears with it "the implication that Seymour was spiritually a failure, unable either to embrace and understand his wife and 'worldly' mother-in-law, or to savor God's first and greatest gift, the gift of life" (38). Quagliano translates the negative interpretation of "Hapworth" into the following universal statement: "The story of Seymour Glass then would be a story about the impossibility of saintliness in contemporary American culture" (38). But Quagliano rejects this interpretation in favor of the view of Seymour as a modern *bodhisattva*, an enlightened man. However, this positive interpretation does not enable him to arrive at a universal statement such as the one about saintliness in contemporary America.

Unlike Arthur Quagliano, Howard Harper is able to derive a universal message from a positive interpretation of "Hapworth." In a chapter of his book *Desperate Faith*, Harper says that "Hapworth" is "a sermon" which reveals "the religious position ... toward which the Glass saga seems to be moving" (92). According to Harper, the Glass Family Series as a whole is pointing to "the revelation that whatever is, is right; that everything—even evil—is all part of God's mysterious plan" (92). Harper acknowledges that this is not an original idea and that "its most eloquent advocate was John Milton" [in "Paradise Lost"]. But Harper points out a difference when he says: "Salinger's recent protagonists do not try to reform a corrupt world as Milton did, but find instead that its corruption is, in the blinding light of religious revelation, irrelevant" (92).

CONCLUSION

In "Hapworth 16, 1924," Salinger again combined an expository and a narrative framework as he had done in "Seymour—An Introduction," and he also did not break new ground in terms of narrative perspective, not even if we assume that Buddy is an unreliable narrator and impersonated Seymour in writing this letter from camp. Where the innovation lies in "Hapworth" is in its preposterous style and in the almost unbelievable characterization of Seymour as a young genius and clairvoyant who was obsessed with God but had serious character flaws.

The style of "Hapworth" is extremely unusual and has no precedent in Salinger's fiction. It fluctuates between the pretentiousness of a young genius who worries about his "dégringolade" as a poet and the slang of a seven-year-old New York City brat, who says that a style manual he has been studying (Strunk and White?) is "alternately priceless and sheer crap." To lovers of the subtleties of language, this style is undoubtedly a delight, but to most other readers it probably gets a bit tedious because of the great length of the letter.

Even if the style of the seven-year-old Seymour does not hold the interest of all readers, there are aspects of his characterization which are bound to fascinate both the casual reader and the Salinger aficionado. For one thing, "Hapworth" shows Seymour to have supernatural metal powers; for another thing, it shows Seymour to have serious character flaws.

Readers of "Hapworth" who have read only one or two previous stories about Seymour Glass will know that he was a child prodigy, that he appeared on the national radio quiz show "It's a Wise Child," and that he was a freshman at Columbia University when he was only fifteen. However, the earlier stories do not illustrate how utterly amazing Seymour's mental powers were. "Hapworth" shows that Seymour had a photographic memory and had already read more great works of Western literature and religion by the time he was seven years old than most college professors read in a lifetime. He was also able to acquire foreign languages very quickly and was already fluent in French, Spanish, and Italian. His extensive religious studies involved Western as well as Eastern texts and reveal just how consuming Seymour's love of God and his quest for spiritual advancement were. But the most astonishing thing about Seymour's mental powers is his ability to have "glimpses" of his and other people's past incarnations as well as of his and other people's future. In "Hapworth," Seymour mentions a half-dozen such glimpses including one of the party at which he and Buddy will be signed up for the radio quiz show "It's a Wise Child" and another glimpse of Buddy, many years later, writing a story about his very party.

For students of the Glass Family Series the unique thing about "Hapworth 16, 1924" is not that it illustrates Seymour's superhuman mental powers but that it illustrates in detail three character flaws that previous stories had only hinted at. In "Seymour—An Introduction," Buddy Glass asks rhetorically if Seymour was a saint and if he had no grievous flaws or meannesses. Those questions are not answered in the "Introduction," but they are answered in "Hapworth." Seymour's letter from camp shows that he was aware of three problems that were serious obstacles on his path of spiritual advancement because he foresaw that they would trouble him throughout his life. These problems were his sensuality, his mental instability, and his malice toward unspiritual people.

Laughable though the seven-year-old Seymour's precocious sexual attraction to the wife of the camp director may seem to us, it was no laughing matter to Seymour because he had left this streak of sensuality uncorrected in previous incarnations, and he was afraid that it would continue to hamper his spiritual advancement in this particular lifetime. Seymour's problem here is similar to that of his fellow child prodigy Teddy McArdle in the story "Teddy" because Teddy tells us that in his previous incarnation he got involved with a woman and "sort of stopped meditating" ("Teddy" 188). As a result of his surrender to sensuality, Teddy took a step backward in his spiritual advancement and was reincarnated as a person living in America, the land of sensuality. Seymour's struggle with his sensuality in "Hapworth" sheds light on his later relationships with Charlotte Mayhew and Muriel Fedder in "Raise High the Roof Beam, Carpenters" and "A Perfect Day for Bananafish," because both of them seem to have inflamed Seymour's sensuality.

A second character flaw and obstacle to Seymour's spiritual progress is his emotional instability which he says runs through his character like a turbulent river. It not only makes him break down and weep several times while he is writing the letter from camp; more importantly, it makes him lose his temper when the head counselor Roger Pittman insults Buddy and when he, Seymour, injures his leg as a result of the negligence of the camp director, Mr. Happy.

But the most serious character flaw that "Hapworth" reveals is Seymour's contempt of and malice toward unspiritual people. During his confrontation with Mr. Happy, Seymour says that he was surprised at the supplies of hidden malice in his character. He thought he had worked this problem out of his system long ago, but his malice keeps reappearing later on in his life as we can see when he hits Charlotte Mayhew in the face with a stone ("Raise High the Roof Beam, Carpenters") and when he decides to blow his brains out while sitting on a bed near his sleeping wife, Muriel ("A Perfect Day for Bananafish").

"Hapworth" is an important part of the Glass Family Series because it answers Buddy's two questions in "Seymour–An Introduction" if Seymour had no grievous faults and meannesses and if he was perhaps a saint. "Hapworth" demonstrates that Seymour did indeed have serious character flaws. Other parts of the Glass Family Series show that as he grew into adulthood, Seymour was not able to work these flaws out of his spiritual system and that he was very far from sainthood when he killed himself. For this reason it seems that "Hapworth 16, 1924" ought to be republished in a volume together with the story of his suicide, "A Perfect Day for Bananafish."

For the Salinger buff who wants to know everything there is to know about Seymour and Buddy Glass, "Hapworth 16, 1924" is a treasure trove. For the average reader, however, it is a daunting task to read this letter. Even some critics have felt overwhelmed by it. For instance, John Wenke, the author of *J.D. Salinger: A Study of the Short Fiction*, says that "Hapworth" is "virtually unreadable" (107), and he therefore devotes less than two pages to it.

Because of the length of "Hapworth," its bizarre style, and the lack of action, it is my recommendation to new readers of Salinger's fiction not to read it until they have read all the other installments of the Glass Family Series, but above all to read first the story "Teddy" which also deals with a young clairvoyant genius and God-seeker.

Students of Salinger's fiction who are looking for topics that have not been adequately explored will find quite a few in "Hapworth" and in the relationship between "Hapworth" and the other parts of the Glass Family Series. First of all, Seymour talks a lot about his brother Buddy and what a "young genius" he is at the age of five, but no one has explored what "Hapworth" adds to our understanding of the character of Buddy Glass and of Buddy's relationship to Seymour. Secondly, Seymour's relationship to his parents needs to be studied in connection with what we know about the relationship of child prodigies to their parents. Also, since Seymour talks so much about God in his letter from camp, his religious outlook needs to be examined in detail. Above all, Seymour's admission of his three major character flaws—his sensuality, his emotional instability, and his malice—merits a re-examination of the Charlotte Mayhew incident, of Seymour's relationship with his bride Muriel in "Raise High the Roof Beam, Carpenters," and of his suicide in "A Perfect Day for Bananafish." And finally, the lack of any references to Zen Buddhism in "Hapworth" and the positive statements about Jesus Christ, Taoism and Vedanta Hinduism suggest that a re-examination of the religious underpinnings of the Glass Family Series is in order.

WORKS CITED

Fosburgh, Lacey. "J.D. Salinger Speaks About His Silence." *New York Times* (3 November 1974): 1, 69.

Harper, Howard. "J.D. Salinger—Through the Glasses Darkly." In *Desperate Faith*. Chapel Hill: U of North Carolina P, 1967, 65-95.

Miller, James. E. *J.D. Salinger*. Minneapolis: U of Minnesota P, 1965.
"People." *Time* (25 June 1965): 52.
Quagliano, Anthony. "'Hapworth 16, 1924': A Problem in Hagiography." *University of Dayton Review* 8 (1971): 35-43.
Salinger, J.D. *Franny and Zooey* [1961]. New York: Bantam, 1964.
___ . "Hapworth 16, 1924." *New Yorker* (19 June 1965): 32-113.
___ . *Raise High the Roof Beam, Carpenters and Seymour—An Introduction* [1963]. New York: Bantam, 1965.
___ . "Teddy." In *Nine Stories* [1953]. New York: Bantam, 1964, 166-198.
Schulz, Max. "Epilogue to 'Seymour—An Introduction': Salinger and the Crisis of Consciousness." *Studies in Short Fiction* 5 (1968): 128-138. Rpt. in *J.D. Salinger*. Ed. Harold Bloom. New York: Chelsea House, 1987, 53-61.
Slethaugh, Gordon. "Seymour: A Clarification." *Renascence* 23 (1971): 115-128.
Wenke, John. "'Hapworth 16. 1924': 'Continuing at Blissful Random...'." In *J.D. Salinger: A Study of the Short Fiction*. Boston: Twayne, 1991, 107-108.

SUGGESTIONS FOR FURTHER READING

Bellman, Samuel. "New Light on Seymour's Suicide: Salinger's 'Hapworth 16, 1924'." *Studies in Short Fiction* 3 (1966): 348-351.
French, Warren. "Hapworth 16, 1924." In *J.D. Salinger, Revisited*. Boston: G.K. Hall, 1988, 109-116.
Goldstein, Bernice, and Sanford Goldstein. "Ego and 'Hapworth 16, 1924'." *Renascence* 24 (1972): 159-167.
Metcalf, Frank. "The Suicide of Salinger's Seymour Glass." *Studies in Short Fiction* 9 (1972): 243-246.
Rupp, Richard H. "J.D. Salinger: A Solitary Liturgy." In *Celebration in Postwar American Fiction 1945-1967*. Coral Gables: U of Florida P, 1970, 113-131.

Chapter 10

The Glass Family Series

> I love working on these Glass stories. I've been waiting for them most of my life.
>
> J.D. Salinger

THE SHAPE OF THE SERIES

In "A Perfect Day for Bananafish"—the story in which Seymour Glass kills himself—we can tell that Salinger had not yet decided to make Seymour the focus of a narrative series about Seymour and his family because, aside from Seymour's wife Muriel, the story mentions no other members of the Glass family. And in "Franny"—the story in which the title character has a nervous breakdown—we can tell that Salinger had not yet decided to make Franny a member of the Glass family because he does not mention her last name, and there is no mention by name of any her family, let alone to Seymour's suicide which is mentioned in all the other Glass stories. But in "Raise High the Roof Beam, Carpenters"—the story in which Seymour doesn't show up for his own wedding and instead elopes with his bride, Muriel—we can tell that Salinger had now formulated a plan for the Glass Family Series because he now introduced us to all nine Glasses, the parents and the seven siblings.

Over the years Salinger's plans for the Glass series changed. This is apparent from what Buddy Glass says about the series in "Seymour—An Introduction," from what Salinger himself said about it in the dust cover notes for two of his books, and from the way he changed the characterization of Seymour from story to story.

In "Seymour—An Introduction," Buddy Glass, Salinger's alter ego, talks about his plans for a narrative series about Seymour. He says that before he conceived of "Seymour—An Introduction," he had planned a short story entitled "Seymour One" which would be followed by a "Seymour Two," a "Seymour Three," and perhaps a "Seymour Four." However, he says that he has given up those plans in favor of writing a long "thesaurus of undetached prefatory re-marks," namely the "Introduction." But he also says that additional stories about Seymour might pop up later when they're ready.

Elsewhere in "Seymour—An Introduction," Buddy says that he has written about Seymour before, and he refers specifically to "A Perfect Day for Banana-fish" and to "Raise High the Roof Beam, Carpenters." However, Buddy also reports that his family has complained about his portrayal of Seymour in "Ba-nanafish" because the Seymour in that story was not the Seymour they knew but someone with an uncanny resemblance to Buddy himself. Then Buddy admits that that his family is right and that his craftsmanship leaves something to be desired. This comment suggests that Buddy misrepresented his brother in "Ba-nanafish" because he, Buddy, projected his own dislike of Muriel on Seymour so as to blame her for Seymour's suicide. Buddy's admission suggests that Seymour did not kill himself out of despair over his marriage to a superficial and materialistic person but for some other reason. Moreover, Buddy's admis-sion that he misrepresented Seymour in "Bananafish" is also necessary so that Salinger can make Seymour credible as the spiritual guide of his younger sib-lings in "Raise High the Roof Beam, Carpenters," and "Zooey" and as a near saint in "Seymour—An Introduction."

Salinger's own comments on the Glass Family Series give added insight into his evolving plans. Here is the advertising blurb he wrote for the dust cover of *Franny and Zooey* (1961):

The author writes: FRANNY came out in *The New Yorker* in 1955, and was swiftly followed, in 1957, by ZOOEY. Both stories are early, critical entries in a narrative series I'm doing about a family of settlers in twentieth-century New York, the Glasses. It is a long-term project, patently an ambitious one, and there is a real-enough danger, I suppose, that sooner or later I'll bog down, perhaps disappear en-tirely, in my own methods, locutions, and mannerisms. On the whole, though, I'm very hopeful. I love working on these Glass stories, I've been waiting for them most of my life, and I think I have fairly decent, monomaniacal plans to finish them with due care and all-available skill.

A couple of stories in the series besides FRANNY and ZOOEY have already been published in *The New Yorker*, and some new material is scheduled to appear there soon or Soon. I have a great deal of thoroughly unscheduled material on paper, too, but I expect to be fussing with it, to use a popular trade term, for some time to come. ("Polishing" is another dandy word that comes to mind.) I work like greased light-ning, myself, but my alter-ego and collaborator, Buddy Glass, is insufferably slow.

It is my rather subversive opinion that a writer's feelings of anonymity-obscurity are the second-most valuable property on loan to him during his working years. My wife has asked me to add, however, in a single explosion of candor, that I live in Westport with my dog.

When Salinger mentions that two stories in the series, aside from "Franny" and "Zooey," had already been published, he is probably referring to "Raise High the Roof Beam, Carpenters" and "Seymour—An Introduction." It is curious that Salinger should mention only two other Glass stories besides "Franny" and "Zooey" and omit the very first one in the series, "A Perfect Day for Banana-fish." This is particularly odd since Seymour's suicide is mentioned in all

Glass stories except "Franny" and because the "Introduction" mentions "Bananafish" as a story written by Buddy Glass. This omission suggests that Salinger was perhaps planning to drop "A Perfect Day for Bananafish" from the series or to revise Buddy's account of Seymour's suicide.

After *Franny and Zooey* had been published, a cover story on Salinger in *Time* magazine quoted an unnamed "friend" of Salinger's as saying that "Salinger intends to write a Glass trilogy" (Skow 16). If this is indeed what Salinger intended at that time, then the two books, *Franny and Zooey* (1961) and *Raise High the Roof Beam Carpenters and Seymour—An Introduction* (1963), are the first and second parts. And if these first two parts are an indication, the third part of the trilogy could be expected to consist of another pair of stories or novellas collected in one volume.

However, in the dust cover notes for *Raise High the Roof Beam, Carpenters and Seymour—An Introduction*, Salinger said that he had "several new Glass stories coming along," and this suggests that his plans for the Glass series called for a format larger than a trilogy:

> The author writes: The two long pieces in this book originally came out in *The New Yorker*—RAISE HIGH THE ROOF BEAM, CARPENTERS in 1955, SEYMOUR—An Introduction in 1959. Whatever their differences in mood or effect, they are both very much concerned with Seymour Glass, who is the main character in my still-uncompleted series about the Glass family. It struck me that they had better be collected together, if not deliberately paired off, in something of a hurry, if I mean them to avoid unduly or undesirably close contact with new material in the series. There is only my word for it, granted, but I have several new stories coming along—waxing, dilating—each in its own way, but I suspect the less said about them, in mixed company, the better.
>
> Oddly, the joys and satisfactions of working on the Glass family peculiarly increase and deepen for me with the years. I can't say why, though. Not, at least, outside the casino proper of my fiction.

Salinger here seems to promise that he would publish "several new stories" about the Glass family, but he actually published only one more, and that was "Hapworth 16, 1924" in 1965.

James Bryan reported that after "Hapworth," Salinger submitted another Glass story to the *New Yorker* but withdrew it at the last minute (Bryan 75). The preface to "Hapworth" suggests that this might have been the story that Buddy says he was working on but dropped in order to type up and publish an "exact copy" of a letter that young Seymour wrote home from Camp Hapworth. Buddy says that the story he was working on was about a party that he and Seymour and his parents attended in the winter of 1924 or 1925, and he says that this party was very consequential. In the letter from Camp Hapworth, Seymour reports that he had a "glimpse" into the future which revealed to him that at the very party that Buddy mentions in the preface, he and Buddy would be made an important offer concerning their careers. We know from "Seymour—An Introduction," that it was at this party that Seymour and Buddy were signed up for the radio quiz show "It's a Wise Child." It may well be that this was the story that Salinger wrote for the *New Yorker* but then withdrew.

Salinger has said that he continues to write but doesn't intend to publish anymore during his lifetime because "Publishing is a terrible invasion of [his] privacy" (Fosburgh 1). Salinger's daughter Margaret sheds light on this cryptic comment when she quotes her Aunt Doris as saying: "Not publishing all these years. What a crazy business. It's because he can't stand any criticism" (*Dream Catcher* 428). However, Margaret Salinger also said in a radio interview that her father plans to publish posthumously and has a number of stories ready for publication. Given Salinger's earlier comment that he enjoys working on the Glass family, it is probable that at least some of the posthumous stories will be additional installments of the Glass Family Series.

No matter what unpublished Glass stories may repose in Salinger's safe, by having stopped publishing in 1965, Salinger has given the Glass Family Series a *de facto* closure. Originally Salinger may have had other plans, but the Glass Family Series did wind up—at least temporarily—as a trilogy consisting of three pairs of stories and novellas. They are *Franny and Zooey* (1961); *Raise High the Roof Beam, Carpenters and Seymour—An Introduction* (1963); "A Perfect Day for Bananafish" (1948); and "Hapworth 16, 1924" (1965). If Salinger never publishes anything again—not even posthumously—then it is only a matter of time until someone else will publish "Bananafish" and "Hapworth" between their own hard covers, because those two pieces really belong together just like "Franny" and "Zooey."

Although the plot that connects the six parts of the Glass Family Series is fragmentary, and although there are radical differences between the form of the early stories and the later novellas, the series has more coherence than, for instance, Ernest Hemingway's short story cycle *In Our Time* or William Faulkner's *Go Down, Moses*. One linking element that pulls the parts of the Glass Family Series together is that the pieces all deal either with Seymour's life and death or with his influence on his siblings. In addition, the pieces are held together by a web of shared references to events in the lives of the Glasses. Moreover, the reader's interest in the series is held by two pervasive questions: "Why would an advanced God-seeker such as Seymour kill himself?" And, "Why do Seymour's siblings consider him a near-saint despite his suicide?" But most importantly, the Glass Family Series also achieves coherence because its stories and novellas develop three major clusters of themes, a philosophical one that arises out of the conflict between the spiritual values of the Glasses and the material values of average unspiritual people, an aesthetic one that arises out of Buddy's changing views of art and the creative process, and a religious one that arises out of Seymour's quest for spiritual perfection and union with God.

THREE LEVELS OF MEANING

Whether we see the meaning of the Glass Family Series as being primarily philosophical, aesthetic or religious depends on our own interests. But how much of this meaning we will be able to understand depends on how much time and effort we are willing to expend, because an understanding of any part of the overall meaning of the series requires a considerable intellectual commitment.

An understanding of the Glass series requires, first of all, a willing suspension of disbelief, because we cannot possibly come to terms with the meaning of the stories and novellas unless we are willing to accept Seymour's superhuman intellect and his supernatural psychic powers. But accepting Seymour is not enough. The complexity of the Glass series requires that we read the six parts of it at least twice. But even such re-readings will permit only a basic understanding of the series. For a deeper understanding of the overall meaning, we must familiarize ourselves with the works of literature, aesthetics, and religious philosophy to which Seymour, Buddy, and Zooey refer. In short, an understanding of the Glass series requires as much effort as do, for instance, T. S. Eliot's "The Waste Land," James Joyce's *Ulysses*, William Faulkner's *The Sound and the Fury*, or, more recently, Thomas Pynchon's *Gravity's Rainbow*.

The reader who does not care to delve into any of the texts that Seymour, Buddy and Zooey refer to will find that the meaning of the Glass series is essentially philosophical because what is most obvious in the stories and novellas is that they all develop conflicts between the values of Glasses and the values of the people around them. Typical conflicts are those between Seymour and Muriel in "A Perfect Day for Bananafish," between Franny Glass and Lane Coutell in "Franny," and between Buddy Glass and the Matron of Honor in "Raise High the Roof Beam, Carpenters." These conflicts and the characters who function as the antagonists of the Glasses are so designed that we are made to sympathize with the intellectual and spiritual values of the Glasses and to condemn the superficiality and materialism of their antagonists.

The values of the Glasses reveal a vision of life according to which the physical world is merely a transitory world of appearances while the metaphysical world—the eternal world of ideas and essences—is the ultimate reality. In other words, the vision of life in the Glass stories is one which, to a reader more familiar with Western than Eastern thought, will appear to be very similar to the philosophical idealism of the nineteenth-century romantics. The favorable comments that Salinger makes in several stories about such romantics as William Blake, William Wordsworth, John Keats, Percy Bysshe Shelley, Walt Whitman, and Henry David Thoreau suggest that there is indeed a kinship between the vision of life of the Glass series and that of nineteenth-century romanticism. This kinship becomes even more apparent when we read the Glass series as a *Künstler-Roman*, a composite novel about Buddy's struggle to come to terms with his art.

Buddy's development as a writer, the changes in the form of his fiction from the early stories to the later novellas, and his growing understanding of Seymour's view of art reveal the aesthetic meaning of the Glass Family Series. To understand this aspect of the series, a reader needs to have a basic familiarity with nineteenth- and twentieth-century theories of art, enough, at any rate, to understand that a romantic such a William Blake had a very different view of the creative process than a realist such as Gustave Flaubert, and that romantic theories of art resurfaced in twentieth-century writers such as Rainer Maria Rilke and Franz Kafka.

The form of Buddy's early stories shows that Buddy was initially very much concerned with turning out stories which had a Flaubertian polish, followed conventional story patterns, and pleased large audiences. Gradually, however, the form of Buddy's fiction became less rigid and its content more esoteric and less appealing to the average reader. These changes are due to the influence of

Seymour's romantic ideas. Buddy eventually came to adopt Seymour's belief that all great art is created spontaneously, from the heart rather than the head, with the artist serving as the instrument of divine inspiration. This is a notion very similar to the romantic concept of the artist as an Aeolian harp: The wind which blows through the instrument and makes its strings tremble is divine inspiration. In this view of the nature of art, inspiration determines not only the content but also the form, for since the work originates with God, the artist should not impose any arbitrary form on it but should allow the form to grow organically out of the content. The belief that the artist should follow his heart and not his head explains not only the irregular form of the later Glass novellas, it also explains their religious content.

Related to Seymour and Buddy's view that the nature of all great works of art is determined by divine inspiration is the idea that the purpose of art is to communicate the truths that the artist grasps when "all his stars are out," when he is truly inspired. The Glasses' view of the purpose of art is well expressed in Buddy's statement that the best poems are "utterances that please or enlighten or enlarge the invited eavesdropper to within an inch of his life." This statement reveals Buddy's acceptance of the time-honored concept that art should delight and instruct and that it is the function of the artist to serve his fellow man.

Like Plato and the nineteenth-century romantics, Seymour and Buddy believed that the instruction that art provides should be philosophical or religious in nature. It should point out the divine essence of all things, the Tao of the Taoists or the *Brahman* of the Hindus, something that Seymour once called "the main current of poetry that runs through things, all things." Thus, according to the Glasses, great art is always religious, and true artists are God's servants and spokesmen.

And this brings us to the religious core of the Glass Family Series. To understand what the series has to say on this level of meaning, a reader has to have some knowledge of the New Testament, classical Taoism, Zen Buddhism, and Vedanta Hinduism. The more a reader knows about these four sources of Salinger's religious thought, especially Vedanta, the better will be his or her understanding of the religious meaning of the Glass Family Series.

This religious meaning arises, paradoxically, both out of the failure of Seymour's quest for God and out of Seymour's teachings. Because Seymour killed himself in despair, he clearly serves as a negative example, and yet the stories all present his ideas as extraordinary insights. This apparent contradiction resolves itself when we realize that Seymour was not as saintly as Buddy tries to make him out to be in "Seymour—An Introduction." In Seymour's letter from Camp Hapworth we find that he was very much troubled by three problems, his sensuality, his emotional instability, and, above all, by "supplies of hidden malice." These tendencies which he says he left "uncorrected in [his] last two appearances" continued to plague him and eventually stopped his advancement toward his goal of *mukti*, full enlightenment and union with God.

Seymour's failure as a God-seeker is chiefly due to his estrangement from common humanity, and this estrangement in turn is a result of the self-directed ways in which he pursued his spiritual development. Born a genius, Seymour made the quest for enlightenment the purpose of his life when he was still a child. At the age of seven he found that his precociousness as "poet and private scholar" and his "consuming admiration for God" had estranged him from normal people to such a degree that his interactions with them led to conflicts which brought out his negative tendencies, especially his malice. He therefore decided to pursue his spiritual quest along the self-directed paths of study and meditation and to avoid interaction with unspiritual people as much as possible.

By the time Seymour was in his early twenties, his contempt for unspiritual people had brought his spiritual progress to a halt, and he attempted to kill himself by slashing his wrists. But then he realized that he might be able to resume his spiritual advancement if he pursued his quest for God via a different path than the paths of study and meditation. He therefore embraced *karma yoga*, the path of action and service as taught by the *Bhagavad Gita*. At that time, he inscribed a key passage from the *Gita* as the top entry on a panel of quotations on the door of his and Buddy's room:

> You have the right to work, but for the work's sake only. You have no right to the fruits of work. Desire for the fruits of work must never be your motive in working. Never give way to laziness, either.
> Perform every action with your heart fixed on the Supreme Lord. Renounce attachment to the fruits. Be even-tempered in success and failure; for it is this evenness of temper which is meant by yoga.
> Work done with anxiety about results is far inferior to work done without such anxiety, in the calm of self-surrender. Seek refuge in the knowledge of Brahman. They who work selfishly for results are miserable. (Prabhavananda 40-41; "Zooey" 177)

The *karma yoga* concept expressed in this passage is the essence of Seymour's teachings and of the religious meaning in the Glass series. This concept consists of three related ideas which recur in the later Glass novellas. These three ideas are that our work becomes an act of worship and a means of spiritual advancement if we perform it for God or for others; if we perform it as best as we can; and, above all, if we perform it with detachment.

"Raise High the Roof Beam, Carpenters" and "Zooey" both illustrate the basic notion of service to others as a means of spiritual development. In "Carpenters," Seymour explains his hope that his marriage will help him resume his spiritual progress when he summarizes a miscellany of Vedanta: "Marriage partners are to serve each other. Elevate, help, teach, strengthen each other, but above all serve." And by serving each other, so Vedanta teaches, the marriage partners are serving God. The service ideal of *karma yoga* also comes out in "Zooey" when Zooey tells Franny she is so concerned with her own spiritual development that she is missing out on every single religious action going on around her. She doesn't even realize that the chicken soup that her mother offers her is "consecrated" chicken soup, that Bessie is in fact serving God by serving others. Zooey therefore tells Franny not to use the Jesus Prayer as a substitute for doing her duty in life, or just her daily duty, but to make her work on the stage her religion and become God's actress.

The second aspect of the *karma yoga* concept, the idea that our work becomes our means of spiritual advancement if we perform it to the best of our abilities, is expressed both in "Zooey" and in "Seymour—An Introduction." In the "Introduction," Seymour tells Buddy that writing is not really his profession but that it has never been anything but his religion. Therefore, Buddy's duty is to write his heart out whenever he is writing anything. Buddy passes this advice on to Zooey when he tells him that since Zooey has decided to become an actor, he should act with all his might. And Zooey, in turn, passes this idea along to Franny, telling her that if she wants to be God's actress, she should aim for perfection whenever she is on the stage.

The most important aspect of *karma yoga* and of Seymour's teachings is the idea of detachment. This idea is illustrated in all four later Glass novellas. In "Carpenters," the idea of detachment appears when Seymour summarizes the Vedanta view of marriage and says that marriage partners should raise their children lovingly but with detachment because a child is a guest in the house who should be loved and respected and never possessed since the child belongs to God. Zooey also stresses the importance of the concept of detachment when he tells Franny that the only thing that is really important in the religious life is detachment. And then he defines detachment in the same terms as the *Bhagavad Gita* as, "Desirelessness. Cessation from all hankerings!" The idea that detachment means desirelessness is also illustrated in Seymour's letter from Camp Hapworth when he writes that he would like to be able to miss his family without hoping that they miss him in return. He says: "I am utterly convinced that if A's hat blows off while he is sauntering down the street, it is the charming duty of B to pick it up and hand it to A without examining A's face or combing it for gratitude."

Perhaps the best illustration of the concept of detachment occurs in "Seymour—An Introduction" when Seymour gives Buddy advice on how to shoot marbles. He asks him: "Could you try not aiming so much?" And then he explains that if Buddy aims too much, that is, if he is more interested in winning marbles than making perfect shots, then it will be pure accident if he hits the other marble. But if he can overcome his hankering for winning, then his chances of making perfect shots are much greater.

Buddy later gives a further illustration of the concept of detachment when he compares Seymour's marble-shooting method with the fine art of pitching a cigarette butt into a waste basket way across the room. Buddy says that most people will only be able to hit the waste basket if they don't care whether the butt goes in the basket or if the room has been emptied of eyewitnesses, including the ego of the person who is trying to hit the basket with the cigarette butt. Thus the detachment that Seymour advocates is detachment from the tangible results of one's actions. Buddy drives this point home when he says that after Seymour heard his marble hit its target, he was never sure whether the winning click he heard was that of his own marble. In fact, someone always had to pick up the marble he'd won and hand it to him.

The essence of Seymour's teachings and of the religious meaning of the Glass Family Series is expressed when Seymour tells the seven-year-old Zooey to shine his shoes for the Fat Lady before he goes to perform on the radio quiz show "It's a Wise Child." This is a typical Salinger idea because it seems so illogical. To young Zooey it doesn't make sense to shine his shoes for a radio audience that can't see him. When Zooey reluctantly does what Seymour asks him to do, it is only because his eldest brother has "a very Seymour look" on his face. But 17 years later, when Zooey relates the anecdote to Franny, he understands that while Seymour's Fat Lady represents the less attractive members of the radio audience for whom he was performing on "It's a Wise Child," she also represents Christ Himself. This insight relates Seymour's teachings not only to the New Testament and to Christ's statement that what we do for the least of His brothers we do for Him; it also relates Seymour's teachings to the three key ideas in the excerpt from the *Bhagavad Gita* that Seymour posted on the door of his and Buddy's room. The Fat Lady parable as explained by Zooey tells us that we should worship God through unselfish service to others, that we should perform our everyday work with all our might—even down to shining our shoes for people that can't see them—and that we should perform that work with detachment, that is, for the sake of doing it as well as we can and not for the sake of any rewards.

WORKS CITED

Bryan, James. "Salinger and His Short Fiction." Diss. U of Virginia: Charlottesville, 1968.

Fosburgh, Lacey. "J.D. Salinger Speaks About His Silence." *New York Times* (3 November 1974): 1, 69.13

Prabhavananda, Swami, and Christopher Isherwood, trans. *The Song of God: Bhagavad Gita* [1944]. New York: Signet, 1972.

Salinger, J.D. *Franny and Zooey* [1961]. New York: Bantam, 1964.

___ . "Hapworth 16, 1924." *New Yorker* (19 June 1965): 32-113.

___ . *Raise High the Roof Beam, Carpenters and Seymour—An Introduction* [1963]. New York: Bantam, 1965.

Salinger, Margaret. *Dream Catcher*. New York: Washington Square, 2000.

Skow, John. "Sonny: An Introduction." *Time* (15 September 1961): 84-90. Rpt. in *Salinger: A Critical and Personal Portrait.* Ed. Henry A. Grunwald. New York: Harper, 1962, 3-18.

SUGGESTIONS FOR FURTHER READING

Bufithis, Philip H. "Salinger and the Psychiatrist." *West Virginia University Philological Papers* 21 (December 1974): 67-77.

Cotter, James F. "Religious Symbols in Salinger's Shorter Fiction." *Studies in Short Fiction* 15 (1978): 121-132.

Glazier, Lyle. "The Glass Family Saga: Argument and Epiphany." *College English* 27 (1965): 248-251.

Hamilton, Kenneth. "The Interplay of Life and Art." In *J.D. Salinger: A Critical Essay.* Grand Rapids, MI: Eerdmans, 1967, 11-21.

Hinkle, Warren. "J. D. Salinger's Glass Menagerie." *Ramparts* 1 (1962): 4-51.

Nikhilananda, Swami. *Hinduism: Its Meaning for the Liberation of the Spirit* [1958]. New York: Ramakrishna-Vivekananda Center, 1992.

O'Connor, Dennis L. "J.D. Salinger: Writing as Religion." *Wilson Quarterly* 4 (Spring 1980): 182-190.

Seed, David. "Keeping it in the Family: The Novellas of J.D. Salinger." In *The Modern American Novella.* Ed. A. Robert Lee. New York: St. Martin's, 1989, 139-161.

Slethaugh, Gordon E. "Form in Salinger's Shorter Fiction." *Canadian Review of American Studies* 3 (1972): 50-59.
Vivekananda, Swami. *Karma Yoga and Bhakti Yoga.* New York: Ramakrishna-Vivekananda Center, 1955.

Conclusion

The Persistence of Salinger's Reputation

Publishing is an invasion of my privacy.

J.D. Salinger

Although Salinger stopped publishing in 1965, *The Catcher in the Rye* continues to sell 250,000 copies a year world-wide; his work continues to be studied in high schools, colleges, and universities; and his private life continues to be scrutinized in newspapers and popular magazines. The persistence of Salinger's reputation is astonishing in view of his small output, all published between 1940 and 1965: one novel, three volumes of short fiction, and 21 uncollected magazine stories. It is especially astonishing when we consider that critical opinion began to turn against Salinger in the late fifties and that the reviews of his narrative series about the Glass family became more negative with each installment.

Salinger's popularity peaked in 1961. That year his face appeared on the cover of *Time* magazine, and the critic Alfred Kazin dubbed him "Everybody's Favorite" (43). During the following two years, five books and over 100 articles were published about Salinger, the largest number in any two-year period of Salinger's career. However by 1962—the year after *Franny and Zooey* was published—quite a bit of the criticism had turned negative.

In terms of Salinger's relationship with the critics, his halcyon days were between the publication of *Nine Stories* in 1953 and the publication of "Zooey" in 1957. In fact, the early reception of Salinger's work was so enthusiastic that in 1959 George Steiner complained about the "Salinger Industry" whose chief aim it supposedly was to over-praise its author. To make his point, Steiner quoted from articles that compared Salinger's *The Catcher in the Rye* to such masterworks of world literature as Homer's *Odyssey*, Virgil's *Aeneid*, Mark Twain's *The Adventures of Huckleberry Finn*, Scott Fitzgerald's *The Great Gatsby*, and James Joyce's *Ulysses*. Salinger should not be treated as if he were one of the great writers of world literature, so Steiner argued, just because he is "a gifted and entertaining writer with one excellent short novel and a number of memorable stories to his credit" (361).

Aside from the somewhat too enthusiastic early criticism, it was the religious themes of the Glass Family Series that alienated the big-name critics. For instance, Maxwell Geismar judged "Zooey" to be "an appallingly bad story" which epitomizes everything that is wrong with Salinger, "the narrow range of his literary orbit, its uneasy base, its superstructure of sham." Geismar didn't even like *The Catcher in the Rye* because he saw its main concerns as "the revolt of the rich child, the conspicuous display of leisure-class emotions, the wounded affections never quite faced, of the upper-class orphan" (199). The only Salinger story that Geismar liked was "A Perfect Day for Bananafish" because in that story "Salinger's philosophical and mystic preoccupations had not yet gotten the better of him" (201). Like Geismar, Alfred Kazin also deplored Salinger's preoccupation with things metaphysical. He assessed Salinger as a writer who is "competent and interesting" but who "lacks strength" because "he identifies himself too fussily with the spiritual aches and pains of his characters." Salinger therefore lost sight of "the drama of our social existence" (130).

Not all critics deplored the religious direction in which Salinger's fiction had begun to go after *The Catcher in the Rye*. Among the well-known critics, Ihab Hassan, Granville Hicks, and Arthur Mizener remained sympathetic and resolutely judged Salinger's work on its own terms. And younger scholars such as Bernice and Sanford Goldstein, Dennis O'Connor, Eberhard Alsen, and James Lundquist wrote articles and books analyzing the role of the Zen Buddhist, Taoist, and Vedanta ideas mentioned in the Glass Family Series.

While the majority of critics who have written about Salinger have approached his work with the respect and thoughtfulness that a major writer deserves, there have been others who have argued that much of Salinger's fame is due to his having become a media figure who is best known for not publishing and for not wanting any publicity. These conflicting views of Salinger become apparent when we look at the many reassessments of Salinger's work that have been published ever since he let it be known that he continues to write but doesn't plan to publish any more during his lifetime.

Two representative reappraisals are those of Bruce Bawer and Janet Malcolm. In a 1986 *New Criterion* article entitled "Salinger's Arrested Development," Bawer claims that Salinger's "love of privacy has, in the years since his departure from the literary scene, made him a 'legend' in a way that his work alone could never have done" (34). Bawer admits that *The Catcher in the Rye* is "one of the few small classics of postwar American fiction," but he doesn't like *Nine Stories* because of their protagonists' negative attitudes toward everyone except an innocent child or two, and he likes the Glass stories even less because of their "blithe equation of religion and misanthropy" (45). Bawer sums up his negative assessment of Salinger's work when he says that "the bulk of Salinger's fiction is seriously weakened by the fact that he is congenitally less interested in getting to the bottom of his characters' emotionally retarded behavior than he is in celebrating it" (47). Bawer then indulges in an *ad hominem* argument when he accuses Salinger of snobbery and of contempt for his audience.

He says that "it is dismaying, but should not be surprising, that so contemptuous a man, however considerable his talent, was unable to produce a more consequential body of work than that which he has bequeathed us." Bawer concludes by acknowledging "the immense esteem in which Salinger is held by
literate Americans," but he says that this esteem stands in "disproportion to the
actual level of his literary achievement." He then explains away Salinger's continued literary reputation by blaming it on "the current literary climate, in which
cultish devotions and sentimental attachments often count as strongly as sensi-
ble critical evaluation" (47).

A more recent and more positive reassessment of Salinger's stature as a writer
is that of Janet Malcolm in a 2001 issue of the *New York Review of Books*. It
is entitled "Justice for J.D. Salinger." Malcolm begins by reviewing the decline
of Salinger's reputation with the literary establishment. She points out that by
the late fifties, "Salinger was no longer the universally beloved author *of The
Catcher in the Rye*; he was now the seriously annoying creator of the Glass family" (16). Malcolm then comments on the negative reviews of Salinger's Glass
stories by critic Alfred Kazin and fellow novelists Mary McCarthy, Joan Did-
ion, and John Updike. The "mistakes" and "excesses" that these reviewers deplored in Salinger's work are "often precisely the innovations that give the work
its power." Malcolm adds that what all of Salinger's detractors have in common is "their extraordinary rage against the Glasses" and that she can't think of
another case "where literary characters have aroused so much animosity" (16).

Malcolm sees as the most important innovation in Salinger's work his characterization of the extraordinary Glass siblings, Seymour, Buddy, Zooey, and
Franny because they are as different from normal mortals as the giant bug that
Gregor Samsa is transformed into in Franz Kafka's story "The Metamorphosis."
Because the Glasses are so unique in mid-century America, their stories are all
what Malcolm calls "fables of otherness" (16). Among the Glass stories, the
paradigmatic one is "A Perfect Day for Bananafish" because it is "a kind of
miniature and somewhat oversharp version of the allegory that the [later] Glass
family stories would enact" (16). Like "Bananafish," all the later Glass stories
communicate "the view of the world as a battle ground between the normal and
the abnormal, the ordinary and the extraordinary, the talentless and the gifted,
the well and the sick" (18).

Malcolm singles out the novella "Zooey" (1957) as being "arguably Salinger's masterpiece." She notes that contemporary critics complained that it was
too long and too dated, but she finds that "rereading it and its companion piece
'Franny' is no less rewarding than rereading *The Great Gatsby*." Like *Gatsby,*
so Malcolm says, "Zooey" is a work of fiction that "remains brilliant and is in
no essential sense dated. It is the contemporary criticism that is dated" (16).

Because Salinger deliberately kept his output small, literary histories have
not accorded him the significance as a writer that his admirers think he deserves.
If we go back to the time when Salinger's fame had just peaked and consult the
1963 edition of *The Literary History of the United States* by Spiller, Thorp,
and Johnson, we will find that it devotes only one paragraph to Salinger, albeit
a paragraph of praise. Ihab Hassan, the author of the chapter entitled "Since
1945," calls *The Catcher in the Rye* "the testament of the postwar generation"
and recognizes Salinger as "a virtuoso of the short story." What's more, he sees

value in "the myth of the Glass family" because, by that myth, "the actualities of America life may be gauged, criticized, and upheld." Hassan arrives at this conclusion about Salinger: "The essential quality of his work was sentiment and irony rooted in a quixotic gesture of the spirit which reaches to mystical love but falls back again to redeem with humor the vulgarity of life below" (1425).

Over a decade later, in the 1979 *Harvard Guide to Contemporary American Writing*, Salinger occupies twice as much space as in the 1963 *Literary History*, but the treatment he receives is far less complimentary. Leo Braudy, the author of the chapter on "Realists, Naturalists, and Novelists of Manners," calls Salinger "as much a cult figure as a literary one" and he says that Salinger is "feted as a master by critics and cultists alike." It is Braudy's opinion that "Salinger was the perfect *New Yorker* writer" because he created "a hovering effect that promised more in atmosphere than it delivered in substance." Another problem with Salinger is that his work "grew increasingly gnomic and involved with wisdom literature." Braudy sums up his judgment by saying that Salinger's fiction is "a tantalizing literature of psychologic nuance and moral suggestion rather than an aggressively clarifying literature of plot, observation, and moral analysis" (144-145).

Yet another decade later, Salinger is dismissed with a sentence here and there in Emory Elliott's *Columbia Literary History of the United States* (1988). However, he is accorded a whole paragraph in Elliott's *Columbia History of the American Novel* (1991). The author of the chapter on "Society and Identity," David Van Leer, totally ignores the Hindu-Buddhist ideas in Salinger's fiction and treats Salinger as "most representative" of what he calls "popularized existentialism." Van Leer concedes that in *The Catcher in the Rye* "Salinger captured the voice of adolescent anxiety," and he admits that Holden Caulfield "came to symbolize the disorientation of a generation searching for authenticity in a culture deemed (by Holden's dismissive reckoning) 'phony'." Van Leer sums up his negative estimation of Salinger's importance as a writer by saying that the suicide of Seymour Glass and Salinger's refusal to publish after 1965 suggest that "the elevation of the individual over society did not lead to a constructive program for growth or change" (492).

Salinger fared much better in the more recent *Cambridge History of American Literature* (1999). The discussion of Salinger's work takes up over two pages—more than in any previous literary history—but the judgment of Salinger's accomplishment is based chiefly on *The Catcher in the Rye*. The author, Morris Dickstein, calls Salinger "a wicked satirist with a cool eye and perfect ear," and he says that Salinger "lampoons the vulgarity and duplicity of adults while endowing his powerless young with amazing verbal virtuosity" (172). On the one hand, Dickstein says that *The Catcher in the Rye* isn't as original as it may seem because it "brings together three of the main tropes of the fifties counterculture" which appeared in any number of novels, namely "the youthful misfit, the road, and mental illness as a form of social maladjustment and intuitive wisdom." On the other hand, Dickstein admits that "only Salinger successfully captured the exact accent and rhythm of the adolescent voice and sensibility; only in his work did the young recognize themselves as they were or as they dreamed of being" (172-173).

Dickstein is aware that in his later work "Salinger's theme is spiritual," and he tries to make a connection between his view of Salinger as a writer for the young and the Glass Family Series. He says: "His young people and his sainted dead (especially Seymour Glass) are eternal innocents who cannot adjust to society or accept its compromises" (173). However, Dickstein thinks that the Glass series is ill-conceived because "such fiction can turn precious and narcissistic, reposing on a sentimental vision of the elect, but with little sense of the society that frustrates their needs." He considers *The Catcher in the Rye* a more successful work of art than any of Salinger's later fiction because when he wrote *Catcher,* "Salinger still had his ear tuned to wider frequencies." Dickstein's opinion of the Glass series, therefore, is that "Salinger's later work needs more Muriel and less Sybil, more of the world's variety and less obsession with saintliness" (173).

As we can see from the treatment that Salinger has received in the literary histories of the last 40 years, his reputation has fluctuated but not diminished. It is a small reputation because Salinger chose to stop publishing in mid-career. But he has continued to write for over three decades, and his daughter Margaret reported in a radio interview that he has prepared a number of manuscripts for posthumous publication ("Margaret Salinger on J.D. Salinger"). It is therefore too early to make any conclusive statements about Salinger's place in American literature.

If Salinger were to change his mind and burn everything he has written since 1965—after all, his alter ego Buddy Glass says that he has "histrionically burned at least a dozen stories"—we would still be left with a small but exquisite body of work. Salinger's place in American literature would then be pretty much as John Skow defined it in his 1961 *Time* magazine feature story:

If he were to stop writing now, *The Catcher in the Rye* would be judged a small masterpiece—say about the size of [Stephen Crane's] *The Red Badge of Courage*—the *Nine Stories* a collection unmatched since Hemingway's *In Our Time,* and *Franny and Zooey* a glowing minor work. (18)

But Salinger has not stopped writing. And who knows, maybe the best is yet to come.

WORKS CITED

Bawer, Bruce. "Salinger's Arrested Development." *New Criterion* 5 (September 1986): 34-47.

Braudy, Leo. "Realists, Naturalists, Novelists of Manners." In *Harvard Guide to Contemporary American Writing.* Ed. Daniel Hoffman. Cambridge, MA: Belknap, 1979, 84-152.

Dickstein, Morris. "On and Off the Road: The Outsider as Young Rebel." *The Cambridge History of American Literature.* Volume 7. *Prose Writing 1940-1990.* Ed. Sacvan Bercovitch. Cambridge, England, and New York: Cambridge UP, 1999, 165-223.

Elliott, Emory, ed. *The Columbia Literary History of the United States.* New York: Columbia UP, 1988.

Geismar, Maxwell. "The Wise Child and the New Yorker School of Fiction." In

American Moderns: From Rebellion to Conformity. New York: Hill and
    Wang, 1958, 195-209. Rpt. in Grunwald 87-101.
Grunwald, Henry A., ed. *Salinger: A Critical and Personal Portrait.* New York:
    Harper, 1962.
Hassan, Ihab. "Since 1945." In *Literary History of the United States.* Ed. Robert
    Spiller et al. New York: Macmillan, 1963, 1412-1441.
Kazin, Alfred. "The Alone Generation: A Comment on the Fiction of the Fifties."
    Harper's Magazine 209 (October 1959): 127-131.
___ . "J.D. Salinger: Everybody's Favorite." *Atlantic Monthly* 208 (August 1961):
    27-31. Rpt. in Grunwald 43-52.
Malcolm, Janet. "Justice to J.D. Salinger." *New York Review of Books* (21 June
    2001): 16-22.
"Margaret Salinger on J.D. Salinger." *The Connection.* National Public Radio.
    WBUR Boston. 14 September 2000. <http://the connection.org archive/
    2000/09/9914b.shtml>
Skow, John. "Sonny: An Introduction." *Time* (15 Sept. 1961): 84-90. Rpt. in Grun-
    wald 3-18.
Steiner, George. "The Salinger Industry." *Nation* 189 (14 November 1959): 360-363.
    Rpt. in Grunwald 82-85.
Van Leer, David. "Society and Identity." In *The Columbia History of the American
    Novel.* Ed. Elliott Emory. New York: Columbia UP, 1991, 485-509.

SUGGESTIONS FOR FURTHER READING

Bloom, Harold. "Introduction." In *Modern Critical Views: J.D. Salinger.* New York:
    Chelsea House, 1987, 1-4.
Blotner, Joseph. "Salinger Now: An Appraisal." *Wisconsin Studies in Contempo-
    rary Literature* 4 (Winter 1963): 100-108.
Coles, Robert. "Reconsideration: J.D. Salinger." *New Republic* (28 April 1978): 30-
    32.
Costello, Donald P. "Autopsy of a Faded Romance: Salinger and His Critics." *Com-
    monweal* (25 October 1963): 132-135.
Gardner, James. "J.D. Salinger, Fashion Victim." *National Review* (7 April 1997):
    51-52.
Lodge, David. "Family Romances." [London] *Times Literary Supplement* (13 June
    1975): 642.
Romano, John. "Salinger Was Playing Our Song." *New York Times Book Review* (3
    June 1979): 11, 48.
Teachout, Terry. "Salinger Then and Now." *Commentary* 84 (September 1987): 61-
    64.

Epilogue

Salinger's Non-Sequiturs

In the prologue, I said that my purpose in this book is to guide the reader toward an understanding of the vision of life in Salinger's fiction. I also said that we get an indication of that vision of life in Salinger's many non-sequiturs. That is why I begin each chapter in the book with one of those seemingly nonsensical statements.

The Latin phrase *non sequitur* means "it doesn't follow." A statement is called a non-sequitur either if it violates the logic of cause and effect (he threw the stone at her because she was so beautiful), or if it equates two things that are not equal (he competently blundered), or if it is an illogical follow-up to another statement (You're not kind at all, Zooey—I wish you'd get married).

Salinger's fondness for non-sequiturs explains why he likes Zen koans and Taoist sayings. They also are statements that are seemingly nonsensical. In "Raise High the Roof Beam, Carpenters," Seymour Glass tells the story of a Zen master who was asked what the most valuable thing in the world was, and the master answered that "a dead cat was because no one could put a price on it." And in "Seymour—An Introduction," Salinger quotes the following saying by Chuang-tse: "The sage is full of anxiety and indecision in undertaking anything, and so he is always successful."

Even more to the point, Salinger apparently felt drawn to Advaita Vedanta Hinduism because it is a belief system which requires that a person gives up Western-style logic. In the story "Teddy," Teddy McArdle explains it this way:

You know that apple that Adam ate in the Garden of Eden, referred to in the Bible? ... You know what was in that apple? Logic. Logic and intellectual stuff. That was all that was in it. So—this is my point—what you have to do is vomit it up if you want to see things as they really are.

Some readers can achieve this open state of mind without help because they can intuitively grasp the meaning of Salinger's non-sequiturs and the essence of his vision of life. Others may have to do some reading in the Buddhist, Taoist, and Vedanta texts that Salinger mentions in his fiction.

Appendix I

Index of Salinger's Fictional Characters

THE UNCOLLECTED STORIES 1940-1948

Aigletinger, Miss — Corinne von Nordhoffen's elementary school teacher in "The Inverted Forest."

Barbara — Eighteen-year-old central character in "A Young Girl in 1941 with No Waist at All."

Burke, Sergeant — Title character of "Soft-Boiled Sergeant."

Burke, Slicer — Prison inmate in "The Heart of a Broken Story."

Burns, Philly — Narrator of "Soft-Boiled Sergeant."

Camson, Dickie — Central character in "Once a Week Won't Kill You."

Camson, Rena — Aunt of the central charcater in "Once a Week Won't Kill You."

Camson, Virginia — Wife of the central character in "Once a Week Won't Kill You."

Carpenter, Hanson — Married man with whom Helen Mason starts an affair in "Go See Eddie."

Caulfield, Holden — Central character in "I'm Crazy" and "Slight Rebellion Off Madison." In "Slight Rebellion," his middle name is

"Morrisey." Mentioned as missing in action and presumed dead in "Last Day of the Last Furlough" and "This Sandwich Has No Mayonnaise."

Caulfield, Kenneth — Vincent Caulfield's younger brother who died in childhood. Mentioned in "The Stranger."

Caulfield, Vincent — Holden Caulfield's twenty-nine-year-old brother and central character in "This Sandwich Has No Mayonnaise." Minor character in "Last Day of the Last Furlough" and "The Stranger."

Caulfield, Viola — Holden Caulfield's baby sister in "I'm Crazy."

Cooney, Elaine — Sixteen-year-old central character in "Elaine."

Cooney, Evelyn — The central character's mother in "Elaine."

Croft, Bunny — Mary, née Gates. Thirty-one-year-old admirer of Raymond Ford who runs off with him in "The Inverted Forest."

Croft, Howie — Bunny Croft's husband in "The Inverted Forest."

Curfman, Carl — Second husband of Lois Taggett in "The Long Debut of Lois Taggett."

Delroy, Jack — The most popular young man at the party in "The Young Folks."

Elmendorf, Miss — Elaine's middle school teacher in "Elaine."

Elsie — Helen Mason's maid in "Go See Eddie."

Ferrero, Ratface — Prison inmate in "The Heart of a Broken Story."

Ford, Raymond — Poet and English instructor at Columbia University. One of the two central characters in "The Inverted Forest."

Frances — Girl whom Babe Gallagher loves in "Last Day of the Last Furlough." Also mentioned in "A Boy in France."

Gladwaller, Jack — Biology professor. Father of Babe Gallagher in "Last Day of the Last Furlough."

Gladwaller, Babe — John F. Twenty-four-year-old central character in "Last Day of the Last

	Pearl Harbor in "Personal Notes of an Infantryman."
Leah	Jewish girl in Vienna that John, the young American, falls in love with in "A Girl I Knew."
Leggett, Doris	The prettiest girl at the party in "The Young Folks."
Lester, Shirley	The girl after whom Justin Horgen-schlag pines in "The Heart of a Broken Story."
Lisbeth-Sue	The prison warden's eight-year-old daughter in "The Heart of a Broken Story."
Luce, Carl	A schoolmate of Holden's from Pencey Prep in "Slight Rebellion Off Mad-ison."
Mason, Bob	The brother of the central character in "Go See Eddie."
Mason, Helen	The adulterous actress who is the central character in "Go See Eddie."
Miller, Mr.	Baron Von Nordhoffen's secretary in "The Inverted Forest."
Monahan, Monny	Frank Vitrelli's girlfriend in "Elaine."
Moore, Peggy	Rudford's elementary school friend in "Blue Melody."
Odenhearn, Mrs.	Barbara's mother-in-law to be in "A Young Girl in 1941 with No Waist at All."
Pettit, Harry	Army recruit in "The Hang of It."
Pettit, Bobby	Colonel in the Army and narrator in "The Hang Of It."
Phillips, Edna	Central character in "The Young Folks."
Polk, Helen	Née Beebers. Vincent Caulfield's former girlfriend in "TheStranger."
Rizzio, Mrs.	The woman who gets Raymond Ford interested in poetry. In "The Inverted Forest."
Rocco	Hit man who kills Joe Varioni in "The Varioni Brothers."
Rudford	Nine-year-old central character in "Blue Melody."
Schmidt, Teddy	He marries Elaine Cooney in "Elaine."
Smith, Sarah	Née Daley. Admirer of the college instructor, song lyricist, and would-be

	novelist Joe Varioni in "The Varioni Brothers."
Spencer, Mr.	Holden Caulfield's history teacher in "I'm Crazy."
Stone, Phil	Married man with whom Helen has an affair in "Go See Eddie."
Taggett, Lois	Central character in "The Long Debut of Lois Taggett."
Tedderton, Bill	The first husband of Lois Taggett in "The Long Debut of Lois Taggett."
Varioni, Joe	English instructor at Waycross College. Writer of song lyrics and frustrated novelist. One of the two central characters in "The Varioni Brothers." Also mentioned in "Blue Melody."
Varioni, Sonny	Composer of popular songs and one of the two central characters in "The Varioni Brothers." Also mentioned in "Blue Melody."
Vitrelli, Frank	Minor character in "Elaine."
Von Nordhoffen, Corinne	One of the two central characters in "The Inverted Forest."
Von Nordhoffen, Otho	Baron. Corinne's millionaire father in "The Inverted Forest."
Vorhees, Professor	English professor at Waycross College in Wisconsin. Admirer of Joe Varioni in "The Varioni Brothers."
Vullmer, Billy	Nineteen-year-old husband and father in "Both Parties Concerned."
Vullmer, Ruthie	Née Cropper. Billy Vullmer's seventeen-year-old wife in "Both Parties Concerned."
Waner, Robert	Friend of Connie von Nordhoffen's and one of the narrators in "The Inverted Forest."
Warbach, Mrs.	Mother of Andrew Warbach, a student at Pentey [sic] Prep in "I'm Crazy." Holden tells her that Andrew is very popular.
Widger, Mrs.	The Vullmers' baby-sitter in "Both Parties Concerned."
Woodruff, Diane and Fielding.	Elderly couple on board the cruise ship in "A Young Girl in 1941 with No Waist at All."

THE CATCHER IN THE RYE

Ackley, Robert	Holden Caulfield's dorm neighbor at Pencey Prep.
Aigletinger, Miss	Holden Caulfield's elementary school teacher.
Antolini, Mr.	Holden's former English teacher at Elkton Hills. He now teaches at New York University.
Atterbury, Selma	Classmate of Phoebe Caulfield.
Banky, Ed	Basketball coach at Pencey Prep.
Bernice Crabs or Krebs	Girl from Seattle that Holden dances with in the Lavender Room of the Edmont Hotel.
Birdsell, Eddie	Princeton student who gave Holden the address of a stripper.
Brossard, Mel	Wrestler and dorm mate of Holden's at Pencey Prep.
Castle, James	Student at Elkton Hills who committed suicide by jumping out of a second floor window.
Caulfield, Allie	Holden's younger brother who died of leukemia in 1947.
Caulfield, D.B.	Holden's older brother. He is a fiction writer who works in Hollywood.
Caulfield, Phoebe Josephine	Holden's ten-year-old sister.
Campbell, Paul	One of the few classmates at Pencey Prep whom Holden liked.
Cavendish, Faith	Stripper that Holden can't get a date with.
Charlene	The Caulfields' live-in maid.
Childs, Arthur	Quaker classmate of Holden's at Whooton.
Coyle, Howie	Basketball player at Pencey Prep.
Cudahy, Mr.	Jane Gallagher's alcoholic stepfather.
Cultz, Jeanette	Friend of Sally Hayes.
The Dicksteins	The Caulfields' same-floor neighbors in New York.
Ernie	Black pianist in a New York jazz club.
Fallon, Bobby	Maine friend of Holden and Allie.
Fencer, Harry	President of Holden's class at Pencey Prep.
Fletcher, Estelle	Black jazz singer whose record Holden buys for Phoebe.

Gale, Herb — Robert Ackley's roommate at Pencey Prep.

Gallagher, Jane — Friend of Holden's who keeps her kings in the back row when playing checkers.

Goldfarb, Raymond — Scotch-drinking student at the Whooton School.

Haas, Mr. — Headmaster at Elkton Hills Prep School.

Hartzell, Mr. — Stradlater's English teacher at Pencey Prep.

Hayes, Sally — "The queen of the phonies." Holden's girlfriend.

Hoffman — One of Holden's dorm neighbors at Pencey Prep.

Holmborg, Alice — Classmate of Phoebe Caulfield.

Horwitz — Cab driver that Holden asks about the ducks in Central Park.

Kinsella, Richard — Pencey Prep student who always digressed in his speeches during Oral Expression.

Laverne — Girl from Seattle that Holden dances with in the Lavender Room of the Edmont Hotel.

Leahy — Dorm neighbor at Pencey Prep.

Levine, Gertrude — Classmate of Holden in grade school.

Luce, Carl — Classmate of Holden at the Whooton School.

Macklin, Harris — Elkton Hills roommate of Holden's who was a great whistler.

Margulies, Phyllis — Classmate who gives Phoebe Caulfield belching lessons.

Marsala, Edgar — Flatulent classmate of Holden's at Pencey Prep.

Marty — Girl from Seattle that Holden dances with in the Lavender Room of the Edmont Hotel.

Maurice — Pimp and elevator operator at the Edmont Hotel.

Morrow, Mrs. — Mother of the Pencey Prep student, Ernest Morrow. Holden lies and tells her that Ernie is very popular.

Ossenburger, Mr. — Wealthy undertaker and Pencey Prep alumnus.

Pete	Night elevator boy in the apartment building where Holden's parents live.
Pike, Al	Choate student that Jane Gallagher dated.
Robinson, Bob	Pencey Prep student who has an inferiority complex.
Singer, Buddy	Band leader whose band plays in the Lavender Room of the Edmont Hotel.
Schmidt, Rudolf	Janitor at Pencey Prep.
Shaney, Louis	Catholic classmate of Holden's at Whooton.
Sherman, Anne Louise	Girl that Holden necked with.
Simmons, Lillian	Former girlfriend of D.B., Holden's brother.
Slagle, Dick	Holden's roommate at Elkton Hills. He had cheap suitcases.
Smith, Phyllis	Former date of Stradlater's.
Spencer, Mr.	History teacher at Pencey Prep.
Stabile, Phil	The Elkton Hills student who drove James Castle to suicide.
Steele, Jim	False name that Holden gives to the three girls from Seattle and to the prostitute, Sunny.
Stradlater, Ward	Holden Caulfield's roommate at Pencey Prep.
Sunny	Sixteen-year-old prostitute who works in the Edmont Hotel.
Thaw, Bud	Student at Pencey Prep.
Thurmer, Mr.	The headmaster at Pencey Prep.
Thurmer, Selma	Daughter of the Pencey Prep headmaster.
Tichener, Robert	Pencey Prep classmate whom Holden liked.
Valencia	Lounge singer at the Wicker Bar.
Vinson, Mr.	Holden's Oral Expression teacher at Pencey Prep.
Walsh, Roberta	Girl that Holden once dated.
Weintraub, Curtis	Classmate of Phoebe Caulfield.
Woodruff, Frederick	Pencey Prep student who buys Holden's typewriter.
Zambesi, Mr.	Holden's biology teacher at Pencey Prep.

NINE STORIES

Agadganian, Robert	The central character's stepfather in "Daumier-Smith."
Arthur	Young lawyer, husband of Joanie in "Pretty Mouth."
Booper	The central character's six-year-old sister in "Teddy."
Carpenter, Sybil	Three-year-old friend of Seymour Glass in "Bananafish."
Charles	Esmé's five-year-old brother in "For Esmé."
Clay, Corporal	Sergeant X's jeep driver in "For Esmé."
De Daumier-Smith, Jean	His real name is probably John Smith. Nineteen-year-old painter and central character in "Daumier-Smith."
Eric	Franklin Graff's homosexual friend in "Just Before the War."
Esmé	Thirteen-year-old British girl in "For Esmé."
Gedsudski, John	Central character in "Laughing Man."
Glass, Muriel	Wife of the central character in "Bananafish."
Glass, Seymour	Central character in "Bananafish." Also mentioned in "Down at the Dinghy."
Glass, Webb	One of Boo Boo Tannenbaum's brothers in "Down at the Dinghy." He is probably Buddy Glass.
Grace	Black live-in maid of the Wengler's in "Uncle Wiggily."
Graff, Franklin	The young man of twenty-four that fifteen-year-old Ginnie Mannox has a crush on in "Just before the War."
Graff, Selena	Ginnie's tennis partner in "Just Before the War."
Hudson, Mary	John Gedsudski's girlfriend in "The Laughing Man."
Jimmereeno, Jimmy	One of Ramona Wengler's imaginary friends. He's the one who gets "runned over" in "Uncle Wiggily."
Joanie	Arthur's wife with whom Lee is having an affair in "Pretty Mouth."

Lee	Gray-haired lawyer. Central character in "Pretty Mouth."
Lipschutz, Sharon	Rival of Sybil Carpenter in "Bananafish."
Loretta	Corporal Clay's girlfriend in "For Esmé."
Mannox, Ginnie	Virginia. Central character in "Just Before the War."
Mannox, Joan	Ginnie's sister in "Just Before the War."
McArdle, Teddy	Ten-year-old central character in "Teddy."
Megley, Miss	Esmé and Charles' governess in "For Esmé."
Mary Jane	Eloise's former college roommate in "Uncle Wiggily."
Mickeranno, Mickey	One of Ramona Wengler's imaginary friends in "Uncle Wiggily."
Nicholson, Bob	Education professor in "Teddy."
Sandra	The Tannenbaum's maid in "Down at the Dinghy."
Sister Irma	A nun who takes art lessons from the central character in "Daumier-Smith."
Sivetski, Dr.	Muriel's mother's psychiatrist in "Bananafish."
Snell, Mrs.	The Tannenbaum's kitchen help in "Down at the Dinghy."
Tannenbaum, Boo Boo	Beatrice, née Glass. Twenty-five-year-old central character in "Down at the Dinghy."
Tannenbaum, Lionel	Boo Boo's four-year-old son in "Down at the Dinghy."
Walt	Eloise's former lover in "Uncle Wiggily." He got killed in an accident at the end of World War II. Mentioned as a Glass sibling in "Carpenters," "Zooey" and the "Introduction."
Wengler, Eloise	Central character in "Uncle Wiggily."
Wengler, Lew	Eloise's husband in "Uncle Wiggily."
Wengler, Ramona	Eloise's four-year-old daughter in "Uncle Wiggily."
X, Mrs.	Girlfriend of the central character's stepfather in "Daumier-Smith."
X, Sergeant	Central character in "For Esmé."

| The Yashotos | Couple who run the correspondence art school in "Daumier-Smith." |

THE GLASS FAMILY SERIES

Bloomberg	The Glass's cat in "Zooey."
Burwick, Bob	Lieutenant. The husband of the Matron of Honor in "Carpenters."
Burwick, Edie	Muriel's Matron of Honor in "Carpenters."
Campbell, Wally	Friend of Lane Coutell in "Franny."
Caulfield, Curtis	School friend of Seymour and Buddy in the "Introduction."
Coutell, Lane	Franny's boyfriend in "Franny."
Culgerry, Miss	Nurse in "Hapworth 16, 1924."
Deaf-mute old man	Muriel's un-named great-uncle in "Carpenters."
Fedder, Rhea	Muriel's mother in "Bananafish": and "Carpenters."
Fraser, Mr.	Miss Overmans boss at the public library in "Hapworth."
Glass, Bessie	Née Gallagher. Former vaudeville performer. Mother of the seven Glass siblings. She appears in "Zooey" and is mentioned in the "Introduction" and "Hapworth."
Glass, Boo Boo	Beatrice. Third oldest of the Glass siblings in "Carpenters."
Glass, Buddy	Webb Gallagher (?). Second oldest Glass sibling. Co-protagonist with Seymour in "Carpenters" and the "Introduction." Narrator of "Zooey." Transcriber of "Hapworth."
Glass, Franny	Frances. The youngest of the Glass siblings. Central character in "Franny," co-protagonist in "Zooey."
Glass, Les	Former vaudeville performer, now a talent scout in Hollywood. Father of the seven Glass siblings. He appears the "Introduction," and is mentioned in "Zooey" and "Hapworth."
Glass, Muriel	Née Fedder. Seymour's wife. She appears in "Bananafish" and "Carpen-

ters, and is mentioned in "Zooey" and the "Introduction."

Glass, Walter F. The older of the Glass twins (by 12 minutes). He died in a freak accident at the end of WW II. He is mentioned in "Carpenters," "Zooey," and the "Intro-duction."

Glass, Waker The younger of the Glass twins. He gives away his new Davega bicycle in the "Introduction." Later he becomes a Roman catholic priest. Mentioned in "Carpenters," "Zooey," the "Intro-duction," and "Hapworth."

Glass, Zooey Zachary. Second youngest Glass sibling. One of the two central characters in "Zooey."

Hess, Dick Writer of TV scripts in "Zooey."

Hammersmith, Griffith Seymour and Buddy's bed-wetting fellow camper in "Hapworth."

Happy, Mr. and Mrs. Camp director and wife in "Hapworth."

Kolb, John Fellow camper of Seymour and Buddy in "Hapworth."

LeSage. Mr. Zooey's boss at the TV studio in "Zooey."

Mayhew, Charlotte She needed nine stitches in her face after the ten-year-old Seymour hit her with a stone in "Carpernters" Also mentioned as "Charlotte the Harlot" in the "Introduction."

Nelson, Mr. & Mrs. The loutish cooks in "Hapworth."

Pittman, Roger Nicknamed "Whitey." Counselor in "Hapworth."

Overman, Miss Librarian mentioned in the "Intro-duction" and "Hapworth."

Silsburn, Mrs. Muriel Fedder's fifty-year-old aunt in "Carpenters."

Sims, Dr. Mrs. Fedder's psychiatrist in "Car-penters."

Tupper, Professor An Oxford professor whom Franny despises. Mentioned in "Zooey."

Yankauer, Ira Buddy's opponent in curb marbles in the "Introduction."

Zabel, Miss Student in one of Buddy's writing classes in the "Introduction."

Appendix II

A Glass Family Chronology

1917	February. Seymour Glass is born, the first child of the vaudeville performers Les Glass and Bessie Gallagher ("Zooey" 181-182).
1919	Buddy, W. G. (Webb Gallagher ?) Glass, is born ("Hapworth" 112).
1920	Boo Boo (Beatrice) Glass, is born ("Introduction" 115).
1921	The twins, Walter F. and Waker Glass, are born ("Hapworth" 80).
1921-1923	The Glasses tour Australia ("Introduction" 145).
1922	Seymour, 5, is taken for a ride all over a Brisbane stage on Joe Jackson's nickel-plated trick bicycle ("Introduction" 148).
1923	Early spring. Seymour, 6, begins to frequent a branch of the New York Public Library and systematically reads everything he can find on God and religion ("Introduction" 125; "Hapworth" 88).
1923	May. Seymour, 6, begins to see the "magnificent light" mentioned in Vivekananda's *Raja Yoga* meditation manual and tries to teach his mother one of the breathing exercises from that manual ("Hapworth" 58, 77, 92).
1924	January. Seymour, 6, begins to acquire limited clairvoyance. He mentions "an abominable glimpse [he] had at recess period right after Christmas" during which he was able to see that in a previous incarnation his and Buddy's relationship with Les was "fraught with discordancy" ("Hapworth" 50).

1924	July 1. Seymour, 7, and Buddy, 5, arrive at Camp Simon Hapworth in Maine (This date is suggested by comments in "Hapworth" on pp. 34, 35, 40, 42, 44, 68, 86, 112).
1924	July 16. Seymour, 7, injures his leg and snaps the communication of pain between his leg and his brain so he can take 11 stitches without anesthesia ("Hapworth" 73).
1924	July 17. Seymour, 7, spends seven-and-a-half hours writing an enormous letter to his parents. In his letter, he mentions over a dozen "glimpses" into previous "appearances" and into the future. He predicts, for example, that he will not live much beyond the age of thirty ("Hapworth" 60-61).
1925	January. During their parents' retirement party, Seymour, 8, and Buddy, 6, meet a man who later signs them up for the radio program "It's a Wise Child" ("Hapworth" 61).
1925	Spring. Les and Bessie Glass retire from vaudeville ("Introduction" 119, 145).
1926	Seymour, 9, outraces Buddy, 7, to the drugstore at Broadway and 113th Street ("Introduction" 211).
1927	Fall. Seymour, 10, advises Buddy, 8, to try "not aiming so much" when playing curb marbles ("Introduction" 202).
1927	Seymour, 10, and Buddy, 8, become regulars on the radio quiz show "It's a Wise Child" ("Carpenters" 7).
1927	Seymour, 10, helps Charlotte Mayhew get on "It's a Wise Child" ("Carpenters" 81).
1928	Seymour, 11, writes the John Keats poem ("Introduction" 124).
1928	Seymour, 11, discovers Chinese poetry and begins to imitate poets such as P'ang, Tang-li and Ko-huang ("Introduction" 122).
1929	On "It's a Wise Child," Seymour, 12, says that his favorite word in the Bible is "Watch" ("Introduction" 152).
1929	Summer. Seymour, 12, injures Charlotte by hitting her in the face with a stone ("Carpenters" 89).
1929	Charlotte Mayhew leaves "It's a Wise Child" ("Carpenters" 80).
1929	The Glasses move to an apartment in the East Seventies ("Zooey" 74).
1930	Zachary (Zooey) Martin Glass, is born ("Introduction" 146).
1930	Seymour, 13, is examined by a group of Freudian psychologists for over six hours ("Introduction" 98).

1930	Waker, 9, gives away his brand new bicycle ("Introduction" 205)
1932	Seymour, 15, enters Columbia University as a freshman ("Carpenters" 26).
1933	Buddy, 14, writes a story in which all the characters have Heidelberg dueling scars ("Introduction" 98).
1933	Seymour, 16, is "bounced off" the "It's a Wise Child" program because of his comment about President Lincoln. Buddy, 14, also leaves "It's a Wise Child" ("Carpenters" 44, 73-74).
1935	Franny (Frances) Glass, is born ("Introduction" 146).
1935	January or February. Seymour, 17, reads a Taoist tale to ten-month-old Franny ("Carpenters" 3).[1]
1936	Seymour, 18, receives his Ph.D. from Columbia University and starts teaching there ("Introduction" 156).
1937	Zooey, 7, gets on "It's a Wise Child" ("Zooey" 153).
1937	Seymour, 20, tells Zooey, 7, to shine his shoes for the Fat Lady before going to the broadcast studio ("Zooey" 200).
1938	Seymour, 21, is now "a near full professor of English" ("Introduction" 186).
1938	Summer. Seymour, 21, is able to trace, apparently during meditation, that he and Buddy and Zooey "have been brothers for no fewer than four incarnations, maybe more" ("Introduction" 158).
1939	Buddy, 20, urges Seymour, 22, to publish some of his poetry, but Seymour refuses ("Introduction" 124).
1940	Seymour, 23, and Buddy, 21, move to their own apartment on 79th Street, near Madison Avenue ("Zooey" 181; "Introduction" 160).
1940	Buddy takes a short story writing course from a professor B. at Columbia University ("Introduction" 154).
1940	Seymour writes a long comment about one of Buddy's stories and tells him not to be too clever but to trust his heart when writing short stories ("Introduction" 161).
1940	December. Seymour, 23, and Buddy, 21, register for the draft ("Introduction" 160).
1941	Boo Boo, 21, gives birth to a baby boy, Lionel ("Dinghy" 76).
1941	Seymour, 24, is drafted and begins basic training at Fort Monmouth, New Jersey ("Carpenters" 9, 26).
1941	Seymour, 24, attempts to commit suicide by slashing his wrists ("Carpenters" 70).

1941	Winter. Seymour, 24, meets Muriel Fedder and comes to New York almost every night to be with her ("Carpenters" 9, 72-73).
1941	Seymour, 24, now drinks quite a bit. He says that he can't discuss an unpleasant topic, his injuring Charlotte Mayhew, "over just one drink" ("Carpenters" 66-67, 74, 77).
1942	February. Buddy, 23, begins basic training at Fort Benning, Georgia ("Carpenters" 6).
1942	Les Glass is "hustling talent for a motion picture studio" in Los Angeles ("Carpenters" 6).
1942	After completing basic training, Buddy, 23, has "walking pleurisy for over three months" ("Introduction" 117, "Carpenters" 6).
1942	Spring. Seymour, 25, is transferred to a B-17 base in California ("Carpenters" 7).
1942	Spring. Boo Boo, 22, is an ensign in the Navy and is stationed at the Brooklyn Navy base ("Carpenters" 6).
1942	May 22nd or 23rd. Buddy, 23, gets a letter from Beatrice asking him to attend Seymour's wedding ("Carpenters" 8)
1942	June 4. Seymour, 25, fails to show up for his own wedding but later that day "elopes" with Muriel ("Carpenters" 9,13, 86)
1944	Seymour, 27, is shipped to the "European Theater of Operations" ("Introduction" 113).
1945	Seymour, 28, is "getting very bald" ("Introduction" 171).
1945	Seymour, 28, has a nervous breakdown and is treated in an Army hospital in Germany ("Bananafish" 6).
1945	October. Boo Boo, 25, convinces her son Lionel, 4, not to run away from home ("Dinghy" 77).
1945	Late Autumn. Waker 24, is killed in an accident while serving with the army of occupation in Japan ("Carpenters" 6).
1946	Buddy, 29, leaves New York City and moves to the country ("Introduction" 138).
1947	Buddy, 30, starts teaching college writing courses ("Introduction" 137).
1945-1948	Seymour remains in psychiatric wards of Army hospitals for most of the last three years of his life ("Introduction" 114).
1948	Around March 12, Seymour returns to New York on a commercial flight ("Introduction" 113, 134).
1948	Between March 12 and 15, Seymour spends a few days with Muriel's family. During that time he is rude to Muriel's grandmother; he rips up some of his

	in-laws' family photographs; he calls Muriel names; he wrecks his in-laws' car in an apparent suicide attempt; and he reads to Buddy a poem he wrote about a widower and a white cat ("Bananafish" 5-6; "Introduction" 132).
1948	March 17. Wednesday morning. Seymour and Muriel arrive in Florida ("Bananafish" 5).
1948	March 19. Friday, early afternoon. Seymour writes a poem (in Japanese) on the desk blotter in his hotel room. It is about a little girl and her doll ("Zooey" 64; "Introduction" 134).
1948	March 19. Friday, around 3:30 p.m. Seymour, 31, sits down on his hotel bed, looks at the sleeping Muriel, and fires a bullet through his right temple ("Bananafish" 18).[2]
1948	Buddy, 29, publishes "A Perfect Day for Bananafish" ("Introduction" 112).
1951	Buddy, 32, publishes *The Catcher in the Rye* ("Introduction" 112).
1953	Buddy, 36, publishes "Teddy" ("Introduction" 176).
1955	November. Franny Glass, 20, has a nervous breakdown and comes home to be counseled by Zooey, 25 ("Zooey" 50).
1956-57	Buddy, 37-38, writes "Zooey" ("Zooey" 47-50).
1959	Boo Boo, 39, gives birth to a baby girl ("Introduction" 147).
1959	While writing "Seymour—An Introduction," Buddy, 40, falls ill and spends nine weeks in bed with acute hepatitis ("Introduction" 150).
1965	Bessie Glass sends Buddy, 46, a letter that Seymour, 7, wrote home from summer camp in 1924, and Buddy decides to publish that letter rather than a story he was working on ("Hapworth" 32).

---

[1]   There is a discrepancy concerning the year of Franny's birth. It is given as 1934 in "Carpenters" and 1935 in the "Introduction." In "Carpenters," we are told that Seymour was 17 when he read the Taoist tale to the 10-month-old Franny ("Carpenters" 3). That means he must have read that tale to Franny in January or February of 1935, because Seymour turned 18 in February of 1935. ("Zooey" 181-182). Therefore according to "Carpenters," Franny must have been born in March or April of 1934. But in the "Introduction," Buddy Glass states that Franny was born in 1935 ("Introduction" 146).

[2]   Another discrepancy concerns the day of Seymour's suicide which given as a Friday in "A Perfect Day for Bananafish" and as a Thursday in "Zooey." In "Bananafish," Muriel tells her mother that she and Seymour arrived in Florida on a

Wednesday and that Seymour played the piano in the Ocean Room of their hotel both nights that they've been there. ("Bananafish" 5, 7). That makes the day of the suicide a Friday. However, in "Zooey," Buddy Glass writes a letter to Zooey that is dated "3/18/51" and he says that it is three years to the day that Seymour killed himself ("Zooey" 56, 62). That makes the date of Seymour's suicide March 18, 1948. However, March 18, 1948, was a Thursday and not a Friday.

Appendix III

Salinger's Philosophy of Composition

> The true poet has no choice of material. The material plainly chooses
> him, not he it.
>
> Buddy Glass

Although J.D. Salinger's *The Catcher in the Rye* (1951) is undeniably one of the classics of twentieth-century American fiction, some critics rate Salinger's short stories even higher. His collection *Nine Stories* (1953) contains two pieces, "A Perfect Day for Bananafish" and "For Esmé—With Love and Squalor," which have been ranked with the best stories of Ernest Hemingway, F. Scott Fitzgerald, and William Faulkner.

However, in the late 1950s, Salinger began to write experimental short fiction which received more negative than positive reviews. What critics objected to in the novellas "Zooey" (1957), "Seymour—An Introduction" (1959), and "Hapworth 16, 1924" (1965), was not only the length, looseness of structure, and whimsical style but also an increasing preoccupation with religious ideas derived from Vedanta Hinduism, Taoism, and Zen Buddhism. Because of the negative responses to his fiction, Salinger stopped publishing.

The radical change that occurred in Salinger's fiction becomes apparent when we compare "A Perfect Day for Bananafish:" (1948) and "Hapworth 16, 1924" (1965). "Bananafish" is a very compact short story which combines brevity of detail and compression of incident. Moreover, it is told from a mostly objective point of view which forces readers to draw their own conclusions about what is going on in the minds of the characters. The style of the story adds to its compactness, for it has a Flaubertian polish that reveals painstaking craftsmanship and innumerable revisions. Every word is *le mot juste*, and there is virtually not a sentence in the whole story that can be omitted without changing the overall meaning. By contrast, the form of "Hapworth 16, 1924" is in every respect the opposite. The piece is more than seven times as long as "Bananafish," and it contains much detail that could be omitted without detriment to the overall meaning. Told in the first person, it is extremely subjective because the writer spends considerable time analyzing his own thoughts and emotions. And the style is so unbalanced, so involuted, and so full of verbal *faux pas* that serious ideas often appear ridiculous. Moreover, the structure of "Hapworth" shows that Salinger has deliberately gone beyond the tradition of the short story and created a type of fiction which combines expository and narrative elements.

The changes in Salinger's fiction are due to a change in his view of art. This change is revealed in comments by Buddy Glass, the narrator of the Glass Family Series, whom we can safely consider to be Salinger's spokesman in these matters. After all, Salinger called Buddy Glass his "alter-ego" (in the dust cover notes for *Franny and Zooey*), and he made Buddy claim authorship of "A Perfect Day for Bananafish," "Teddy," "Raise High the Roof Beam, Carpenters" and *The Catcher in the Rye* ("Introduction" 111-112, 176). The changes in Salinger's philosophy of composition parallel the changes in Buddy's views, and those were influenced chiefly by the advice Buddy received from his older brother Seymour.

In "Seymour—An Introduction," Buddy Glass reproduces seven brief memos and one long letter in which his brother Seymour gives him criticism and advice on some of his early stories. Seymour's letter and memos contain the core of a philosophy of composition which Buddy Glass fleshes out with additional comments of his own elsewhere in the "Introduction." This philosophy of composition is expressed in the following 10 statements:

1. Writers should allow themselves to be "seized" by their inspiration (98).
2. The artist is "the only true seer we have on earth" (104).
3. Great literature should "please or enlighten or enlarge" the reader (118).
4. "The true poet has no choice of material. The material plainly chooses him, not he it" (121).
5. A writer should make sure to "shut out as few of his old librarians as humanly possible" (126).
6. The writer's madness should be "a madness of the heart" and not a madness of the head (140).
7. Writers produce their best work when "all [their] stars are out" (159).
8. A writer should "follow [his/her] heart, win or lose" (160).
9. If a writer is "a deserving craftsman," his "heart will never betray him" (161).
10. A writer should be detached from the fruits of his work and follow the principle of "Aiming but no aiming" (207).

These 10 statements contain ideas very similar to those expressed by Plato, the nineteenth-century romantics, and Hindu writers on art, as well as the Dutch painter Vincent Van Gogh, the Danish philosopher Søren Kierkegaard, and the Austrian writer Franz Kafka. The 10 statements contain four clusters of ideas.

They concern inspiration and the divine origin of the artist's ideas, the personality of the artist as seer, spontaneous creation and organic form, and the religious and secular purpose of literary art.

INSPIRATION AND THE ORIGIN OF THE ARTIST'S IDEAS

In Salinger's philosophy of composition, the notion that the ideas of great writers are not their own but come from God is implicit in the concepts of inspiration as a divine seizure and in the notion that true artists do not choose their material but that the material chooses them. Plato expressed a similar idea in the "Ion," when he said that in great literature, we do not hear the voice of a specific artist because "God himself is the speaker" ("Ion" 144).

This means that the work of art already exists in its ideal form before the artist's imagination seizes hold of it. As Emerson puts it in his essay "The Poet," "poetry was all written before time was," and all that the poets do is listen to those "primal warblings" and try to write them down. But they always lose words or verses and thus "miswrite the poem." The greatest poets are those who "write down these cadences more faithfully, and these transcripts, though imperfect, become the songs of the nations" (Emerson 322).

However, Salinger's notion of inspiration contains two ideas that are different from what Plato and the nineteenth-century romantics believed. One of these ideas has to do with Salinger's different notion of God and the other with his belief in meditation as a way to get in touch with God.

Salinger disagrees with Plato's notion that inspiration can be compared to the magnetic force that allows us to suspend a number of iron rings from a single magnet. According to Plato, the magnet is God who inspires the artist, the first ring is the artist who inspires the rhapsode, the second ring is the rhapsode who recites and explains the poem, and the third ring is the audience who is inspired by the rhapsode ("Ion" 288-289). While Plato's view of inspiration is based on the dualistic belief that God is separate and different from man, Salinger's view of inspiration is based on the monistic belief that God is immanent in man "in some absolutely nonphysical part of the heart—where the Hindus say that Atman resides" ("Franny" 39).

The notion that divine inspiration does not come from outside but from inside the artist is shared by Kierkegaard, one of the writers to whom Buddy Glass defers when it comes to modern artistic processes. Kierkegaard explains that his work as a writer is the result of "the prompting of an irresistible inward impulse" (Kierkegaard 6). Kierkegaard also says that God is giving him "His assistance" in writing. Kierkegaard labels his divine inspiration "Governance" and says: "[I]t seems to me that if had I a winged pen, yes, ten of them, I still could not follow fast enough to keep pace with the wealth which presents itself" (Kierkegaard 67).

Another difference between Salinger's view of inspiration and that of Plato and the nineteenth-century romantics is due to his belief that meditation is a means of accessing divine inspiration because during meditation, artists can literally receive illumination. This is illustrated in Seymour's letter from Camp Hapworth where he spends much time meditating and writing poetry. He mentions that during meditation he sometimes sees a "magnificent light" ("Hapworth" 58). It is probably to that kind of light that Seymour refers when he that writes do their best work when all their "stars are out."

Although Salinger disagrees with Plato and the nineteenth-century romantics because he believes that the source of inspiration is inside the artist rather than outside, he does agree with that tradition as far the effect is concerned that inspiration has on the artist. In one passage, he refers to that effect as a divine "seizure," and in another passage he calls it a "madness of the heart." This idea that an inspired artist acts like a fool or a madman goes back to Plato and was revived by the nineteenth-century romantics. Plato, for instance, said that when artists are inspired, they abandon themselves entirely to their "heaven-sent madness" ("Phaedrus" 124), and Emerson said that "the poet knows that he speaks adequately then only when he speaks somewhat wildly" (Emerson 332).

These ideas are echoed when Buddy Glass says about the British romantic poet William Bysshe Shelley that he wasn't "quite mad enough" and that his madness was not a madness of the heart but a madness of the head ("Introduction" 140). In short, Buddy Glass believes that Shelley should have followed his heart rather than his head in writing his poetry.

THE ARTIST AS SEER

One of the key ideas in "Seymour—An Introduction" is the notion that the greatest writers are "seers" because their vision is divinely inspired. Similarly, Plato said that true poets have a divine vision akin to that of "the producers of oracles and holy prophets." They are able to see divine truth and beauty "with the eyes of the soul" and they are therefore "the interpreters of the Gods" ("Ion" 144). Echoing Plato, the British romantic poet William Blake, one of Salinger's favorites, said: "One power alone makes a Poet: Imagination, the Divine Vision" (Blake 782).

Salinger's notion of how the artist comes by his divine vision differs slightly from that of other western writers. He does agree with William Blake and other nineteenth-century writers that "Knowledge of Ideal Beauty is Not to be Acquired. It is Born with us" (Blake 459). But while Blake and other romantics assumed that it was pretty much a matter of accident whether or not one was born with poetic genius, Salinger believes that it is determined by karma. According to the law of karma, every one of our physical or mental actions results in a similar reaction either in this life or in a future incarnation. Hence, what we are in this lifetime is determined by our actions and desires in previous lives. As one Indian author explains: "The karma (good and bad deeds) of every man as well as the background of his experience determines his genius" (Anand 59). This idea is expressed by Zooey when he tells Franny that in one incarnation or another she had a hankering not only to be an actress but also to be a *good* one and now she is stuck with the karmic result of that craving. And then Zooey tells his sister that it's all a matter of "Cause and effect, buddy, cause and effect" ("Zooey" 198).

SPONTANEOUS CREATION AND ORGANIC FORM

The belief in spontaneous creation is implicit in the advice that Seymour gives to Buddy when he tells him to follow his heart, "win or lose." Following one's heart means not following any preconceived plan or any established rules. The belief in spontaneous creation in turn implies a belief in organic form. If the artist allows his intuition free rein and does not consciously impose any form on it, then the work will grow its own shape. This idea has been expresses by various romantic and modern artists. Henry David Thoreau, for instance, said that true poetry "is a natural fruit. As naturally as the oak bears an acorn, and the vine a gourd, man bears a poem, either spoken or done" (Thoreau 345). Vincent Van Gogh and Franz Kafka have also expressed the belief that their works of art grow organically. Van Gogh, for example, said that when he created a painting he felt "like a woman in childbirth" (Van Gogh I, 324), and Kafka once said that one of his stories came out of him "like a real birth" (Diaries I, 278). Kafka also explains his belief in organic form when he says that "one should not forget that the story, if it has any justification to exist, bears its complete organization within itself even before it has been fully formed" (Diaries II, 104).

Salinger's belief in organic form is apparent in the later novellas, and it is made explicit in a number of statements by Buddy Glass. For instance, Buddy expresses his disdain for restrictive conventional patterns when he says that he burned some 35 or 50 of his stories because they had a conventional beginning, middle, and end. It is particularly contrived endings which Buddy doesn't like, for he believes that a writer should never impose a conclusion on a story. Instead, he should simply stop writing when the story is finished with him.

Despite his belief that the artist should create spontaneously when he feels inspired, Salinger also believes that in order to express his vision of divine beauty and truth adequately, a writer must be a skilled craftsman. Seymour explains this notion when he urges Buddy to trust his heart: His heart will never betray him because he is "a deserving craftsman."

This emphasis on craftsmanship is more reflective of the Hindu view of art than of the views of Plato and the nineteenth-century romantics. Plato assumes that the poet creates his work only when he is "out of his senses" ("Ion" 144), and this notion implies that the artist does not consciously shape his work. Similarly, among the nineteenth-century romantics we find a de-emphasis of craftsmanship and a belief that the form will take care of itself if the artist listens closely enough to his inspiration. Emerson, for instance, was convinced that the form of a poem grows automatically out of its central idea if that idea is "a thought so passionate and alive that like the spirit of a plant or an animal, it has an architecture of its own, and adorns nature as with a new thing" (Emerson 323).

However, according to Hindu theories of art, years of practice are required before an artist can begin to produce works which reflect the ideal beauty of his divine vision. The Indian author Bharata says in his book *Natya Shastra*, "The one thing most necessary to the human workman is *abhyasa*, 'practice,' otherwise thought of as *anusila*, 'devoted application,' or 'obedience,' the fruit of which is *slistatva*, 'habitus,' or second nature, skill, lit. 'clinginess,' 'adherence'; and this finds expression in the performance as *madhurya*, 'grace' or 'facility'" (Kane 348). Like Bharata, Salinger believes that it is only after an artist has become a "deserving craftsman" that he can begin to "follow his heart" and produce great art.

WORSHIP OF GOD AND SERVICE TO MANKIND

According to Salinger's belief, one of the two major purposes of art is worship of God. The view of art as worship comes out when Seymour says to Buddy that writing was never merely his profession; it has always been his religion. Salinger's view of art as worship can be explained in terms of his eclectic religious philosophy. The basis of this philosophy is Vedanta Hinduism, and at its core lie the teachings of the *Bhagavad Gita*. But as Ananda Coomaraswamy says about the Hindu notion of art as worship, "This is not, of course, exclusively a Hindu view. It has been expounded by many others, such as the Neoplatonists, Hsieh Ho, Goethe, Blake, Schopenhauer and Schiller" (Coomaraswamy 41). And we might add to this list Seymour and Buddy's favorites, Kierkegaard, Van Gogh, and Kafka. Kierkegaard, for example, said that writing to him was "a divine worship" (Kierkegaard 68); Van Gogh labeled one of his later self-portraits "Worshipper of the Eternal Buddha" (Graetz 286); and Kafka referred to writing as "a form of prayer" (*Father* 32).

The second major purpose of art, according to Salinger, is service to mankind. This is a prevalent notion in Western culture ever since Plato demanded that poetry should be "pleasant but also useful to States and to human life" ("Republic" 430). According to Plato, it is the function of the artist to interpret the will of God and thereby to "educate and improve mankind" ("Republic" 434). But since Salinger's philosophy of composition is based on the monistic notion of God's immanence in man, he sees the two aims of worship of God and service to man as essentially identical. Salinger feels that the artist must not only strive for Perfection for its own sake, but that he must also communicate this sense of Perfection to others. This notion is illustrated when Buddy explains that Seymour loved Chinese and Japanese poetry because its aim is to "please or enlighten or enlarge" the reader.

To make sure that a work of art actually pleases or enlightens or enlarges its audience, so Salinger believes, the artist must write in a manner that is designed not to alienate the reader. This is why Seymour Glass never published any of his poetry. He believed that the true poet should write not merely what he feels he must write but he should write what he must write in such a style that he does not shut out people such as his favorite librarian, Miss Overman. And Seymour did not publish any of his poetry because he had not yet found a form of poetry that allowed him to follow his heart and not shut out Miss Overman.

This part of Salinger's philosophy of composition has no direct parallel in Plato's view of art or in that of the nineteenth-century romantics. In Plato's time the poets did not have to worry about their audiences not understanding their work because there were professional rhapsodes such as the title character in the dialogue "Ion" who made a living by reciting literary works and explaining them to the *hoi polloi*, the common people. And most of the nineteenth-century romantics—with the notable exception of Walt Whitman—wrote for an audience whom they presumed to be just as highly educated as they themselves were.

The form and content the last three novellas that Salinger published before falling silent—"Zooey," "Seymour—An Introduction," and "Hapworth 16, 1924"—suggests that Salinger actually wrote them according to the central idea of his philosophy of composition, "follow your heart, win or lose." And as we can see from Zooey's advice to Buddy, Salinger was aware that by following his heart he might "expedite, move up, the day and hour of [his] professional undoing" ("Zooey "48).

It seems to me that in writing "Zooey" Salinger followed his heart and won because he shut out only a few of his old librarians; but in writing "Seymour—An Introduction" and "Hapworth," Salinger followed his heart and lost because he not only shut out all his old librarians but also many readers who are predisposed to like his work. Thus it may well be that Salinger did not publish any more stories after "Hapworth 16, 1924" because he realized that his work was no longer able to "please or enlighten or enlarge the invited eavesdropper to within an inch of his life."

WORKS CITED

Anand, Mulk Raj. *The Hindu View of Art*. Bombay: Asia Publishing House, 1957.

Blake, William. *The Complete Writings of William Blake*. Ed. Geoffrey Keynes. London: Oxford UP, 1966.

Coomaraswamy, Ananda. *The Dance of Shiva*. New York: Noonday Press, 1957.

Emerson, Ralph Waldo. "The Poet." In *The Selected Writings of Ralph Waldo Emerson*. Ed. Brooks Atkinson. New York: Modern Library, 1950, 319-341.

Graetz, H.R. *The Symbolic Language of Vincent Van Gogh*. New York: McGraw-Hill, 1963.

Kafka, Franz. *Dearest Father: Stories and Other Writings*. Trans. Ernst Kaiser and Eithne Wilkins. New York: Schocken, 1954.

___ . *Diaries*. Ed. Max Brod. 2 vols. New York: Schocken, 1948.

Kane, P.V. *History of Sanskrit Poetics*. Delhi: Motilal Banarsidass, 1971.

Kierkegaard, Søren. *The Point of View for My Work as an Author*. Trans. Walter Lowrie. New York: Harper, 1962.

Plato. *The Dialogues of Plato*. Trans. Benjamin Jowett. Chicago: Encyclopedia Britannica, 1952.

Salinger, J.D. "Blue Melody." *Cosmopolitan* 125 (September 1948): 51, 112-119.

___ . *Franny and Zooey* [1961]. New York: Bantam, 1964.

___ . "Hapworth 16, 1924." *New Yorker* (19 June 1965): 32-113.

___ . *Raise High the Roof Beam, Carpenters and Seymour—An Introduction* [1963].
       New York: Bantam, 1965.

Thoreau, Henry David. "A Week on the Concord and Merrimack Rivers." In *Walden and Other Writings*. Ed. Brooks Atkinson. New York: Modern Library, 1950, 301-436.

Van Gogh, Vincent. *The Complete Letters of Vincent Van Gogh*. 3 vols. Greenwich, CT: New York Graphic Society, 1959

Bibliography

FICTION PUBLISHED BY J.D. SALINGER

"The Young Folks." *Story* 16 (March-April 1940): 26-30.
"Go See Eddie." *University of Kansas City Review* 7 (1940): 121-124.
"The Hang of It." *Collier's* (12 July 1941): 22.
"The Heart of a Broken Story." *Esquire* 16 (September 1941): 32, 131-132.
"Personal Notes of an Infantryman." *Collier's* (12 December 1942): 96.
"The Long Debut of Lois Taggett." *Story* 21 (September-October 1942): 28-34.
"The Varioni Brothers." *Saturday Evening Post* (17 July 1943): 12-23, 76-77.
"Both Parties Concerned." *Saturday Evening Post* (26 February 1944): 14, 47-48.
"Soft-Boiled Sergeant." *Saturday Evening Post* (15 April 1944): 18,82, 84-85.
"Last Day of the Last Furlough." *Saturday Evening Post* (15 July 1944): 26-27, 61-
    62, 64.
"Once a Week Won't Kill You." *Story* 25 (November-December 1944): 23-27.
"A Boy in France." *Saturday Evening Post* (31 March 1945): 21, 92.
"Elaine." *Story* 26 (March-April 1945): 38-47.
"This Sandwich Has No Mayonnaise." *Esquire* 24 (October 1945): 54-56, 147-149.
"The Stranger." *Collier's* (1 December 1945): 18, 77.
"I'm Crazy." *Collier's* (22 December 1945): 36, 48, 51.
"Slight Rebellion Off Madison." *New Yorker* (21 December 1946): 82-86.
"A Young Girl in 1941 with No Waist at All." *Mademoiselle* 25 (May 1947): 222-
    223, 292-302.
"The Inverted Forest." *Cosmopolitan* 113 (December 1947): 73-80, 85-86, 88, 90,
    92, 95-96, 98, 100, 102, 107, 109.
"A Perfect Day for Bananafish." *New Yorker* (31 January 1948): 21-25.
"A Girl I Knew." *Good Housekeeping* 126 (February 1948): 178, 186, 188-196.
"Uncle Wiggily in Connecticut." *New Yorker* (20 March 1948): 30-36.
"Just Before the War With the Eskimos." *New Yorker* (5 June 1948): 37-40, 42, 44,
    46.
"Blue Melody." *Cosmopolitan* 125 (September 1948): 51, 112-119.
"The Laughing Man." *New Yorker* (19 March 1949): 27-32,
"Down at the Dinghy." *Harper's* 198 (April 1949): 87-91.
"For Esmé—with Love and Squalor." *New Yorker* (18 April 1950): 28-36.
The Catcher in the Rye. Boston: Little, Brown, 1951.
"Pretty Mouth and Green My Eyes." *New Yorker* (14 July 1951): 20-24.
"De Daumier-Smith's Blue Period." *World Review* 39 (May 1952): 33-48.

"Teddy." *New Yorker* (31 January 1953): 26-36.

Nine Stories. Boston: Little, Brown, 1953.

"Franny." *New Yorker* (29 January 1955): 24-32- 34-43.

"Raise High the Roof Beam, Carpenters." *New Yorker* (19 November 1955): 51-58,
    60-116.

"Zooey." *New Yorker* (4 May 1957): 32-34, 44-139.

"Seymour—An Introduction." *New Yorker* (6 June 1959): 42-111.

Franny and Zooey. Boston: Little, Brown, 1961.

Raise High the Roof Beam, Carpenters and Seymour—An Introduction. Boston:
    Little, Brown, 1963.

"Hapworth 16, 1924." *New Yorker* (19 June 1965): 32-113.

BOOKS ON J.D. SALINGER AND HIS WORK

Alsen, Eberhard. *Salinger's Glass Stories as a Composite Novel.* Troy, NY:
    Whitston, 1983.

Belcher, William F., and James W. Lee, eds. *J.D. Salinger and the Critics.* Belmont,
    CA: Wadsworth, 1962.

Bloom, Harold, ed. *Modern Critical Views: J.D. Salinger.* New York: Chelsea House,
    1987.

Engel, Steven, ed. *Readings on The Catcher in the Rye.* Greenhaven, NY: Greenhaven
    Press, 1998.

Grunwald, Henry Anatole, ed. *Salinger: A Critical and Personal Portrait.* New
    York: Harper, 1962.

French, Warren G. *J.D. Salinger.* New York: Twayne, 1963.

___ . *J.D. Salinger* [rev. ed]. Boston: Twayne, 1976.

___ . *J.D. Salinger, Revisited.* Boston: G.K. Hall, 1988.

Gywnn, Frederick L., and Joseph L. Blotner. *The Fiction of J.D. Salinger.*
    Pittsburgh: U of Pittsburgh P, 1958.

Hamilton, Ian. *In Search of J.D. Salinger.* New York: Random House, 1988.

Hamilton, Kenneth. *J.D. Salinger: A Critical Essay.* Grand Rapids, MI: Eerdmans,
    1967.

Kotzen, Kip, and Thomas Beller, eds. *With Love and Sqiualor: 14 Writers Respond
    to the Work of J.D. Salinger.* New York: Broadway, 2001.

Kubica, Chris, and Will Hochmann, eds. *Letters to J.D. Salinger.* Madison, WI: U of
    Wisconsin P, 2002.

Laser, Marvin, and Norman Fruman, eds. *Studies in J.D. Salinger.* New York:
    Odyssey, 1963.

Lundquist, James. *J.D. Salinger.* New York: Ungar, 1979.

Marsden, Malcolm M., ed. *If You Really Want to Know: A Catcher Casebook.*
    Chicago: Scott-Foresman, 1963.

Miller, James E. *J.D. Salinger.* Minneapolis: U of Minnesota P, 1965.

Pinsker, Sanford. *The Catcher in the Rye: Innocence Under Pressure.* Boston:
    Twayne, 1993.

Ranchan, Som P. *An Adventure in Vedanta: J.D. Salinger's The Glass Family.* Delhi:
    Ajanta, 1989.

Salzberg, Joel, ed. *Critical Essays on Salinger's The Catcher in the Rye.* Boston:
    G.K. Hall, 1990.

Salzman, Jack, ed. *New Essays on The Catcher in the Rye.* Cambridge, England:
    Cambridge UP, 1992.

Simonson, Harold P., and Philip E. Hager, eds. *Salinger's "Catcher in the Rye":
    Clamor vs. Criticism.* Boston: Heath, 1963.

Starosciak, Kenneth. *J.D. Salinger: A Thirty Year Bibliography 1938-1968*. New Brighton, MN: Starosciak, 1971.

Sublette, Jack. *J.D. Salinger: An Annotated Bibliography: 1938-1981*. New York: Garland, 1984.

Wenke, John. *J.D. Salinger: A Study of the Short Fiction*. Boston: Twayne, 1991.

RELIGIOUS TEXTS MENTIONED BY J.D. SALINGER

Aurelius, Marcus. "The Meditations of Marcus Aurelius." Trans. George Long. In *Lucretius: On the Nature of Things. Translated by H.A. Munro. The Discourses of Epictetus. Translated by George Long. The Meditations of Marcus Aurelius. Translated by George Long.* Chicago: Encyclopaedia Britannica, 1955.

Blakney, Raymond B. *Meister Eckhart: A Modern Translation*. New York: Harper, 1941.

Blyth, R.H. *Zen and Zen Classics*. 5 vols. Tokyo: Hokuseido, 1955-1962.

Caussade, Jean Pierre de. *On Prayer: Spiritual Instructions on the Various States of Prayer*. Trans. Algar Thorold. London: Burns, Oates and Washbourne, 1949.

Chuang-tzu. *The Texts of Taoism*. Trans. James Legge. Intro. D.T. Suzuki. New York: Julian, 1959.

Epictetus. *The Discourses of Epictetus*. Trans. George Long. London: Bell, 1912.

French, R.M., trans. *The Way of a Pilgrim and The Pilgrim Continues His Way*. New York: Seabury, 1965.

Herrigel, Eugen. *Zen in the Art of Archery*. Trans. R.F.C. Hull. New York: Pantheon, 1953.

Hui-neng. *The Sutra of Wei Lang (or Hui Neng)*. Trans. Wong Mou-lam and Christmas Humphreys. London: Luzac, 1944.

Kadloubovsky, E. trans. *Writings from the Philokalia*. London: Faber, 1952.

Kierkegaard, Søren. *Fear and Trembling and the Sickness unto Death*. Trans. Walter Lowrie. Garden City, NJ: Doubleday, 1954.

____. *The Point of View for My Work as an Author*. Trans. Walter Lowrie. New York: Harper, 1962.

M [Mahendranath Gupta]. *The Gospel of Sri Ramakrishna*. Trans. Swami Nikhilananda. New York: Ramakrishna-Vivekananda Center, 1942.

McCann, Justin, ed. *The Cloud of Unknowing and Other Treatises*. Westminster: Novena, 1952.

Müller, Max F., ed. *Sacred Books of the East*. 50 vols. Oxford: Clarendon, 1879-1910.

Nikhilananda, Swami, trans. *The Upanishads*. 4 vols. New York: Harper, 1949.

Prabhavananda, Swami, and Christopher Isherwood, trans. *Shankara's Crest Jewel of Discrimination (Viveka Chudamani)* [1947]. New York: Signet, 1970.

____. *The Song of God: Bhagavad Gita* [1944]. New York: Signet, 1972.

Price, A.F., and Wong Mu-lam, trans. *The Diamond Sutra and the Sutra of Hui-Neng*. Berkeley, CA: Shambala, 1969.

Senzaki, Nyogen and Paul Reps, trans. *101 Zen Stories*. London: Rider, 1939.

Shankaracharya. *Self-Knowledge (Atmabodha)*. Trans. Swami Nikhilananda. New York: Ramakrishna-Vivekananda Center, 1946.

Suzuki, Deisetz Teitaro. *Essays in Zen Buddhism*. 5 vols. London: Rider, 1949, 1950, 1953.

Vivekananda, Swami. *Inspired Talks*. New York: Ramakrishna-Vivekananda Center, 1958.

____. *Jnana Yoga*. New York: Ramakrishna-Vivekananda Center, 1955.

____ . *Karma Yoga and Bhakti Yoga*. New York: Ramakrishna-Vivekananda Center, 1955.

____ . *Raja Yoga*. New York: Ramakrishna-Vivekananda Center, 1955.

Yutang, Lin, ed. *The Wisdom of Laotse*. New York: Modern Library, 1948.

CUMULATIVE LIST OF WORKS CITED

"A.G. 'Pete' Bramble. 12th Armored Division." The Twelfth Armored Division and the Liberation of Death Camps.   <http://www. acu.edu/academics/history/12ad/ campsx/bramble.htm>

Alexander, Paul. *Salinger: A Biography*. Los Angeles: Renaissance, 1999.

Alsen, Eberhard. *Salinger's Glass Stories as a Composite Novel*. Troy, NY: Whitston, 1983.

Anand, Mulk Raj. *The Hindu View of Art*. Bombay: Asia Publishing, 1957.

"Backstage with Esquire." *Esquire* 16 (September 1941): 24.

Baro, Gene. "Some Suave and Impressive Slices of Life" [Review of *Nine Stories*]. *New York Herald Tribune Book Review* (12 April 1953): 6.

Barrett, William.   "Reader's Choice" [Review of *Raise High the Roof Beam, Carpenters and Seymour—An Introduction*].   *Atlantic Monthly* 211 (February 1963): 128-130.

Baskett, Sam S. "The Splendid/Squalid World of J.D. Salinger." *Wisconsin Studies in Contemporary Literature* 4 (1963): 48-61.

Baumbach, Jonathan. "The Saint as a Young Man: A Reappraisal of *The Catcher in the Rye*." *Modern Language Quarterly* 25 (December 1964): 461-472. Rpt. in Salzberg 55-64.

Behrman, N.S. "The Vision of the Innocent" [Review of *The Catcher in the Rye*]. *New Yorker* (11 August 1951): 64-68.

Belcher, William F., and James W. Lee, eds. *J.D. Salinger and the Critics*. Belmont, CA: Wadsworth, 1962.

Blake, William, *The Complete Writings of William Blake*. Ed. Geoffrey Keynes. London: Oxford U P, 1966.

Bloom, Harold, ed. *Modern Critical Views: J.D. Salinger*. New York: Chelsea House, 1987.

Bode, Carl. "Salinger, J.D. *Franny and Zooey*" [Review]. *Wisconsin Studies in Contemporary Literature* 3 (Winter 1961): 65-71.

Bramble, A.G. "Kaufering IV, After Being Burned by the Retreating German Soldiers" [Photo]. The Twelfth Armored Division and the Liberation of Death Camps. http://www.acu.edu/academics/history/12ad/ campsx/ burning.gif>

Branch, Edgar. "Mark Twain and J.D. Salinger: A Study in Literary Continuity." *American Quarterly* 9 (Summer 1957): 144-158.   Rpt. in Grunwald 205-217.

Braudy, Leo. "Realists, Naturalists, Novelists of Manners." In *Harvard Guide to Contemporary American Writing*. Ed. Daniel Hoffman. Cambridge, MA: Belknap, 1979, 84-152.

Breit, Harvey. "Reader's Choice" [Review of *The Catcher in the Rye*]. *Atlantic Monthly* 188 (August 1951): 82. Rpt. in Marsden 6-7.

Brickell, Herschel. "J.D. Salinger." In *Prize Stories of 1949: The O. Henry Awards*. New York: Doubleday, 1950, 249.

Bryan, James E.   "The Psychological Structure of *The Catcher in the Rye*." *Publications of the Modern Language Association* 89 (1974): 1065-1074. Rpt. in Salzberg 101-117.

____ . "A Reading of Salinger's 'For Esmé—with Love and Squalor." *Criticism* 9 (19867): 275-288.

____. "Salinger and His Short Fiction." Diss. U of Virginia: Charlottesville, 1968.

____. "Salinger's Seymour's Suicide." *College English* 24 (December 1962): 226-229.

Burger, Nash K. "The Catcher in the Rye." [Review] *New York Times* (16 July 1951): 19.

Burke, Brother Fidelian. "Salinger's 'Esmé': Some Matters of Balance." *Modern Fiction Studies* 12 (Autumn 1966): 341-347.

"Charred bodies discovered upon liberation by US troops" [Photo]. <http://motlc.wiesenthal.com/gallery/pg01/pg7/pg01738.html>

Chester, Alfred. "Salinger: How to Love Without Love." *Commentary* 35 (June 1963): 467-464.

"Contributors." *Story* 16 (March-April 1940): 2.

Coomaraswamy, Ananda. *The Dance of Shiva.* New York: Noonday Press, 1957.

Crane, Stephen. *Maggie: A Girl of the Streets* [1896]. New York: Signet, 1991.

Davis, Tom. "J.D. Salinger: The Identity of Sergeant X." *Western Humanities Review* 16 (Spring 1962): 181-183. Rpt. in Laser and Fruman 261-264.

Detweiler, Robert. "J.D. Salinger and the Quest for Sainthood." In *Four Spiritual Crises in Mid-Century American Fiction.* Coral Gables: U of Florida P, 1963, 36-41.

Dickstein, Morris. "On and Off the Road: The Outsider as Young Rebel." *The Cambridge History of American Literature. Volume 7. Prose Writing 1940-1990.* Ed. Sacvan Bercovitch. Cambridge, England, and New York: Cambridge UP, 1999, 165-223.

Dolch, Martin and John Hagopian. "Down at the Dinghy." In *Insight I: Analyses of American Literature.* Frankfurt: Hirschgraben, 1975, 225-228.

Elliott, Emory, ed. *The Columbia Literary History of the United States.* New York: Columbia UP, 1988.

Emerson, Ralph Waldo. "The Poet." In *The Selected Writings of Ralph Waldo Emerson.* Ed. Brooks Atkinson. New York: Modern Library, 1950, 319-341.

Fiedler, Leslie. "Up From Adolescence." *Partisan Review* 29 (Winter 1962): 127-131. Rpt. in Grunwald 57-62.

Fitzgerald, F. Scott. *The Great Gatsby* [1925]. New York: Scribner's, 1995.

____. "The Rich Boy." In *The Stories of F. Scott Fitzgerald.* Ed. Malcolm Cowley. New York: Scribner's, 1988, 177-208.

Fosburgh, Lacey. "J.D. Salinger Speaks About His Silence." *New York Times* (3 November 1974): 1, 69.

French, Warren. *J.D. Salinger.* New York: Twayne, 1963.

____. *J.D. Salinger* [rev. ed.]. Boston: Twayne, 1976.

____. *J.D. Salinger, Revisited.* Boston: G.K. Hall, 1988.

Geismar, Maxwell. "The Wise Child and the *New Yorker* School of Fiction." In *American Moderns: From Rebellion to Conformity.* New York: Hill and Wang, 1958, 195-209. Rpt. in Grunwald 87-101.

Goldstein, Bernice, and Sanford Goldstein. "Zen and Salinger." *Modern Fiction Studies* 12 (1966): 313-324.

Goodman, Anne. "Mad About Children" [Review of *The Catcher in the Rye*]. *New Republic* 125 (16 July 1951): 20-21. Rpt. in Salzberg 23-24.

Graetz, H. R *The Symbolic Language of Vincent Van Gogh.* New York: McGraw-Hill, 1963.

Green, Martin. "Franny and Zooey." In *Reappraisals: Some Common-Sense Readings in American Literature.* New York: Norton, 1965, 197-210.

Gross, Theodore. "Suicide and Survival in the Modern World." *South Atlantic Quarterly* 68 (1969): 454-462.

Grunwald, Henry A. "Introduction." In *Salinger: A Critical and Personal Portrait*. New York: Harper, 1962, ix-xxviii.

Grunwald, Henry A., ed. *Salinger: A Critical and Personal Portrait*. New York: Harper, 1962.

Gwynn, Frederick L., .and Joseph L. Blotner. *The Fiction of J.D. Salinger*. Pittsburgh: U of Pittsburgh P, 1958.

Hagopian, John V. "'Pretty Mouth and Green My Eyes': Salinger's Paolo and Francesca in New York." *Modern Fiction Studies* 12 (Autumn 1966): 349-354.

Hamilton, Ian. *In Search of J.D. Salinger*. New York: Random House, 1988.

Hamilton, Kenneth. *J.D. Salinger: A Critical Essay*. Grand Rapids, MI: Eerdmans, 1967.

Harper, Howard. "J.D. Salinger—Through the Glasses Darkly." In *Desperate Faith*. Chapel Hill: U of North Carolina P, 1967, 65-95.

Hartwig, Robert T. "Inmates Were Rounded Up and Placed in this Barracks" [Photo]. The Twelfth Armored Division and the Liberation of Death Camps. <http://www.acu.edu/academics/history/12ad/cmpsx/c-ol.gif>

Hassan, Ihab. *Radical Innocence*. Princeton: Princeton UP, 1961.

____ . "Rare Quixotic Gesture: The Fiction of J.D. Salinger." *Western Review* 21 (Summer 1957): 261-280. Rpt. in Grunwald 138-163.

____ . "Since 1945." In *Literary History of the United States*. Ed. Robert Spiller et al. New York: Macmillan, 1963, 1412-1441.

Heiserman, Arthur, and James E. Miller. "J.D. Salinger: Some Crazy Cliff." *Western Humanities Review* 10 (Spring 1956): 129-137. Rpt. in Grunwald 196-205.

Hemingway, Ernest. *Across the River and Into the Trees* [1950]. New York: Scribner's, 1998.

____ . *A Farewell to Arms* [1929]. New York: Scribner's, 1969.

____ . "In Another Country." In *The Short Stories*, 267-272.

____ . *In Our Time* [1925]. New York: Scribner's, 1958.

____ . "Now I Lay Me." In *The Short Stories*, 363-371.

____ . *The Short Stories of Ernest Hemingway*. New York: Scribner's, 1966.

____ . "A Way You'll Never Be." In *The Short Stories*, 402-414.

Hicks, Granville. "Sisters, Sons, and Lovers" [Review of *Franny and Zooey*]. *Saturday Review* 44 (September 1961): 26.

Howe, Irving. "More Reflections in the Glass Mirror" [Review of *Raise High the Roof Beam, Carpenters and Seymour—An Introduction*]. *New York Times Book Review* (7 Apr. 63): 4-5, 34. Rpt. in Irving Howe, *Celebrations and Attacks*. New York: Horizon, 1979, 93-96.

Huber, R.J. "Adlerian Theory and Its Application to *The Catcher in the Rye*—Holden Caulfield." In *Psychological Perspectives on Literature: Freudian Dissidents and Non-Freudians*. Ed. Joseph Natoli. New York: Archon, 1984, 43-52.

Hughes, Riley. "The Catcher in the Rye" [Review]. *Catholic World* 174 (November 1951): 154. Rpt. in Salzberg 31.

Hyman, Stanley Edgar. "J.D. Salinger's House of Glass." In *Standards: A Chronicle of Books of Our Time*. New York: Horizon, 1966, 123-127.

"In Place of the New, A Reissue of the Old" [Review of *Raise High the Roof Beam, Carpenters and Seymour—An Introduction*]. *Newsweek* (28 January 1963): 90, 92.

Johnson, Gerden F. *History of the Twelfth Infantry Regiment in World War II*. Boston: Twelfth Infantry Regiment, 1947.

Jones, Ernest. "Case History of All of Us" [Review of *The Catcher in the Rye*]. *Nation* 173 (1 September 1951): 176. Rpt. in Salzberg 24-25.

Kafka, Franz. *Dearest Father. Stories and Other Writings*. Trans. Ernst Kaiser and
     Eithne Wilkins. New York: Schocken, 1954.
___ . *Diaries*. Ed. Max Brod. 2 vols. New York: Schocken, 1948.
Kakutani, Michiko. "From Salinger, a New Dash of Mystery." *New York Times* (20
     February 1997): C15, C19.
Kane, P.V. *History of Sanskrit Poetics*. Delhi: Motilal Banarsidass, 1971.
Karlstetter, Klaus. "J.D. Salinger, R.W. Emerson and the Perennial Philosophy."
     Moderna Sprak 63 (1969): 224-236.
Kazin, Alfred. "The Alone Generation: A Comment on the Fiction of the Fifties."
     Harper's Magazine 209 (October 1959): 127-131.
___ . *Bright Book of Life*. Boston: Little, Brown, 1973.
___ . "J.D. Salinger: Everybody's Favorite." *Atlantic Monthly* 208 (August 1961):
     27-31. Rpt. in Grunwald 43-52.
Kermode, Frank. "One Hand Clapping" [Review of *Franny and Zooey*]. *New
     Statesman* (8 June 1962): 831-832.
Kierkegaard, Søren. *The Point of View for My Work as an Author*. Trans. Walter
     Lowrie. New York: Harper, 1962.
Kraul, Fritz. "Jerome D. Salingers Roman 'Der Fänger im Roggen' als Pflichtlektüre
     im Deutschunterricht der Oberstufe." *Der Roman im Unterricht* 20 (1968):
     79-86.
Krim, Seymour. "Surface and Substance in a Major Talent" [Review of *Nine Stories*].
     Commonweal 58 (24 April 1953): 78. Rpt. in Grunwald 64-69.
Laser, Marvin, and Norman Fruman, eds. *Studies in J.D. Salinger*. New York:
     Odyssey, 1963.
Levine, Paul. "J.D. Salinger: The Development of the Misfit Hero." *Twentieth
     Century Literature* 5 (October 1958): 92-99. Rpt. in Belcher and Lee 107-
     115.
Lodge, David. "Family Romances." [London] *Times Literary Supplement* (13 June
     1975): 642.
Longstreth, Morris. "Review of *The Catcher in the Rye*." *Christian Science Monitor*
     (19 July 1951): 7. Rpt. in Salzberg 30-31.
Lundquist, James. *J.D. Salinger*. New York: Ungar, 1979.
Malcolm, Janet. "Justice to J.D. Salinger." *New York Review of Books* (21 June
     2001): 16-22.
"Margaret Salinger on J.D. Salinger." *The Connection*. Natl. Public Radio. WBUR
     Boston.   14 September 2000 <http://www.the connection.org/archive/
     2000/09/ 0914b.shtml>.
Marsden, Malcolm, ed. *If You Really Want To Know: A Catcher Casebook*. Chicago:
     Scott, Foresman, 1963.
McCarthy, Mary. "J.D. Salinger's Closed Circuit." *Harper's Magazine* 225 (October
     1962): 45-48. Rpt. in Laser and Fruman 245-250.
Mellard, James. "The Disappearing Subject: A Lacanian Reading of *The Catcher in
     the Rye*." In *Critical Essays on Salinger's The Catcher in the Rye*. Ed. Joel
     Salzberg. Boston: G.K. Hall, 1990, 197-214.
Miller, James E. *J.D. Salinger*. Minneapolis: U of Minnesota P, 1965.
Mizener, Arthur. "The American Hero as Poet: Seymour Glass." In *The Sense of Life
     in the Modern Novel*. Boston: Houghton Mifflin, 1963, 227-246
___ . "In Genteel Traditions" [Review of *Nine Stories*]. *New Republic* 23 May 1953:
     19-20.
___ . "The Love Song of J.D. Salinger." *Harper's Magazine* 218 (February 1959):
     83-90. Rpt. in Grunwald 23-36.
Nikhilananda, Swami. *The Essence of Hinduism*.   New York: Ramakrishna-
     Vivekananda Center, 1946.

"Nine By Salinger" [Review of *Nine Stories*]. *Newsweek* (6 April 1953): 98.

O'Connor, Dennis. "Salinger's Religious Pluralism: The Example of 'Raise High the Roof Beam Carpenters'." *Southern Review* 20 (April 1984): 316-332. Rpt. in Bloom 119-134.

Ohmann, Carol, and Richard Ohmann. "Reviewers, Critics, and *The Catcher in the Rye*." *Critical Inquiry* 3 (Autumn 1976): 15-37. Rpt. in Salzberg 119-140.

Paniker, Sumitra. "The Influence of Eastern Thought on 'Teddy' and the Seymour Glass Stories of J.D. Salinger." Diss. U of Texas: Austin, 1971.

"People." *Time* (25 June 1965): 52.

Peterson, Virgilia. "Three Days in the Bewildering World of an Adolescent" [Review of *The Catcher in the Rye*]. *New York Herald Tribune Book Review* (15 July 1951): 3. Rpt. in Marsden 3-4.

Phelps, John. "A Writer Who Talks To, and Of, the Young" [Review of *Franny and Zooey*]. *New York Herald Tribune Book Review* (17 September 1961): 3, 14.

Phillips, Paul. "A Look at a Best-Seller: Salinger's *Franny and Zooey*" [Review]. *Mainstream* 15 (1962): 32-39.

"Plain and Fancy" [Review of *Franny and Zooey*]. *Newsweek* (18 September 1961): 109-110.

Plato. *The Dialogues of Plato*. Trans. Benjamin Jowett. Chicago: Encyclopaedia Britannica, 1952.

Posset, Anton. "Die amerikanische Armee entdeckt den Holocaust." *Themenhefte Landsberger Zeitgeschichte* 2 (1993): 35-41.

Prabhavananda, Swami and Christopher Isherwood, trans. *The Song of God: Bhagavad Gita* [1944]. New York: Signet 1972.

Purcell, William F. "World War II and the Early Fiction of J.D. Salinger." *Studies in American Literature* (Kyoto) 28 (1991): 77-93.

Quagliano, Anthony. "'Hapworth 16, 1924': A Problem in Hagiography." *University of Dayton Review* 8 (1971): 35-43.

"Robert T. Hartwig, 12th Armored Division." The Twelfth Armored Division and the Liberation of Death Camps. <http://www. acu.edu/academics/ history/12ad/ campsx/hartwig.htm>

Russell, John. "Salinger: From Daumier to Smith." *Wisconsin Studies in Contemporary Literature* 4 (Winter 1963): 70-87.

Saks, Julien, Colonel. "GI's Discover the Holocaust." In *Hellcats* [WW II Combat History of the 12th Armored Division]. Paducah, KY: 1987, 117-120

Salinger, J.D. "Backstage with Esquire." *Esquire* 25 (September 1945): 34.

___ . "Blue Melody." *Cosmopolitan* 125 (September 1948): 51, 112-119.

___ . "Both Parties Concerned." *Saturday Evening Post* (26 February 1944): 14, 47-48.

___ . "A Boy in France." *Saturday Evening Post* (31 March 1945): 21, 92.

___ . *The Catcher in the Rye* [1951]. New York: Bantam, 1964.

___ . Contributors." *Story* 25 (November-December 1944): 1

___ . "De Daumier-Smith's Blue Period." In *Nine Stories* [1953]. New York: Bantam, 1964, 130-165.

___ . "Down at the Dinghy." In *Nine Stories* [1953]. New York: Bantam, 1964, 74-86.

___ . "Elaine." *Story* 26 (March-April 1945): 38-47

___ . "For Esmé—with Love and Squalor." In *Nine Stories* [1953]. New York: Bantam, 1964, 87-114.

___ . *Franny and Zooey* [1961]. New York: Bantam, 1964.

___ . "A Girl I Knew." *Good Housekeeping* 126 (February 1948): 37, 186, 188-196.

___ . "Go See Eddie." *University of Kansas City Review* 7 (December 1940): 121-124.

___ . "The Hang of It." *Collier's* (12 July 1931): 22.

____ . "Hapworth 16, 1924." *New Yorker* (19 June 1965): 32-113.

____ . "The Heart of a Broken Story." *Esquire* 16 (September 1941): 32, 131-133.

____ . "I'm Crazy." *Collier's* (22 December 1945): 36, 48, 51.

____ . "The Inverted Forest." *Cosmopolitan* 113 (December 1947): 73-80, 85-86, 88, 90, 92, 95-96, 98, 100, 102,107, 109. Rpt. in *Cosmopolitan* 150 (March 1961): 111-132.

____ . "Just Before the War With the Eskimos." In *Nine Stories* [1953]. New York: Bantam, 1964, 39-55.

____ . "Last Day of the Last Furlough." *Saturday Evening Post* (15 July 1944): 26-27, 61-62, 64.

____ . "The Laughing Man." In *Nine Stories* [1953]. New York: Bantam, 1964, 56-73.

____ . Letter to Ernest Hemingway. [nd.] Ernest Hemingway Collection. Princeton, NJ: .Princeton University Library.

____ . Letter to Whit Burnett. 28 June 1944. Archives of Story Magazine and Story Press. Princeton, NJ: Princeton University Library.

____ . "The Long Debut of Lois Taggett." *Story* 21 (September-October 1942): 28-34.

____ . "Once a Week Won't Kill You." *Story* 25 (November-December 1944): 23-27.

____ . "A Perfect Day for Bananafish." In *Nine Stories* [1953]. New York: Bantam, 1964, 3-18.

____ . "Personal Notes of an Infantryman." *Collier's* (12 December 1942): 96.

____ . "Pretty Mouth and Green My Eyes." In *Nine Stories*. [1953]. New York: Bantam, 1964: 115-129.

____ . *Raise High the Roof Beam, Carpenters and Seymour—An Introduction* [1963]. New York: Bantam, 1965.

____ . "The Skipped Diploma: Musings of a Social Soph." *Ursinus Weekly* (10 October 1938): 2.

____ . "Slight Rebellion Off Madison." *New Yorker* (21 December 1946): 82-86.

____ . "Soft-Boiled Sergeant." *Saturday Evening Post* (15 April 1944): 18, 82, 84-85.

____ . "The Stranger." *Collier's* (1 December 1945): 18, 77.

____ . "Teddy." In *Nine Stories* [1953]. New York: Bantam, 1964, 166-198.

____ . "This Sandwich Has No Mayonnaise." *Esquire* 24 (October 1945): 54-56, 147-149.

____ . "Uncle Wiggily in Connecticut." In *Nine Stories* [1953]. New York: Bantam, 1964, 19-38.

____ . "The Varioni Brothers." *Saturday Evening Post* (17 July 1943): 12-13, 76-77.

____ . "The Young Folks." *Story* 16 (March-April 1940): 26-30.

____ . "A Young Girl in 1941 with No Waist at All." *Mademoiselle* 25 (May 1947): 222-223, 292-302.

Salinger, Margaret. *Dream Catcher*. New York: Washington Square, 2000.

Salzberg, Joel, ed. *Critical Essays on Salinger's The Catcher in the Rye*. Boston: G.K. Hall, 1990.

Schriber, Mary Suzanne. "Holden Caulfield: C'est Moi." In *Critical Essays on Salinger's The Catcher in the Rye*. Ed. Joel Salzberg. Boston: G.K. Hall, 1990, 226-238.

Schulz, Max F. "Epilogue to 'Seymour—An Introduction': Salinger and the Crisis of Consciousness." *Studies in Short Fiction* 5 (1968): 128-138. Rpt. in Bloom 53-61.

Schwartz, Arthur. "For Seymour—With Love and Judgment." *Wisconsin Studies in Contemporary Literature* 4 (1963): 88-99.

Seitzman, Daniel. "Therapy and Antitherapy in Salinger's 'Zooey'." *American Imago* 25 (Summer 1968): 140-162.

Sharma, Som P. Ranchan. "Echoes of the *Gita* in Salinger's 'Franny and Zooey'." In *The Gita in World Literature*. Ed. C.D. Verma. New Delhi: Sterling, 1990, 214-219.

Skow, John. "Sonny: An Introduction." *Time* (15 September 1961): 84-90. Rpt. in Grunwald 3-18.

Slethaugh, Gordon. "Seymour: A Clarification." *Renascence* 23 (1971): 115-128.

Smith, Harrison. "Manhattan Ulysses, Junior" [Review of *The Catcher in the Rye*]. *Saturday Review of Literature* 34 (14 July 1951): 12-13. Rpt. in Salzberg 28-30.

Stein, William Bysshe. "Salinger's 'Teddy': *Tat Tvam Asi* or That Thou Art." *Arizona Quarterly* 29 (Autumn 1973): 253-265.

Steiner, George. "The Salinger Industry." *Nation* 189 (14 November 1959): 360-363. Rpt. in Grunwald 82-85.

Stern, James. "Aw, the World's a Crummy Place" [Parody/Review of *The Catcher in the Rye*]. *New York Times Book Review* (15 July 1951): 5. Rpt. in Marsden 2-3.

Strauch, Carl F. "Kings in the Back Row: Meaning Through Structure—A Reading of Salinger's *The Catcher in the Rye*." *Wisconsin Studies in Contemporary Literature* 2 (Winter 1961): 5-30. Rpt. in Laser and Fruman 143-171.

Strong, Paul. "Black Wing, Black Heart—Betrayal in J.D. Salinger's 'The Laughing Man'." *West Virginia University Philological Papers* 24 (Mar. 1988): 91-96.

Thoreau, Henry David. "A Week on the Concord and Merrimack Rivers." In *Walden and Other Writings*. Ed. Brooks Atkinson. New York: Modern Library, 1950, 301-436.

Updike, John. "Anxious Days for the Glass Family" [Review of *Franny and Zooey*]. *New York Times Book Review* (17 September 1961): 1, 52. Rpt. in Grunwald 53-56.

____ . "Franny and Zooey" [Revised Review]. In *Studies in J.D. Salinger*. Ed. Marvin Laser and Norman Fruman. New York: Odyssey, 1963, 227-231.

"US Soldiers View Burned Bodies at Landsberg Nazi Camp." Photo Album. Simon Wiesenthal Multi Media Learning Center <http://motlc.wiesenthal.com/albums/palbum/p00/a0048p2.html>.

Van Gogh, Vincent. *The Complete Letters of Vincent Van Gogh*. 3 vols. Greenwich, CT: New York Graphic Society, 1959.

Van Leer, David. "Society and Identity." In *The Columbia History of the American Novel*. Ed. Emory Elliott. New York: Colmubia UP, 1991, 485-509.

Vivekananda, Swami. *Karma Yoga and Bhakti Yoga*. New York: Ramakrishna-Vivekananda Center, 1955.

____ . *Raja Yoga*. New York: Ramakrishna-Vivekananda Center, 1955.

Wakefield, Dan. "Salinger and the Search for Love." *New World Writing No. 14*. New York: New American Library, 1958: 68-85. Rpt. as "The Search for Love" in Grunwald 176-191.

Welty, Eudora. "Threads of Innocence" [Review of *Nine Stories*]. *New York Times Book Review* (5 Apr. 1953): 1. Rpt. in Eudora Welty, *A Writer's Eye: Collected Book Reviews*. Jackson, MS: UP of Mississippi, 1974, 109-110.

Wenke, John. "Sergeant X, Esmé, and the Meaning of Words." *Studies in Short Fiction* 18 (1981): 251-259.

____ . *J.D. Salinger: A Study of the Short Fiction*. Boston: Twayne, 1991.

West, Nathanael. *Miss Lonelyhearts* [1933]. New York: Avon, 1964.

Wiegand, William. "Salinger and Kierkegaard." *Minnesota Review* 5 (1965): 137-156.

____ . "Seventy-eight Bananas." *Chicago Review* 11 (1958): 3-19. Rpt. in Grunwald 123-136.

Wordsworth, William. "Ode: Intimations of Immortality." In *The Norton Anthology of British Literature*. 7th ed. Vol. 2. Ed. M.H. Abrams et al. New York: Norton, 2000, 287-292.

SUGGESTIONS FOR FURTHER READING

Aitkant, Satish C. "From Alienation to Accommodation: Salinger's 'Franny and Zooey'." *Kyushu American Literature* 28 (October 1987): 39-44.
Antico, John. "The Parody of J.D. Salinger: Esmé and the Fat Lady Exposed." *Modern Fiction Studies* 12 (Autumn 1966): 325-340.
Baskett, Sam. "The Splednid/Squalid World of J.D., Salinger." *Wisconsion Studies in Contemporary Literature* 4 (Winter 1963): 48-61.
Bellman, Samuel. "New Light on Seymour's Suicide: Salinger's 'Hapworth 16, 1924'." *Studies in Short Fiction* 3 (1966): 348-351.
Bloom, Harold. "Introduction." In *Modern Critical Views: J.D. Salinger*. New York: Chelsea House, 1987, 1-4.
Blotner, Joseph. "Salinger Now: An Appraisal." *Wisconsin Studies in Contemporary Literaure* 4 (Winter 1963): 100-108.
Bryan, James. "The Admiral and Her Sailor in Salinger's 'Down at the Dinghy'." *Studies in Short Fiction* 17 (Spring 1980): 174-178.
Bufithis, Philip H. "Salinger and the Psychiatrist." *West Virginia University Philological Papers* 21 (December 1974): 67-77.
Chuang-tzu. *The Texts of Taoism*. Trans. James Legge. Intro. D.T. Suzuki. New York: Julian, 1959.
Coles, Robert. "Reconsideration: J.D. Salinger." *New Republic* (28 April 1978): 30-32.
Costello, Donald P. "Autopsy of a Faded Romance: Salinger and His Critics." *Commonweal* 25 (October 1963): 132-135.
___ . "The Language of *The Catcher in the Rye*." *American Speech* 34 (October 1959): 172-181. Rpt. in Salzberg 44-53.
Cotter, James F. "Religious Symbols in Salinger's Short Stories." *Studies in Short Fiction* 15 (1978): 121-132.
Davison, Richard Allen. "Salinger Criticism and 'The Laughing Man': A Case of Arrested Development." *Studies in Short Fiction* 18 (Winter 1981): 1-9.
French, R.M. trans. *The Way of a Pilgrim and The Pilgrim Continues His Way*. New York: Seabury, 1965.
French, Warren. "Franny." In *J.D. Salinger. Revisited*. Boston: G.K. Hall, 1988, 89-93.
___ . "Hapworth 16, 1924." In *J.D. Salinger, Revisited*. Boston: G.K. Hall, 1988, 109-116.
___ . "The House of Glass." In *J.D. Salinger, Revisited*. Boston: G.K. Hall, 1988, 89-99.
___ . "Recollection." In *J.D. Salinger*. New York: Twayne, 1963, 148-153.
Galloway, David D. "The Love Ethic." In *The Absurd Hero in American Fiction*. Austin, TX: U of Texas P, 1966, 140-169. Rpt. in *J.D. Salinger: Modern Critical Views*. Ed. Harold Bloom. New York: Chelsea House, 1987, 29-51.
Gardner, James. "J.D. Salinger, Fashion Victim." *National Review* (7 April 1997): 51-52.
Genthe, Charles V. "Six, Sex, Sick: Seymour, Some Comments." *Twentieth Century Literature* 10 (January 1965): 170-171.
Glazier, Lyle. "The Glass Family Saga: Argument and Epiphany." *College English* 27 (1965): 248-251.

Goldstein, Bernice, and Sanford Goldstein. "Ego and 'Hapworth 16, 1924'."
    Renascence 24 (1972): 159-167.
____ . "'Seymour—A Introduction': Writing as Discovery." *Studies in Short Fiction*
    7 (1970): 248-256.
Hamilton, Kenneth. "Hell in New York: J.D. Salinger's 'Pretty Mouth and Green My
    Eyes'." *Dalhousie Review* 47 (1967): 394-399.
____ . "The Interplay of Life and Art." In *J.D. Salinger: A Critical Essay.* Grand
    Rapids, MI: Eerdmans, 1967, 11-21.
____ . "One Way to Use the Bible: The Example of J.D. Salinger." *Christian Scholar*
    47 (1964): 243-251.
Hassan, Ihab. "Almost the Voice of Silence: The Later Novelettes of J.D. Salinger."
    Wisconsin Studies in Contemporary Literature 4 (Winter 1963): 5-20.
Haveman, Ernest. " The Search for the Mysterious J.D. Salinger: Recluse in the Rye."
    Life (3 November 1961): 129-144.
Herrigel, Eugen. *Zen in the Art of Archery.* Trans. R.F.C. Hull. New York: Pantheon,
    1953.
Hinkle, Warren. "J.D. Salinger's Glass Menagerie." *Ramparts* 1 (1962): 4-51.
Hoban, Phoebe. "The Salinger File." *New York* (15 June 1987): 36-42.
Korte, Barbara. "Narrative Perspective in the Works of J.D. Salinger." *Literatur in*
    Wissenschaft und Unterricht 2 (1987): 343-351.
Lundquist, James. "Against Obscenity: *The Catcher in the Rye.*" In *J.D. Salinger.*
    New York: Ungar, 1979, 37-68.
Lyons, John O. "The Romantic Style of Salinger's 'Seymour—An Introduction'."
    Wisconsin Studies in Contemporary Literature 4 (Winter 1963): 62-69.
M. [Mahendranath Gupta]. *The Gospel of Sri Ramakrishna.* Trans. Swami
    Nikhilananda. New York: Ramakrishna-Vivekananda Center, 1942.
McIntyre, John P., S.J. "A Preface for 'Franny and Zooey'." *Critic* 20 (1962): 25-28.
Metcalf, Frank. "Form in Salinger's Shorter Fiction." *Canadian Review of American*
    Studies 3 (Spring 1972); 50-59
____ . "The Suicide of Salinger's Seymour Glass." *Studies in Short Fictio*n 9 (1972):
    243-246.
Nikhilananda, Swami. *Hinduism*: *Its Meaning for the Liberation of the Spirit*
    [1958]. New York: Ramakrishna-Vivekananda Center, 1992.
O'Connor, Dennis L. "J.D. Salinger: Writing as Religion." *Wilson Quarterly* 4
    (Spring 1980): 182-190.
Oldsey, Bernard. "The Movies in the Rye." *College English* 23 (December 1961):
    209-215. Rpt. in Salzberg 92-99.
Panichas, George A. "J.D. Salinger and the Russian Pilgrim." In *The Reverent*
    Disciple. Knoxville: U of Tennessee P, 1974, 372-337.
Piwinski, David J. "Salinger's 'De Daumier-Smith's Blue Period': Pseudonym as
    Cryptogram." *Notes on Contemporary Literature* 15 (October 1985): 32-
    39.
Prigozy, Ruth. *"Nine Stories*: Salinger's Linked Mysteries." In *Modern American*
    Short Story Sequences. Ed. J. Gerald Kennedy. Cambridge, England, and
    New York: Cambridge UP, 1995, 114-132.
Romano, John. "Salinger Was Playing Our Song." *New York Times Book Review* (3
    June 1979): 11, 48.
Rosenbaum, Ron. "The Man in the Glass House." *Esquire* (June 1997): 41-53, 116-
    121.
Rupp, Richard H. "J.D. Salinger: A Solitary Liturgy." In *Celebration in Postwar*
    American Fiction 1945-1967. Coral Gables: U of Florida P, 1970, 113-131.
Russell, John. "Salinger's Feat." *Modern Fiction Studies* 12 (Fall 1966): 299-311.
Salinger, J.D. "The Children's Echelon." [nd.] Archives of Story Magazine and Story
    Press. Princeton, NJ: Princeton University Library.

___ . "The Last and Best of the Peter Pans." [nd.] Archives of Story Magazine and Story Press. Princeton, NJ: Princeton University Library.

___ . "The Magic Foxhole." [nd.] Archives of Story Magazine and Story Press. Princeton, NJ: Princeton University Library.

___ . "The Ocean Full of Bowling Balls." [nd.] Archives of Story Magazine and Story Press. Princeton, NJ: Princeton University Library.

___ . "Two Lonely Men." [nd.] Archives of Story Magazine and Story Press. Princeton, NJ: Princeton University Library.

Seed, David. "Keeping it in the Family: The Novellas of J.D. Salinger." In the *Modern American Novella*. Ed. A. Robert Lee. New York: St. Martin's, 1989, 139-161.

Seitzman, Daniel. "Salinger's 'Franny': Homoerotic Imagery." *American Imago* 22 (1965): 57-76.

Seng, Peter J. "The Fallen Idol: The Immature World of Holden Caulfield." *College English* 32 (December 1962): 203-209. Rpt. in Marsden 73-81.

Shulevitz, Judith. "Holden Reconsidered and All." *New York Times Book Review* (29 July 2001): 23.

Suzuki, Deisetz Teitaro. *Essays in Zen Buddhism* [1948]. New York: Grove, 1986.

Teachout, Terry. "Salinger Then and Now." *Commentary 84* (September 1987): 61-64.

Vanderbilt, Kermit, "Symbolic Resolution in *The Catcher in the Rye:* The Cap, the Carrousel, and the American West." *Western Humanities Review* 17 (Summer 1963): 271-277.

Weinberg, Helen. "J.D. Salinger's Holden and Seymour and the Spiritual Activist Hero." In *The New American Novel: The Kafkan Mode in Contemporary Fiction*. Ithaca, NY: Cornell UP, 1970, 141-164.

Wenke, John. "The Uncollected Stories." In *J.D. Salinger: A Study of the Short Fiction*. Boston: Twayne, 1991, 4-7.

Yutang, Lin, ed. *The Wisdom of Laotse*. New York: Modern Library, 1948.

Index

About the Author

EBERHARD ALSEN is Professor Emeritus of the State University of New York, Cortland. His previous works include *Romantic Postmodernism in American Fiction* (1996), along with articles in such journals as *American Literature, Studies in Short Fiction,* and *Emerson Society Quarterly.*